CONTENTS

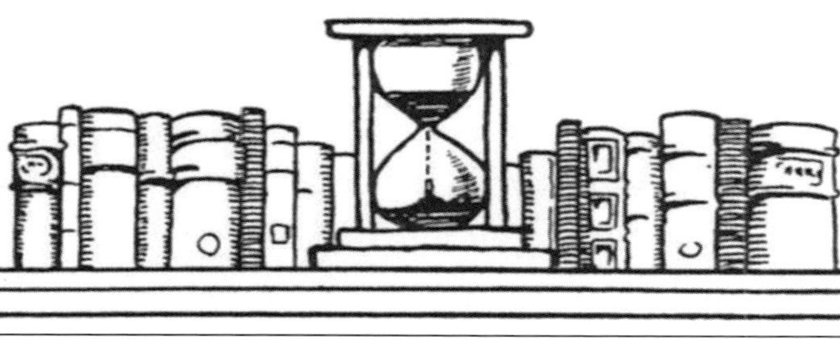

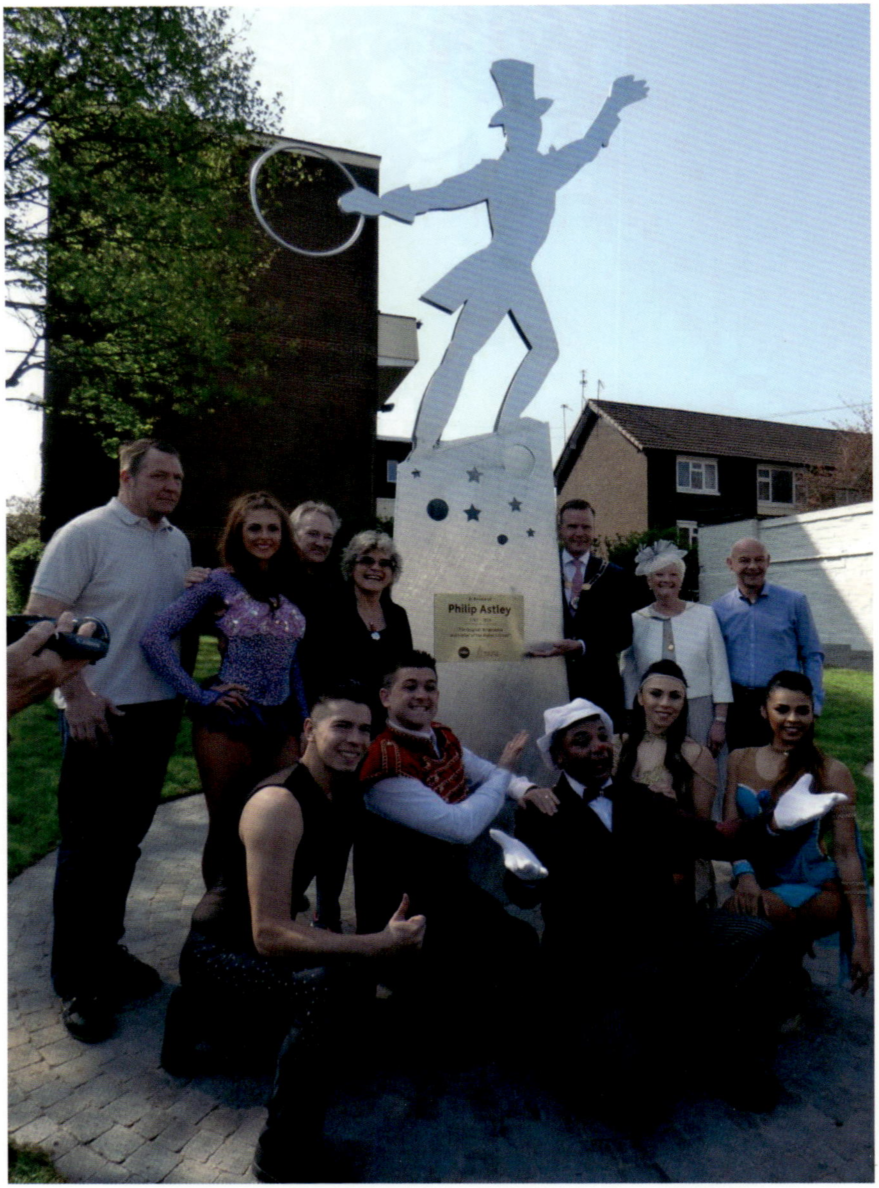

Celebrating 250 years of the circus in 2018: On 21st April 2018 this statue of Philip Astley was unveiled in Newcastle-under-Lyme – Astley's birthplace. Philip Astley (1742 – 1814) first presented an equestrian show to the public in 1768 – from this grew the entertainment form we know as the circus. The picture includes Andrew Van Buren who made the whole thing happen, Clown Chico Rico, representatives of No Fit State Circus, Suzzanna Mata, and the Mayor of Newcastle Under Lyme, Councillor. Simon White. The statue was designed by Candida Kelsall and was made by Liam Robinson. This book is dedicated to all those who strive to keep traditional forms of entertainment alive while giving them fresh appeal and relevance. Long live the circus, the fairground, the theatre and the cinema!

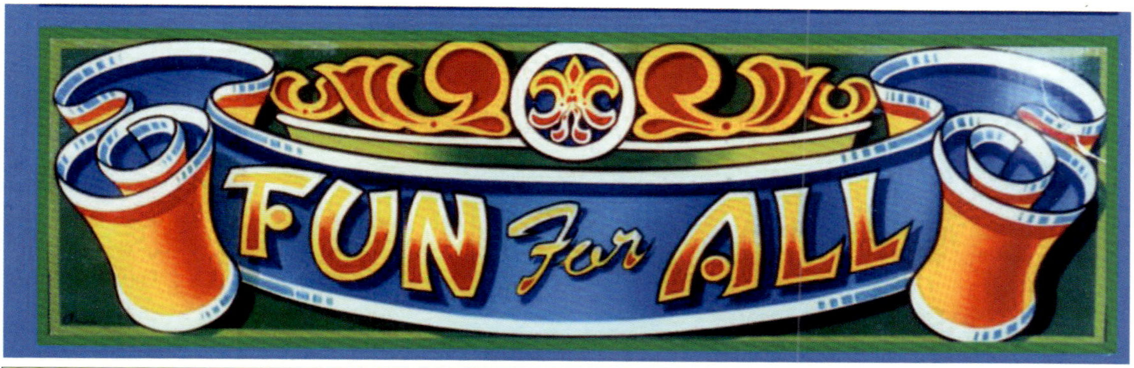

Ned Williams

Presents

Four Swallows And Two Elephants

Seven "Hidden Biographies" of men and women who lived and worked in the Entertainment World and whose lives criss-crossed the Black Country

ISBN: 978-1-5272-3052-1

URALIA PRESS

23 Westland Road, Wolverhampton, WV3 9NZ
2018

Four Swallows and Two Elephants
Published by Uralia Press, 2018.
23 Westland Road, Wolverhampton, WV3 9NZ

ISBN: 978-1-5272-3052-1

Printed by John Price,
Bilston

Introduction

Call me Ned

Let me introduce you to this book which just happens to appear in 2018 – the year in which we celebrate the two hundred and fiftieth anniversary of the invention of the circus. Way back in 1768 Philip Astley established the entertainment form which we now call the circus, but maybe you had never heard of him until now. Why is he so relatively unknown? The answer is that his biography has been "hidden".

Welcome to this book, which I had originally called "Hidden Biographies". That was a reasonable working-title and gave me a sense of what it was that I wanted to write, but I still found myself having difficulties when it came to explaining it to anyone else. I may have found a more poetic title, but now that it is materialising as a book, I still feel a need to explain what it's all about!

This book is about seven people for whom their real name or assumed name played a significant part in their life. In some cases it was a name used for a specific time or purpose, in other cases it seemed to be a major exercise in identity building. These people were not quite who they said they were, so the quest to know more about them begins with the task of unravelling the mystery surrounding their identity. The other thing that these people had in common was that their lives criss-crossed the Black Country.

Even the name "Black Country" is worthy of attention and explanation, but to examine all the issues surrounding that name would need another book all to itself. These two aspects of their lives (Their "obscurity" and their local connections.) are what have driven my interest in researching the stories of these people's lives and trying to tell their narratives.

Perhaps I better explain my interest in the business of "names". My parents chose to give me the name John Edward Williams and during my childhood I was normally called John. At about the age of twelve I awoke one day with the conviction that "John" was not my real name and that henceforward I wanted to be known as "Ned". This provided me with a lesson in the mystery and power of names, and the interesting matter of the relationship between a name and identity. In the end, what is a person's real name? All the characters in this book moulded their lives and careers to some extent by adopting a new name, but they all did it in slightly different ways. Eliza Bennett simple became "Mrs. Patch" by marriage, but Broncho Bill, Ben Kennedy and Irving Bosco took on their names in more mysterious ways. "Southdown" and "JBT" used pen-names partly because it was a convention in the area of journalism in which they worked.

In the case of Brenda Jones, she made no show-business use of her married name, Cuttin, but often appeared with a name that was created to identify a particular act in the circus world. Circus artistes sometimes appear under at least two "act-names" within one show, while also existing in their real names when selling you some candy-floss during the interval!

The other factor that led to these characters playing with names is that they all existed in the world of entertainment, and by the word "entertainment", I mean the worlds of the fairground, the circus, the theatre and the cinema. Their lives are proof of the "inter-connectedness" of these worlds, while also demonstrating that they can be considered separately. Add all this to the fact that the Black Country is a background to these stories and I think you can begin to see why all this has interested me. Having experienced a "name change" at the beginning of my teens, I was then very fortunate to experience that sense of adventure that can be introduced into life by changing home. At the age of eighteen, almost overnight, I ceased being an "Essex Boy" or an "East Ender" and became a "Furriner" living in the Black Country – a role that has been exciting for more than half a century. I followed in the footsteps of Ben Kennedy or Irving Bosco in discovering The Midlands! So this is a book of names and places.

"JBT" and Mrs. Patch spent most of their lives in and around the Black Country. "Southdown" and Brenda Jones experimented with finding new lives away from the Black Country, but always returned to it at fairly frequent intervals. Broncho Bill adopted Wolverhampton as the ideal home for his sons and his elephants. Irving Bosco earned himself a place in Black Country history, but then chose to retire elsewhere.

One reason I have for believing that this book will interest you is the evidence of the popularity of genealogy and of television programmes like "Who Do You Think You Are?". Genealogy, and the TV programmes that utilise it, both celebrate the excitement of research and its revelations. In this book I first set out to find out who the person behind the name really is, and then set out to try and tell that person's story in the light of research. I can describe their achievements, or if they are writers, I can include examples of their work. Research goes on in archives and on the Internet but is augmented by the search for people who are descended from the characters described here in the hope that they can add to the story.

Meeting descendants of the people in this book also raises another interesting question: to what extent has the person described in these pages left a legacy that survives for subsequent generations. In the first instance, is the person remembered, or recorded in family archives, or are they forgotten? How are they remembered or "archived", or how are they forgotten? Responses to my research have varied from meeting the grand-daughter of "Southdown" who had very deliberately tried to preserve details of the life of her grandfather, to trying to find descendants of Ben Kennedy which has been almost, but not entirely, impossible! Although I traced three of Ben Kennedy's grandchildren, none of them could tell me much about him. (However: one granddaughter was able to produce an "archive" which has greatly enhanced the range of images used in that chapter!)

Writing biographical material is immensely satisfying – I learnt that when I came to write a biography of Pat Collins, the well-known "King of Showmen". I worked with Freda Allen on the project and we both felt that we had known Pat despite the fact that he was "before our time". We probably knew more than we could refine into a text, and in the process of getting to know him we encountered that strange phenomenon: the more one knows, there's a whole lot more to know! A biography is never finished; answers simply pose more questions.

Another aspect of "hidden biography" arises from the fact that we all wish we had been more genealogically astute in our own lives. We all wish we had asked the previous generation more questions. In my case I had a grand-mother who died when I was one and a half years old. I can look at a photograph in which I see myself sitting on her lap, and yet nearly everything about her life is a mystery to me! The details that I do know only make my ignorance of other matters more irritating. Obviously I can then extend this to the

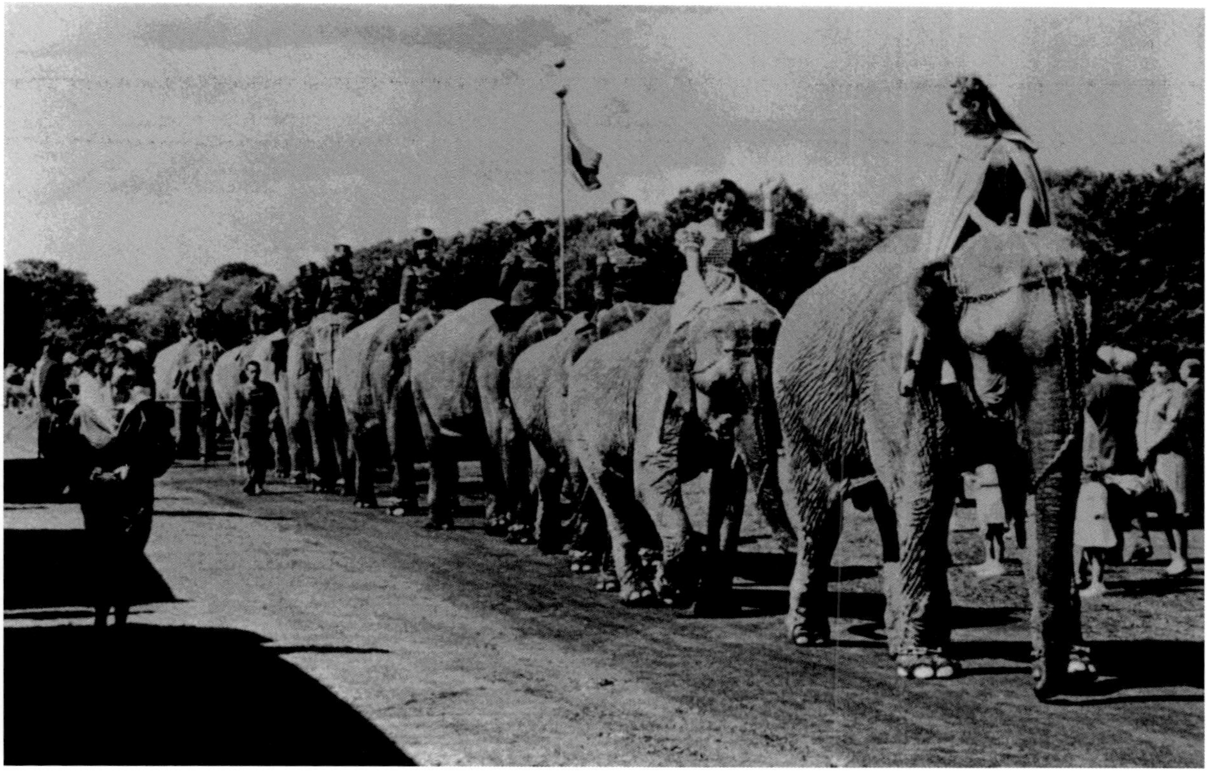

mystery that surrounds other adults I once "knew", but about whom I now know so little. For example, two men had quite an influence on me: Francis Ashley and Jack Nelson. At the time, I took knowing them for granted, but years later questions arise and it is suddenly clear that their biographies are "hidden".

Above: On the second elephant from the front, Marianne Preece joins the Billy Smart's Circus parade into Walsall Arboretum in July 1965. It was her first public duty as the newly crowned Bloxwich Carnival Queen. She later told me that she was very worried about it but had been reassured that her elephant would be sympathetic and helpful – and that turned out to be the case, and Marianne never forgot the excitement and pleasure of the occasion.
Such scenes no longer have a place in the life of the Black Country, but the image is a reminder that the circus, the fair, the theatre and the cinema often enhanced our daily lives. Meeting an elephant or enjoying a show could transport us into another world in which the exotic, and magical, and wildly entertaining could exist on our doorstep.

Francis Ashley (1910 – 1991) was my mentor from about the age of ten onwards and at one time I used to visit his home on a weekly basis for induction into the world of railway modelling. After doing whatever had to be done in the railway department, we always sat down to a cap of tea before my departure, and the conversations covered a wide range of subjects. Francis Ashley's' past came out in dribs and drabs but never in any systematic way. He had played the violin in Mantovani's pre-war orchestra and travelled the world in ships' orchestras. In the war he had become a PoW, having been captured by the Japanese in Burma. After the war he resorted to all sorts of schemes to survive financially and to plan a massive railway modelling project – his life's great work which later he would leave to me to complete. I always felt that I knew him well, but now I look back and realise just how much of his biography is hidden from me. A little contemporary research soon threw up some interesting mysteries!

Jack Nelson (1909 – 1979) invented the Ilford Junior Railway Club and in my teens I became secretary of that club. We met every Friday evening in Jack's flat and I think it was his contribution to the cause of keeping young lads off the streets and out of mischief! We met from 7.30 till 9.00.pm and that hour and a half was an intense exchange of information and inspiration on all matters related to our obsession with railway modelling. Jack had his own fairly refined views on this subject but he did not push them, rather he let us inter-act in our anarchic way. There was little time for anything else, and certainly for nothing personal about ourselves or Jack. Nevertheless, Jack did share a few stories about his other lives and we guessed that his "day job" was that of a prison psychiatrist. Those of us who have kept in touch often reminisce about those days but all admit how little we really knew about Jack. As it turns out someone has risen to the challenge of trying to assemble Jack's biography. (The story is told by Richard Foster in a book called "Forty Years of the London & North Western Railway Society".) To have Jack "explained" to us after all these years is wonderful, but once again this is a reminder of how little we know about the people who have contributed to our lives, and the value of unearthing "hidden biographies". (As it turns out Jack had a very technical "day job" and his encounters with prisoners were a result of his Christian commitment to voluntary work as a prison visitor.)

Neither Francis Ashley nor Jack Nelson was "famous" in the sense that I could hope that hordes of readers might want to learn about their lives. Even the people I have described in this book are not "famous" compared with Hollywood film stars, world leaders or media and sport personalities, but they did lead lives that created some kind of footprint that makes their stories reach out to a wider world. Something has made them stand out from the ranks of many possible candidates waiting for their stories to be told. You may not relate to all seven of the people described here, but at least one will make an indelible impression on you, and you may feel compelled to embark on your own search for further hidden biographies.

I have to admit to having written about some of these people before, but what has made it a new experience in recent times has been the application of new technology to the world of archives and genealogical information. The emergence of genealogical websites like "Ancestry" and "Findmypast" have opened new horizons and the gradual digitalisation of newspaper collections accessible via the Internet have been extremely important. For example, many years ago I spent hours poring over the fine print of "The Era" in Birmingham Reference Library searching for minute advertisements submitted by Bennett & Patch, but now you can sit at home with your laptop and conduct a word search that will produce a mountain of obscure information. This facility has made it possible to explore the life and background of Broncho Bill in an entirely new way. We look forward to the day when all old newspapers are digitised and await inspection on the Net.

Researching the stories told in this book, and meeting people associated with that search, have been rewarding and sometimes exciting. Having brought all this information together it is my wish that you will also find it interesting, intriguing and stimulating whether you are interested in Black Country history, entertainment history or the wonders of genealogy. Please make contact if you have anything to add!

Ned Williams. Autumn 2018.

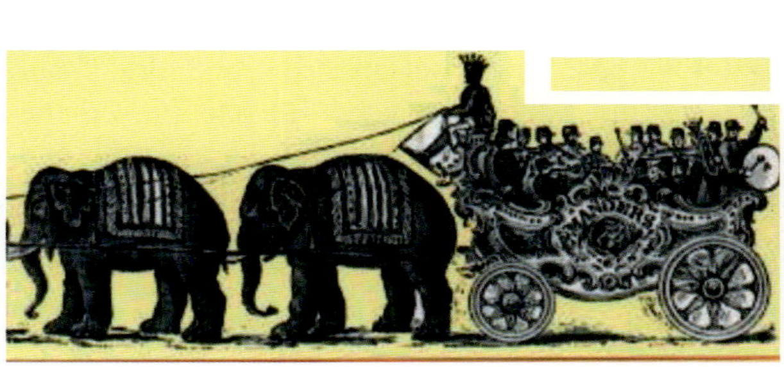

Sources

This book has used genealogical sources such as census material, the indexes to births, marriages and deaths etc., usually reached by the Internet sites mentioned above. Information has also been collected from newspapers, both those kept in local archives and the National Newspaper Collection in its digital form. A visit to the National Newspaper Collection at Colindale was always an exciting prospect. The modern "word-search" methods of using the Internet do not trawl such a comprehensive collection of papers but have their own advantages. Access to old newspapers via the Internet has been a major component in the creation of this book. The two newspapers which have inspired this book, as well as being sources of information, are "The Era" and "World's Fair!

"The Era" was published weekly from 1838 to 1939 and covered the entertainment world, often in the form of advertisements and notices placed by people in the business, as well as "news" collected by the paper. Its definition of "entertainment" was wide, and for a time even included the world of the fairground.

Without "The Era" we would have almost no record of enterprises like the portable theatres. "World's Fair"; the showman's newspaper, has been published weekly from its headquarters in Oldham from 1903 up to the present day. In its time it has covered all sorts of subjects, not just the fairground world. The paper built up a unique army of regular correspondents, many of whom adopted "pen-names". "JBT" and "Southdown" were two "World's Fair" correspondents who are described in this book. "World's Fair" has not yet been digitised and made available via the Internet. It can be read at Colindale or at the National Fairground & Circus Archive which is part of Sheffield University Library. The archive itself has built up a huge collection and has contributed greatly to taking such history seriously.

Each area of entertainment described in this book has developed its own language. I realise that the use of "jargon" can be an obstacle to good communication, but often the distinctive characteristics of each specialist world are best conveyed by use of its own language. So welcome to the world of "bioscopes", ghost shows, animated pictures, the sawdust ring and the concept of "cine-variety".

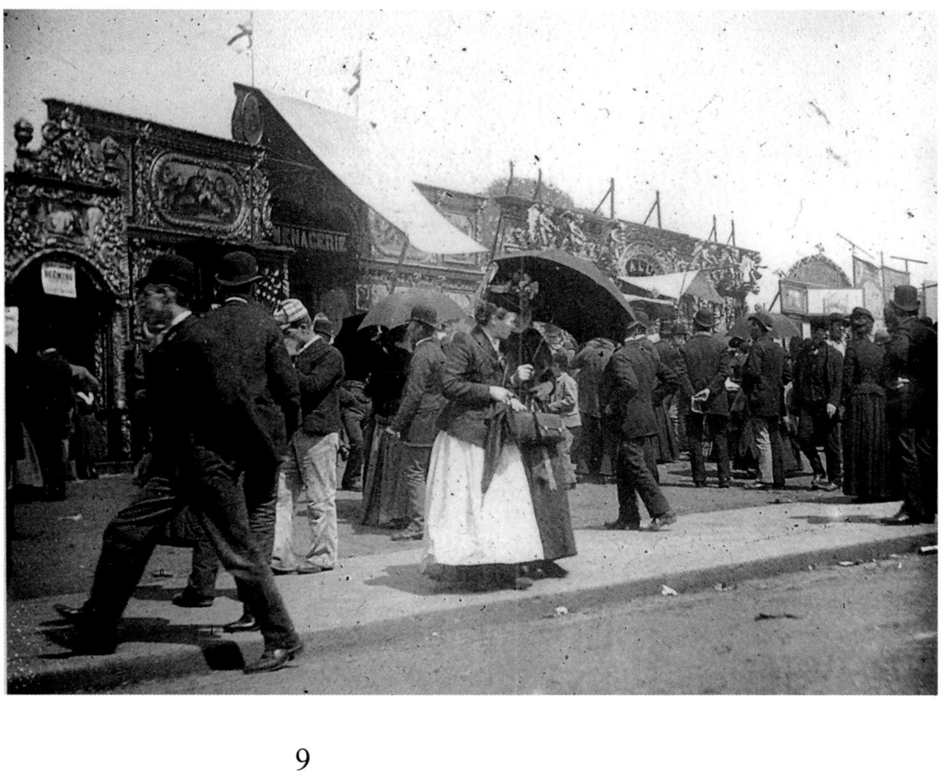

Right: Wolverhampton people, in Victorian times, come to see the shows lined up for their inspection. By the following day the shows would have moved on and life would return to normal! Note the carved and gilded woodwork of the front of a menagerie.

Glossary

Travelling shows were very popular in the second half of the 19th Century, either as part of the fair, or travelling independently. The show front was usually created by lining up two or three horse drawn wagons, often with an organ on one side and an engine/generator on the other. Shutters extended to the ground and carved woodwork or banners extended the height of the frontage. A shallow stage provided space for pre-show entertainment, enticing the potential audience and persuading them to cross the stage and enter the auditorium. The latter was usually a wooden frame, often with wooden side walls and a roof consisting of a canvas tilt. It is important to have some idea of the variety of shows that could be found in this kind of environment to appreciate the background to this book.

Ghost Shows
Ghost shows took Britain by storm in the 1880s. "Ghosts" were presented to the audience via an optical illusion using projected light and images refracted through a sheet of glass. Travelling ghost shows tended to use the "wagon-fronted" show front as seen on page 12.

Dioramas
A number of travelling shows developed in which the audience watched a series of painted scenes or "back-cloths", paraded before them. Sometimes these could be partially animated and presented in more elaborate tableaux such as navel battles or epic Biblical scenes. Narratives were explained by a "lecturer", and sometimes there was musical accompaniment. Examples included: Pooles' Mryrioramas, Hamilton's Excursions, and Kingston's Excursions mentioned in Chapter 6.

Bioscopes
From 1897 onwards cinematography was presented in travelling shows, and some shows which had presented earlier forms of entertainment converted to the new medium. The bioscopes went through rapid development from the wagon-fronted show format to huge elaborate frontages with well-furnished auditoria. They used a variety of terms to describe the new medium: phantascopes, animated pictures, electroscope, bio-graphs as well as cinematography. Films shown were short but production values soon improved, and film-making contractors such as Mitchell &Kenyon, of Blackburn, started making films for showmen. These could be specific to the town in which the show was presented and formed part of a "Come and see yourselves in the bioscope show tonight" campaign. The film-stock was "silent" and highly inflammable.

Travelling Menageries
Exhibiting animals, particularly exotic animals, played a major part in nineteenth century entertainment, introducing animals from all over the world to the British public. One of the most well-known shows was Bostock & Wombwell's which frequently visited Black Country towns.

Waxworks
The cage-like wagons used to present live animals could be used just as effectively to house tableaux consisting of waxwork figures. By the time the public tired of such entertainment the showmen were able to convert their shows to bioscopes, and some eventually moved on to become early permanent cinema proprietors.

Marionette Shows
It is easy to forget that in the nineteenth century puppets were presented as adult entertainment and the showmen who presented them became legends in their own time although now largely forgotten. Southdown, our hero of Chapter 4, was obsessed by them and was keen to keep memories of them alive. The Black Country was often visited by Wilding's Marionettes, as featured in a display at the Museum of the Chase, at Hednesford.

Portable Theatres
Very few permanent theatres existed outside London until the second half of the nineteenth century apart from a few "Theatre Royals" authorised by Royal Patent. Theatrical entertainment was provided by a few companies who travelled with their own props, minimal scenery and costumes to appear in assembly halls etc… The proprietors of travelling "portable" theatres went one step further and actually moved their entire theatre-building from place to place. They occasionally built up as part of a fair, but generally operated independently. There were many such family enterprises, and many that were popular in Black Country towns. In this book the chapter on "Bennett & Patch" will introduce you to this forgotten world.

Cinemas
Showing films to a paying public in permanent premises devoted to that activity became a reality after the passing of the 1909 Kinematograph Act. It came into force on 1st January 1910. Many of the characters described in this book had to respond to the new framework established to regulate the presentation of cinematography, and bioscopes had faded away by the outbreak of the First World War.

Cine-Variety

Once cinematography was established in Britain In 1896, showing films became a popular form of entertainment. However, some people doubted whether the public had sufficient "attention span" to deal with long periods of watching films and therefore presented short films alternated with live variety entertainment. Ben Kennedy and Irving Bosco were particular showmen who embraced this concept of "cine-variety". Irving Bosco also had experience of showing film as an "act" in a circus environment.

The Circus

When "invented" by Philip Astley this entertainment form was centred around the presentation of equestrian skills. As it developed, acts from the worlds of the menagerie, and variety-type acts, were added, and circuses have traditionally blended a unique mix of entertainment usually presented in a ring, but also sometimes on stage. In the nineteenth century circuses were presented in tents and sometimes in temporary buildings. The invention of the "Big Top" helped cement our expectation that circuses belong in a particular type of tent. The small circus could also be presented behind the "showfront" associated with the world of the fairground and numerous examples of these appeared in the Black Country – thus crossing the paths of the people featured in this book. It remains a vibrant entertainment form to this day although some people might want you to believe otherwise!

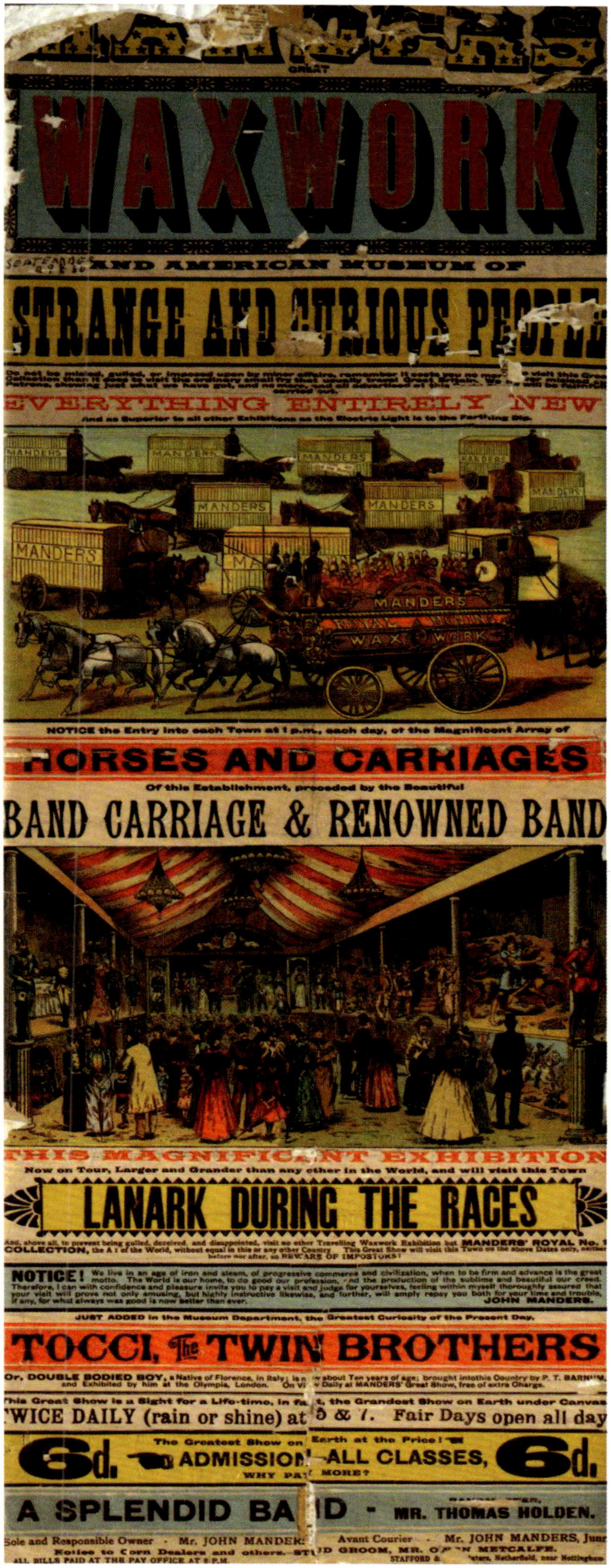

Right: A colourful poster produced for Mander's Waxworks. Two branches of the Manders family travelled menageries but John Manders (1839 - 1905) and his wife who came from a family associated with travelling marionette shows, decided to present a waxworks shows. The poster includes a picture of the show in its wagons, used for transport and mounting a parade, and a picture of the interior of the show as patrons walk round the tableaux of "Strange and Curious People". A band and a few live acts added to the entertainment. After 1899 films were also presented. John's son, also called John (1870 – 1947) was part of the generation who would move into the permanent cinema business. His brother James (1872 – 1933) also went into the bioscope business. Other Manders went into the fairground world, and some of them are to be found in the Black Country today. Others married well-known showmen – all adding up to a complex picture where many strands of entertainment intermingle.

(Poster reproduced by permission of SCRAN.)

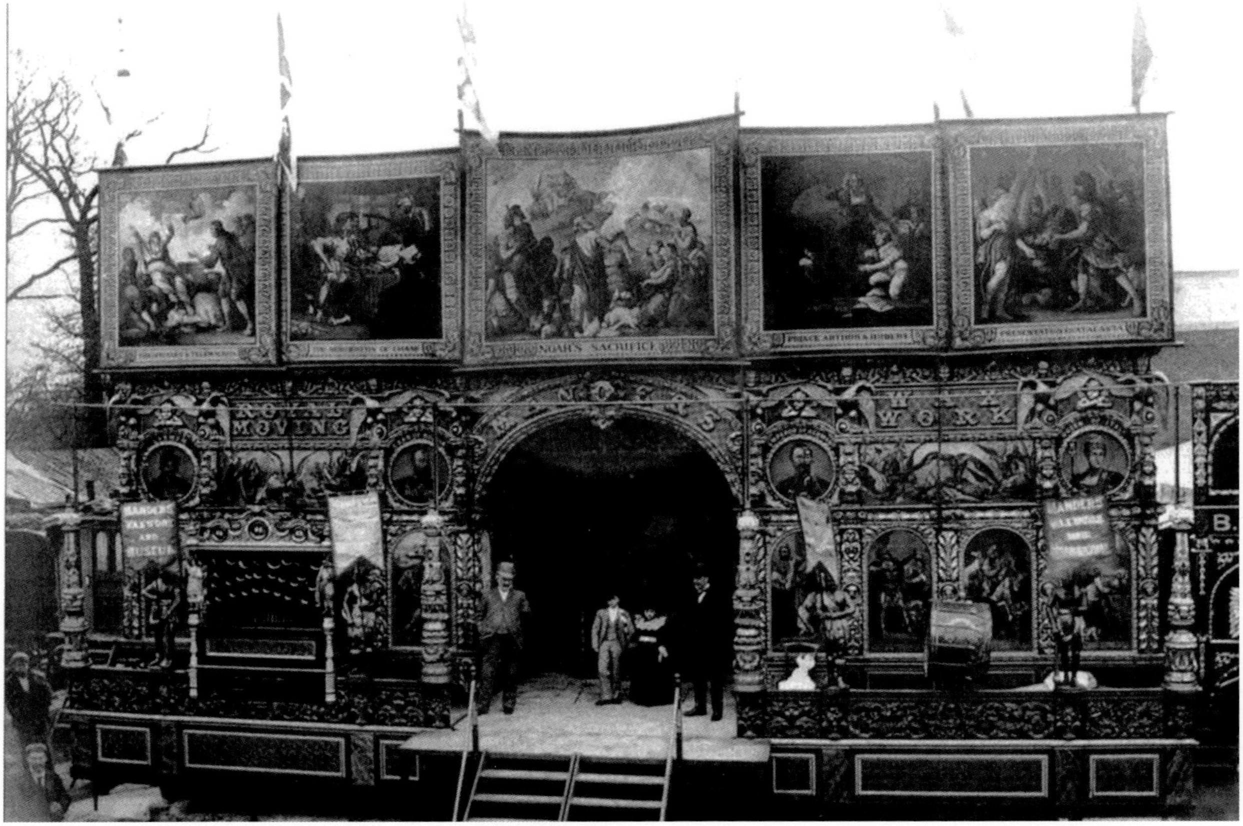

Above: John Manders' Royal Moving Waxworks" was a typical "wagon-fronted show" in which the three horse-drawn wagons were parked in a line, with the central wagon at right angles to the other two, forming the entrance and exit to the show. (Sometimes there were side entrances reached via a fold-out arch as seen at the right hand side of the picture.) One side-wagon would be obscured by a trumpet organ, as seen on the left, and the other side traditionally became the spot occupied by a "light engine" which generated electricity to light the show front. Panels could be unfolded to extend the frontage vertically, and shutters folded down to obscure the wheels. In this picture we can see that banners even more dramatically added to the height of the frontage. Most shows used a small stage area to present live entertainment to lure patrons into the show, and the arch behind the stage led into the auditorium; a canvas-roofed, wooden framed construction erected behind the frontage. Waxworks, menageries, circuses, bioscope shows and theatrical shows etc. all used variations of such frontages.

The Mirror Show

This was just one of many types of "show" that could be presented in the fairground environment. Patrons are invited to enter the show and admire themselves as revealed in a range of distorting mirrors. Joe Bate, our hero of Chapter 3, became associated with travelling such a show.

The Whale Show

Exhibiting exotic animals – alive or dead – was "big business" in the nineteenth century and took many forms. Whale Shows earn a mention as such a show plays a part in the story told in Chapter 5. The last "whale" to travel in Britain came off the road in the 1950s.

Fairground rides

Mechanised rides became increasingly important on the fairground just as many of the shows began to decline in popularity. Steam provided propulsion on early rides, then came electricity, which also provided light. In the text you will encounter the term "Scenic" – used to give a generic name to the large circular "scenic railways" or "circular switchbacks" that dominated the world of fairground rides up until the First World War.

Showfronts and Portables

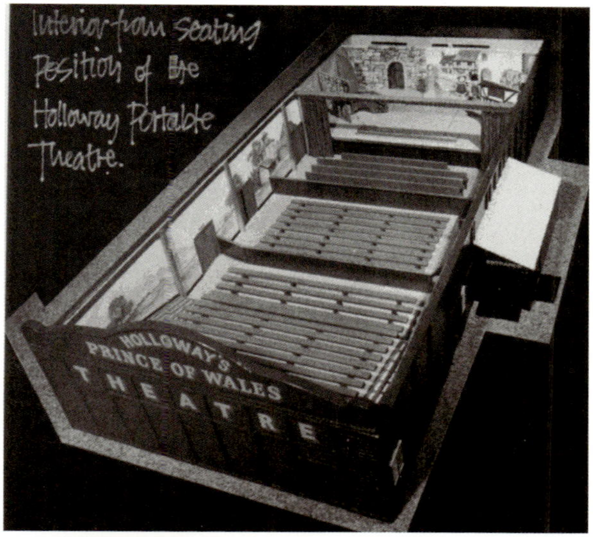

Although many shows featured fronts like that shown on page 12, some showmen favoured a "walk-in" style with a less elaborate frontage. This model of Holloway's "Prince of Wales" portable theatre, built by Geoff Holloway, illustrates the layout of the show, with a raked set of seats at the back, forms, in the centre and rails for patrons to lean on while standing in the "pit". The stage curtains and the stage itself are very basic and all dressing rooms would have to be in vans parked at the rear of the show. The Holloways presented live theatre in this structure and then progressed to films. With the arrival of "sound" they reverted to live drama. until 1939.

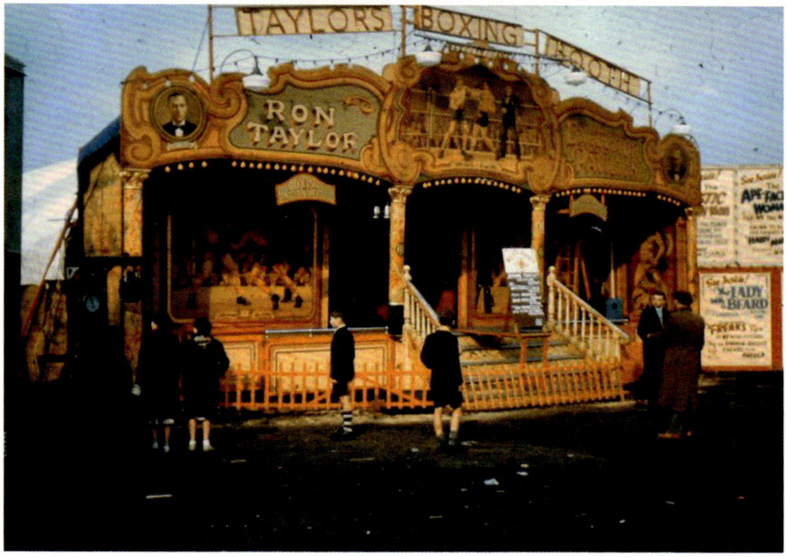

The elaborate showfronts loved by JBT and Southdown, who feature in this book, were becoming a thing of the past by about 1910. However shows on the fairground continued to feature interesting frontages until they, in turn, began to become a thing of the past by the 1960s. The boxing booth, "wild west show", girl-show, and to some extent the Wall of Death, continued the traditions of the shows for some time. Ron Taylor's Boxing Show can be seen here in the early 1960s in a picture taken by Fred Richardson at the Birmingham Onion Fair. It continued to be used until the 1990s and is now preserved.

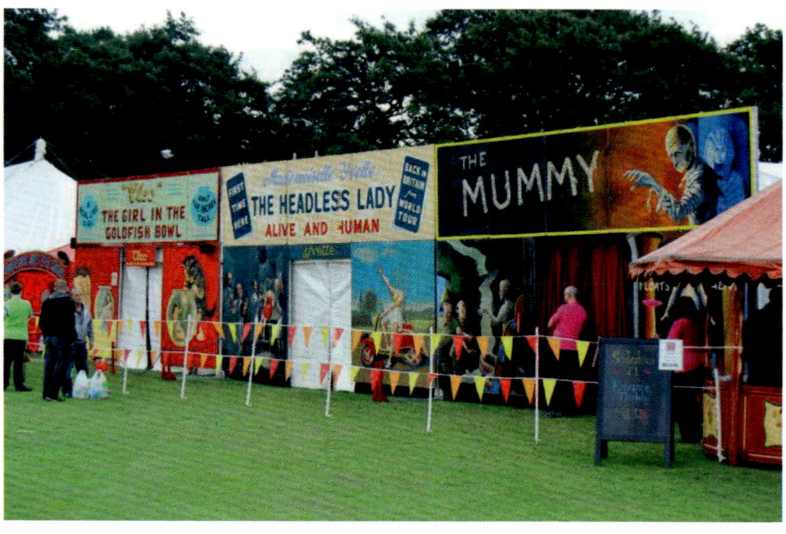

A more basic showfront was used by the small "walk-in" shows, but they too have largely disappeared. Here at Sheffield in August 2014 we see a "show-line" reconstructed to celebrate the 21st birthday of the National Fairground Archive, providing a new opportunity to see The Headless Lady, The Mummy, and The Girl in the Goldfish Bowl. A "flea circus" was also present.

Four Swallows And Two Elephants

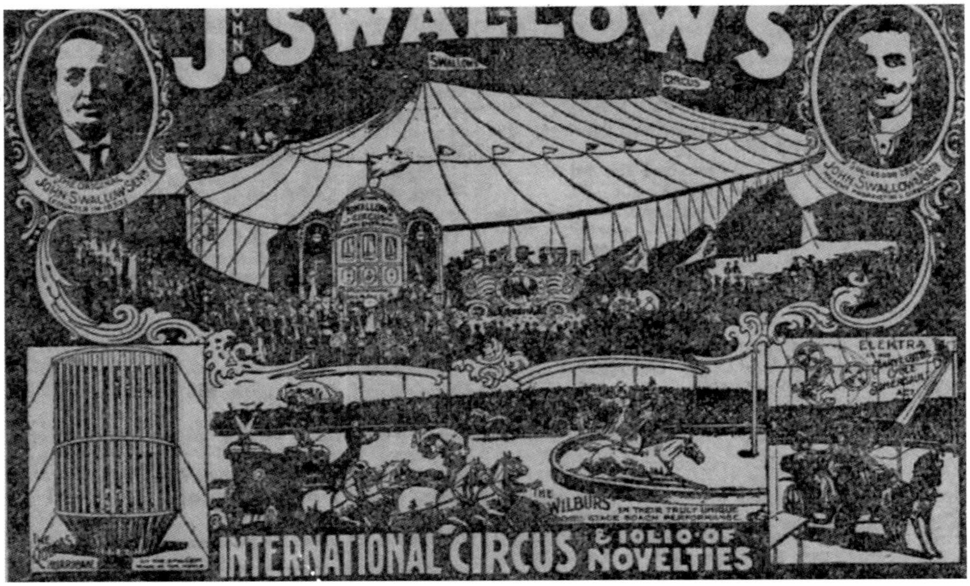

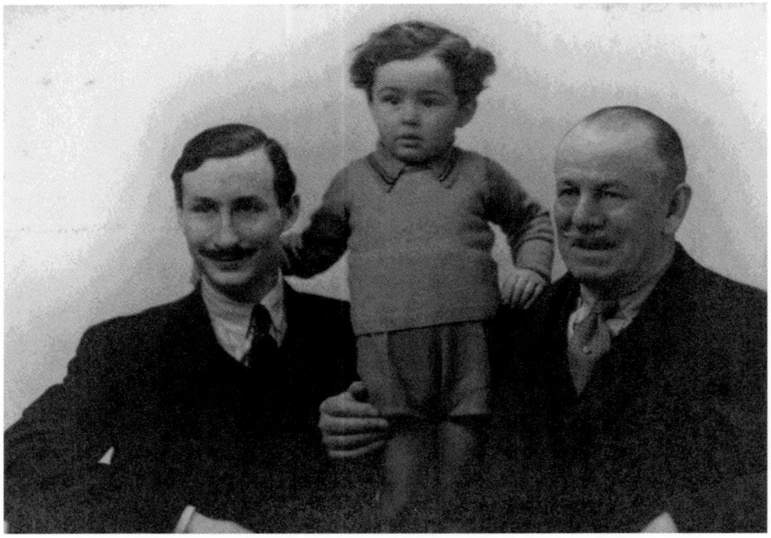

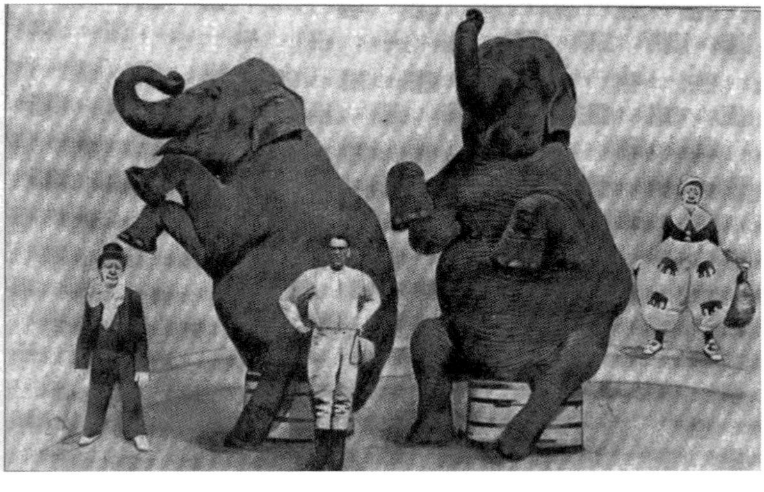

Above: A newspaper advertisement of 1910 vintage from Dundee uses a likeness of John Swallow I (1820 – 1895) (Top left), and a likeness of John Swallow II (1875 – 1945) to emphasise the continuity maintained by the Swallow family in the circus business.

Left: A photograph surviving in the family archive presents John Swallow III (1916 to 1987) (left) and John Swallow II (1938- 2008) (right) with young John Swallow IV in the centre. The picture must have been taken about 1940.

Left: Salt and Sauce, John Swallow II's elephants who travelled with John (aka Broncho Bill) from the early 1920s until 1945, becoming a local legend in Wolverhampton where their winter quarters were in Gorsebrook Road.

Chapter 1

Four Swallows and Two Elephants

Broncho Bill

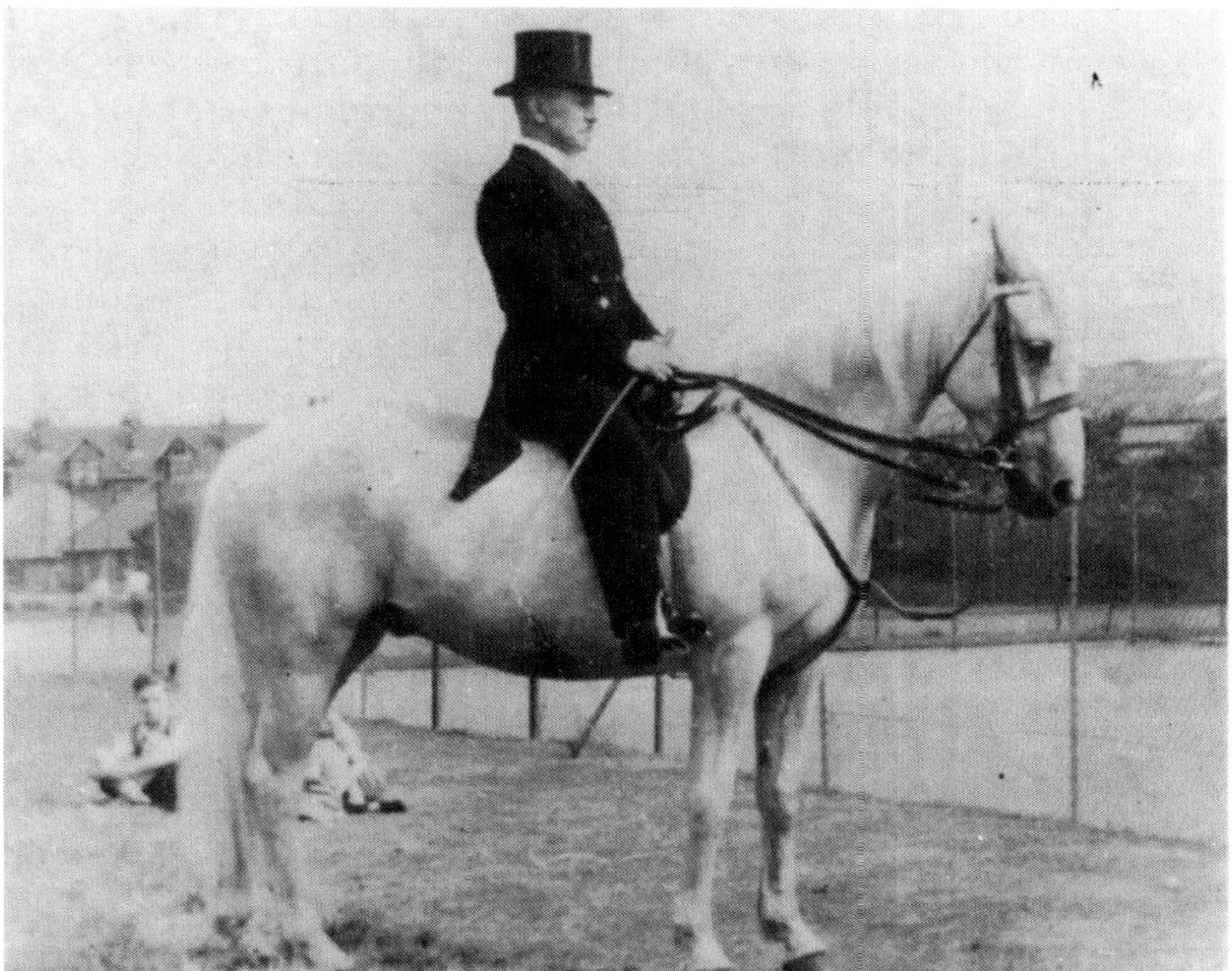

A Swallow Tree

William Swallow (1794 – 1838) married Frances Swallow, nee Moran.
They had seven children, including John Swallow I, born 1819.

John Swallow I (1819 – 13th May 1895) = Elizabeth Maugham (1844 – 24th April 1921)

Elizabeth	Amelia	Ada	John II	William	Adele	Lilian	Gilbert
b. 1865	b.1868	b.1874	b. 1875	b. 1878	b. 1880	b.1883	b.1885
d. 1887	d. 1942	d. ?	d. 1945	d. 1900	d. 1961	d.1965	d. 1948

Notes on John Swallow II's siblings:
Elizabeth married Frank Anderson on 26th. Oct. 1886 in Glasgow
Amelia married Sam Anderson in 1894.
Ada married John Henry Walton (known as "Jackles") in 1892
William died at the age of 22.
Adele married Arthur Stapley (Known as "Comical Walker") in 1917.
Lilian married James Whittaker in 1925
Gilbert married Florence

Lilian and Gilbert were both born on 4th October, Lilian in 1883 in Liverpool, Gilbert in 1885 in Glasgow.

John Henry Swallow II* = Annie Peck
1875 – 1945 1886 - 1969
Married 5th August 1910 (Copenhagen)
*BRONCHO BILL

Amy Adele	William Charles	John David*	Pat
b. 21st Dec 1912	b. 13th June 1913	b. 26th May 1916	b. 1924
d. 1989	d. 1979	d. 1987	d. 1958
Known as Doree		=Kathleen Postens	
=Alexander Campbell		*John Swallow III	

John Swallow IV
b. Dec 1939, d. 2008
= Gillian Dunning in 1962

Kate, b. 1966 | Verity, b. 1972

Searching for Elephants

After three of four years intensive work on the biography of Pat Collins, the Black Country Showman, published 1991, there was a short period of respite in which I could reflect on the way that the project had taken me into an entirely new world. Freda Allen who had been my colleague on that project did not wish to proceed any further into the fairground world, but I thought the project had revealed that there were many other stories waiting to be told. My thoughts were reinforced by the fact that some local showmen felt "left out" by our intense focus on the Pat Collins' empire. They encouraged me to feel that another project should follow in which we looked at the lives of other showmen with Black Country connections. Exploring the fairground world had also led me to become interested in the circus. It is essential to see the fairground and the circus as two entirely separate worlds, but really there are several interesting links between them. Such thoughts led to the production of another book: *"Fairs & Circuses in the Black Country"*, published in 1994. (This, in turn, led to a bigger project which resulted in the publication of *"Midland Fairground Families"* in 1996.)

While researching the material for *"Fairs & Circuses in the Black Country"* I was desperate to identify a circus with solid Black Country connections. I did not have to look very far! While talking to local people in Wolverhampton and mentioning my new interest in the circus, I was often treated to anecdotes and memories relating to two circus elephants that had once lived in the town. Sometimes these stories were very vague but sometimes people were able to give me more precise information which led to building up a picture of what this was all about. Eventually I was directed to the home of Sid and Winifred Watts in some high rise flats at the junction of Waterloo Road and Stafford Road. I interviewed them on 18th September 1993 and they had an interesting tale to tell which eventually made its way into the text of *"Fairs & Circuses in the Black Country"*.

Sid Watts was a Londoner, born in 1906. He first worked for Broncho Bill's Circus when it was making its annual New Year appearance at the Islington Agricultural Hall in the early 1920s. He travelled to Wolverhampton with the show and was given a job as "elephant groom". He shared the job with Jack Lowe and found that he would have to live with Jack and the elephants in their "winter quarters" in Gorsebrook Road. I learned for the first time that the elephants were called Salt and Saucy. Sid confirmed many of the stories that others had told me – particularly that the elephants were exercised in the Stafford Road/Dunstall area and were well known to local people. Sid often took the elephants to Mrs. Brick's grocery shop in Stafford Road where he could have a cup of tea and the elephants could graze. Mrs. Brick's daughter was Winifred, who eventually became Sid's wife. Mr. Brick was able to find Sid a job at Wolverhampton Gas Works

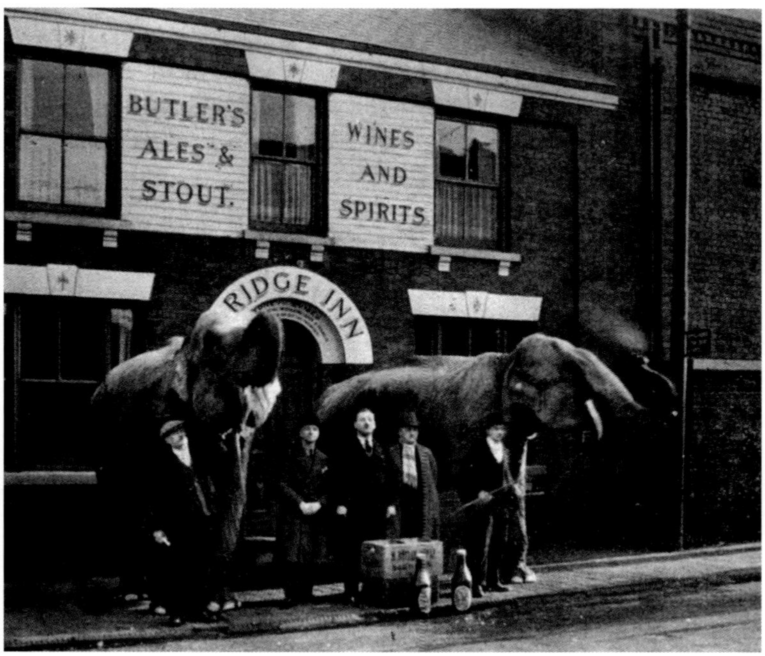

Salt and Sauce pose outside the Bridge Inn on Stafford Road, Wolverhampton in the 1920s. When staying in their quarters on Gorsebrook Road, they often walked the local streets and socialised with local people. The building to the right of the picture was part of the Great Western Railway's Stafford Road works.

that enabled him to "retire" from elephant keeping about 1934. After meeting Sid Watts Wolverhampton's elephants ceased to be shadowy legends and became very real to me.

Learning about Salt and Saucy quickly led me into the world of Broncho Bill's Circus. I then found out that Broncho Bill was really John Swallow – grandfather to the John Swallow we all knew at the time as a reporter at Central Television. He specialised in local stories with a curiosity value or human interest theme. On two occasions I had worked with John Swallow in presenting a story. For example, we concocted a short film about Wolverhampton's decision to put up signs at the town's border claiming that it was part of the Black Country. This was a very divisive and contentious matter and one short news item was not going to settle the matter but John handled it all in an amusing manner. As soon as I realised John Swallow's circus ancestry I phoned him and arranged to go and see him. At first he seemed unsure about whether he wanted his ancestry to be explored, but on becoming more enthusiastic about memories of Salt and Saucy, he produced a large black box of photographs and the story started to unfold. His willingness to share some of his family archive enabled me to include the story of Broncho Bill's Circus in the book *"Fairs & Circuses in the Black Country"*, but I was left a number of questions unanswered. (I seemed to know more about the elephants than about Broncho Bill!)

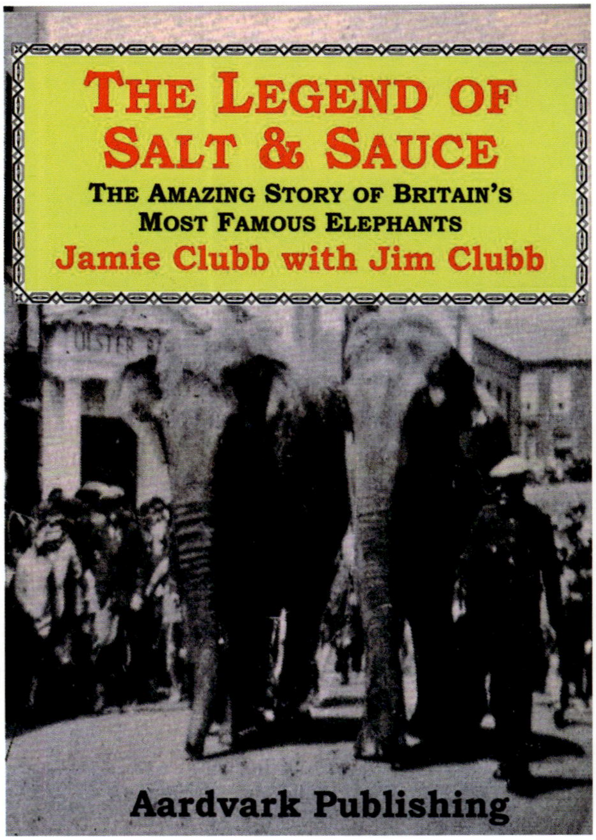

After the book's publication I felt that a more comprehensive account of Broncho Bill's life should be attempted, and that maybe Salt and Saucy deserved a proper shared biography. Although both projects simmered on a "back burner" neither made significant progress. In the end I was relieved to learn that someone else was preparing to tackle the production of a biography of the two elephants particularly because they would bring some expertise to the task that I lacked.

Jamie Clubb, and his father, Jim Clubb, published their biography of Wolverhampton's elephants in 2008, to which I was able to make a small contribution. The elephants' correct names were "Salt" and "Sauce", but I met so many people who called the latter "Saucy" I tend to perpetuate the mistake! Neither I, nor the Clubbs, were successful in contacting John Swallow while the book was being produced. He had moved from Wolverhampton to Maldon and was not enjoying good health. After the book came out, I sent John a copy and he died shortly afterwards, but not before he had scribbled me a note to say how much he had enjoyed reviving memories of the elephants, and the part they had played in his childhood. John's death meant we had lost a valuable connection to the untold story of his grandfather: Broncho Bill.

At my first meeting with John Swallow I was directed to his grandfather's grave in Jeffcock Road Cemetery, not far from my Wolverhampton home. To my surprise there was no mention of the name "Broncho Bill" on the headstone. I was also surprised to find another John Swallow buried in the same cemetery: the grave of the man I have called "John Swallow I" It was becoming necessary for me to number the Swallows as a prelude to making further enquiries. These enquiries then faltered for lack of good progress and were overtaken by other projects, but Broncho Bill remained one of the mysterious characters connected with entertainment and connected with the Black Country that needed to be looked at as soon as circumstances made it possible. The search for Swallows had begun, slipped onto the back burner for a while, and then surfaced as this book began to take shape.

Left: The cover of the Clubbs' book: "The Legend of Salt and Sauce". Published in 2008.

Right: Jim Clubb, Ivor Rosaire, and Jamie Clubb, brought together at a meeting of the Circus Friends Association, promoting the Clubbs' book about Salt and Sauce and also celebrating Ivor's long career as an animal presenter and trainer. Ivor Rosaire (1911 – 2006) was a man of many talents. When John Swallow II joined Rosaire's Circus in 1931 the twenty three year old Ivor was entrusted with presenting Salt and Sauce three years later, eventually working with many elephant troupes for Chipperfields, Fossetts and others.

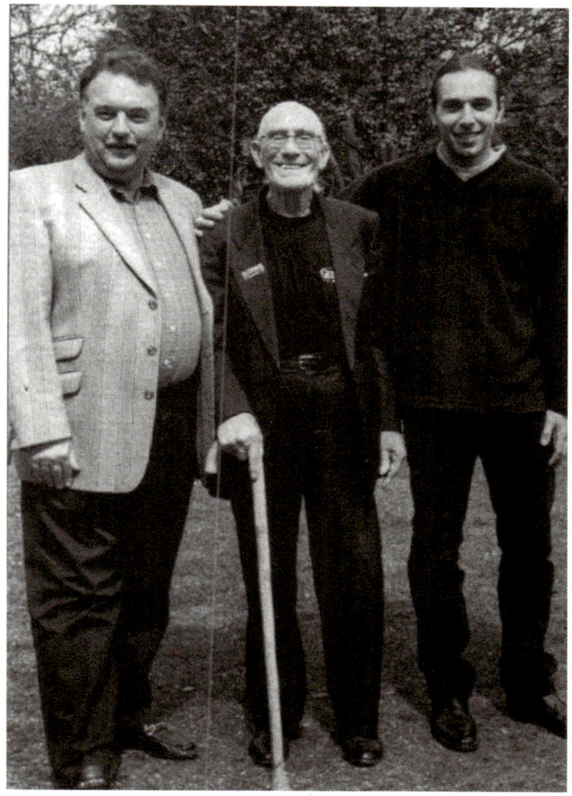

Below left: John Swallow II's grave in Jeffcock Road, Cemetery, Wolverhampton. The name "Broncho Bill" is not featured. He shares the grave with Annie who died 25th October 1969 and their son William who died 9th August 1979.

Below Right: In the same cemery: the grave of John Swallow I who died 13th May 1895, his wife Elizabeth, who died 24th April 1921 and their son William who died 23rd August 1900.

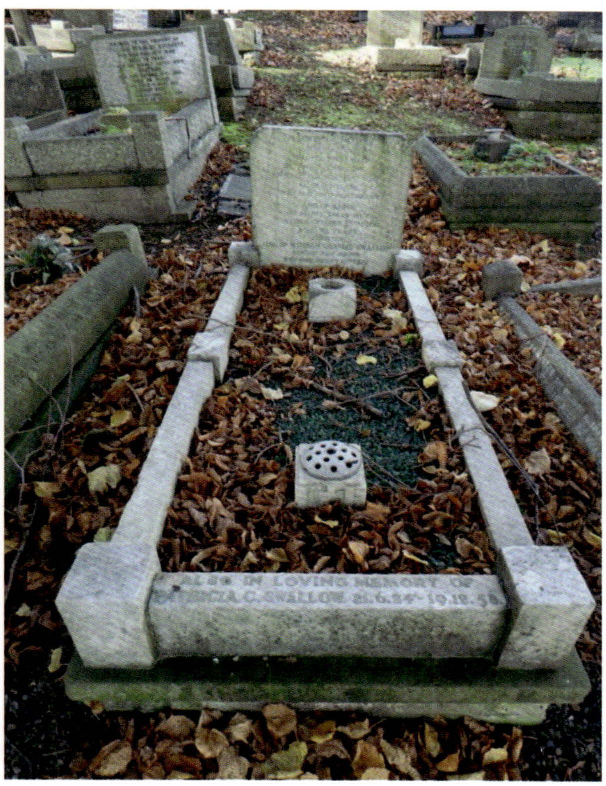

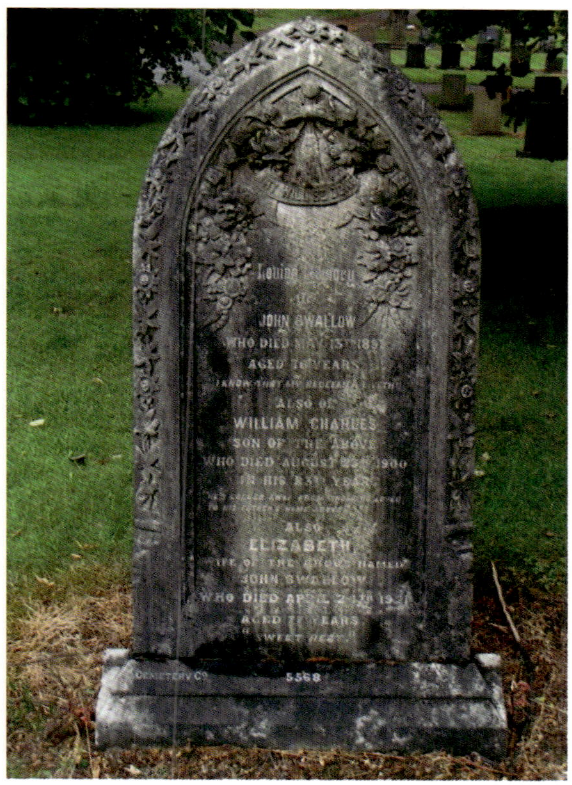

Searching for Swallows

The task of setting out the story of Broncho Bill begins with establishing his real identity. His real name was John Henry Swallow, born in 1876 and died in 1945. The next problem is that his father, his son and his grandson were also named John Swallow so the first step is to number them from "I" to "IV", thus making the central character of our story: 'John Swallow II'. As it turns out, he only really used the name 'Broncho Bill' for a relatively short time.

There could never really be any doubt that John Swallow II would become an "equestrian" and possibly the proprietor of a circus because he was the son (but fourth surviving child) of John Swallow I whose life had exactly followed such a path. We therefore have to begin our story by looking at the life of John Swallow I. John Swallow I was born in 1819 or 1820, probably in Yorkshire. It seems impossible to find out much about his early life. He was the son of William and Frances Swallow, and although his father had spent much of his life in the clothing and shoe trade, he was described as a "showman" at the time of his death.

Some writers have stated that his circus was established as early as 1841 when John was in his early twenties, but unfortunately no evidence has yet been found in the 1841 or 1851 censuses. One account found in The Era of 17th September 1910 suggests the circus began as early as 1830 when John Swallow I was only about eleven years old! This gives us an important clue: the original circus was probably created by his father; William Swallow. Little is recorded about William Swallow until his death, at the age of forty five, on 30th December 1838 at Bolton. An inquest reached the strange conclusion he had suddenly died "by the visitation of God", but from our point of view the inquest usefully notes that he was a "travelling showman". Maybe it was he who started a show in 1830 and introduced several of his children to the business.

In the 1861 census John Swallow I appears as a "visitor" at the home of his sister; Mary Ann Clough in Gomersal, Yorkshire, with his occupation clearly stated as "equestrian". Soon after that, in 1864, he married Elizabeth. This event is more difficult to pin down in the public records. However we know that her maiden name was Maugham but there is still some mystery surrounding such information. What seems more certain is that she was born in 1844 and came from Newcastle, thus she was twenty years old at the time of marriage and John Swallow I was about forty. On the birth certificates of his first children John is described as "A performer at a circus" rather than "circus proprietor". Some documentation of John Swallow I's travels is to be found in local papers. For example, in 1865 several papers report on a case heard at the Stockton Borough Police Court brought by a Mr. Waldron, manager of Stockton's Theatre Royal. He had complained to the authorities that John Swallow's presentation of "Dick Turpin's Ride to York" contravened the "Regulation of Theatres Act" because it was a "play" for which John Swallow had no licence. Apparently John Swallow had opened in Stockton, and rivalry with the Theatre Royal had led to all this.

Six magistrates deliberated for twenty minutes and were divided equally on whether the performance was a play or not. The case had to be dismissed as there was no clear decision on the matter. Once reported in the Newcastle Journal the story spread rapidly to other newspapers – as far away as The Wolverhampton Chronicle which ambiguously explained to local readers that… "This piece is a play of melodrama originally produced at Astley's".
In the mid 1860s John Swallow I began placing occasional adverts in The Era, sometimes giving us an idea of the breadth of his travels. For example, while the circus is in Macclesfield in February 1866 he advertises: "Wanted: Male and Female Equestrians and a Good Band for tenting season."

The Rise and Fall of John Swallow I

John Swallow's circus seems to have been a great success, some of which was in Scotland. It has been said that his show was patronised by Royalty on several occasions – possible it had been seen by Queen Victoria while at Balmoral. From the 1870s onwards his children appeared in the show as proved by the 1871 census when the family is observed on the cattle market in Burton-on-Trent. Elizabeth, aged five and Amelia, aged 3 are described as "equestrian apprentices"! As the family grows, the diversity of their birthplaces reveals that they were very definitely a "travelling family" – for example Elizabeth, born towards the end of 1866 was born in Birkenhead, Amelia, born in 1868 was born in Manchester, and their first son to be called John was born in Whitehaven in 1870, but died in infancy. (The second son to be called John, the subject of our story, was born in Edinburgh in 1876.)

Although the 1871 census finds the family in Burton-on-Trent, we know, from advertising in the Dundee Courier of 29th August of that year that the show was once again touring Scotland. In the summer of 1872 we find John Swallow in Glasgow, the following year in Edinburgh. It would be wonderful to have a more detailed picture of his travels as many things are unclear. For example at the end of the 1870s we find newspaper evidence of John Swallow using a "recently erected" building in Paisley (later converted to a theatre by a Mr. T.C. Howitt) leaving us to speculate on the degree to which John Swallow experimented with wooden buildings as an alternative to a circus tent.

The 1881 Census finds the Swallow family "in their vans" on some land in Liverpool. On that occasion John Snr. (61) and Elizabeth (37) are joined by six children as well as two servants, one of whom looks after the horses. Of the children: Elizabeth (15), Amelia (13) and Ada (7) are all described as "equestrians", presumably performing in the ring for their father.

In November 1885 the Western Morning News gives a glowing account of the show while it was appearing at Plymouth: *"After all that has been said, or can be said, in commendation of Mr. Swallow's Circus, now occupying St. James' Hall, Plymouth, full justice would scarcely be done to the company. The entertainment is everything that the proprietor claims for it, and the hearty manner in which the entertainers are applauded after each of the sixteen events of the programme, supplies proof that the crowds have been well satisfied with what had been given to them in exchange for their money."*

However, within a year of this report the family's fortunes were changing. For example, in the Autumn of 1887 John and Elizabeth lost their oldest daughter, Elizabeth, at the age of twenty-two. Back in October 1866 good news had prevailed when Elizabeth had married Frank Anderson who worked for Henglers Circus, in Glasgow. On 29th November 1887 she had delivered their son, but the good news was followed by her death, in London, on Christmas Eve. John Swallow II was in his teens by this time and had presumably had joined his sisters Amelia and Ada, in the ring.

By 1889 John Swallow I faced catastrophe. And the story was told in The Era when Amelia was taken to court in the February of that year:

The Era of 16th February 1889 reported on a court case heard at Stockport County Court on 8th Feb 1889 – all the parties concerned being connected with circuses. The plaintiff was Paddy Watson, a singing clown; the defendant was John Swallow, and claimant, Amelia Swallow, equestrienne, daughter of John Swallow. Paddy Watson had worked for the Swallows and claimed he had not been fully paid. As John Swallow, Amelia and Ada gave evidence the sad story of John's declining fortunes emerged and were described in The Era as follows:

…… "John Swallow had been a circus proprietor nearly all his life. He used to run a travelling concern and was accompanied by his daughters Amelia, Ada and one deceased, and his sons, who performed. In 1887 he began to go downhill, and, getting into debt, borrowed money from his daughters. Wishing to borrow from Amelia in October 1887, she would only agree to purchase two horses from him, one being Princess, and another called Forrest, for £28….

The family continued to keep together, and the claimant used the horses professionally. While at Redditch, at Easter 1888, Forrest became lame, and as the defendant was then pressed by a creditor, he handed over the horse, along with the van, to the creditor, on the understanding that he was to give his daughter Amelia another horse called Blackie….

In August 1888 the defendant came to grief altogether. His goods and chattels were swept away under a bill of sale, and he ceased to have a single thing to call his own but his clothes. From that time on he had travelled about with his children, taking care of their baggage, teaching the boys to ride, and being kept by them entirely."

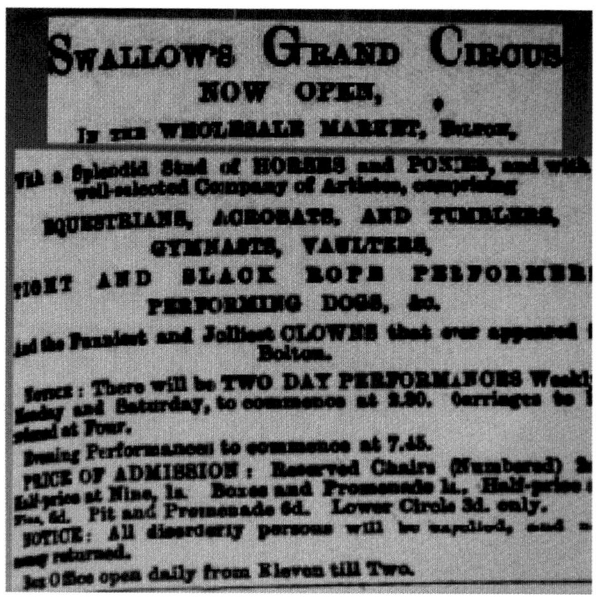

Photographs of John Swallow I's circus do not seem to have survived but newspaper adverts can be found such as this one advertising the show in Bolton in November 1873.

Amelia Swallow, barely in her twenties, must have taken control of the business, but John Swallow I could no longer call himself "circus proprietor". In 1891 we can again turn to the census to tell us about the Swallow family, but they are now found in two quite separate entries. John Swallow I is to be found as a lodger in the home of Thomas and Margaret Maugham in Newcastle on Tyne. The seventy-two year old now simply describes himself as "equestrian" – as do the children: Amelia (23), Ada (18), John Swallow II (16), and William (14). Adele, at the age of eleven is still a "scholar". However, what is interesting is to find out about John's wife, Elizabeth, and the rest of the family.

The Wolverhampton Connection

A trawl through the 1891 Census helps us find the other part of the Swallow family: they are to be found in Wolverhampton. The strange thing is that John Swallow I appears in both entries – apparently in Newcastle and Wolverhampton at the same time! In the Wolverhampton entry he modestly describes himself as "circus artist". He, and Elizabeth (now 47), are now lodgers at No. 6 Thornley Street, along with the two youngest children: Lilian (7) and Gilbert (5). Just for good measure Eugene and Elizabeth Foot are also lodging at the same address and describe themselves as "circus artists", along with their six-month old daughter. No. 6, Thornley Street, in 1891, was the home of Theodore Fitzwood (40) and his wife Mary (26). He describes himself as "horsebreaker and trainer" but the enumerator has over-written the entry simply with the word "groom". Theodore apparently had come to Britain from Africa, and his wife came from Jersey in the Channel Islands. They are difficult to trace in any other public record, but their home in Thornley Street continues to play a part in our story.

Thornley Street is close to the centre of Wolverhampton, just north of Broad Street, and was "civilised" with new housing in the 1880s onwards – replacing a run-down area known locally as "The Caribee" or "Caribee Island". In 1910 the Quigley family opened Wolverhampton's second cinema, the Olympia, in Thornley Street and the section between Whitmore Street and Broad Street now shows no trace of its one-time residential nature. Residential development must have only been on one side of the street as the other was occupied by the rear of the Drill Hall. With John Swallow I's decline in fortunes it seems that he and Elizabeth chose to "retire" to Thornley Street, thus cementing the Swallows connection with Wolverhampton.

On 13th May 1895 John Swallow I died at 6 Thornley Street, aged 76. He was buried in Jeffcock Road Cemetery. Five years later, in 1900, he was joined in this grave by his son William who had died at the age of twenty-two. What remained of his circus by 1895 is not clear but in theory it was bequeathed to his son, John II. No. 6, Thornley Street certainly seemed capable of holding a number of people. In the 1901 census we find John's widow, Elizabeth in charge, along with her daughters, Ada (26), Adele (20), Lilian (17) and son Gilbert (15). Ada Swallow had married John Henry Walton on 17th October 1892 – at High Wycombe and she brought along three children. (John Walton was also known as "Clown Jackles".) Just for good measure a "music hall artiste" named Edwin Rockett was also a guest in the Thornley Street household.

It seems that Elizabeth Swallow remained at Thornley Street for the rest of her life, and her son John Swallow II used the address as a base and contact address for some of that time. Elizabeth died on 24th April 1921 and joined her late husband in the grave at Jeffcock Road Cemetery.

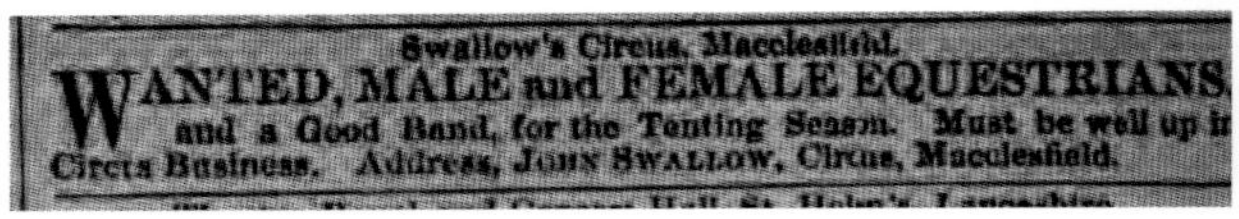
Swallow's Circus, Macclesfield.
WANTED, MALE and FEMALE EQUESTRIANS, and a Good Band, for the Tenting Season. Must be well up i
Circus Business. Address, JOHN SWALLOW, Circus, Macclesfield.

This advertisement placed in "The Era" in 1866 had to use the temporary circus location as its point of contact. Once the base in Thornley Street, Wolverhampton, was established, that address could be used. In the advert appearing below we can see that as late as 1937 adverts could be used to find further engagements for Salt and Sauce, using John Swallow II's Waterloo Road address.

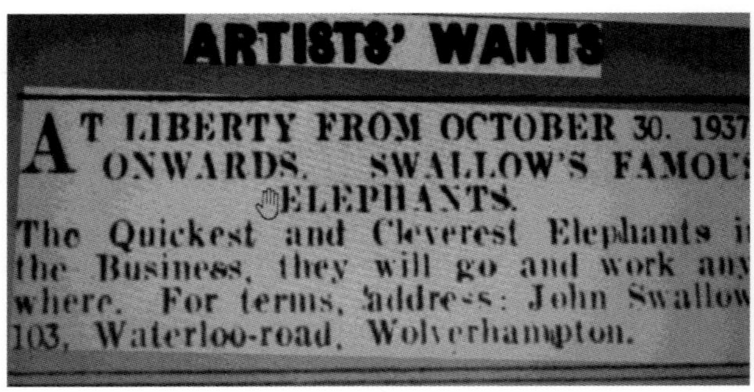
ARTISTS' WANTS

AT LIBERTY FROM OCTOBER 30. 1937 ONWARDS. SWALLOW'S FAMOU ELEPHANTS. The Quickest and Cleverest Elephants i the Business, they will go and work any where. For terms, address: John Swallow 103, Waterloo-road, Wolverhampton.

John Swallow II / Broncho Bill

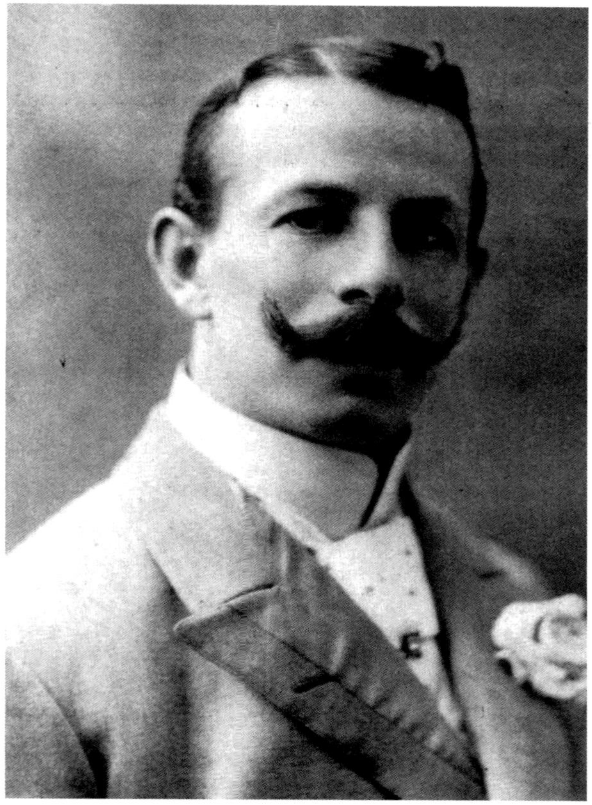

John Henry Swallow on his way to becoming "Broncho Bill".

John Henry Swallow II was born 21st November 1875 in Edinburgh. The first child of John and Elizabeth Swallow had been a son called John, born in Whitehaven in 1870, but this child had not survived – and, in the Victorian tradition, his name was used again when the next son arrived.

By the age of three it is said that he was strapped to the back of a horse, and by the age of six could stand while riding a horse bare-back. Within a year or two he could somersault to and from the horse's back. There could be no doubt that he would follow in his father's footsteps as an equestrian and eventually as a circus proprietor. As we have seen above, his father's circus faltered in the 1880s while John Swallow II was still in his teens, and at that time his older sisters, Amelia and Ada, seemed to take charge, so it is interesting to try and work out when John took a greater responsibility for the show. To some extent it seems that he was also keen to work independently of his family and to earn recognition in his own right as a great equestrian. Although the circus was bequeathed to him on his father's death in 1895, it seems that there was precious little to pass on. Perhaps we should regard the years from the late 1880s onwards as the time in which John Swallow II pursued an independent career.

It is possible to come across glimpses of John Swallow's activities during this period in reports and advertisements printed in "The Era" – that encyclopaedic nineteenth century "showbiz" weekly newspaper that is often our only window into worlds that have now vanished. It is a difficult paper to read as it is so densely packed with information but modern "word search" technology and the digitisation of newspaper archives has made life easier! Quite obscure references to John Swallow's life can now be picked up. For example, on 23rd November 1895 we find a one-line comment on the fact that John Swallow II was appearing as part of a troupe called "The Trojan Youths" in Harry Boswell's Circus in Hanley. We find similar minimal references to John Swallow II's career in a paper called The Music Hall and Theatre Review. For example, in February 1893 he is recorded as appearing in Ginnett's Circus at Portsmouth and two years later is mentioned again when Ginnett's show was being presented in Belfast.

In April 1896 an article appears in The Era on the circus career of Bob Carlisle who had advertised for a partner following a decision to go into the circus business. John Swallow answered the call from Dundee and they opened for the first time as partners in Leith. Apparently all went well while they travelled in Scotland, but they were less successful in England and finally parted company in Preston.

On 27th February 1897 "The Era" tells us that John Swallow II was appearing with Claude Ginnett's Circus again in Derby where *"Mr. John Swallow continues is sensational feats of horsemanship."* The Ginnetts were a major circus dynasty and it seems that John Swallow made many friends with such families. On 26th August 1900 William Swallow, John's brother, died and the Ginnetts attended the funeral. Many years later two members of the Ginnett family attended John's modest funeral. This gives us a picture of John Swallow's life being always on the move – not just geographically but also in terms of the variety of ways in which he provided a basic continuity to his career as an equestrian.

William, only two years younger than John, had died in Wolverhampton – this reminds us that while John's career took him far and wide while in his twenties, his family was fairly solidly based at 6 Thornley Street, Wolverhampton, as described in the 1901 census, as set out above. That John Swallow cannot be found in the 1901 census is a mystery but we know from an advert in "The Era" that during March – just before the census was taken – that he was appearing in Ohmi's Circus at Castleford. In the December of 1901 he was with Algie's Circus in Carlisle. This circus was owned by a P.E.Veitch, but managed by Mr. C. Algie. In a report John Swallow II is described as *"giving a clever display of horsemanship, Sam Anderson was performing daring somersaults while riding bareback and Miss Amelia and Miss Lilian were "successful equestriennes"*. These snippets of information tell us that John was sometimes appearing in shows alongside his sisters and his brother-in-law.

The period from 1901 to 1905 can only be described by snippets of information supplied from the advertising columns of "The Era" – sometimes giving us no more than a place name and a date. For example June 1902 John Swallow was in Greenock, in November 1902 he was in Wigan with Adele and Sam once more. At the beginning of 1903 John was looking for work, offering to not only put on "Dick Turpin's Ride to York", but also to provide costumes and scenery…. "and the best-trained Bess in the world." Apparently they had just completed a very successful season in Southport.

An advertisement appearing in September 1904 confirms the existence of work opportunities in Continental Europe as we find John is touring with Cirque Pinder in France while telling us that he is looking for work during the winter of 1904 into 1905.

The Arrival of the Wild West

Two great American touring shows came to Britain at the turn of the century. Barnum and Bailey's circus toured in 1898, coming to Wolverhampton on 7th and 8th of November. Buffalo Bill's Wild West Show toured in 1903 and 1904, following different routes. The 1903 journey took them from Worcester to Kidderminster, to Dudley, to Wolverhampton and onwards to Stafford on successive nights in June. In April 1904 the show came to Walsall and Wollaston, just outside Stourbridge. These shows raised audience expectations and set new standards of equestrian skill as well as scale of production. 'Dick Turpin's Ride to York' faded a little after seeing hordes of Wild West characters on horseback in these shows. It is interesting to speculate on to what extent local artistes joined these shows, and to what extent British artists joined the troupe on the European legs of their tours.

It does seem certain that John Swallow joined the Barnum & Bailey tour of Europe. George Sanger Coleman watched John Swallow rehearsing a routine in the Barnum & Bailey show and wrote a paragraph about it in his book, "The Sanger Story". The rehearsal was also watched by John Bailey himself. Coleman felt it was an impressive display of equestrian skill but John Bailey felt it lacked "passion", even although it was only a rehearsal, and subsequently dismissed John Swallow!

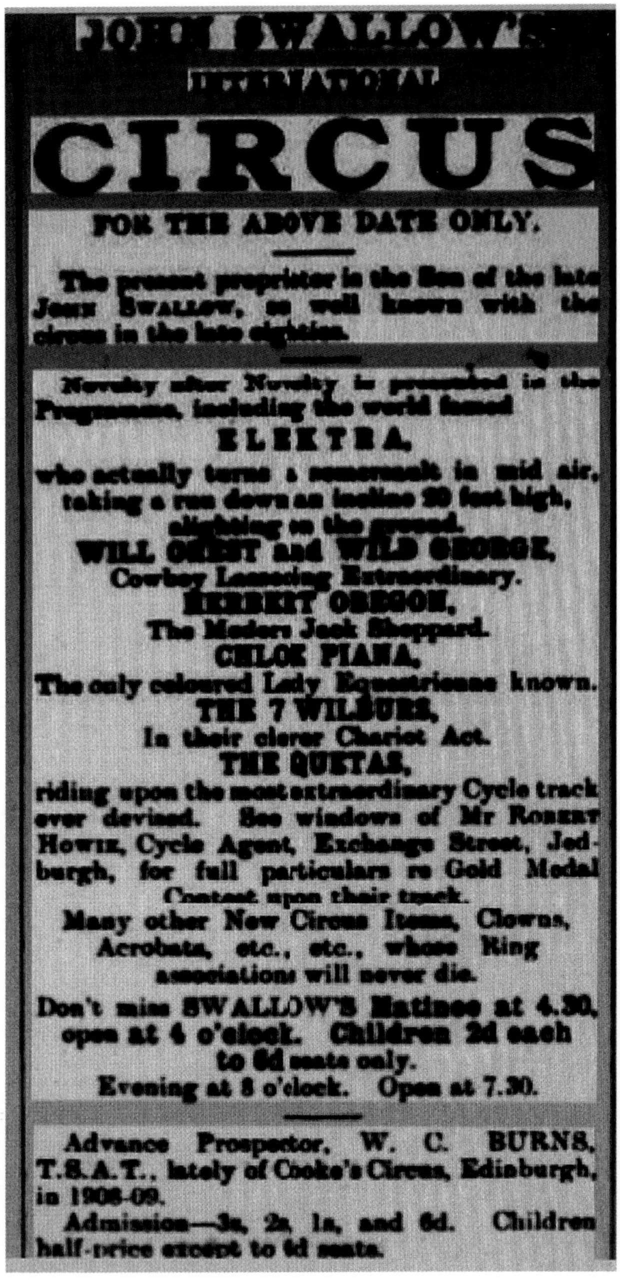

Several accounts of John's life also present him as travelling to America during the 1900s, where again he may have rode on Barnum and Bailey's show. It is said that he drove the Deadwood Stagecoach in the show's Wild West finale. In the report of John's funeral his son, John David Swallow, states that his father was in America from 1904 to 1908 and was then touring in Europe for two years. As I have shown above, the advertisements in "The Era" would suggest a slightly later departure for America. Consulting shipping records so far has only produced an account of a John Henry Swallow travelling across the Atlantic to New York on The Minneapolis in 1905 and a plain John Swallow heading for New York in August 1906 on The Minnetonka.

1910 onwards…

It does not seem that John Swallow simply returned from America and immediately set up his own Wild West Show. However, it does seem that he was running his own circus from 1910 onwards, simply calling it John Swallow's International Circus. For example, The Era of 27th May 1910 reports that the circus of that name had been seen in Hawick, stating, *"The present proprietor is the son of the late John Swallow, well know circus proprietor of the 1880s".*

This explanation of the circus's pedigree is repeated in most descriptions of its appearances. Its appearance at Hawick was part of a series on one-night stands as the circus travelled from Jedburgh, to Hawick and on to Selkirk, Inverleithin, Stow, Galashiels, Melrose, Earlstown and on into Central Scotland. Two shows were presented at each venue.

There is a much bigger report in The Era of 17th September 1910 after the circus had appeared for two nights in Dundee. The review is very positive about the show and mentions a number of the acts, including wire-walking, acrobats, an escapologist, trick cycling and a "stage coach act" – perhaps a sign of American influence. Miss Amelia, John's sister, earns a mention, and his brother-in-law; Comical Walker. Even the bandleader, Robert Horrocks, is commended! Historically it is interesting to note a mention of Miss Chloe Diana, "the only black lady equestrienne", Could this be someone else that John Swallow had met in America? John's brother Gilbert Swallow, then twenty five, is described as "the capable manager". The stand in Dundee produced the advertising "block" featuring portraits of John Swallow and his father – once again emphasizing the continuity from one generation of the family to the next. (See page 12)

The Era told its readers, *"This old established circus concluded a two day visit to Dundee on Monday evening 12th September. The huge tent was pitched on The Esplanade and large audiences were attracted to the two performances given daily. Mr. John H Swallow Jnr. worthily upholds the reputation of his father who established the show in 1830. The entertainment is of a high-class order, a pleasing feature being the entire absence of anything pertaining to vulgarity. The highly trained mare, Elizabeth, a beautiful piebald animal trained and introduced by Mr. John Swallow reflects the utmost credit on its trainer."*

On 5th August 1910 John II married Annie Peck in Copenhagen, Denmark, perhaps marking the end of a short continental tour. Annie Peck seems to have come from a large family based in Aberdeen and was at least eleven years younger than John Swallow. They had probably met on Ginnett's Circus where she appeared under the professional name of Mdle. D'Alma – a well-regarded rider in her own right. Although the family legend is that she was of Irish background, she appears to be the daughter of a trawler fisherman and was born in Scarborough in 1888. In the 1891 and 1901 census she and her sisters are living in Aberdeen.

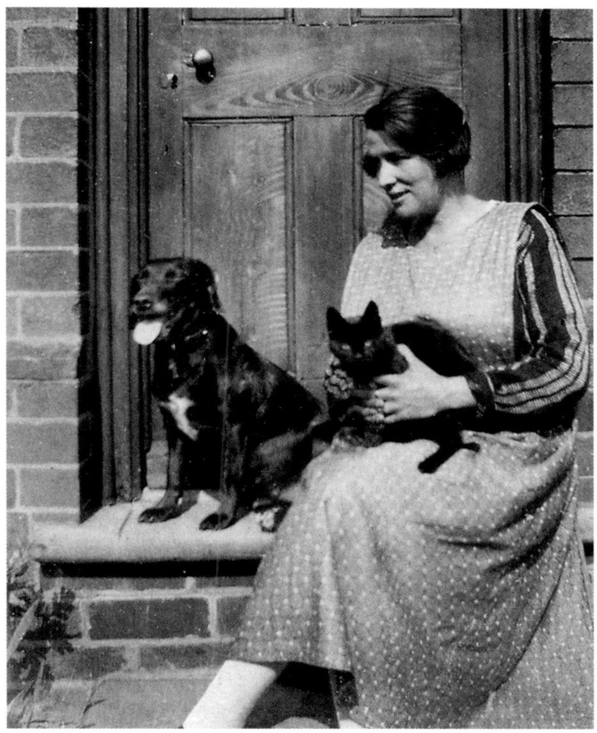

Above: Annie Swallow, nee Peck.
Opposite page: John Swallow's International Circus advertised in Jedburgh, 20th May 1910.

John Swallow's International .. **CIRCUS**

And IOLIO of Novelties.

Established by the late John Swallow in 1830.
Present Proprietor, JOHN H. SWALLOW, Junr.

PROGRAMME, One Penny.

Subject to Alterations.

1. Musical Discourse by the Band.
2. **Zemoe** and **Auguste**, Ring Experts.
3. The Game of Polo, on Horseback by **Six Mounted Gents**.
4. **Victoria and Elena,** Wire Dancers.
5. **Miss Amelia, Trick Act on Horseback**. Clown, **Funny Bibby**
6. Entree. Five minutes fun with **Bibby**.
7. Five Horse Liberty Act, introduced by **M'ddle Anita or J. Swallow**.
8. **Globbela** on the moving Sphere.
9. Quick Change Act of Equestrianism, by **Miss Amelia.**
10. **Will Oresto** and **Wild George,** Lassoo and Knot Experts.
11. **Herbert Oregon,** the modern Jack Sheppard, who will be manacled, put in a sack and dragged around the Arena by a horse, freeing himself in a remarkably short time.
12. The Highly-trained Mare, **Elizabeth,** trained and introduced by **John Swallow.**
13. **The Papillios.** The Daring Teeth Performers.
14. **Miss d'Almer,** Equestrienne. Clown, **Comical Walker**.
15. Comic Interlude by **Walker** the **Fool**.
17. **THE QUETAS.** in their Cycle Hurricane Racing upon the smallest possible track ever ridden. A Solid Gold Medal, Hall-marked, will be given to any local amateur rider who can ride around once upon the track without falling off.
18. Finale—Comicalities throughout the Performance by numerous fools.

Sole Proprietor and Manager - - - - JOHN H. SWALLOW.

During 1910 John Swallow used this phrase: "Circus and Iolio of Novelties" to describe his show. Note that Amelia appears in the show, and Adele's husband, "Comical Walker, plus the Queta cycling team who regularly travelled with John Swallow.

FIRST VISIT TO THIS COUNTRY!

BRONCHO BILL'S GREAT

WILD WEST

EXHIBITION and MAMMOTH TWO-RING CIRCUS

Will Positively Visit

JACKSON'S MEADOW, HITCHIN STREET, BIGGLESWADE

FRIDAY, October 22nd (For 1 Day Only).

Nothing Ever Seen Like This Gigantic Show in England Before. The Real Thing! You have seen the Pictures of the Great Wild West. Come and see the reality

COWBOYS and COWGIRLS! INDIANS! PRAIRIE MUSTANGS! The World's Champion Lassoo Throwers! The Great Stockwhip Crackers! BRONCHO BUSTERS! Thrilling Indian and Cowboy's Ride for Life! Breath-Taking Log Chariot Racing by Backwoodsmen!

THE GREAT SPECTACLE

The Attack on the Deadwood Coach, in which over 150 HORSES, COWBOYS, INDIANS, Etc., appear at one time.

In addition to our WILD WEST EXHIBITION, we present our

GREAT CIRCUS SHOW IN TWO LARGE RINGS

All should See

THE GREAT AERIAL BEKETOW TROUPE

In their marvellous performance on their high revolving trapeze and ladder. Nothing ever seen like this in a travelling concern before.

PRAIRIE BOB'S GREAT COWBOY BAND

---

2 EXHIBITIONS DAILY (Rain or Shine). At 3 and 8. Doors open 2.15 and 7.15

Seating Accomodation for 10,000

Prices of Admission : 3s., 2s., 1s., and 6d.

Children admitted to 3 o'clock Exhibition only at Half-price to all seats.
8 o'clock Exhibition, Children Half-price except to 6d. Seats

---

The whole of the Entertainments will take place under one of the latgest tents ever erected A VERITABLE TOWN OF CANVAS.

The 1914 show featuring its Wild West theme.

The 1911 Census:

When the 1911 census was taken in the spring of 1911 we find some of the Swallows are still living at 6 Thornley Street, Wolverhampton. Elizabeth, the sixty seven year old widow of John Swallow I is joined by two of her daughters; Amelia and Lilian, her son Gilbert and granddaughter; Lina Anderson (Amelia's daughter) who was then six. Both Amelia and Gilbert declare that they are working in the circus world. There is no mention of John Swallow II because he was elsewhere.

John Swallow II and his wife Annie are to be found in Manor Street, Waterford, in Ireland. They were obviously travelling Ireland with the circus because the other members of the "household" are John's sisters; Ada and Adele and Adele's three children; Ada, Mille and Jack. Sixteen year old Nellie Peck, Annie's sister, is also present and they all seem to be involved in the show.

Broncho Bill at last

It has always been interesting to speculate on exactly when John Swallow became Broncho Bill. The 1911 Irish Census entry confirms that during that year he was touring a circus and later in the year there are reports of the show travelling in England. For example, the Warwick Advertiser of 14th October 1911 reports his "first visit" to the town and the show is presented as John Swallow's International Circus and Novelty Hippodrome. Special mention is made of a trick cycling act presented by "The Quetas".

By 1912 Broncho Bill Anderson films were filling many of Britain's new cinema screens – popularising the name and the mythology of the American Wild West. John Swallow's travels are well recorded by local newspapers through 1912 but the show resolutely sticks to calling itself "John Swallow's International Circus", sometimes adding "And Iolio of Arenic Realisations"! "The Quetas" stay with the show and are joined by "The Papelions": two girls who are suspended from a wire rope gripped in their teeth as they revolve at great speed at the top of the circus tent… a feat we will return to in a later story in chapter 7. Comical Walker stays in the show and Gilbert Swallow remains in a management role.

Occasionally a local paper informs the local readers of John Swallow's recent history. For example The Cornishman of 2nd May 1912 states, *"Mr. Swallow has been for several years with the great Barnum show in America and also with the greatest continental circuses."*

1913/14

From the available evidence it seems that the commencement of the 1913 travelling season was the moment when John Swallow II became Broncho Bill. An advert in The Era of mid April exclaims: *"Wanted – at once: three or four smart cowboys, tentmen grooms and ring performers. Applicants should contact the show at Brecon."* At the same time The Era comments on the fact that three circuses were currently touring South Wales: John Sangers, Fossett's Wild West Show, and Broncho Bill's Wild West Show."

Having spent some time in South Wales the show seems to move to Derbyshire and from there to the North East. The Northern Daily Mail of 17th July 1913 comments on the show coming to Hartlepool – *"Many years have elapsed since the town has received a visit from a typical Wild West Exhibition, and therefore the arrival today of Broncho Bill's two ring circus is eagerly awaited.*" Comical Walker, the Papelions, and the Quetas are still in the show but must by now have been joined by a number of cowboys, cowgirls and Indians, plus Prairie Bob's Cowboy Band. A report from Beverley, in Yorkshire, states that the show included 150 such artists! Later there are press reports of the show in Whitby, Filey. Lincoln, Grantham etc. Sometimes these reports add other details such as references to the Deadwood Stage act, or the size of the two-ring marquee, claimed to hold 10,000 people! The show featured twenty two separate turns.

Towards the end of August 1913 the show is back in the Midlands with reports appearing in the Lichfield, Coventry and Walsall papers. The show normally did one-night stands so it is not clear how many venues might be visited in one week, nor to work out the entire itinerary. Towards the end of the season they appear in Banbury in October and Abingdon in November by which time some of the artists are leaving the show. From an item appearing in The Era of 29th October 1913 concerning Comical Walker (John's bother-in-law), we learn that he has just completed a 34 week tour <u>in the fourth season</u> of Broncho Bills Wild West Circus. (As the circus had only become a "Wild West show" that year we must assume The Era is counting the seasons from 1910 onwards.) To travel a two-ring show with a large number of artists must have been a major logistical exercise. As far as we know all this was achieved without motorised transport.

If anything the 1914 season's show set out to be even "bigger and better", once again presenting itself as a two-ring circus in the American style, and a non-stop series of turns in each ring. Prairie Bob's Cowboy Band and Comical Walker returned to the show but there were a number of new circus acts added. On 31st March 1914 the Western Daily Press recorded the show's appearance at Bristol saying: *"Everything in connection with this show is done on a big scale. The equipment is extensive, those taking part form quite a colony, and the equine force is not only strong in number, but of an excellent standard of quality."* This "colony" of cowboys and Indians touring the country gives us plenty to think about: Were they all genuine cowboys and "native Americans" as we would now call them? As the 1914 tour unfolds we learn more about one or two of them, but ultimately our questions about their identities will probably never be answered.

The tour seems to have begun in the Midlands with visits to Tamworth and Warwick being mentioned by the press in March. The show then moved on to Cheltenham and Bristol before headed into Somerset and the south-west. At Glastonbury there was trouble when an "indian" was involved in a fight with a local citizen. Later, in Taunton there was a dispute concerning the use of the field that the circus wished to occupy. At Barnstaple, in May, there was a fire in a wig-wam in which two people died. Louisa Denley and her son Henry were described as Sioux Indians when their deaths were examined in the inquest. At Portsmouth an "Indian Chief" was thrown from his horse and fractured his leg. He was identified as Rajani Majunda, suggesting that perhaps not all the "Indians" were American!

The show later travelled along the south coast without further incident: Portsmouth – Bognor – Hastings etc., but trouble occurred at Bexhill when one of the equestrian directors, William Weaver of Edgbaston, suffered theft from his living van. All these things were going on as events in Europe were building up to the outbreak of war. Many of the incidents were extensively and widely reported, but John Swallow/Broncho Bill is never mentioned. We can have no idea of how he felt about his show: was it a dream now realised, or a huge and unwieldly headache? And how did he feel about the impending war?

Once the war began we find there was no let-up in the pace at which the show travelled. A week in mid August saw them travelling through Essex with the following schedule; Monday: Romford, Tuesday: Grays, Wednesday: Southend, Thursday: Chelmsford, Friday: Maldon. The following week they were travelling through Suffolk.

Below: Broncho Bill's Wild West Circus on tour with its large "two ring" tent.

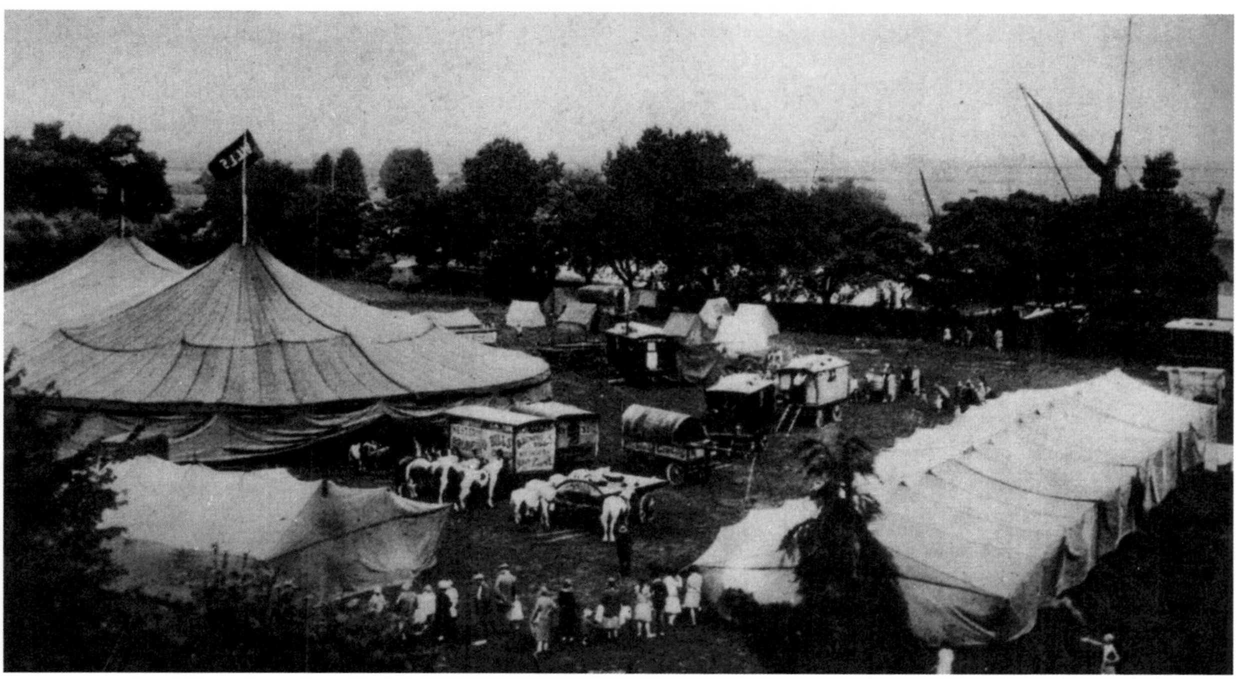

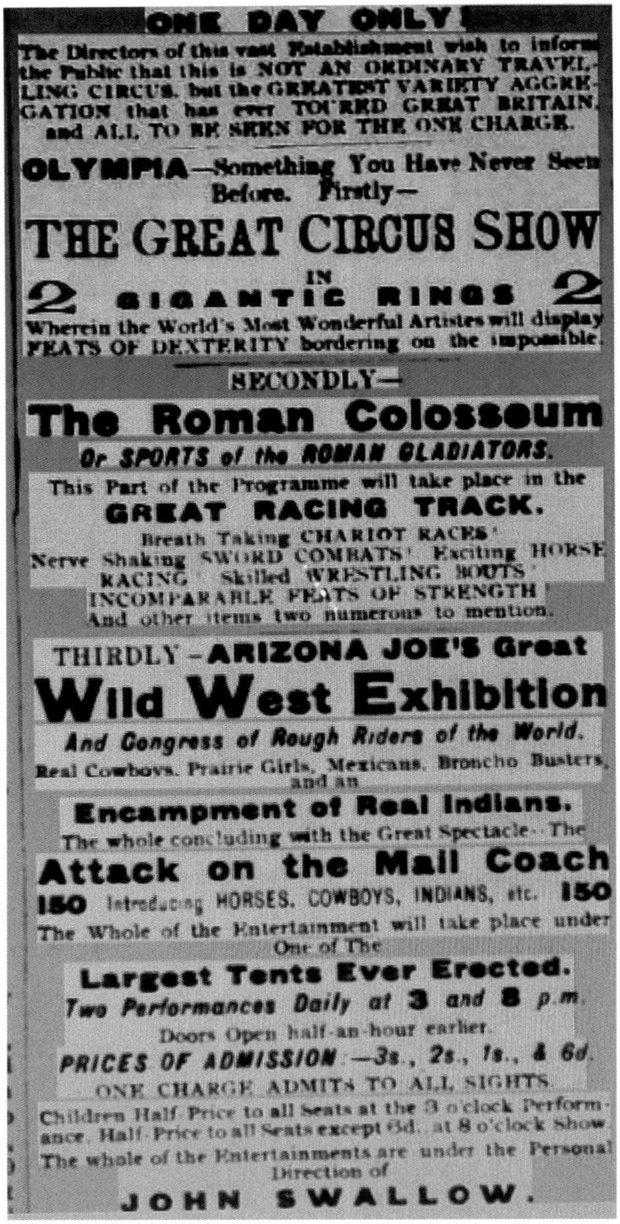

Above: As this advertisement makes clear, from 1916 onwards John Swallow was providing an ambitious "three shows in one" presentation. Using his two ring tent he was providing a "Roman Colosseum" show, his "Wild West Exhibition" and the "great circus show" itself, despite the fact that all this had to be organised while Britain was at war. As 1916 progressed John Swallow started using the name "Olympia" as the 'umbrella name' for the entire show,

The First World War

When the First World War commenced in August 1914 there was great uncertainty about the fate of the travelling entertainment industry and an expectation that many horses would be recruited for military service. In the end it seemed that Broncho Bill's show was reckoned to be part of maintaining a "business as usual" approach to the business of entertainment, and that John Swallow himself was able to offer the government help in the training and buying of horses etc. Even so, it was soon apparent that finding men and women to keep the show going was not going to be easy.

Although the Autumn of 1914 was as busy as usual we know that John Swallow took one day off in September to visit the Birmingham Onion Fair in Aston. This fair was a flagship event for Pat Collins, the Black Country showman, and I am often asked if the two men met. John's visit was mentioned by the World's Fair but we can only guess what the two men might have discussed. By early 1915 John Swallow was desperately advertising in The Era. People wanted included equestrians, gymnasts, acrobats, clowns, speciality acts plus cowboys, cowgirls, sharp shooters, knife throwers, Indians, Mexicans, stud grooms and a tent-master. Musicians were also hard to find. The season began on 1st March and he was still advertising his need for "two good speciality acts". At the end of that month, while the circus was travelling through Cheshire musicians were still being sought. The adverts carried a warning: "No fancy salaries will be entertained as the state of the country will not allow the same". Close to Broncho Bill's adverts are similar adverts placed by Ben Kennedy, described later in this book, for his Gaiety Theatre in Birmingham and the Empires in West Bromwich and Smethwick.

This situation must have continued throughout the war, yet somehow the show remained on the road, and no.6 Thornley Street, Wolverhampton, remained the show's administrative base. Maybe members of the family continued to work on the show, and it seems likely that the over-all female proportion of the staff increased. John and Annie's first two children arrived during this period – William Charles was born at Thornley Street on 13th June 1913, and John David was born on 26th May 1916.

Although travelling a circus became increasingly difficult as the War progressed, John Swallow seemed determined to expand his show rather than reduce it in size and seek economies. The 1916 season was more ambitious than ever and took the form of "Three Shows in One": a Roman Arena, a Mammoth two ring circus and a Wild West Exhibition – all presented in one huge tent. At first the marketing department simply called it "Broncho Bill's Shows" but as the season progressed John Swallow adopted the name "Olympia" as an umbrella title for the show. Extensive advertising in the local press emphasised the magnitude of the show and boldly stated, *"The Directors of this establishment wish to inform the Public that this is not an ordinary circus, but the greatest variety aggregation that has ever toured Great Britain – and all this to be seen for one charge."*

Conscription to the armed services began in 1916 and John Swallow applied for exemption for his "show superintendent" in March, but Dudley magistrates rejected his application. As before, the show generally presented one-night stands consisting of two performances. The tour began in the Midlands and we know, for example, that it was open in Lichfield on 28th April. By the middle of May it had reached the East Midlands and found itself competing with other touring shows. For example when opening on Salt's Meadow in Belper on 17th May, they found that Bostock's Circus had been on exactly the same ground one week earlier! On reaching Nantwich in May they were followed by Bostock's Circus again and by Lord John Sanger's. Bostocks called themselves "The Greatest Show in Britain", adding that it came "Directly from France"!

At the end of May successive days were spent in Nantwich, then Crewe, then Northwich, and finally in Chester on the Little Roodee – the ground on which Pat Collins had presented his fair a few weeks earlier. (Pat was born in Chester and regarded this fair as an important annual event in his travels.) Very often the show had come and gone before the local press could report on it, but in Cheltenham on the 1st September a glowing report of the show was printed in the Gloucestershire Echo in which it was described as a show that had come directly from America. It continued from Cheltenham down to Wells, on to Shepton Mallet, Trowbridge and then turned north again to travel through the Cotswolds. The entire 1916 season ran for thirty weeks, and when the family returned to Wolverhampton at the end of November Adele Swallow and Arthur Stapley-Walker ("Comical Walker") celebrated by getting married.

For some reason the 1917 and 1918 seasons ran without so much publicity and apparently without the "Roman Arena" ingredients of the show, but it was still the second biggest tenting show on the road in Great Britain.

By the summer of 1919 life had returned to normal and when Broncho Bill's Circus and Wild West Show appeared in Dundee in the June of that year, huge audiences were noted. The stars of the show were Miss Ida and Miss Ausonia, both equestriennes, and the Royal Tokiwa Family. The show still concluded with the attack on the stage coach. Miss Ida was none other than Adele, John's sister, but there is no mention of her husband, the clown Comical Walker. John Swallow had always seemed keen on Japanese acrobatic troupes. By this time one of the Mizouno Troupe had settled in Wolverhampton, not far from John's base, and was about to become a famous local chip shop proprietor!

The strength of John's own association with Wolverhampton was no doubt affected by the fact he could seldom have been there. There even seems to be a period at the end of the war when an address in Brighton became his base. Maybe all these things were about to change.

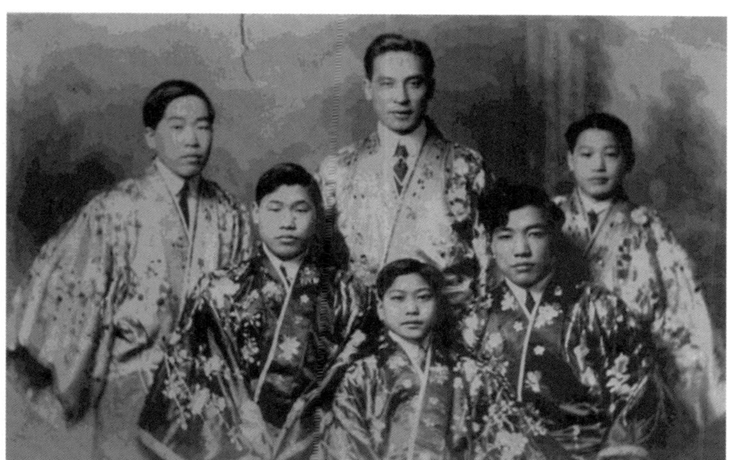

The Mizuno Troupe was just one of several Japanese Acrobatic troupes that appeared in John Swallow's circus. One member of the troupe married a local girl, settled in Wolverhampton, and ran a fish and chip shop.

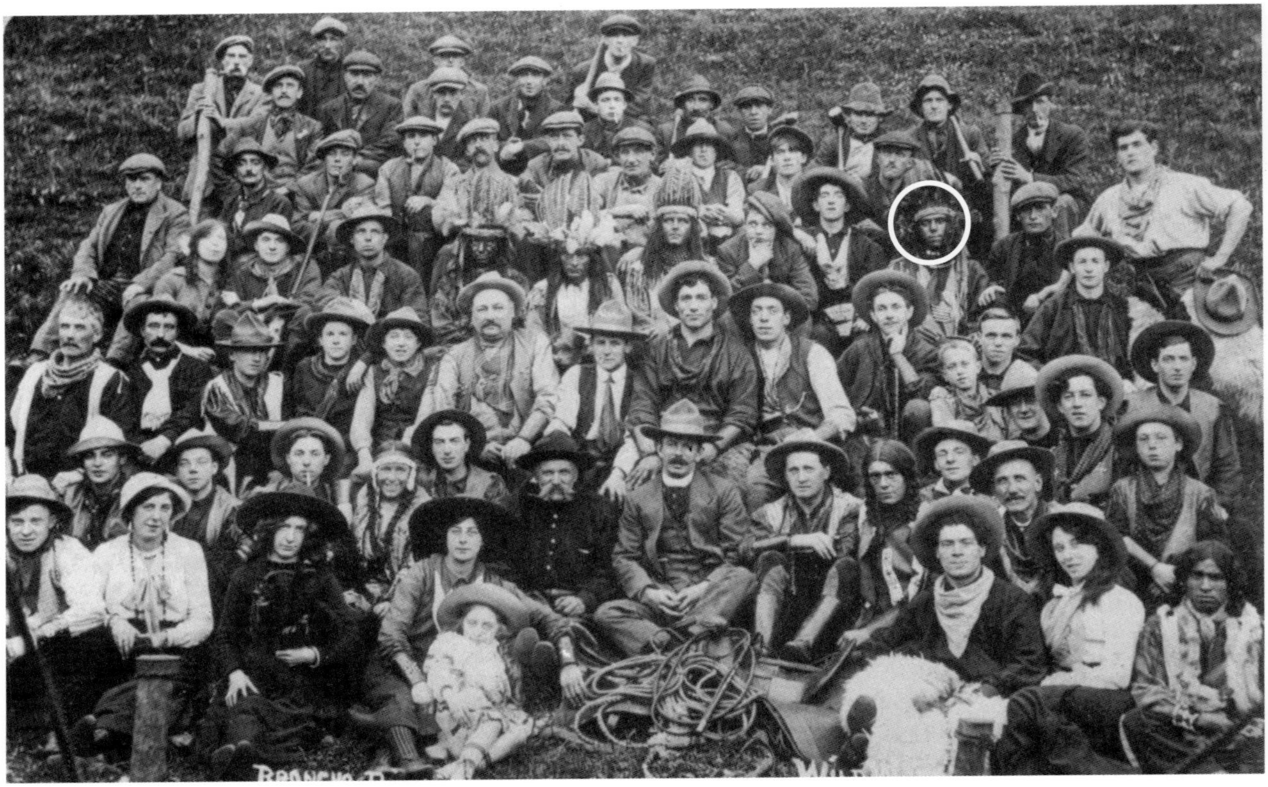

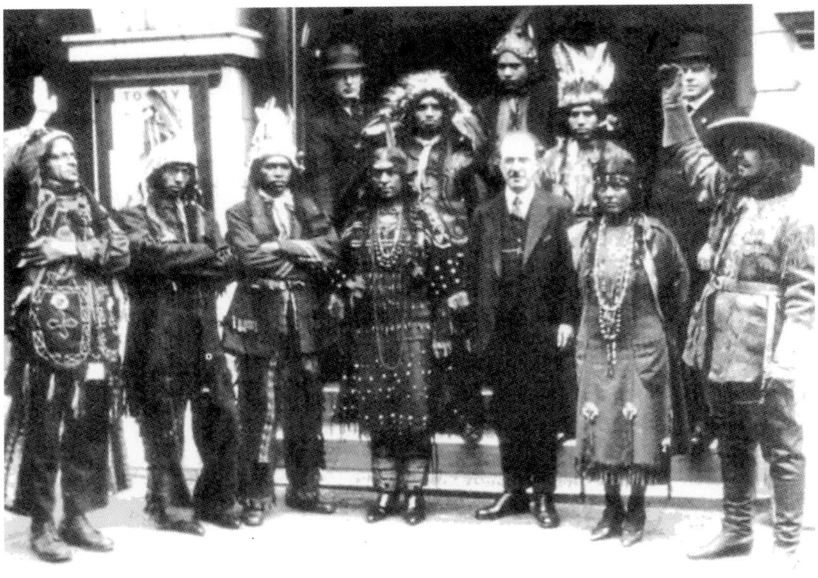

Above: John Swallow II sits in the centre of this picture of the "Wild West" stars of his show. How many came from America, and how many were "authentic" cowboys or Indians is an interesting matter.

A correspondent identified the gentleman "circled" as her grandfather whom she thought was a Canadian "Indian"! Amazingly someone else thought she recognised him, and told me that his name was Hasan Ali – not a name I might have expected. I would love to know if any other Swallows appear in the picture, and whether anyone else can be identified.

Above: John Swallow followed the example of Buffalo Bill and used his "Cowboys and Indians" to seek publicity for his show while on tour. In this picture everyone is posed with Tom Shaw outside the Sheffield Picture House.

The Roaring Twenties

During the Early 1920s John Swallow II bought a house at 90 Waterloo Road, Wolverhampton, and, at the same time, may have acquired the yard in Goosebrook Road which could become a Winter headquarters for his circus. (Later he is recorded as having a home at 103 Waterloo Road but I don't know whether this indicates a move or is simply a case of houses being re-numbered!) At the beginning of 1920s he was still advertising in The Era's wanted columns for every kind of artist for the next tenting season – including yet another troupe of Japanese acrobats. The contact address was still 6 Thornley Street so it is possible that he house continued to be used by some of the Swallows until after Elizabeth Swallow's death in April 1921.

The 1920 season began by travelling to Yorkshire, reaching Shipley, near Bradford, at Easter (3rd April), then passing through places like Hebden Bridge before going on to Leeds and Sheffield. The new Japanese troupe was called the "Royal Nikki Family", but some of the Swallow family still appeared in the show – for example Adele and her husband, Comical Walker, had now returned but they were now joined by their daughter Lina, representing the next generation. She performed a wire-walking act.

It also seems that John Swallow joined forces with Sir Garrard Trrwhitt-Drake, and David Taylor, during 1920 to present another circus using the name "Ringland's Circus and Menagerie" – borrowing another American circus name in an attempt to impress potential audiences. John's own "Broncho Bill "show continued to travel through 1920, but it is not clear how much time he was able to devote to this other venture. The Ringlands Circus does receive attention from the press as it travelled, but not to the same extent as Broncho Bill's, although some of the material is in the same boastful style! Instead of having a Wild West component, Ringland's seemed to use its large menagerie to complement its traditional circus content. Animals included lions, bears, camels and monkeys – and a baby elephant. This was possibly the beginning of John Swallow's interest in elephants. However, this was a costly show to put on, and although it was deemed a success, it struggled to make itself pay.

Years later two people wrote about their memories of Broncho Bill's Circus during and after the First World War: Bill Ward (in the September 1971 "King Pole", and Hal Thomas in the September 1980 issue.) Bill Ward felt that Boncho Bill's claims were rather an exaggeration, and what was seen in the ring could be quite a disappointment. Hal Thomas took a positive view, but it is interesting that John Swallow was a very ardent publicist for his own show, made great claims in his adverts, and often supplied copy to newspapers describing the show in glowing terms. (The "copy" was often identical from one local newspaper to another, suggesting a single authorship!). The show was said to include 150, men, women and horses, but is not clear if this meant fifty of each, and whether it included the horses used by the show's transport.

In September 1921 a charge of "obtaining money by false pretences" was brought against Broncho Bill at Holyhead. The prosecution stated that only twenty horses appeared in the ring – no sign of 150, or even 50. The defence argued that this had been a result of the bad weather and the need to trim the show in case of the tent being blown down. After some argument the case was dismissed, but it does remind us of the difficulty of now being able to have a precise understanding of the size of Broncho Bill's show, even allowing for the fact that it probably varied.

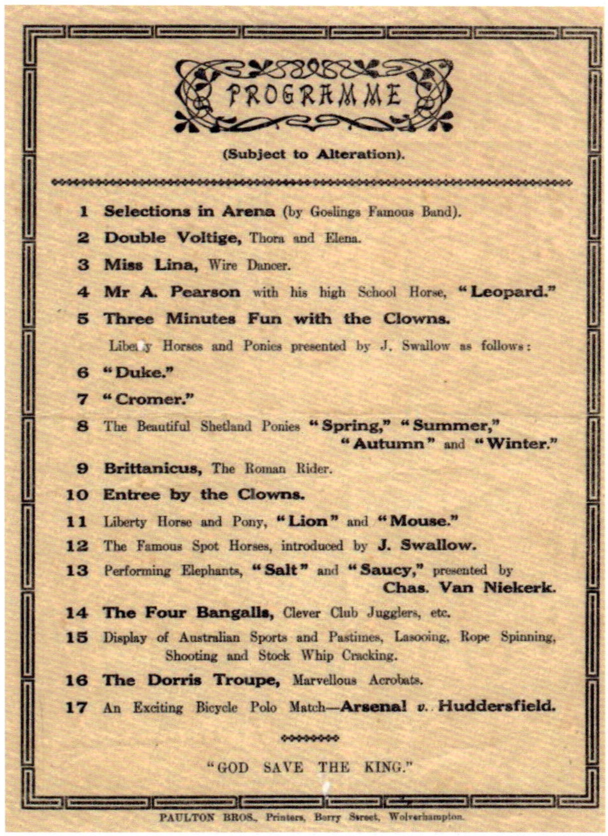

PROGRAMME

(Subject to Alteration).

1 **Selections in Arena** (by Goslings Famous Band).
2 **Double Voltige,** Thora and Elena.
3 **Miss Lina,** Wire Dancer.
4 **Mr A. Pearson** with his high School Horse, **"Leopard."**
5 **Three Minutes Fun with the Clowns.**

Liberty Horses and Ponies presented by J. Swallow as follows:

6 **"Duke."**
7 **"Cromer."**
8 The Beautiful Shetland Ponies **"Spring," "Summer," "Autumn"** and **"Winter."**
9 **Brittanicus,** The Roman Rider.
10 **Entree by the Clowns.**
11 Liberty Horse and Pony, **"Lion"** and **"Mouse."**
12 The Famous Spot Horses, introduced by **J. Swallow.**
13 Performing Elephants, **"Salt"** and **"Saucy,"** presented by **Chas. Van Niekerk.**
14 **The Four Bangalls,** Clever Club Jugglers, etc.
15 Display of Australian Sports and Pastimes, Lasooing, Rope Spinning, Shooting and Stock Whip Cracking.
16 **The Dorris Troupe,** Marvellous Acrobats.
17 An Exciting Bicycle Polo Match—**Arsenal** *v.* **Huddersfield.**

"GOD SAVE THE KING."

PAULTON BROS., Printers, Berry Street, Wolverhampton.

A 1920s "running order" sheet shows John Swallow II presenting his horses and Charles Van Niekerk presenting the elephants. Lina, Johns' granddaughter, is also in the show.

The new decade also began with John Swallow II becoming associated with the presentation of a circus at the annual "World's Fair" event held at the Agricultural Hall, Islington, every December/January. The event was a showcase for whatever was new in the world of travelling entertainment – both fairground and circus, was a social event for those associated with the trade, and provided plenty of amusement for Londoners. The "World's Fair" was organised by T.E. Reid and it was he who arranged for John Swallow to organise circus or menagerie content.

By 1922 John Swallow's life was following a routine consisting of the winter show at Islington's Agricultural Hall, with a tenting season from March to late Autumn. Something "new" was provided by the arrival of the elephants: Salt and Sauce.

Salt and Sauce were two elephants that had once been part of a troupe presented by George Lockhart as "The Cruet Set". As well as having some claim to national fame, they also became a major "local legend" in Wolverhampton. In 2008 they became the subject of their own biography: "The Legend of Salt and Sauce" by Jamie and Jim Clubb. The authors of this fascinating birth-to-death account of their lives do admit that there are some parts of the story that are more difficult to tell than others. This is particularly true of the period just before they are purchased by Broncho Bill.

Broncho Bill seems to have bought Salt and Sauce from Captain Joe Taylor, who may have continued to present them on some occasions after this transaction. Whatever the story, they become part of Broncho Bill's Wild West Circus as it sets out in the spring of 1922. The Lichfield Mercury of 24th March 1922 contains a review

"Most of us retain a lingering fancy for the good old fashioned circus... It is certainly healthier and more full-blooded then the 'pictures'. Be that as it may, Broncho Bill's Wild West Circus called at Lichfield last Monday, attracted large audiences, and did not disappoint them.

The two outstanding features were undoubtedly the elephants, Salt and Saucy, and the Mizuno troupe of Japanese acrobats. The elephants went through their performance with a ludicrous air of aloofness, and almost human intelligence, whilst the Japanese were simply and unbelievably super-human."

Of course, it is interesting that the Mizuno Troupe re-appear on Broncho Bill's circus, but it more important to note that the elephants steal the show, and that they are going to be referred-to as "Salt and Saucy" as often as "Salt and Sauce"

While preparing *"Fairs and Circuses in the Black Country"* in 1994 I was able to interview Sid Watts who had started work as an elephant groom with Salt and Saucy at the Agricultural Hall for the 1921 season. He came with them to Wolverhampton, plus another groom named Jack Lowe. Sid stayed with the elephants from then until 1934 when he "settled down" and married a Wolverhampton girl. Obviously he was able to provide a wonderful first-hand account of travelling and working with Salt and Sauce. Unfortunately for us, Sid Watts died in January 1997, at the age of ninety, so it has not been possible to ask him lots of other questions about the life and times of Broncho Bill's circus.

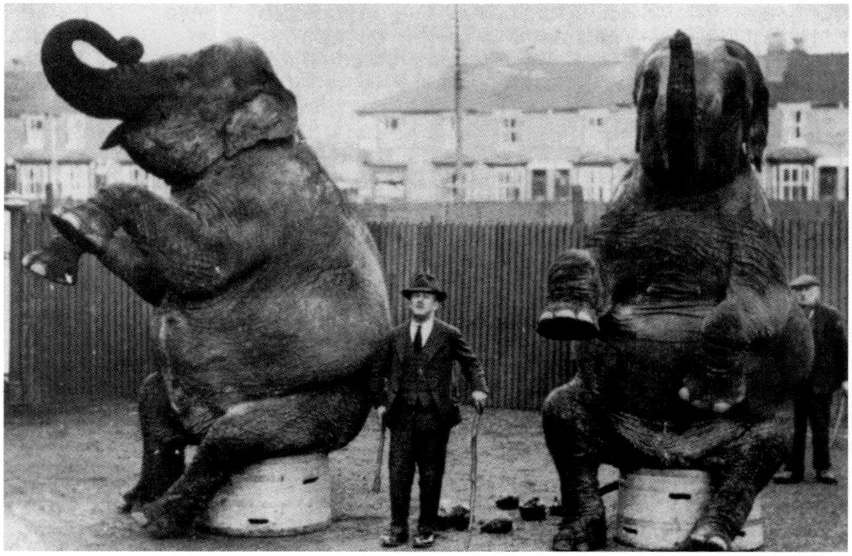

Charles Van Niekirk poses with Salt and Sauce in the yard at Gorsebrook Road, Wolverhampton.
The road in the background is Jones Road and still looks the same today. Just to the left of the picture the yard was overshadowed by the railway viaduct carrying the line from Wolverhampton to Shrewsbury.
The site of the yard has recently been redeveloped but it is still possible to identify its location.

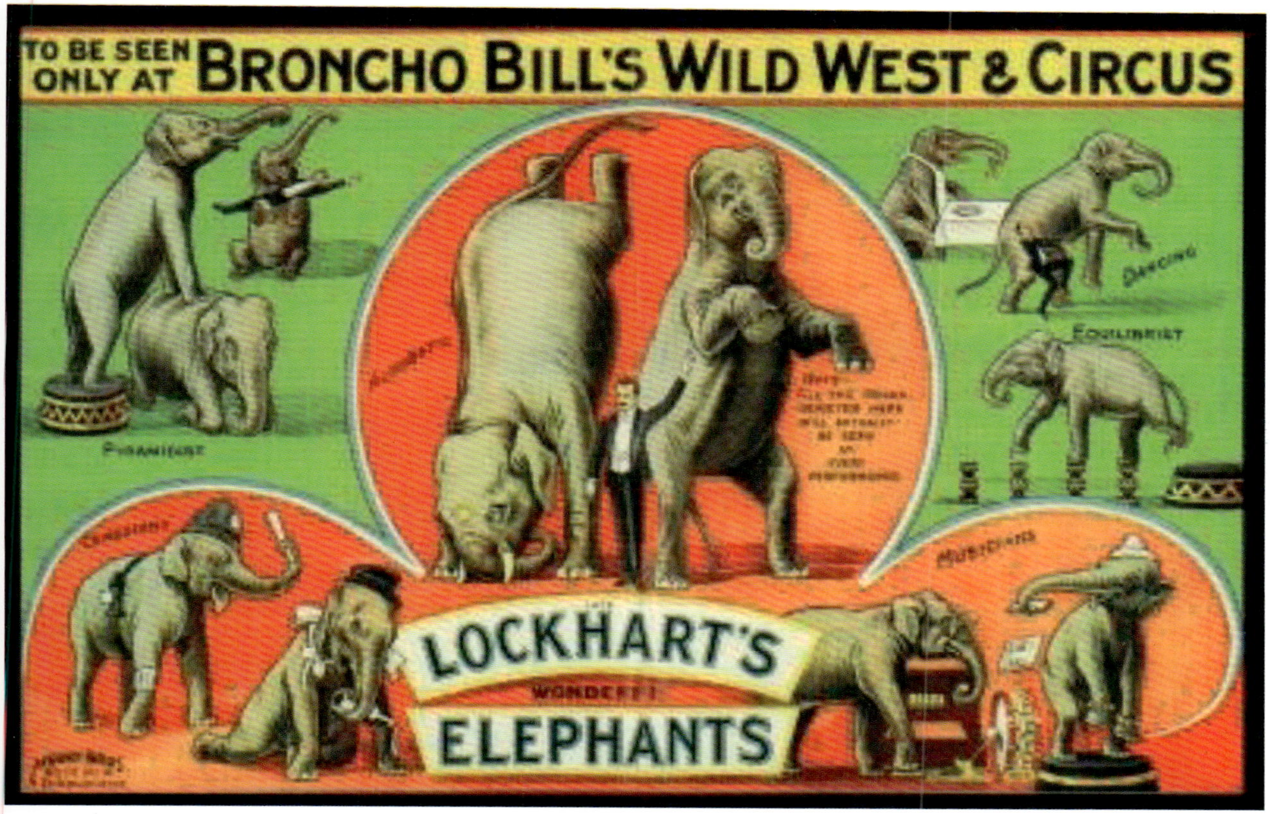

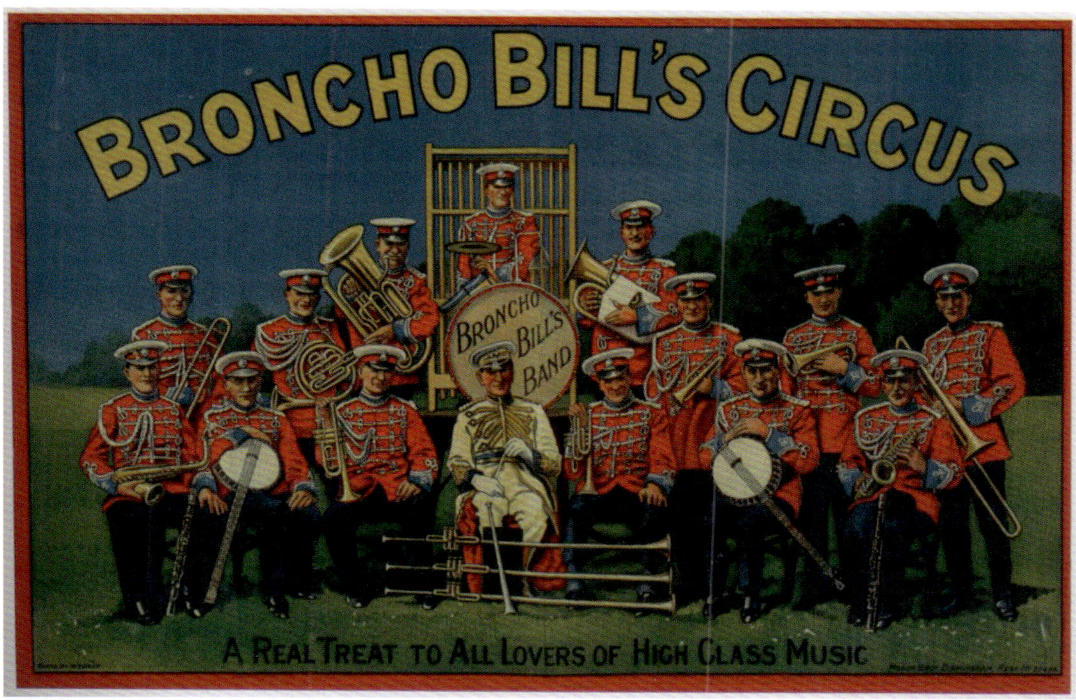

Colourful artwork relating to Broncho Bill's Circus of 1920s vintage reprcduced from Ken Rattenbury's collection

Two Elephants

From 1922 onwards John Swallow's story, ie Broncho Bill's story, is also the story of his two elephants: Salt and Sauce. It is the most documented part of their lives, and of John Swallow's life. Sid Watts and Jack Lowe also had little time for anything other than caring for the elephants in that period. However, looking after the elephants was not the same as presenting them in the ring. That task generally fell to Charles Van Niekirk, who appears to have come from South Africa.

The elephants' home, when not travelling, was in corrugated iron sheds in Gorsebrook Road, Wolverhampton, almost under the railway viaduct that dominates the area. There they learnt new tricks and routines and enjoyed forays into neighbouring parts of Wolverhampton for exercise and "treats" provided by local shopkeepers, and publicans. In this way they became well known to a number of Wulfrunians.

The elephants generally travelled between shows on foot, wearing special boots provided by John Swallow. However they also sometimes travelled by rail, and I received an interesting letter from the late Alex Chatwin about this. He wrote:

"When the circus went on tour the elephants sometimes travelled by train. The LMS railway company converted an old passenger coach for them. During those years my father was Parcels Clerk at the High Level Station, and because elephants travelled "passenger" rather than "goods", they had to be considered as "parcels", and my father had to be present when they were being loaded into their carriage. On one occasion I happened to be at the station and was able to watch the operation. Most of the compartment partitions had been removed, leaving just a couple for Mr. Swallow and his staff. The elephants walked up a ramp and entered the carriage through large doors in the side, and so to their stalls where they were secured.

One year I was on holiday with my parents, staying with relatives at Highworth, near Swindon, when it was announced that Swallow's Circus was 'coming to town'. Dad bought the tickets and we had ringside seats, but when the elephants started their act by trotting round the ring, they refused to pass Dad until he stood up, spoke to them, and patted their trunks. They knew him even though he was so far away from his usual environment."

Salt and Sauce appeared in the first half of the show among the other circus routines, the Wild West "exhibition" forming the second half of the show. Van Niekirk, who presented them in the ring, returned at the end of the show to become a horse-back sharp-shooter, in the Deadwood Stage routine. Sid Watts also eventually appeared in the ring during a routine they developed in which he put his head in Sauce's mouth and was lifted off the ground. Meanwhile Broncho Bill's publicity department advertised them as "The most wonderful animals in the "World", or "The most famous animals in the Universe having visited every town and city in the World".

Among all the adverts and their extravagant claims, and the reviews possibly written in glowing terms by Broncho Bill himself, there are occasional items in the press that give a slightly different insight into these times. For example in June 1923 John Swallow actually gives an interview to the local paper, the Western Chronicle, and it went like this:

"Broncho Bill, whose Wild West is visiting Yeovil on 15th June, gave our representative a few interesting particulars about elephants. "Elephants," said Broncho Bill, live to 100 years of age. Our performing elephants, Salt and Sauce, are 28 years old. They have been performing for 20 years in all the great cities of the world. This is their first time in Great Britain with a circus. It took three years to teach Sauce to stand on her head – the only elephant in the world doing this wonderful stunt.

They weigh two tons each now, and will keep on growing until they are 50 years of age when they will weigh nearly four tons each. Besides Salt and Sauce there is a baby elephant. We carry them from town to town on the railway on all journeys more than twelve miles.

Our elephants have their toe nails manicured every three weeks, they are filed and polished just like those of a human being. This is an important matter especially when they are performing – they have to be spic and span in the limelight.""

The mid twenties were a period of relative stability for Broncho Bill and the elephants. There was a tendency for the tours to repeat certain routes, visit some towns almost every year for example, but always some variation to make life interesting. Setting off through Gloucestershire, Somerset and down to Devon and Cornwall was often followed by a journey back along the south coast through Sussex and Kent. Sometimes this led on to tours of Essex and East Anglia. On many occasions the autumn saw visits to Tamworth, Coventry, Leamington, and Banbury. Other tours went over to the East Midlands and then up into Yorkshire and Lancashire. One strange thing is that the tours sometimes seem to have been interrupted by lightening visits to towns which were not in the sequence! At least in alternate years the tour would include a visit to Scotland.

Not surprisingly the twenties also saw the introduction of motorised transport. For example in March 1924 The Era carried an advert in which a "window biller" was wanted, stating that he would have to be able to drive a Ford van. Interestingly, this advert seems to be the first to use the 90 Waterloo Road address as a point of contact. Meanwhile the people travelling with the show remained fairly constant with the Mizouno troup being billed as almost important as "Lokhart's elephants". T.W.Cooke was often named as equestrian director and ring master; Reginald Gosling took over from George Coe as bandmaster, although the band ceased to be a "prairie cowboy band"! (Reg Gosling was a young bandmaster, and died at the age of 37 in 1930.) Towards the end of the twenties Thomas Culleen was the advance billing agent, but he died in April 1930. John Swallow's brother-in-law, Arthur Stapley, continued to appear as Comical Walker and his daughter Lina continued to appear in the show. Annie Swallow appears to have remained at home in Wolverhampton with the intention that the boys, William and John, would go to Wolverhampton Grammar School.

From the beginning of 1929 onwards the Wild West half of the circus was dropped and Broncho Bill's troupe of spotted prairie horses began to share the top of the bill with Salt and Sauce. The latter carried on, regardless of the general decline of everybody's financial well-being towards the end of the decade. One night in 1928 Sauce was hit by a motor-cyclist near Newmarket. (By this time Sid Watts had decided to settle down in Wolverhampton and his place was taken by F. Bailey, with F.Hawkins looking after Salt.)

1930 began with a tour that took in the Birmingham area for a change, opening in Stechford, Bordesley Green, Washwood Heath, Erdington, Handsworth and Stirchley, before heading for Morecambe and on into Scotland, and back into Lancashire. Of course the advertising was as positive as ever, but the show seemed to be becoming more modest in content. One interesting feature of the 1930 tour was that the principle clown was "'Appy 'Arry", also known as Harry Reco. His real name was Herbert Wroe – another character with an assumed name! His story has recently been told in King Pole extra, no. 215.) The journey ended with a performance in Stafford on 25th October and then it was but a short journey back to Wolverhampton. During that final week they had opened for two shows nightly in Wilmslow, Congelton, Ashbourne and Uttoxeter before reaching Stafford. The pace had never slackened.

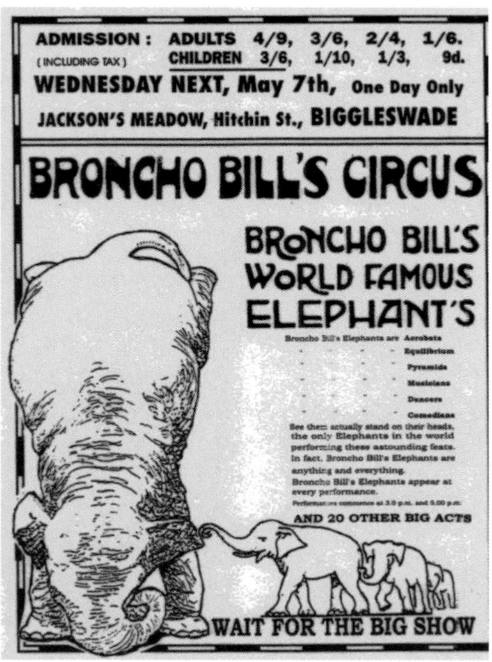

Throughout the 1920s the elephants featured in the show's advertising.

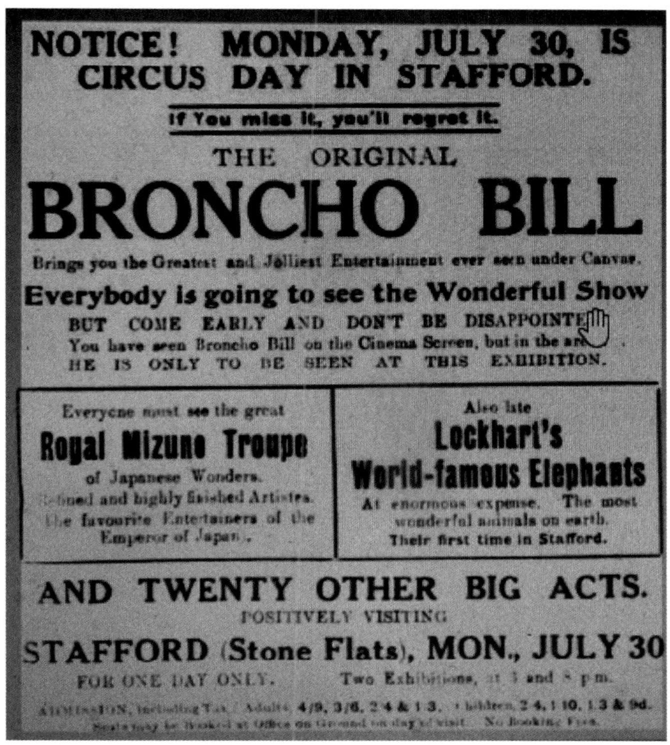

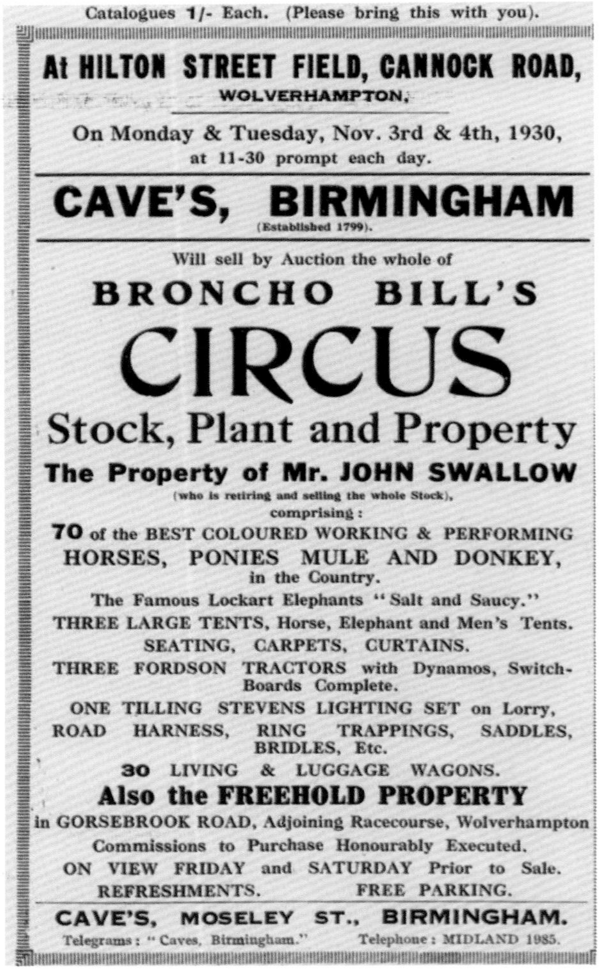

Broncho Bill's circus goes up for sale in November 1930 and John Swallow contemplates retirement.

Retirement and an Auction

As soon as he reached Wolverhampton John Swallow II, aka Broncho Bill, announced his retirement, after fifty five years in the circus business. His retirement statement observed how much life had changed since the First World War. He noted the rise of motoring and changes in public taste regarding entertainment. He emphasised that business had always been better "in the north" and in Scotland in particular, yet his tours had always made repeated visits to the South Coast! He mentioned that his sons had tried their "apprentice hands" in the business and were both good horsemen without adding that they were probably also showing no sign of any wish to take over the business. In Wolverhampton, John had joined the Freemasons, and the Albrighton Hunt, so perhaps he had also developed a vision of his retirement.

With great haste an auction was organised for the 4th and 5th November 1930, to take place in a field just off the Cannock Road, in Wolverhampton. This should not have taken observers by surprise for the Birmingham-based auctioneers, Messrs Caves, had visited the circus at Ayr in the September, and had discussed the creation of an inventory of Broncho Bill's property to prepare for its disposal.

The auction was described in detail by the Express and Star, but unfortunately the reporter is not identified. The report of the first day comments on the sale of the circus equipment such as costumes, sets, props, tenting and seating and living vans. A cowboy and a clown were interviewed about the prospects of unemployment. The Express and Star moved on to much more detailed account of the second day when the animals were auctioned:

"Beneath the green and white canopy of a massive marquee in a field at Hilton Street, Wolverhampton, this afternoon, a remarkable collection of horses and ponies, some no taller than Alsatian dogs, and two Indian elephants were sold in the presence of some of the oddest and picturesque gatherings ever seen.

Broncho Bill's circus went out of the hands of Mr. J. Swallow, of Wolverhampton, and into the possession of a host of strange people coming, according to the dialects heard of the bidders, from all parts of the British Isles. Gypsy women decked in jewellery and flamboyantly dressed had their children bound them by gaudy plaid shawls, and horse-breakers in check suits and caps had sleek whippets at their heels. Girls in hunting attire and showmen wearing grey top hats, white spats and big cravats, mingled with horse-dealers who wore corduroy suits and scarlet neckerchiefs...
No reserve price was placed on any lot, the highest bidder in each case getting the animals concerned. Some of the horses sold were considered by experts to be among the finest in Europe.

Mr. Swallow, who watched the proceedings, several times warned men who used sticks on the horses as they were run up the gauntlet between bidders. "I have never used a whip or a stick on any of them. They are going out of my possession today, but while I have them, I will see that they are not ill-treated." Throughout the sale, Mr. Swallow, even when he admitted that certain animals were going for ridiculously low prices, seemed more concerned in ascertaining that they would have good homes, than the money obtained. Several of his horses he let go to friends for nominal prices for sentimental reasons.

Pasha, a blue and white gelding known throughout the country for its clever ring turns, fetched the highest price among the horses, Mr. John Duffy, the proprietor of Duffy's Circus of Cork, paying 140 guineas. Mr. Duffy also bought Gypsy, a skewbald bare-backed riding horse, for 100 guineas, and gave 200 guineas for a troupe of spotted performing horses named Felix, Pinto, Pepper and Salt. Mr. Fossett bought Nero, a fine skewbald gelding for 100 guineas and for Henley and Arden, two spot stallions well known for their clever acts, he gave 105 guineas. (These horses became a well-known feature of Sir Robert Fossett's Circus into the late 1940s.)

Paul, a piebald horse which has pulled Mr. Swallow's private wagon, went for 26 guineas, while Jack, a black and white mule, raised 20 guineas. Dilly, Mr.Swallow's hunter is well-known at Albrighton Hunt, and which can jump seven feet, was sold for the ridiculously low sum of 25 guineas. There were 72 horses sold altogether.
The two elephants, Salt and Sauce, which attracted a great deal of attention, were chained up in a small tent, and attended by Mr. Bailey. The elephants, Mr. Swallow, told me would have to be sold together, because otherwise they would not perform. When they entered the marquee a photographer took a flashlight photograph of them, which rather startled them, and then the bidding began. Unfortunately no one took up the auctioneer's suggested bid of 1000 guineas, but at the last minute Harry Wilding put in the bid." (Harry Wilding was a Birmingham based journalist and amateur showman with a huge knowledge of the fairground and circus world, and it would seem that he made this bid when he was dismayed to find no other bidder. He must have thought his action would simply start the bidding, from which he would retire.)

Equipment related to presenting "The Roman Gladiators" was sold to Billy Russell a well- known variety theatre comedian who had a life-long interest in the fairground. He had learnt fairground painting as a child from his father, and had looked after some of Pat Collins's equipment for a while. His theatrical career lasted until the early 1960s and I knew him briefly as a Vice President of the Black Country Society in its early days. I have also mentioned him when writing about the Dudley Hippodrome!

The last item to be sold was the yard in Gorsebrook Road but this was withdrawn when the bidding only reached £750. As it turned out this was fortuitous. Just as John Swallow must have felt that the show was over, and his retirement could begin, it became obvious that Harry Wilding could not raise the funds to pay for Salt and Sauce. Mr. Bailey had to take them back to the unsold yard in Gorsebrook Road, and John Swallow had to think about what would happen next.

There was one job that had to be given his attention right away because once again he would be directing the circus at the World's Fair event at the Royal Agricultural Hall at Islington. The event opened on Christmas Eve and ran through to 7th February. As director of the show he would have organise it, produce it, and then supervise performances, although I don't think he took on the role of ring master. "Vigilant" reviewed the show for World's Fair and it is pretty clear that Salt and Saucy did not take part in it – perhaps they were appearing in a stage circus somewhere else, or just "resting" in Wolverhampton. Vigilant notes that the band was led by George Coe who had often been John Swallow's bandmaster. On 19th January 1931 the audience at the afternoon performance included a party made up of World's Fair correspondents, including "Southdown".

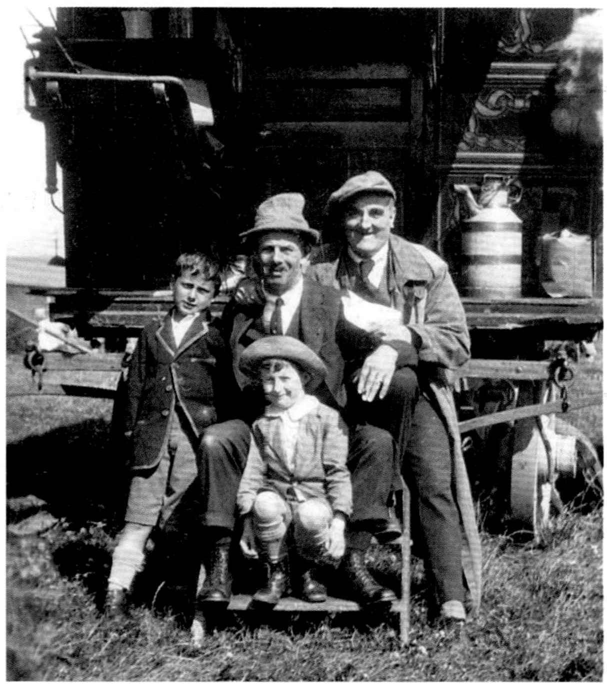

John Swallow II sits on the living van steps in the centre of the picture, in the mid 1920s. On the left is John Swallow III, his son. The latter attended the sale of his father's circus and later wrote about the event. The other people in the picture have not been identified.

Off to Ireland

It is interesting to see that John Duffy, the Irish circus proprietor, played such a significant part in the auction of John Swallow's effects in the November of 1930. As it turned out he was able to provide a future for Salt and Sauce by incorporating them in his show, appearing as "Broncho Bill's Wonderful Performing Elephants". They joined the show at Larne and in July their photograph was featured on the front page of "World's Fair" as they made their way round Ireland, finishing at Trim, County Meath in October.

It seems likely that they then returned to England and were taken to The Agricultural Hall, Islington for the late 1931/Jan 32 show, where John Swallow was also organising a Circus Reunion. It seems they then went back to Ireland for s second season with John Duffy, only to return home at the end of the year for a season with the Birmingham's Bingley Hall Circus organised by Pat Collins. Meanwhile John Swallow's "Prairie Horses" had begun a career with a circus confusingly called "Broncho Bill & Bailey's Circus" which had nothing to do with John Swallow at all.

By this time John Swallow had worked out a way forward, however it would result in "retirement" being completely abandoned. The idea was that John Swallow would offer Salt and Sauce as potential circus stars in return for him becoming a partner in the circus, helping to manage and improve it, and earning 50% of the takings. Charles Van Niekirk would also come along, not only to present the elephants but to add his sharp-shooting act to the show! He would even take the tickets on the door if necessary.

In this way John Swallow and the two elephants joined Rosaire's Circus – a small family-run circus led by Fred Ross, presenting himself to the world as Count Rosaire. Salt and Sauce became "Rosaire's Wonderful Elephants". The book on Salt and Sauce goes on to describe how eventually Ivor Rosaire took on Van Niekirk's task of presenting Salt and Sauce – a useful sequence of events because until his recent death Ivor has been around to give us a first-hand account of life with Salt and Sauce, and the many other elephants he eventually met in his extraordinary career. John Swallow's partnership with the Rosaires lasted until 1939, at which point they amicably parted.

Below: John Duffy (centre) provided Salt and Sauce with a 1931 tour of Ireland

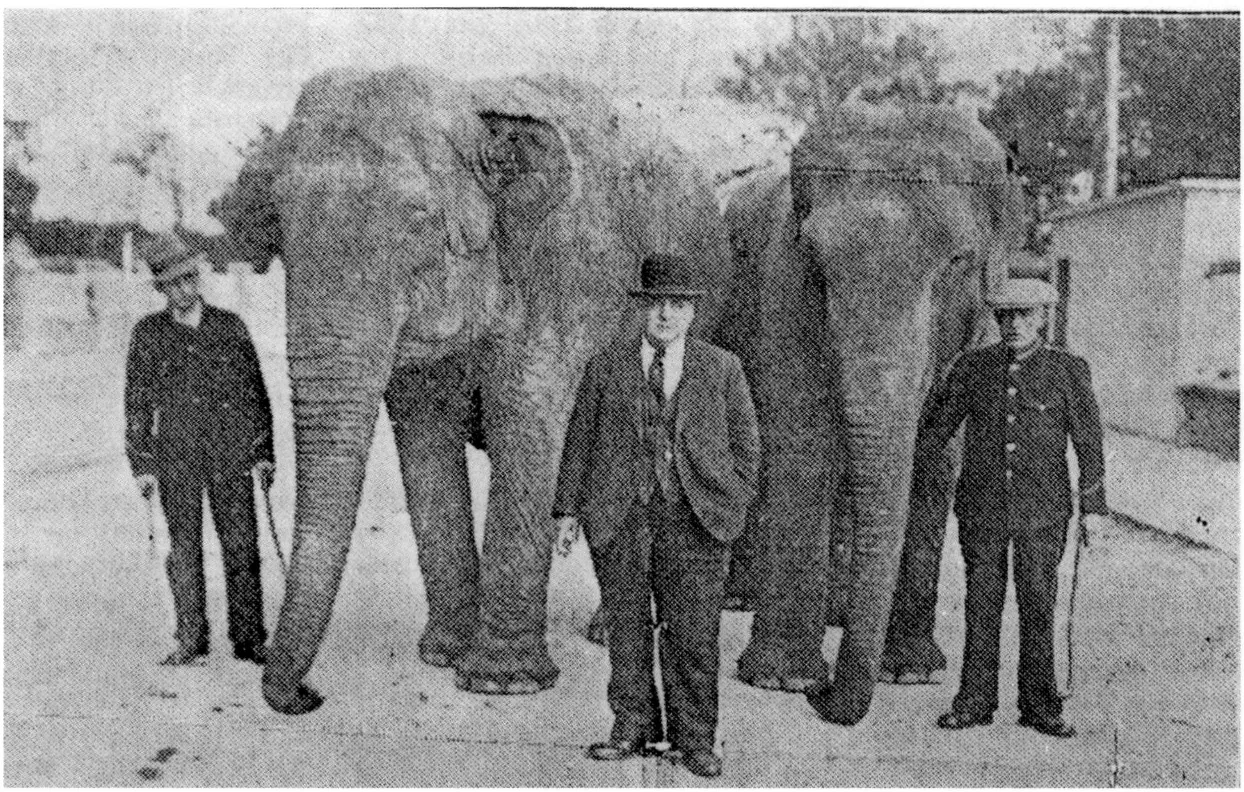

During 1939 John Swallow entered an agreement to work with Madame Clara Paulo, of Paulo's Circus – another family business of which Clara was the "guvnor". Another connection was that John Swallow's brother Gilbert had worked as an advance agent for Paulo's. Although the Second World War began in the September of that year, Paulo's Circus continued to travel and enjoy some success. When not travelling with Paulo's the elephants appeared at events like the Belle Vue Christmas shows in Manchester, or even in stage-based circus presentations in theatres. On many occasions it was John Swallow himself who presented them and who took on the strain of moving them from place to place. Meanwhile people began to notice a decline in his health, associated with heart problems.

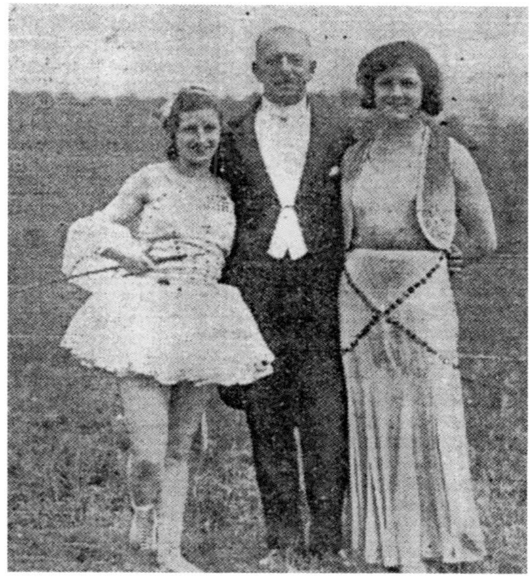

The September 1939 census found John Swallow II and his wife Annie in a caravan at Kingswood Farm just outside Wolverhampton.

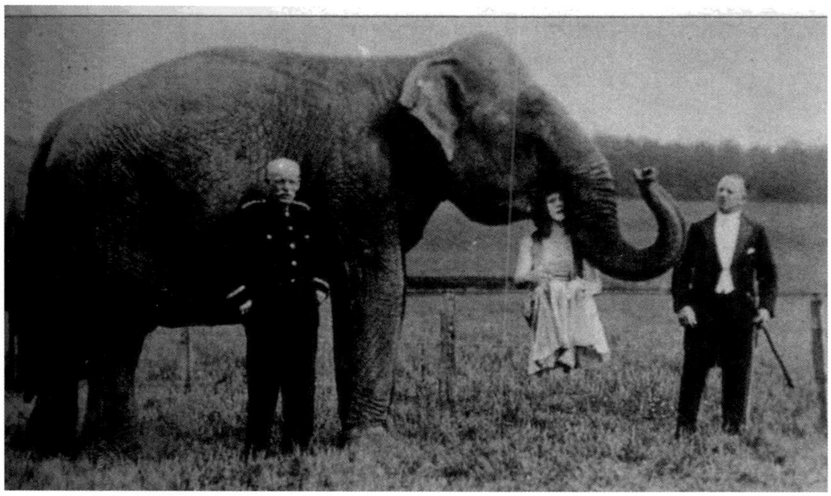

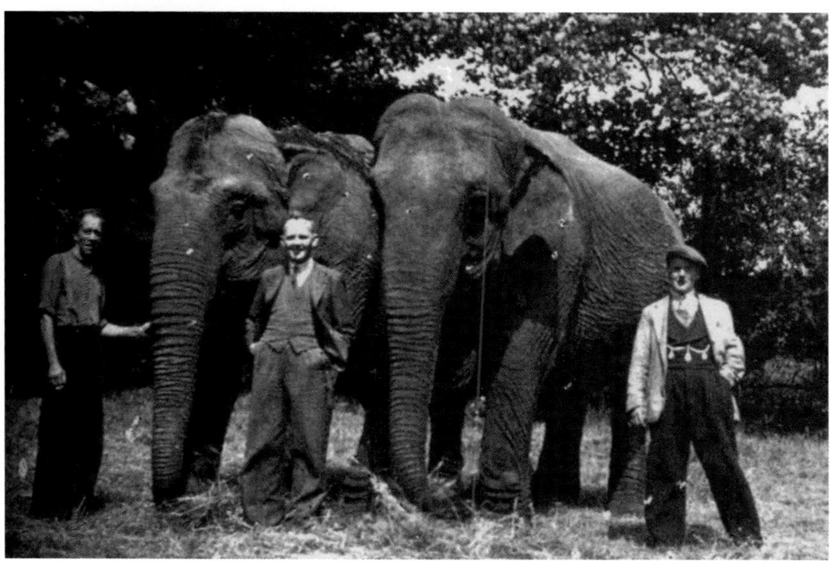

Top right: John Swallow in 1934 with Vivian and Cicely Rosaire.

Centre right: John Swallow on the right and Jack Lowe with Sauce performing the head carry with Zena Rosaire in 1933 – the first year of John's travels with the Rosaire Family and their circus.

Bottom right: Salt and Sauce photographed while on their travels with Madame Clara Paulo's Circus. The man on the left is thought to be Billy Thompson and the man on the right is Jack Mellor who was a World's Fair correspondent – using the pen name: "Wanderer" partly as a reference to his base in Wolverhampton.

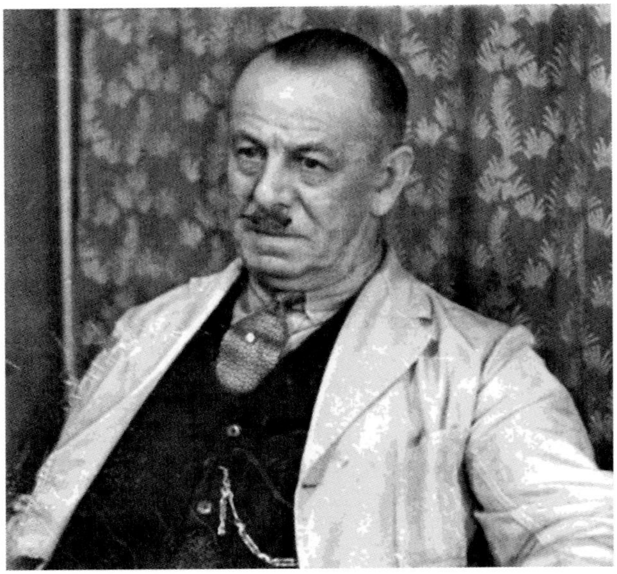

John Swallow II in later years.

Dark Times

Early in 1945 a World's Fair correspondent using the pen-name, "Southdown" visited the yard in Gorsebrook Road, Wolverhampton to discover that Paulo's Circus was wintering there. We reveal the identity of "Southdown" later in this book, and explain why he was familiar with the elephant's relationship with Wolverhampton. When Paulo's left the yard they took the circus to its first stand in Dudley in mid-March. By the summer of 1945 they were in Kent.

One day in Canterbury John Swallow had an argument with someone from the RSPCA about the health of Sauce who was suffering from the effects of an abscess on her leg. This incident was then woven into the account of John's death because not long after this he collapsed and died. On his death certificate it is stated that John Henry Swallow, age sixty nine, died at Wincheap Grove in Canterbury on 2nd August 1945. The cause of death is described as heart disease.

John's death was reported in the Express & Star, Wolverhampton's nightly newspaper, immediately – no doubt a result of the fact that John's son, John David Swallow, was involved in the production of the paper. The report included a very "potted" history of John Swallow's circus concentrating on the period from 1910 till 1930. We shall call John David Swallow, "John Swallow III" and he was the one who then took charge of the situation, knowing that Salt and Sauce had been left to his mother – Annie Swallow.

John Swallow III lived at 196 Coalway Road, Wolverhampton, and had married Kathleen Postons early in 1938. About eighteen months later their first son was born and he was also called John (John Swallow IV). It seems that John Swallow III offered to sell the elephants to Emily Paulo but she declined to take them. However it seems that it was resolved to leave them with Paulo's Circus for the time being. When Paulo's Circus reached Sutton Coldfield on 29th September 1945 it was arranged to hand them over to Dudley Zoo where John Swallow III gave them to the zoo's director, Edwin Wilson , on behalf of Annie. Obviously this was reported in the Express & Star.

However John Swallow IV gave me a slightly different account – suggesting that Salt and Saucy had been kept for a short while in the back garden in Coalway Road. Young John had been a pupil at Woodfield Primary School at the time and raided the school scrap food bins to feed the elephants. His head mistress has not believed his explanation for this, but then found it was true! If there was a time when Salt and Sauce had visited Coalway Road, it must have been in the winter of 1944/45, when John would have barely started school. Nevertheless John's accounts of visits to Dudley Zoo to see Grandad's elephants can be better substantiated.

On 8th August 1945 John Swallow II's funeral took place – in the middle of a heatwave. The service was conducted by Rev W. Hassall, the Vicar of St. Stephen's Church, Wolverhampton. It was a fairly modest family affair, but was attended by some of the people we have mentioned, and was reported in that night's Express & Star. John David Swallow and his sister Pat were joined by Mrs A. Campbell (John Swallow II's other daughter, known as Doree) and her husband, Alexander. Gilbert Swallow, John's brother was there, as was Adele Stapley-Walker and her husband Arthur (Comical Walker) plus other nieces and nephews. John's oldest son, William. could not be there as he was an army officer serving in Italy. Clara Paulo represented her family, and a Mr. D. Cooke came from Bennett's Circus. The Circus Friends Association was represented by Jack White, a circus enthusiast who also happened to be the House Manager of Dudley Hippodrome, who had recently been released from the RAF. John Swallow II was buried in Jeffock Road Cemetery, where his grave can still be seen today.

John Swallow II's death was briefly mentioned twice in World's Fair of 18th August. A correspondent using the name "Wanderer" laments the death of "*my old friend*". "Wanderer" was really named Jack Mellor and used the pen-name, when writing in World's Fair, partly as a reference to his own Wolverhampton background.

John Swallow III and John Swallow IV

John Swallow II and his wife Annie had four children. Amy Adele was born on 21st December 1921 in Ormskirk. This latter piece of information suggests that she was born while both her parents were still travelling. William Charles Swallow was born on 13th June 1913 in Dumfries. John Swallow III was born on 26th May 1916 and Pat was born in 1924. Although the lives of John Swallow I and John Swallow II (Broncho Bill) had been so completely focussed on the world of the circus, it is interesting to see how quickly all that became completely buried in the family's past.

William Charles Swallow was at least born at 6 Thornley Street, Wolverhampton, the house which for so long had been the centre of the Swallow empire. As far as we know, some members of the Swallow family continued to live at Thornley Street but John Henry and his wife Annie moved to 103 Waterloo Road just after the First World War, as their sons were growing up. It appears that they were keen for both boys to be educated at Wolverhampton Grammar School. However, it seems that they attended the Grammar School as boarders for at least some of the time so it is not clear to what extent the house in Waterloo Road was used as a family home. It seems most likely that was used during the Winter from the time the travelling season ended and then re-commenced the following year – a break that was interrupted by shows such as the annual event at the Islington Agricultural Hall. Perhaps the relatively settled life and the grammar school education made it inevitable that the boys would not follow their father into the circus world.

William Charles, known as Bill, eventually became a partner in the Wolverhampton Estate Agency business of "Bussey & Swallow", although this was interrupted by six years service in the Army. He later also worked in local industry and in his spare time he was a keen golfer. He died after a short illness on 19th August 1979 at the age of sixty six. His brother John David also went to Wolverhampton Grammar School and went on to a career with the Express & Star, Wolverhampton's daily evening paper. He eventually became General Manager of the Express & Star, moving on to become Company Secretary. For the ten years running up to his retirement in 1958 he was on the board of the Midland News Association – the company which owned the Express & Star. In his retirement he lived in Cornwall where he died in October 1987.

John David Swallow, whom we will refer to as 'John Swallow III', comes across as slightly more linked to his father's life in the circus than Bill. This might be

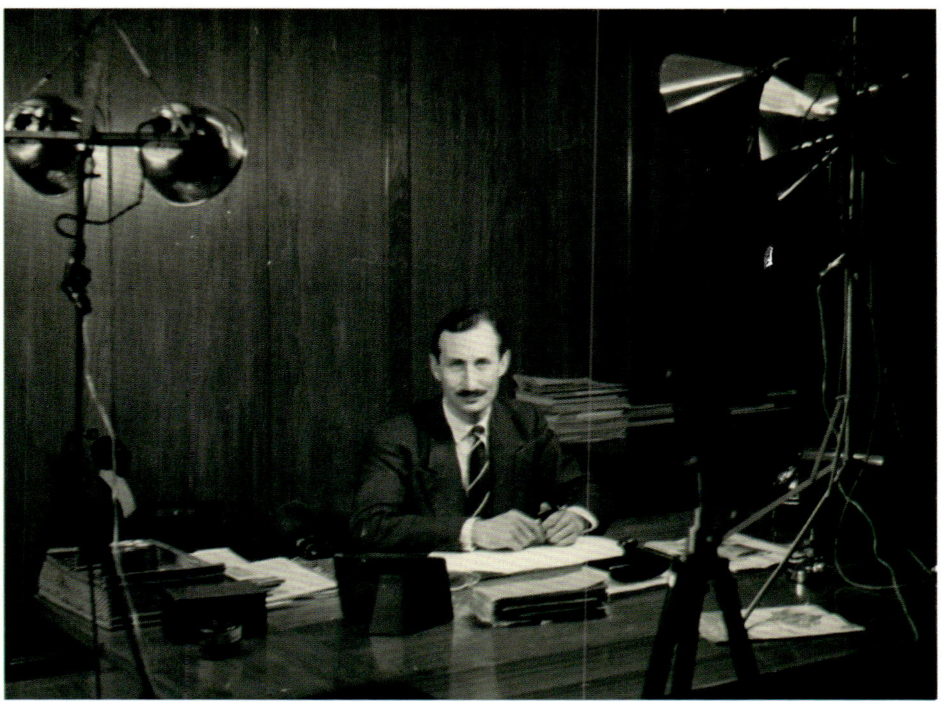

John Swallow III seen while being filmed at his desk at the Express & Star

because he had to deal with events following his father's death, including the fate of Salt and Saucy, because Bill was far way in the Forces. On the other hand he may simply have shared more of his father's interests. For example, Broncho Bill, was an occasional contributor to World's Fair and seemed to have a flair for writing. In 1931, at the age of seventeen, we find John Swallow III writing a piece for World's Fair, possibly encouraged by his father, giving readers a picture of the Wolverhampton Floral Fete of that year. He describes the show's success and the popularity of all its ingredients: band concerts, a circus, Women's League of Health & Beauty display, and the opera, "Merrie England". In mentioning the presentation of the Wembley Empire Circus he identifies George Batty as the Equestrian Director as if familiar with such matters. John Swallow also inherited his father's love of horses, and also had musical talents.

While in retirement in Cornwall it seems that John Swallow III started writing a book about the circus – presumably his father's circus. The sad thing is that this manuscript was lost – denying us access to what might have provided a real close-up account of the show. However, we do have two items which provide proof of John Swallow III's desire to produce the printed word: while in Cornwall he produced a book called "Only Five Survived". This book tells the story of the "Hera", a ship wrecked off the Cornish coast in February 1914.

The title refers to the numbers of men who survived out of a crew of twenty four. The book goes on to describe how the wreck's resting place on the seabed had been discovered and explored by members of the RAF St. Mawgan Sub-Aqua Club – a group that John Swallow first met exactly fifty six years after the wreck. John Swallow III asked his "old school pal", Air Marshall Sir John Lapsley to write a forward. Sir John began by writing: *"I always remember John Swallow as a boy for his great sense of adventure. He could do all those things which most boys would like to do – juggling, knife throwing, lassoing and acrobatics."* It sounds like a boy with a circus background to me!

The other "proof" of John Swallow III's literary aspirations comes in the form of two articles written in 1952 and 1953 for "King Pole" – the quarterly magazine of the Circus Friends Association. They are summarised at the end of this chapter.

John David Swallow married Kathleen Postens early in 1938 and established a home at 196 Coalway Road. Their son, John Swallow IV was born in December 1938. Therefore young John was only six or seven when his grandfather, John Swallow II, died while still touring with Salt and Sauce, his famous elephants. However, it seems that young John grew up with some memories of Salt and Sauce and the wartime problems of keeping them fed. Apparently he was fond of the elephants and was taken to see them on several occasions while they lived at Dudley Zoo. It also seems that John Swallow IV was very close to his grandfather. Even this was not enough to draw him into the circus world, and perhaps his father persuaded him to consider a career in journalism.

After leaving Tettenhall College, in Wolverhampton, John Swallow IV pursued a career in journalism. At one stage he found himself working for the Blackpool Gazette where he probably developed his quirky style and his love of quirky stories. He also worked on a Manchester paper and in 1964 was offered a good job with the Sunday Mirror. At the same time he was being interviewed for a job with ATV. ATV was preparing to launch weekday commercial TV in the Midlands – based in Birmingham. The "ATV Today" programme began on 5th October 1964, and was a twenty minute "magazine" programme following the Midland News. As a result of working for ATV John was able to make Wolverhampton his home.

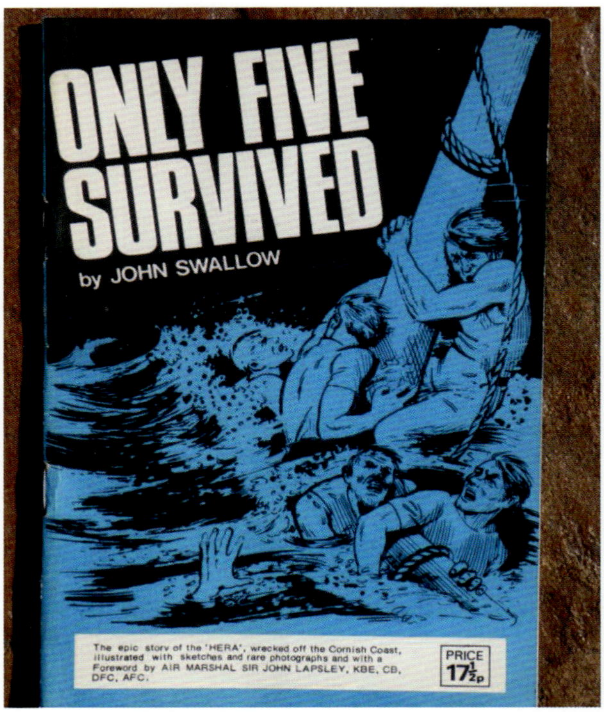

Right: The front cover of "Only Five Survived", by John Swallow III.

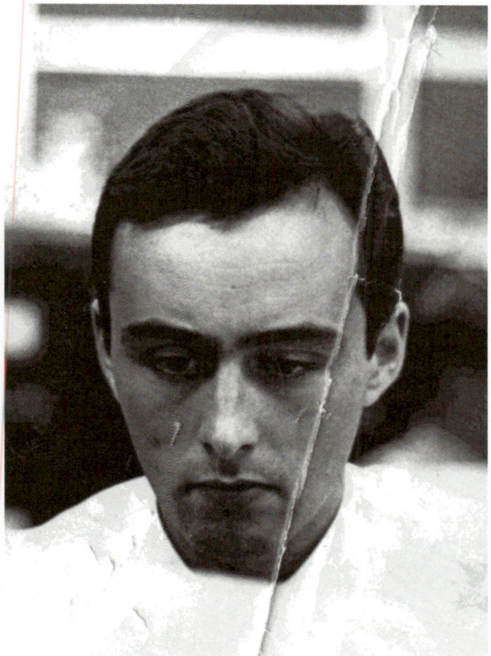

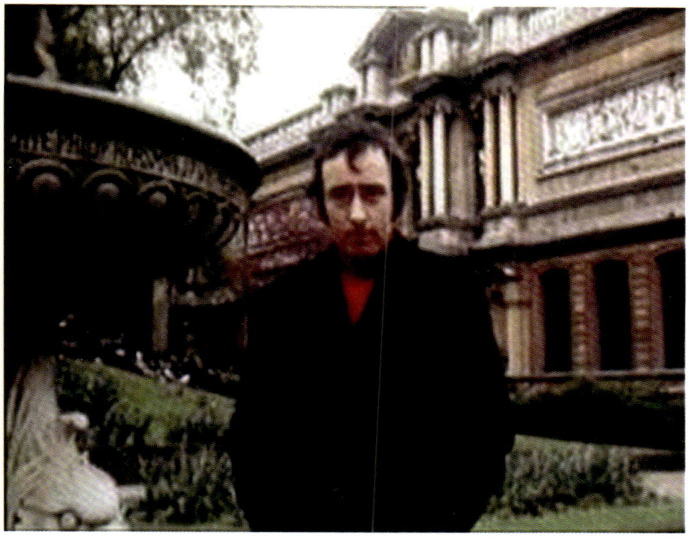

Left: A young John Swallow IV at his typewriter, and above: as he appeared on television, presenting a feature on the merits of holiday-making in Wolverhampton.

John Swallow IV certainly made his name as quirky television reporter with "ATV Today" from 1964 onwards, sometimes working as a double act with Chris Tarrant. Their jokey local stories were very popular in the 1970s but went out of fashion when local news-broadcasting became more serious. (The final edition of "ATV Today" was broadcast on 31st April 1981 and included a compilation of some of John's notable interviews.) However, John went on to work with Central Television until his retirement in the early 2000s.His last appearance on television had been in 1989 when he produced a pilot programme for a series to be called "Swallow This". Unfortunately the series did not proceed.

He subsequently left Wolverhampton and went to live in Maldon, Essex, where he died on 15th July 2008, not long after the publication of the biography of Salt and Saucy. He had been ill for some time and was in Bloomfield Hospital in Chelmsford when he died at the age of sixty eight. The funeral was also held in Chelmsford on 24th July, although his friends in Wolverhampton were informed of this in a notice in the Express & Star. The latter had provided an obituary shortly after his death which concentrated on his television career, and his sense of comedy. His approach to being a reporter was highlighted with the comment that he usually wrote his stories on beer mats or the back of fag packets! Although the paper thought fit to mention that John was the son of paper's one time General Manager, there was no mention of the fact that he was the grandson of Broncho Bill.

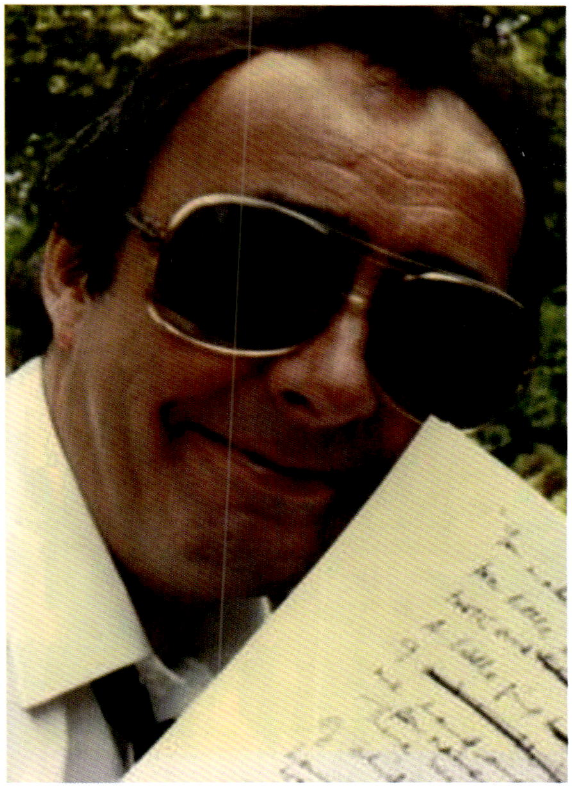

John Swallow IV. Some of John Swallow's television material is now available on a DVD produced by the Media Archive for Central England in "From Headlines to Tight Lines - The Story of ATV Today"

A Broncho Bill Scrapbook

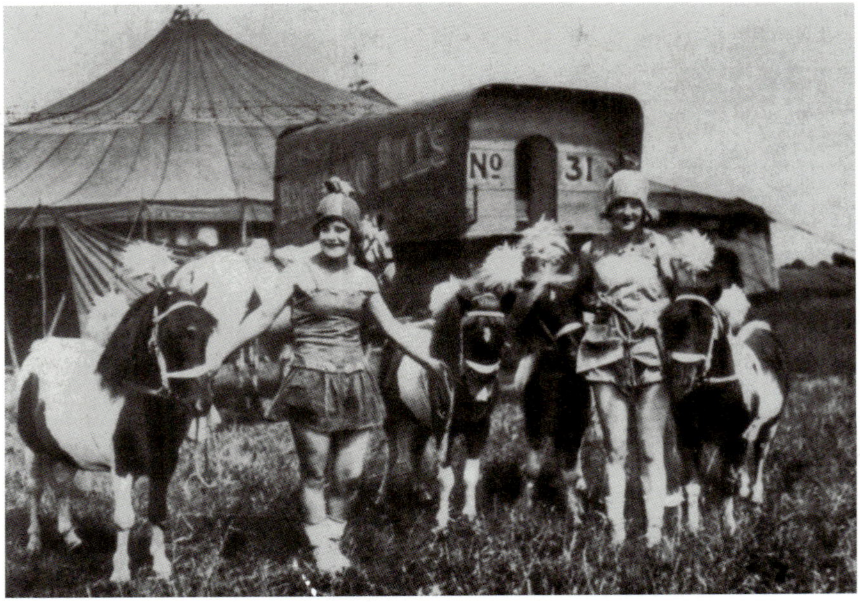

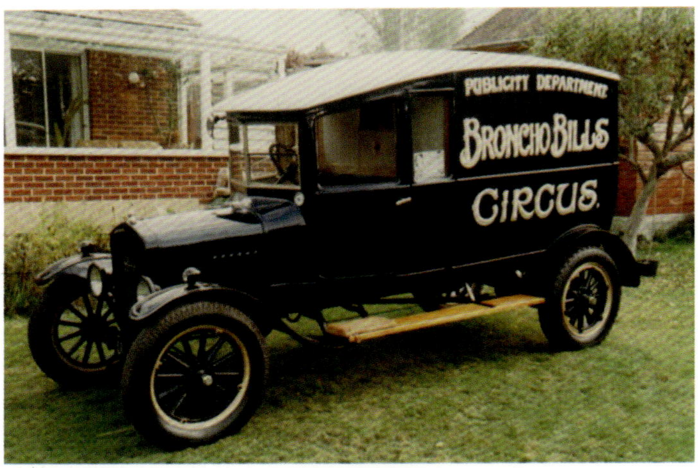

Above: Two girls on Broncho Bill's show photographed with some of the ponies. John Swallow's shows always included a great deal of equestrian entertainment and for most of its life was very much a "horse-drawn show".

Lfet: In the mid 1920s some motor vehicles were introduced to the show and Gilbert Swallow provided the advance-billing department with a Ford van. Amazingly this van survives and has been beautifully restored.

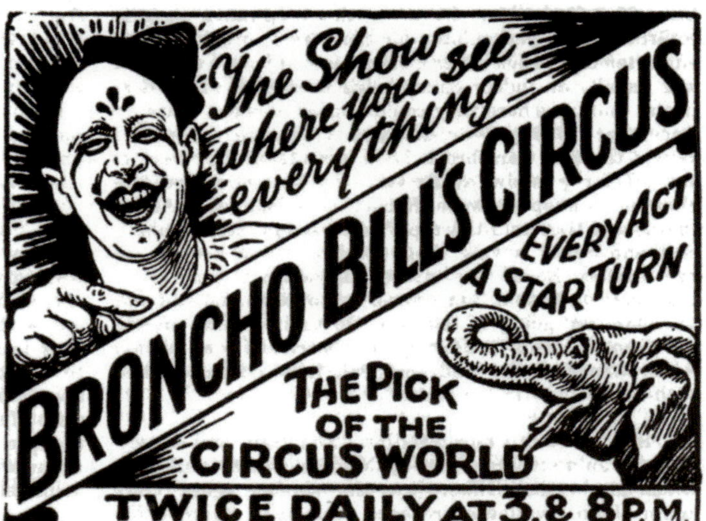

Left: John Swallow provided a printing "block" to local newspapers to reproduce this advertisement for the show. Presumably, the block was always retrieved and passed on to the next user. This is produced from that block.

Many of the photographs used in this chapter were provided by John Swallow IV from his family's collection, and others have been made available by Verity, John's daughter.

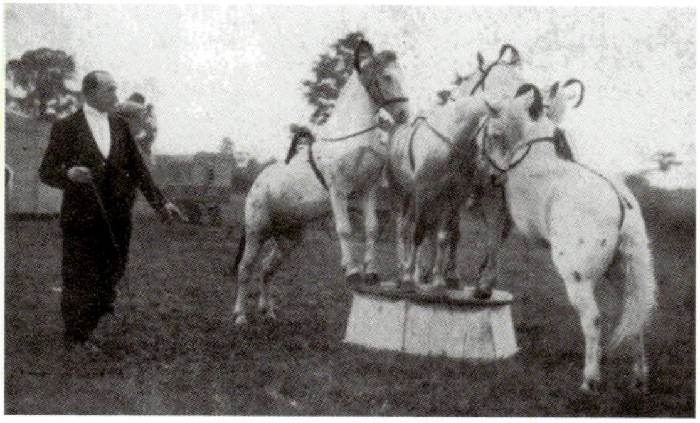

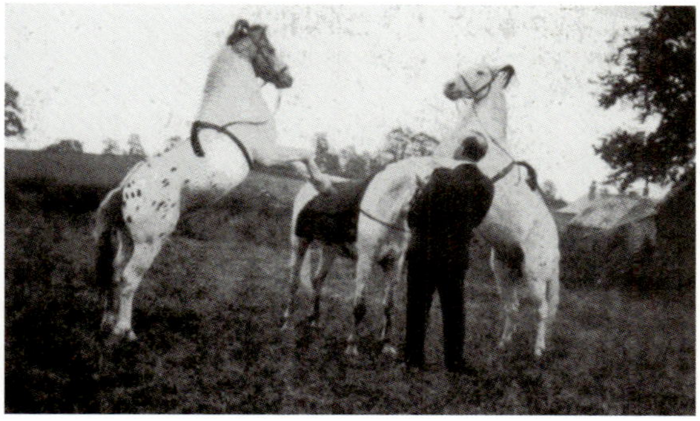

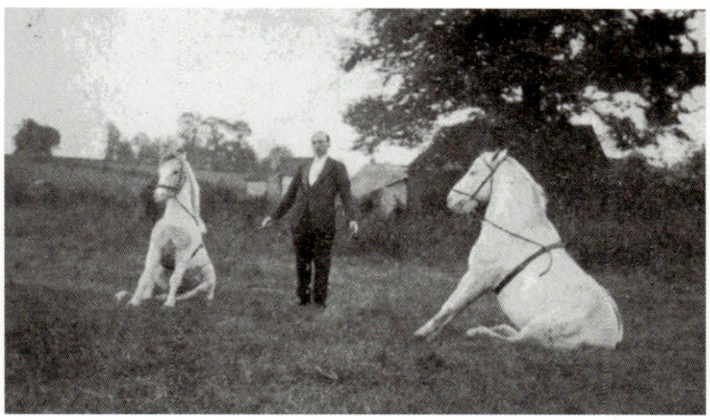

Above: Three postcards produced by Paulton Brothers, a Wolverhampton firm of printers who produced posters and publicity material for John Swallow II. The cards feature John Swallow's ponies.

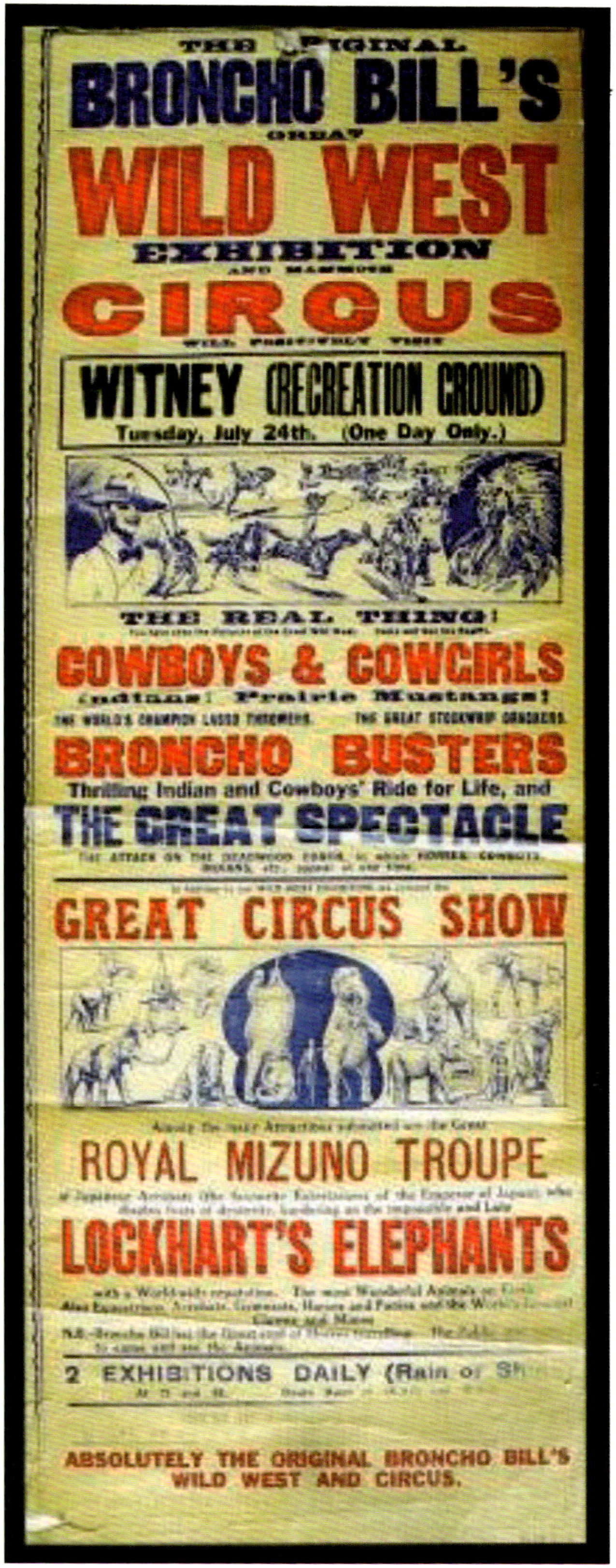

Right: A two-colour Broncho Bill poster thought to be of 1918 vintage, from the Ken Rattenbury collection, featuring the elephants and the Mizuno Troupe.

John David Swallow III's articles for "King Pole".

Although the manuscript of a book about the circus has been lost, the texts of two articles written by John Swallow III for "King Pole" have survived in the archives of that magazine – published quarterly by the Circus Friends Association. The first, "I Nearly Became a Circus Proprietor" was published in the Christmas edition in 1952, the second was published a year later. With the permission of the CFA the articles are presented here in shortened form and with some commentary.

I Might Have Become a Circus Proprietor
John D. Swallow 1952

"Please sir, may I go home for two days?" My housemaster at Wolverhampton Grammar School, Mr. "Jammy" Booth, looked up from a pile of exercise books.
"And why, Swallow, should you go home for two days?
"Because s-s-sir", I stammered, "my father is selling his circus and I want to be there to see it happen."

I waited, quietly optimistic. For once I had a genuine excuse. It was true, only too true, that after fifty five years my father had decided to retire and to sell the big top and all that went with it to the highest bidders. I felt, and probably looked, heart-broken. I felt as if the world was going to end on the morrow, but I wanted to be there to see it happen.

"Jammy" looked up and his smiling eyes gave me my answer. "A most original excuse", he said. "By all means have a couple of days off."

A tear – yes – I am not ashamed to admit it – ran down my right cheek, and I turned to the door. My hand was on the doorknob when Jammy said, "And, Swallow, if the elephants go cheap, please buy me one!"

(Thus began John D Swallow's account of the two-day circus sale held in Wolverhampton on 2nd and 3rd November 1930, including the revelation that the two elephants were the only two items to remain unsold.)

As I approached the sale ground, the past happiness I had found under the cool of the green and white striped big top flooded back to me. To a boy of my tender age – I was fourteen – it seemed like a lifetime of happiness. Without the Fordson tractors, the horses, the clowns, tent men, the Japanese troupe – and Roger, my own horse, which was shortly to be knocked down to the highest bidder – the future was bleak, uncertain, unhappy.

I propped my bicycle against the fence and picked my way through the thick mud which the tractors had churned up in positioning the wagons and lorries, oblivious to the rain which drenched me to the skin. I was in too much haste to notice a little thing like that. I passed the paybox. 'Standing room in all parts,' read a notice in a protruding frame. And inside the big top it was standing room only. Two thousand or more people were packed around the ring, and against one of the king poles was the auctioneer's rostrum.

The crowd was mostly composed of farmers, but there were many circus interests represented from this country and abroad. Dilly, my father's Irish hunter was being paraded up and down, his black, close cropped coat, sleek as a cat's, glistened under the strong arc lamps. I clambered on to a ring prop to better see the proceedings but that collapsed and I took a tumble! Finally I climbed a quarter pole, put my foot through the loop and hung there like a monkey. Fifteen foot above the ring level afforded me a bird's eye view of what was going on.

Bidding had started for Dilly. "Fifteen guineas," sang out the auctioneer, "Twenty guineas". I scanned the faces below. Where was Dad? I spotted him as the bidding reached fifty guineas. He was leaning nonchalantly against the rostrum: a dark figure in a hunting mac. He was a good poker player but I could see by his face that he was bluffing.

Dilly had carried him gracefully over six foot fences, through lovely country in rural Staffordshire, to Brewood, Albrighton, Trysull and Tong. Hunting kept him alive in the winter. It provided him with the excitement he craved, and Dilly was part of that excitement, that love. He looked down at his catalogue, very much as I had looked down when "Jammy" said I could have two days off. Bang went the auctioneer's hammer – and Dilly had a new master.

Slowly but surely the stock in trade of a circus man changed hands. Animals that had been trained by my father were all sold off. I looked away from the unhappy scene and my eyes alighted upon Cocoa the clown. He was sitting by the ring-doors on an elephant tub. Ernie Rowe, for that was the name by which he was christened, appeared to be in the throes of a deep depression. I clambered from my perch and went over to him. "Hello Master John," said the man who earned his living by making people laugh, "I feel awfully unhappy." Just that, and I could have cried again.

And all the time the rain drummed on the tight canvas overhead, like the roll of drum sticks on pig-skin preceding an execution. Crack! Another lot had fallen to the highest bidder.

(John's personal insight into his father's feelings about Dilly offers us a rare opportunity to understand Broncho Bill – the man who had run such a successful wild west circus, and the man, who in retirement continued to travel with his two elephants.)

Those Were the Days
John D. Swallow

The stirring strains of the "Star Spangled Banner" filled the Big Top of my father's circus. The Wild West Show was about to start and behind the ring curtains, horses, cowboys and Indians were assembled to make their spectacular entrance.

I was one of the "Cowboys". Whilst on holiday from school I delighted in spinning ropes, and having reached a reasonable proficiency at it under the skilled and patient tuition of Bill Holmes, I was at last passed "fit for the ring" by my father.

Mounted on Roger, my piebald pony, I sat happily fingering my lasso. In a minute I would be galloping around the arena. It was to be my first public appearance and I was thrilled at the prospect. It was then that my happiness was shattered. A groom sidled up to me and said, "Old Bob is dead."

The memory of that moment is vivid as I write. I slipped off Roger and ran as fast as my spurs would allow to Od Bob's tent. He had been the show's night-watchman for over twenty years, and a more kindly and gentle man I have never known. His manner matched his appearance. He was the personification of Santa Claus; he was everyone's friend.

I pulled back the flap of the bell tent. "Old Bob" was lying on a bed of straw with a rug rolled up as a pillow. The sun, like a spotlight, accentuated the sad beauty of the scene. His face was a picture of serenity framed by the silver grey of his long beard and halo of tousled hair. That drab tent, to my tear-dimmed eyes, became a cathedral and "Old Bob" a saint.

***

Arthur Walker, alias Comical Walker, was better at clowning than doing a straight act on his globe. It used to intrigue my brother and I to see the preparations he made before a performance to ensure the globe would remain static when he did his juggling act standing on it.

Surreptitiously Arthur would dig a small hole in the ring into which he would place a few coloured fragments of paper. The globe once in position would remain completely still.

With the mischief of youth, we decided to sabotage Arthur's act. After he had dug his little hole one day and departed, we removed the pieces of paper, filled in the hole, and replaced the pieces of paper.

That afternoon my brother and I sat in the best seats and on our best behaviour. We could hardly wait for Act 5 – Arthur's act. At last, into the ring came Arthur followed by a prop man pushing his globe. Nonchalantly taking it over he steered to the prepared position over the scraps of paper, and with a confident jump touched down on top of it – but not for long! The globe slipped from under him and down came Arthur, juggling clubs and all. The audience loved it but not nearly as much as my brother and I.

(What John Swallow leaves unexplained was that Arthur Walker was his uncle, Arthur being married to Adele, John Swallow II's sister.)

***

Albert Pearson, our strong man, had a magnificent physique. In a leopard skin loin cloth, with his muscles rippling, he used to thrill the audience with astounding feats of strength. It used to take six prop men to carry his cannon balls and dumb-bells. One day, two little boys, and I am not saying which two – did the job for them and I can assure you we did not find it all fatiguing!

From spinning yarns may I revert to spinning ropes – and Bill Holmes? In my opinion he is the finest exponent of the art of spinning ropes in the country. He was also a good carpenter. When my father "discovered" him he was making coffins. Bill never regretted giving up the circular saw for the spinning rope. And, I am sure, the latter never gave greater pleasure to more people.

Christmas always reminds me of the Royal Agricultural Hall, Islington, and a trumpet. This was given to me by my father, who for many years was the ringmaster at Islington. His dressing room was adjacent to the lady artistes' dressing room and not far removed from Kayes' lions cages.

While my father was in the ring one evening, I remained in his dressing room. I took out my trumpet and endeavoured to emulate the more experienced musicians playing to a packed Boxing Day audience. I made plenty of noise but not much in tune. The ladies in the next room did not complain to my father. However, the man looking after the lions was most concerned. His charges were restless for days afterwards!

Obviously John Swallow III's first article had prompted some correspondence regarding Broncho Bill's experiment with a three-ring circus and the "Wild West Show" – both of which may have been inspired by his visit to America. Commenting on the Wild West Show, John recalled another humorous incident:

This was introduced by Talbot Cooke, who, dressed as a cowboy and mounted on a piebald horse, would say: 'Ladies and Gentlemen, it gives me great pleasure to introduce some of the sports and pastimes of the wild west…'

To my knowledge he had been making this little speech twice a day for many years, but one day he completely forgot his lines, lost his head, and turning to the nearest prop boy shouted, 'Cue, you fool – cue, you fool!' Unfortunately the prop boy was new to the ring and the cue was not forthcoming. I can see Talbot's red and perspiring face as he wheeled round and disappeared through the ring curtains as fast as his horse would take him.

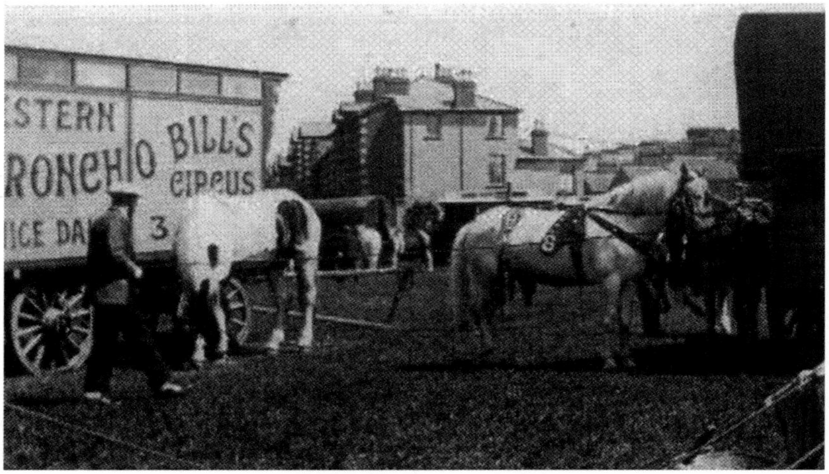

John Swallow IV preserved a large collection of photographs of his grandfather's circus but very few of them were captioned! Almost all the photographs include horses or the elephants, with occasional glimpses of the large tent which was able to contain the two-ring circus.

A rare caption informs us that we can see Doris Yelding in the yard at Gorsebrook Road in the picture below right!

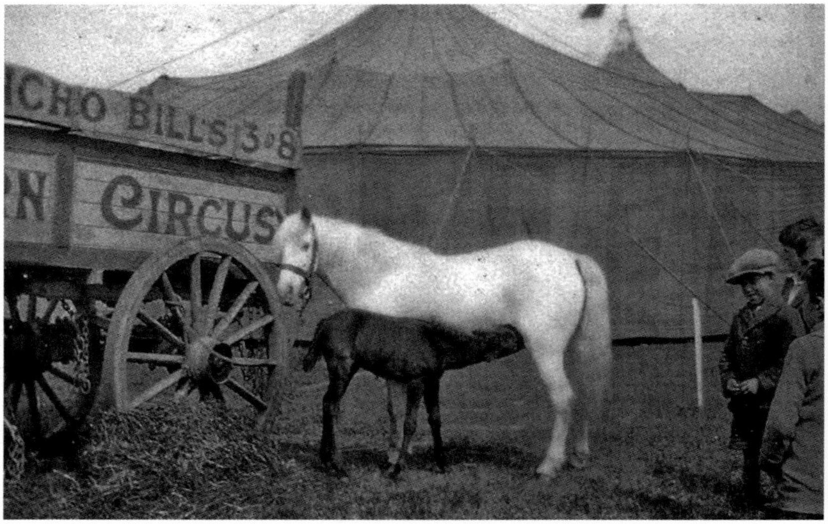

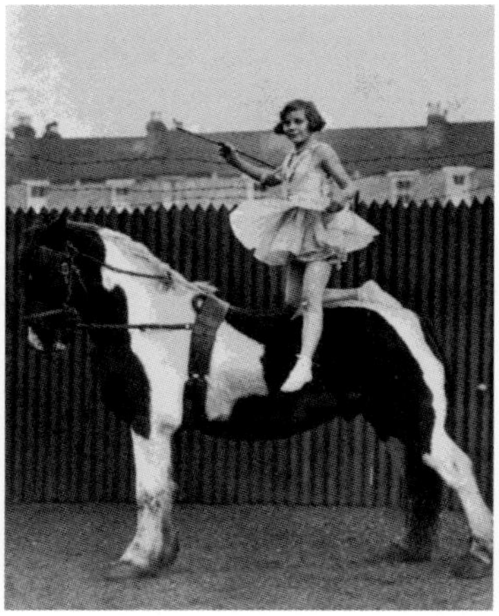

Chapter 2

What's In a Name?

Irving Bosco

Introducing Bosco

Way back in 1979 I came across workers demolishing the remains of the Coliseum cinema in Dudley Road, Blakenhall, Wolverhampton. I went to see what they were doing and found them throwing old ledgers from the former manager's office onto a large bonfire at the front of the stalls. Up until that point they had been burning upholstery off the seats and clearing the auditorium. When I rescued one of the burning ledgers I found it dated from 1913. Most were already destroyed and a search of the office produced no others, but I went home to lunch suddenly feeling very strongly that local cinema history was becoming lost and not much was being done about it.

I had been a film fan since early childhood and also had some leanings towards being interested in the cinemas themselves, nurtured by the variety of cinemas found within reach of my home in East London / Essex Border. I attended Saturday morning matinees at my local Odeon at Gants Hill, and felt that my parents approved of visits to that cinema. I was also attracted to the Essoldo, Manor Park, but sensed that my parents did not approve of that cinema. It was difficult to define this disapproval, but it made the cinema seem even more interesting!

When I came to the Black Country in the Autumn of 1962 I was delighted by the variety of cinemas within reach of my new home in Dudley – particularly if one had a motorbike. A visit to a cinema in far-off Walsall, or Blackheath, often led to asking the cashier to look after my crash helmet, gauntlets, etc. while I watched a film. Sometimes this led to the manager coming to meet the patron who had made such a request and to repay the efforts I had made to visit his cinema I was sometimes given a tour of the premises. Of course, I was far too dumb to have taken photographs at the time, or even to have made notes of what I was told. Even the fact that the cinemas were closing did not make me take proper notice of what was happening.

So that bonfire in the Coliseum in 1979 was quite a wake-up call. I decided that I would immediately start making an inventory of all the locations in the Black Country where films had been shown and make some assessment of what information about them was available. The project quickly grew into becoming a book on the subject – partly inspired by the fact that someone had just published the first regional history of cinemas: "The Picture House in East Anglia" by Stephen Peart. I was also encouraged by Bob Wareing – fellow member of the Wolverhampton Film Society – who made available his comprehensive collection of "Kine Year Books". (Bob was an ardent film and cinema enthusiast, and lived in a bungalow called "Elstree". The Black Country abounded in such characters.)

It was not long before I was on the trail of many key figures in local cinema history – all of whom were completely new to me. For example, it seemed important to find out who were the first people to show films in the Black Country. I soon found out there were two answers to this question: there were the real pioneers who presented bioscope shows from 1897 to 1910, and then there were the first generation of cinema proprietors who showed films in buildings following the introduction of the 1909 Kinematograph Act which took effect on 1st January 1910. Sometimes one person might fit both categories, but that was rare.

I made my enquiries town by town and when I came to look at Dudley's cinema history I found that the first films shown in permanent premises were presented right at the beginning of 1910 in the Public Hall, Wolverhampton Street, by a gentleman named Irving Bosco. I was immediately "hooked" by this name and wanted to find out all about him. Although I had very little success at first in finding out about the man I did find out that he had other claims to fame. The most important claim historically was that he been the first man to operate a cinema in the Black Country, having opened premises in West Bromwich almost a complete year in advance of the Kinematograph Act coming into force. No one in West Bromwich seems to have done much to celebrate Irving Bosco's achievement, but perhaps one day they will.

I found evidence of Irving Bosco's association with several cinemas, taking in such places as Smethwick, Aston, and Harborne as well as Dudley and West Bromwich, but continued to find out little about the man himself. Once again 'coincidence' came to my rescue. I had a letter printed in the Smethwick Telephone (Smethwick's weekly paper) in which I asked if any reader knew anything about Irving Bosco. By then I had found out his real name and the fact that he had once lived in Lordswood Road. A reader replied saying that he had been an electrician and had once been involved in re-wiring the house next door to Bosco's in Lordswood Road. He had been very attracted by 'the girl next door' but she told him that she was about to marry a man called Alex Willington. (This was in 1938!) He believed that she had later gone to live in Solihull. These were just the clues I needed and they enabled me to trace Eva, Bosco's daughter, to her home in Stratford-on-Avon just before putting the finishing touches to "Cinemas of the Black Country" – published in October 1982. Although I still knew relatively little about Irving Bosco, I was able to include a portrait of him, as a young man, in the book.

The family, at that time, were not able to provide very much more information but they were sure that Irving had something to do with a circus in Ireland, and that Waller Jeffs had played a part in Irving's story. Over the next few years it was a bit easier to find out about Waller Jeffs than it was to find out about this legendary Irish circus. It has only become possible to fill-in many gaps in Irving Bosco's life in recent times with genealogical information and old newspapers becoming accessible via The Internet. Having known the name "Irving Bosco" since 1980, for me it was very rewarding in 2018 to meet his grand-daughter to whom he was a real person – not just the subject of research.

The inspiration for researching all this has always been that name: "Irving Bosco". It was a clever name to adopt, and I do my best to explain it in the following text. Perhaps you are already finding there is something special about the name!

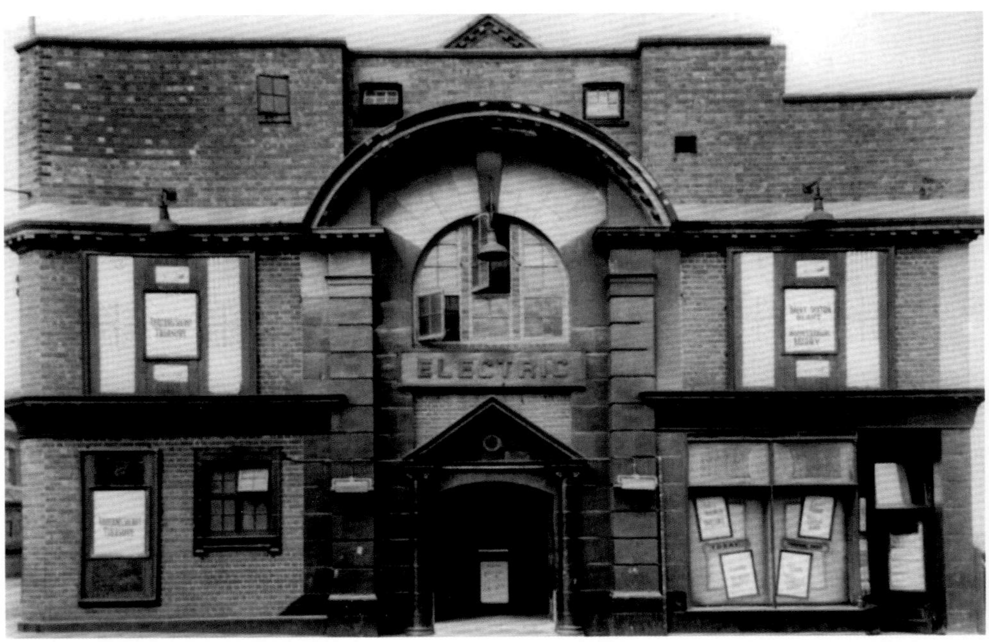

The Cape Hill Electric Cinema, opened by Irving Bosco on Monday 19th June 1911. (CTA Archives)

Joseph **Bainton** (c1841 - ?) = Sarah Jane Morris formerly Sheering (b. c.1843)
Joseph and Sarah Jane had seven children:
Joseph (b. 1870)
WILLIAM (born 13th October 1871)
James (born 24th November 1874)
Ada (b.1878)
Louisa (b.1880)
Frederica (b. 1882)
Ruby (b. 1886)

William Bainton, known as IRVING BOSCO (1871 – 1946), married Margaret Phiducie Sanderson, known as Ducie Saunderson (9th Dec.1883 – 10th Oct. 1963).

Married 27th March 1909 in Birmingham

William Oliver b.1910 – d. 8/12/1970
Married Betty Dalloway in 1940

Eva Margaret b. 20 May 1913 - 2008?
= Alexander Willington.
Married 15 June 1938

Susan b. 7 April 1941

Jill A. b. 17 Dec 1945

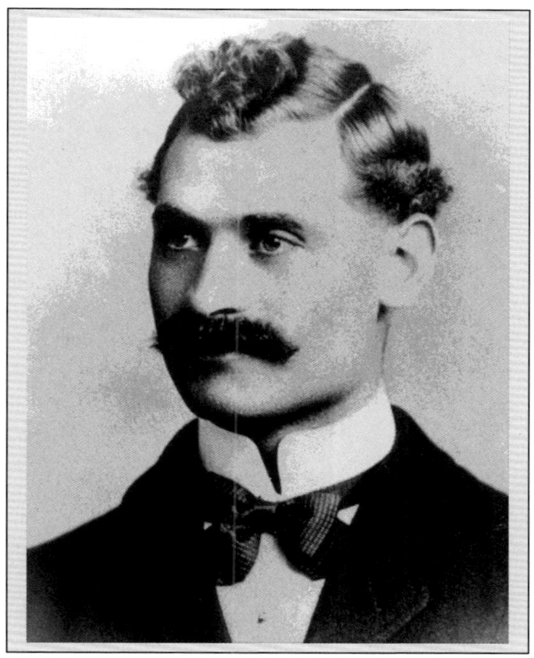

Right: Until recently this was the only picture of Irving Bosco seen by the author.
It was given to him in 1982 by Eva Willington and appears to show him as a young man, perhaps photographed in the late 1890s or early 1900s.

"B" for Bainton

Having a name like "Irving Bosco" would be a great start in life, but of course the truth is that Irving did not begin his life with such a name. He was born as William Morris Bainton, on 13th October, 1871*, at Keighley in Yorkshire. How he adopted the name Irving Bosco is an intriguing mystery, and will be dealt with later. The advantage of being born in October 1871 is that your family may have been recorded in the 1871 census, conducted earlier that year. Sure enough we find the Baintons living in Keighley, listed in the census with Joseph Bainton identified as a vocalist. Joseph's wife is listed as "Annie", while on his birth certificate William's mother is identified as "Sarah Jane" – giving us some intriguing mysteries to resolve. (Reassuringly, William's older brother is confirmed as Joseph, whom we know was born in 1869.)

An advert in "The Era" during April 1881 also mentions Joseph Bainton (i.e. William's father), describing him as a "theatrical agent" and "lately connected with the Britannia Hall, Keighley". Unfortunately there seems to be nothing in "The Era" of the 1870s to provide any other hints of events that may have surrounded William during his early life.

We have to jump to 1881 when we can find the Baintons living at St. Johns Place in Manchester. His forty year old father, Joseph Bainton, is described as a "commission agent", married to thirty-four year old Amy. (Is "Amy" a misreading of the name "Annie"? Once again this provides an element of mystery!) There are five children in the family: Joseph Jnr., aged eleven, William who is said, incorrectly, to be seven years old, James who is six, Ada who is three and one-year-old Louisa. Interestingly each of the children is born in a different place suggesting the family were used to being on the move, as we might expect with a father in show-business.

William's father Joseph is quite an elusive character. He was born in the Marylebone area of London in about 1840. He seems to make an early appearance in an advertisement in "The Era" of 24th July 1859 when he is described as an "Irish Comic & Vocalist" – looking for work after a thirteen week engagement in Chatham. In the following year we find him in Plymouth and Bristol, and by 1862 in Margate. His name does not reappear until the 1881 reference mentioned above, and an 1895 reference to him as "late proprietor of the Peoples' Hall, Keighley. In 1895 he wrote a letter to "The Era", from an address in Manchester, to re-assert his authorship of a song called, "A Young Lady Nineteen Years Old". This music hall song describes the disillusionment of a young bridegroom who watches his new bride remove her wooden leg, wig and false teeth. It exists in a number of versions so I am not sure how Joseph Bainton could have proved he was its author. Nevertheless this dispute underlines the fact that William grew up in the entertainment business in which his father was a player.

The 1891 census helps develop our story. Amy Bainton seems to have stayed in the Manchester area and is now living in the Broughton area of Salford with Joseph Jnr., now twenty one, Ada, Louise, and two further daughters: Frederica and Ruby. However, her husband Joseph and sons William and James are to be found lodging in Paradise Street, Sheffield. They are all listed as "vocalists", and three other residents at the same address are listed as "music hall artists". William's age is given as eighteen, which would have suggested a birth year of 1873. However, the interesting thing is that we now find Joseph and his two sons clearly in the show-business world – the world in which William's life is about to take-off. Their address at 27 Paradise Street, Sheffield, and the house and the house next door, are clearly theatrical lodging houses, emphasising their participation in the theatrical world. By the time we catch up with William in the 1901 census his career and "stage name" will be well established.

Before we refer to the 1901 census it is interesting to try and catch up with William Bainton's progress through the 1890s. It must be at some point during this decade that William Bainton decided to become Irving Bosco but so far it has been impossible to identify that moment. Apparently he is not mentioned in "The Era" until 1896 – a year that is significant in entertainment history. In February 1896 The Lumiere Brothers came over from France to London to show everyone their invention: the cinematograph. Their demonstration was quickly followed by British inventors showing their versions of this new technology, and a number of other inventors rushed to register various patents that would be important in the production of cinematographic equipment. It seems that William Bainton was very excited by the possibilities of this new medium – seen by some as a scientific toy, seen by others as something to do with entertainment. It is even said that our hero took out his own patent but then sold the idea to someone else. (This was probably a device to prevent the image flickering and was developed by Irving Bosco working with Henry Joy.) As 1896 proceeds, cinematographic presentations take place across the provinces of Britain, at first in the large cities, then in large towns and eventually in smaller towns. These presentations often took place in a theatrical setting – ranging from variety theatres to public halls.

*William's birth certificate has been provided by his grand-daughter Susan – once and for all resolving the date of his birth, having seen a number of different years and dates suggested! Although it confirms his date of birth it adds to the mystery surrounding his mother. On the certificate she is identified as Sarah Jane Morris. This reveals why the name "Morris" is part of his name but does not answer the question of whether his parents were married or not. She was born Sarah Jane Sheering in 1836, in Bristol. It appears that she married a Henry James Morris on 24th April 1861, but it is not clear what followed. Although she uses the name Bainton in several census returns, she then creates confusion concerning her first names! By 1901 she is back in Bristol looking after her aging father, James Sheering. With her are the four younger Bainton children: Ada, Louise, Frederica and Ruby.

Becoming Bosco

In the edition of "The Era" published on 19th December 1896 we find a report of a variety show at the Theatre Royal, Birkenhead. Included in the show was "Irving Bosco's Cinematograph". This seems to be the earliest use of this name in print found so far, and clearly proves that this was the kind of entertainment that Irving wished to provide. Why might William Bainton adopt his new name at about the same time? It is reasonable to assume the name "Irving" was inspired by the fame of the great Victorian actor: Henry Irving. Henry Irving was knighted in 1895 – the first actor to receive such an honour and recognition so it was obviously a prestigious name to adopt. (From this book's position it is also interesting that Henry Irving was using an adopted name!) It is more difficult to clarify the name "Bosco". Families of that name, sometimes with Italian ancestry, were to be found in the circus world at that time, and some were to be found in the West Midlands. Although principally interested in cinematography from 1896 onwards, Irving was presenting this in a circus setting and may well have met and admired members of a Bosco family.

By early 1897 Irving Bosco seems to be based at an address in Bristol and is advertising for bookings for his cinematograph. Brief mentions in "The Era" seem to indicate that his cinematograph was presented in Bristol, Bath and Exeter, usually as part of a variety programme. He is therefore using the cinematograph in a theatrical setting just at the same time as some showmen with a fairground background start presenting the same medium in the travelling bioscope shows. The search for shows in which the cinematograph could be included as a ten minute act took Irving Bosco far and wide – sometimes on the stage, and sometimes in the circus ring. In the latter capacity Irving Bosco came to Walsall in December 1897 to provide a conclusion to a show that included a presentation of George Lockhart's elephants. The show was put on by Tommy Transfield in a purpose built temporary wooden building erected at the top of Park Street which was used for five months, during which there was a new show every week. (More information about Transfield's Circus in Walsall during 1897 can be found in my book: "Fairs & Circuses in the Black Country" Uralia Press, 1994.)

Advertisements appear in The Era during 1897 and 1898 in which Bosco seeks engagements for his "Excelsior Cinematograph", and we find evidence of his participation in other people's shows. For example In February 1897 Maggie Morton is presenting her pantomime, "Blue Beard", at the Tamworth Assembly Rooms. We are told: *"In the scene of Blue Beard's Palace Garden" will be introduced the greatest sensation and wonderful invention of the age – THE CINEMATOGRAPH (Irving Bosco's animated pictures)."* Maggie Morton was manageress and proprietor of a large prestigious touring theatre company and was probably then the youngest person to be in such a position. It seems that Irving Bosco toured for ten weeks as part of this show.

The business of presenting his cinematograph on stage or in a circus setting occupies Irving Bosco through 1898 and 1889 in a fairly frenzied state, bringing him into contact with a vast number of people. Unfortunately their names are only familiar to a small band of circus, fairground and circus historians: for example circus names like, Lloyd's, Ohmy's, Batty's and Hoffman's. On stage Irving Bosco would change the name of his cinematograph to suit the occasion. For example, when appearing at the Empire Bristol he was presenting "The Leonograph" as the managing director at The Empire was a Mr. Leon.

During 1899 he travelled with Lloyd's Circus who built a wooden circus building in Dudley which became John Maurice Clement's first theatre in Dudley, while he prepared to build the Opera House.

There seems to be so much going on in Irving Bosco's life at the turn of the century it is difficult to discern any clear underlying direction, however I think we can guess that he was working towards having his own show, rather than being just one act in someone else's show, or even better would be to own or manage one's own theatre or circus. As usual several developments seem to take place simultaneously! Towards the end of 1900 Irving Bosco joins forces with Waller Jeffs who would then become a life-long friend.

Waller Jeffs (1861-1941) mixed a journalistic career with that of "public lecturer", often using magic lantern slides to deliver travel talks etc… The latter activity led him to putting on presentations called "Our Navy" just at a time when Irving Bosco was making a living by showing films related to the Boer War. The two themes could be put together in a "Britain v the Boer and Our Navy" show, with Waller Jeffs providing eloquent commentary while Irving Bosco projected moving images. This takes them from 1900 into 1901. Meanwhile Irving was also setting up his own circus and was apparently preparing to tour Ireland!

In the Irish Census of 1901 we find Irving Bosco lodging at 1 William Street, The Fairgate, Drogheda in County Louth – using the name Irving Bosco, describing himself as a 29 year old "circus proprietor". (So far he has described his age differently in every census!) Making friends in Ireland was important and by 1903 he forms a partnership with George Carter as joint proprietors of the Imperial Hippodrome, Belfast. The two ventures complement one another as this theatre seems to have been a "hippodrome" as originally implied by this name – i.e. it was a variety theatre with facilities for presenting animal acts. In other words circus acts were booked to appear at the Belfast Hippodrome and may well have then gone "on tour" in Ireland with Irving Bosco, an arrangement that lasted for at least the next two years.

Evidence of this appears in "The Showman" of 23rd October 1903 when the paper reports: "On Monday 2nd November the New Imperial Hippodrome, Belfast, opens for a new season under the management of Mr. Irving Bosco, artists include "M. Bosini and his ten performing horses." All the artists listed are presenting circus acts.

From 1900 until the First World War Irving Bosco is also working in a partnership operating as 'Poole & Bosco's Circus'. How this relates to everything else is a puzzle, as is the identity of Mr. Poole, so I will deal with it separately.

While maintaining these activities in Ireland, Irving Bosco also managed to continue working with Waller Jeffs and began regularly appearing for quite long seasons at the Curzon Hall in Birmingham.

Waller Jeffs ran his first season at the Curzon Hall from 6th May to 13th July 1901 showing films in association with the Thomas-Edison Animated Photograph Co. – an organisation set up by a showman named A.D. Thomas, and nothing to do with the American; Thomas Edison! Waller Jeffs ran a second season in the Autumn of 1901 and proved that he could fill the vast Curzon Hill twice nightly with shows that included variety acts, musical items, and with both magic lantern and cinematographic technology. The Curzon Hall itself, at the top of Birmingham's Suffolk Street, had been built in 1864 to provide a home for dog shows, but was soon put to a variety of uses.

When Waller Jeffs returned to the Curzon Hall in 1902 it was under the banner of New Century Animated Pictures – a name used for the rest of the decade. New Century Pictures was actually owned by Sidney H. Carter, based at St. James Hall in Bradford. It is tempting to think that Sidney Carter was related to George Carter, with whom Irving Bosco worked in Belfast. The next thing would be to sort out the relationship of everyone involved – a series of loose "partnerships" and shared responsibilities. Films shown at the Curzon Hall could have been shot by Waller Jeffs himself as New Century Pictures, by contractors like Messrs Mitchell & Kenyon, or even by Irving Bosco. As the seasons progressed Waller Jeffs took greater and greater credit for them, but he and Irving Bosco remained the best of friends and therefore apportioning "credit" was not an issue.

At the end of 1905 Irving Bosco brought his circus from Belfast to Hull, and the Hull Daily Mail commented, *"Mr. Bosco has extensive experience in the circus world and the performance of his company has been highly spoken of."* The paper also revealed that the Ring Master was none other than James Bosco, Irving's brother. Between the partnerships and puzzles of this period there is still the occasional reference to "family", but this will be dealt with separately so as not to further complicate the account of Irving's life and career.

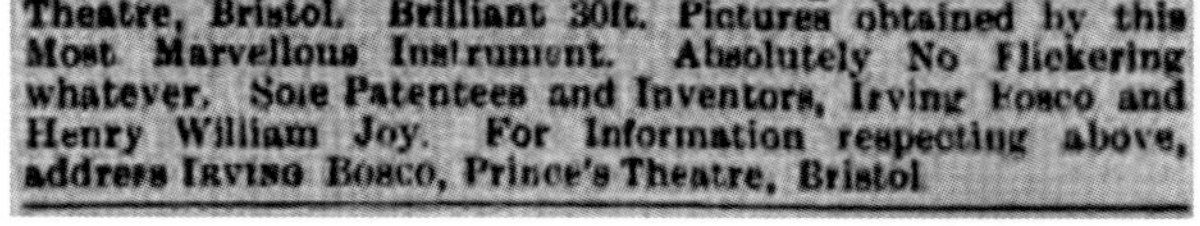
WANTED, Known, Tremendous Success of Irving Bosco's New Cinematograph at Prince's Theatre, Bristol. Brilliant 30ft. Pictures obtained by this Most Marvellous Instrument. Absolutely No Flickering whatever. Sole Patentees and Inventors, Irving Bosco and Henry William Joy. For Information respecting above, address IRVING BOSCO, Prince's Theatre, Bristol

An advert in "The Era" specifically mentioning his "anti-flicker" patent.

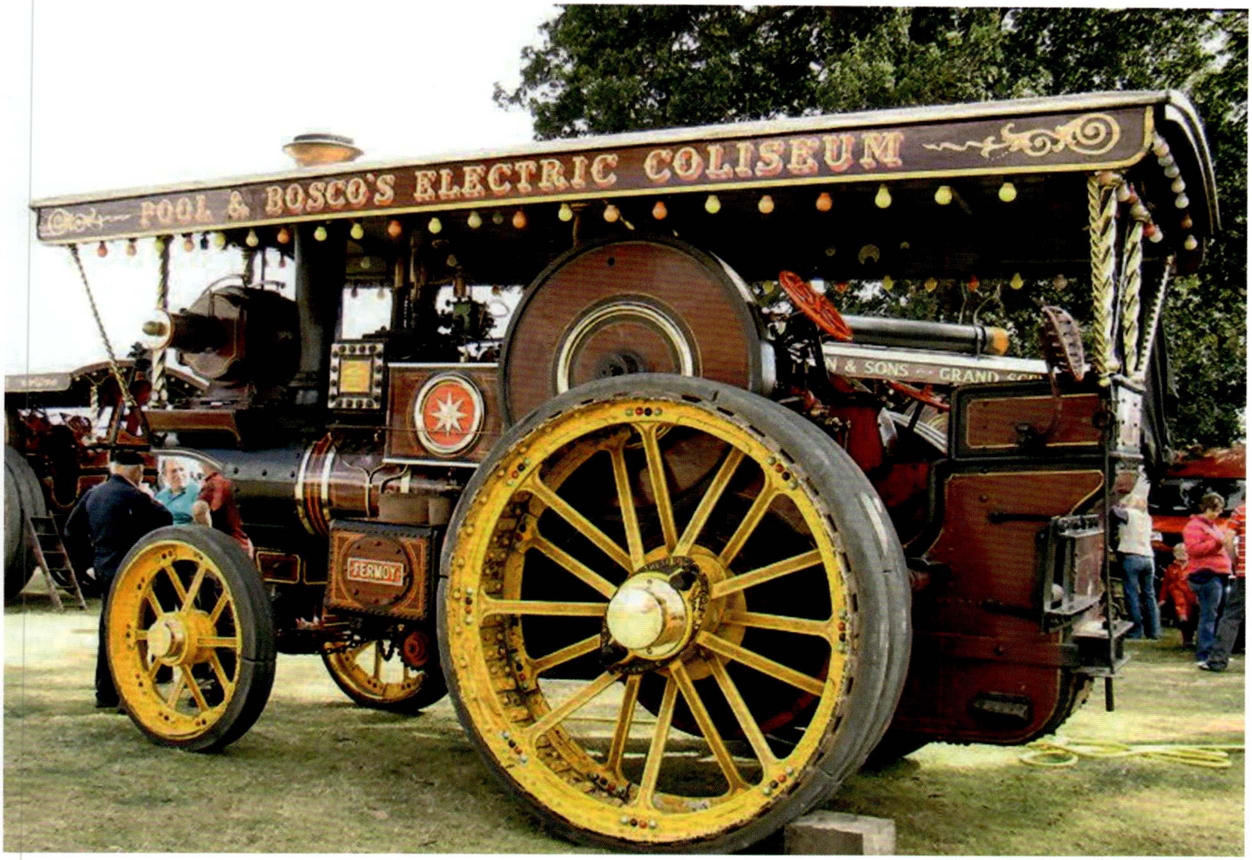

Poole & Bosco's Circus

Above: Poole & Bosco's Burrell engine, now known as "Fermoy", preserved by Russell Cooke who can be seen in front of the engine.
(Picture provided by Traction Time)

At vintage traction engine rallies today you might come across a beautifully preserved Burrell showman's engine called "Fermoy" (Burrell 3090 of 1909) and you would notice that the lettering on the side of the canopy reads: "Pool & Bosco's Electric Coliseum". In this case "Pool" is spelt without an "e", but in references to the show found in "The Era" the name is generally spelt with a final "e". This doubt about how the name is spelt is coupled to the fact that Mr. Pool(e) has been difficult to identify!

As I have already explained, Irving Bosco was involved in touring a circus in Ireland from about 1900 onwards – a show which may have been based at the Hippodrome, Belfast. He is also known to have used the names: "Bosco's Royal Circus", "Pool & Bosco's Great American Circus", The Great National Circus" etc. How these shows over-lapped, or were inter-related to his partnership with Mr. Pool(e) is not at all clear. On top of all this there is also endless confusion surrounding the 'main focus' of these shows – was it the circus acts or the cinematograph?

The earliest reference to "Poole & Bosco's Circus" that I have been able to find in newspaper records goes right back to 1900, and references to the business continue right up until the First World War in 1914. This is a longer period than has generally been assumed by the few people who have tried to investigate the facts behind the name "Pool(e) & Bosco".

During 1900 advertisements appeared in "The Era" and "The Stage" telling readers that there were vacancies for musicians, artistes, grooms and tentmen with Poole and Bosco's Circus. One advert, which specifically asked for grooms who had their own uniform, implied that the tenting season began at Easter 1900, and the contact address given was 1 William Street, Drogheda - the address that we have already noted as the address at which Irving Bosco was "caught" by the 1901 census.
In the Longford Journal of 5th May 1900 appears the comment: *"Mr. Bosco will be remembered as an old*

friend – having visited this town on several occasions with Mr. Jas Lloyd, exhibiting his marvellous living pictures". This one comment reveals that Irving had already become known to Irish audiences prior to 1900 - presenting "living pictures" on other proprietor's shows.

In September 'Poole & Bosco's American Circus' is reported as having been warmly received in Londonderry, and to remind us that Irving was torn between interests in the circus and in cinematography there is a comment on the fact that the show included "Professor Bosco's Biograph" – yet another name invented to describe cinematography. During the same month the show is advertised in the Sligo local paper as Poole & Bosco's Great National Circus. Towards the end of 1900 the following advertisement was placed in the "Wanted Known" column of "The Era" of 20th October: *"The following artistes sincerely wish to thank Poole and Bosco's Circus for a most comfortable tenting season through Ireland: The Rozelles, Douglas and D, Vincent, Leardo, O'Brian, and the band. What oh, the supper!"*

In the Longford Journal of 27th April 1901 we pick up a rare reference to Harry Zanlo – simply the comment: "Zanlo in his great balancing act with four chairs is a marvel". This suggests that Harry Zanlo aka Harry Pool(e) actually appeared in some of the shows and perhaps travelled with the circus when Irving was covering other commitments. Interestingly the same newspaper makes it clear that the cinematograph was used as the finale of the whole show – one of the few accounts of where and how the film presentation was fitted in.

In July 1901 a contact address for Poole & Bosco's Circus is given as 129 Lineker Street, Southport, and in August 1901 "The Stage" mentions that the circus was appearing at Lowestoft. This indicates that the show travelled in England as well as Ireland. Writing in his World's Fair column, "A Few Long Shots", on 11th May 1935, Southdown writes: *"In 1901 Poole & Bosco's Circus was touring in Ireland, and in their show they exhibited - in addition to the usual circus turns – moving pictures on the then new American Biographe depicting De Wet's charge through the British lines, 'The Death of a Spy' and General Botha's great trek."*

No references to the show have been found in The Era and The Stage of 1902, 1903, and 1904, but items can be located in Irish local papers. In a Waterford Times of May 1903 we find the "Great American Circus" travelling through Waterford, Tranmere and Kilmarthomas. In 1904 The Sligo Champion reports on the show, and there are records of the circus appearing at Strabane and Letterkenny. Another appearance – this time at Ballymena, County Antrim produces a newspaper advert that actually clearly states that the show is on tour from the Imperial Hippodrome.

In July 1905 the show is advertised while in Coleraine, and in August 1906 it makes one of several appearances in Derry. Usually the show did one-night stands and the adverts also give us an idea of the changing content of the shows, covering the whole range of what one would expect to find in a large circus of the time, but usually with the addition of the cinematograph. In 1905 we learn that Poole & Bosco's Circus was open at Lurgan on one occasion. The reason this earns a mention is that a woman was mauled by a lion at the show! On several occasions Poole & Bosco's Circus finds itself mentioned in the press as a result of accidents.

Messrs Smith and Scriven's book, "the Travelling Cinematograph Show" (New Era, 1999) reveals that Poole & Bosco formed a limited company in October 1906, using an address at 470, Dudley Road, Birmingham. Soon after this they purchased the front wagons of William Taylor's bioscope show. William Taylor was in the first division of bioscope operation and his show was being presented at the Agricultural Hall, Islington, at the very end of 1906 and into January 1907. It seems that Poole & Bosco saw it while it was there and took the wagons at the end of that season. Such information leaves us with many unanswered questions around the question of how these wagons were used and what transport Messrs Poole and Bosco had at their disposal. Later in 1907 they were advertising another Irish tour and were looking for a "complete seven piece band" and a "first class advance agent".

The 1907 Irish tour does get mentioned in the Waterford Standard of 26th June 1907. Interestingly it is using the name, "Pool & Bosco's Electric Coliseum". An advertisement tells us, "Part of the great road show will be drawn by the latest traction engine." This is two years before the delivery of the Burrell engine and seems to prove that Messrs Pool & Bosco's show did use an engine from the time of becoming "The Electric Coliseum" – and thus presenting itself more like a bioscope show than a circus.One advertisement appearing in the Waterford Chronicle of 13th May1908 carries the name "Pool & Bosco's Great American Coliseum" and tells readers that it is a "Circus, Hippodrome and Menagerie" combined". When it comes to listing the acts in the show it seems to be mainly a "Wild West" show!

Pool & Bosco in Ireland:

WATCH AND WAIT

FOR

POOLE & BOSCOE'S

AMERICAN CIRCUS.

BALLYMENA, WEDNESDAY,

September 26.

The Most Wonderful and Exciting Performance ever brought into this country, Professor Boscoe's New American Biographer, showing 100,000 Animated Living Pictures of the

GREAT BOER WAR.

35 Star Artists..

50 Items on the Programme.

50 Varied Scenes in the Arena. All to be seen for One Ticket.

Two Performances at 2—3 and 7·45.

Admission, 3s, 2s, 1s, and 6d, School Children, 2d each at Day Performance. Workhouse Imates Free.

Wait for this, the Greatest, Grandest, and Most Up-to-Date Circus Travelling. B714

Above: Ballymena 1904.(An 'e' added to both names!)
Below: From the Larne Times, July 1913.
Right: From the Sligo Champion, August 1903.

POOL & BOSCO'S

CIRCUS

AND

HIPPODROME

WILL SHORTLY VISIT CARNLOUGH, LARNE, BALLYCLARE, WHITEHEAD, CARRICKFERGUS.

THE LARGEST AND BEST SHOW TRAVELLING IRELAND. L855

FROM THE IMPERIAL HIPPODROME, BELFAST.

POOL & BOSCO'S

GREAT AMERICAN CIRCUS

WILL VISIT

COLERAINE, FRIDAY, SEPTEMBER 2nd
PORTRUSH, SATURDAY, „ 3rd
BUSHMILLS, MONDAY, „ 5th

DIAVOLO.

LYING THE FLUME, AND 20 OTHER GIGANTIC ATTRACTIONS.

80 HORSES AND ARTISTS 80.

THE GREATEST PROGRAMME EVER SUBMITTED TO THE PUBLIC.

The Largest Waterproof Tent ever erected in Ireland. Comfortably seated and illuminated with Patent Gas.

TWO GRAND PERFORMANCES DAILY. FIRST AT 2.30, SECOND AT 7.30.

ADMISSION, ... 3s, 2s, 1s, and 6d.

The Greatest aggregation of Startling Attractions ever crowded into one Performance.

POOL AND BOSCO'S

— GREAT —

American : Circus,

After an absence of two years, will visit

TOBERCURRY, MONDAY - AUGUST 31st
BOYLE, TUESDAY - - - SEPTEMBER 1st
BALLYMOTE, WEDNESDAY SEPTEMBER 2nd
COLLOONEY, THURSDAY SEPTEMBER 3rd
SLIGO, FRIDAY - - - - SEPTEMBER 4th
GRANGE, SATURDAY - - SEPTEMBER 5th
BUNDORAN, MONDAY - - SEPTEMBER 7th

UNDENIABLY the Biggest and best Circus in Ireland. This Year far Larger, Grander, and Better than ever.

25 Gigantic Attractions 25

The most Colossal Programme ever witnessed. The Greatest Aggregation of startling Wonders ever crowded into one Performance. The Most Gigantic Congress of Arenic Marvels ever seen in Ireland.

80 Horses and Artistes 80.

Two Great Shows combined for one Charge. Remember the value given in previous visits.

THE LEADERS OF ALL SO-CALLED PIONEERS.

The Great London Hippodrome Spectacle, introducing Magnificent Group of Full Grown Lions.

3 Hours Continual Amusement at POOL & BOSCO'S.

Watch for the GREAT FREE SIGHT!

The MODERN BLONDIN, hero of Niagara, and Monarch of the Lofty Wire, will carry a man across the invisible wire at a dizzy height, the same as accomplished by him in 1900, over the Niagara Falls, when he won a wager of 5,000 Dollars, before 300,000 spectators. Remember this is Free at POOL & BOSCO'S, and will take place previous to the Performance when a Gigantic Double Programme will be introduced.

See the life-like representation of the Great Motor Race from start to finish at POOLS & BOSCO'S. See the Royal State Visit to Ireland of their Majesties King Edward VII and Queen Alexandra, showing Royal Procession through Dublin.

Remember One Ticket to all.

Two Grand Performances daily. Midday at 2.30.

In Irving Bosco's busy year of 1909 the circus took delivery of the Burrell steam road locomotive mentioned at the beginning of this section. The address to which the engine was consigned was 470 Dudley Road, Birmingham. This in itself is a mystery as it was the address of a lock-up shop, one of a terrace of such shops, and not showing any signs of being HQ of a circus operation! As the engine appears to have carried the reference to "Pool & Bosco's Electric Coliseum" we have to wonder whether it was intended to work with a standard bioscope show or with the circus – or was that one and the same thing? The item in the Waterford Standard of June 1907 does to some extent answer such questions.

Advertisements appearing in 1910, again using the 470 Dudley Road address, indicate that the show was once again touring Ireland. The Burrell engine was sold in 1911, but the Irish tours continued during the years, 1912, 1913, and 1914. Press advertising is more modest during this period and goes back to simply using the title: "Pool & Bosco's Circus" while describing itself as the "largest and best show in Ireland". Even in August 1914 they were looking for a good agent while appearing in Athlone. This was during a period when Irving Bosco was extremely busy building a cinema empire in the Midlands so one assumes that the circus was managed by Harry Pool.

The most enduring mystery surrounding Poole & Bosco's Circus is the identity of Mr. Poole. In the early 1990s the late John Turner tried to collect and collate biographical information about circus folk gleaned from the pages of "World's Fair" and "The Era". His work resulted in the publication of two books: "Victorian Arena – parts One and Two". (He explained his work by subtitling the books: "A Dictionary of Circus Biography"). John Turner recorded the existence of Poole and Bosco's Circus and stated that Mr. Poole was one Harry Poole, also known as Harry Zanlo.

Harry Zanlo was principally a clown, and we encounter him in a "work wanted" advertisement in The Era of 23rd February 1895. He shares the advert with Annetta Hart, and describes himself as a "tumbling, talking and singing clown" with a contact address in Rochdale. He also appears in a report about the Royal Circus in Manchester in May 1891 when his real name, Harry Poole, is used but the acts in the show's programme list "Zanlo, Bobby and Harry – French Grotesques". I have found virtually no other references, but a Harry Poole (with an "e" on this occasion) does turn up as the manager of The New Alhambra Variety Theatre in North Street, Belfast, when it reopens on 24th December 1900. Apparently the theatre had changed hands and had been substantially refurbished and its reopening was described by the Northern Whig newspaper as a "magnificent success". The paper went on to say, *"Mr. Harry Poole, the General Manager, carried out the various arrangements in such manner as to draw forth praise from many admirers."*

Harry Poole remained as manager of the New Alhambra in Belfast until the summer of 1901 when he appears to have suffered an illness. We cannot be certain that this is the same Harry Poole who joined Irving Bosco in presenting an Irish touring circus but it is tempting to think that the two men met in Belfast at this time, while Irving Bosco was managing the Imperial Hippodrome.

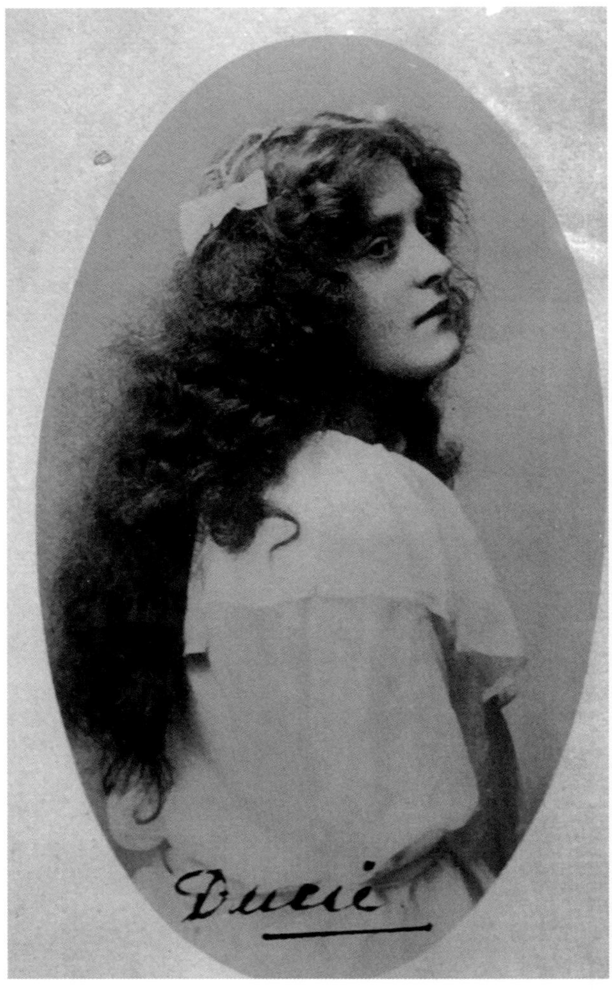

Above: Miss Ducie Saunderson

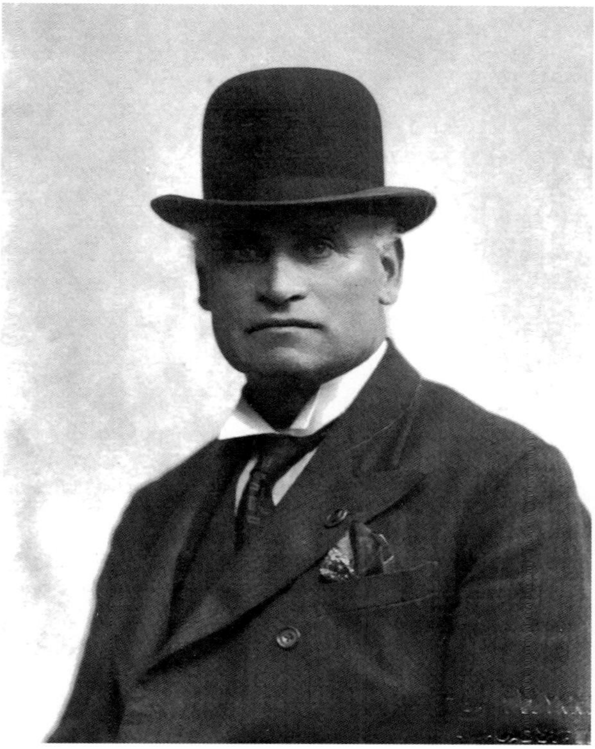

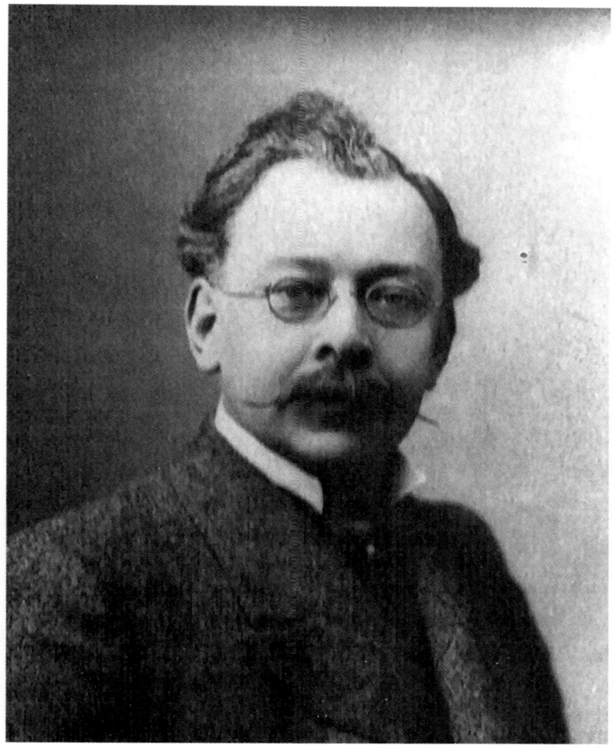

Above left: Mr. Irving Bosco, Cinematographer and circus proprietor, Above right: Mr. Waller Jeffs.(Lecturer and presenter of cinematographic entertainment.)

1909 and all that…

1909 seems to have been an important year in the life and career of Irving Bosco. It began with the usual four month "season" with Waller Jeffs at the Curzon Hall, but while working at the Curzon Hall, Irving Bosco took a pioneering step into the world of "cinema" – i.e. the presentation of film to a paying audience in permanent premises, built or adapted for that purpose. On Saturday 23rd January 1909 The Picture Palace, in Queen Street, West Bromwich, opened its doors. In doing this, Irving was almost a year ahead of his time. The first Kinematograph Act, designed to regulate and control such businesses, did not take effect until 1st January 1910 and most towns did not have a cinema until on or after that date – so it's significance cannot be overestimated: this was the Black Country's first cinema, nine months ahead of cinema licensing. How did Irving Bosco look after such a venture? – well it seems that he appointed his brother James to run the place.

Back at the Curzon Hall, the star of the twice-nightly shows in 1909 was Miss Ducie Saunderson, an outstanding mezzo-soprano singer, and accomplished dancer. Like Irving Bosco she was not using her real name and there are a few mysteries surrounding her biography! She was born on 9th December 1883 at Shildon in County Durham. She was the daughter of John and Eva Sanderson and was given the name of Margaret Phiducia Sanderson. This unusual middle name and its correct spelling was a promising start. Somewhere along the way she made use of her middle name and slightly altered the spelling of her surname, and became Ducie Saunderson.

Ducie's progress can be followed through the 1891 and 1901 censuses. In 1891 she and her family have moved from Shildon to Bowling, in Bradford. Her father, John Sanderson, has ceased to be a railway porter and has become a wool comber. As a seven-year-old in 1891 she is a "scholar" like her two older sisters, but in 1901 she is a "pattern-marker" and is earning her living. We also know that by 1901 she had joined the Eccleshill Dramatic and Music Society and was taking part in their shows. The Bradford Observer of 8th January 1901 reports that, *"Miss Ducie Saunderson is again the principal boy in the pantomime, "Roger of Manningham'".* The show was being presented at the

St. Georges Hall, in Bradford, and this comment implies that it was not the first time that Ducie had been the principal boy despite only being 17+. It is also interesting that she had already adopted a "stage name", using her middle name and a slight amendment to her surname.

A year later, in January 1902 Ducie appeared as "girl babe" in the society's annual pantomime which this time was "The Babes in Heaton Woods". Once again the show was presented at the St. Georges Hall, Bradford, and on this occasion the Bradford paper tells us that such shows were organised by Mr. Sidney Carter. One is left to wonder if this is the same man who later became Chairman of the Cinema Veterans Association, and who may have had connections with Irving Bosco's shows? Reports in the 1903 and 1904 papers suggest that Ducie Sanderson's appearances had become professional, but she seems to disappear from newspaper records until we encounter her again in 1908 when appearing with Waller Jeffs' 'New Century Pictures' presentation at the Assembly Rooms, Leamington Spa. The Leamington Circular of 29th September 1908 reports briefly on the show and mentions *"The continued success of Miss Ducie Sanderson"*.

Although it is not possible to give a full account of Ducie's career, we do have a picture of her progress from amateur music and drama in Bradford to the moment when she joins Waller Jeff's shows, inevitably meeting Irving Bosco. Just for good measure, the Leeds Mercury of 29th March 1909 provided a little biography when telling its readers: *"Miss Saunderson is a native of Bradford, and is quite as popular in the Yorkshire towns as she is in Birmingham. She is an accomplished vocalist and a charming and expert dancer. She made her first appearance in pantomime at the age of nine at the Theatre Royal, Bradford. She has also appeared in musical comedy"*

On 27th March 1909 the thirty-eight-year-old Irving Bosco married twenty-six years-old Ducie Sanderson, the singer who had sang every night at Waller Jeff's Curzon Hall shows. They both used their real names, as opposed to their stage names, and both claimed to be living at 44 Bristol Road, Edgbaston. Irving identifies himself as a "Theatrical Manager" – the role he played in Waller Jeff's shows – and Ducie identifies herself as a "Vocalist". It is interesting to note that Irving's late father – Joseph Bainton – was also identified as a "Theatrical Manager", further confirmation that there was some family background to Irving's journey into show business. The wedding was witnessed by John Sanderson, Ducie's father, and Waller Jeffs. One of Ducie's sisters was a bridesmaid.

The marriage service was conducted by Rev. Joseph Wood, Unitarian Minister of the Old Meeting Church, in Birmingham's Bristol Street. The season at the Curzon Hall must have been coming to an end, because the couple appeared at that evening's show and then left for a short honeymoon in Ireland. We have no way of knowing whether the choice of the Old Meeting Church was one of convenience or conviction. Like many Unitarian churches the place had an interesting history going back to the beginnings of Non-conformity in the 1660s. The hall used by Unitarians up until 1881 was demolished by the London & North Western Railway to facilitate development of New Street Station. Four years later, in 1885, the Unitarians opened the large Gothic building in which Irving and Ducie were married.

The wedding was reported in "The Era" of the following week and the report included a rather dark photograph of the couple – who both appear to be wearing dark glasses! Most striking is the fact that the bridegroom towers above the bride.

After the wedding and reception the couple embarked on a honeymoon at Killarney in Ireland – or was this an opportunity for Irving to introduce Ducie to his business operations in Ireland? The wedding occurs right at the time when Irving's work seems at it most diverse and most intense – working for Waller Jeffs, opening his cinema in West Bromwich, and running circus activities in Ireland.

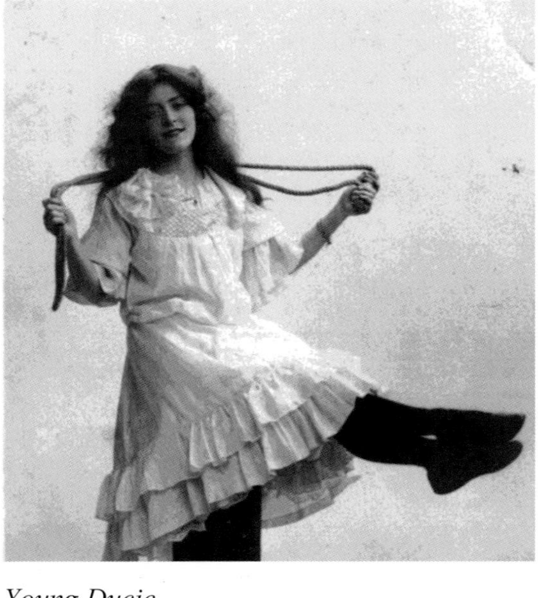

Young Ducie

Irving Bosco and Ducie Saunderson on their wedding day: 27th March 1909.As Irving was very tall and Ducie was rather petite, the photographer obviously thought the groom should be seated and the bride should stand! Until Irving Bosco's granddaughter, Susan, produced this photograph the only picture I had ever seen of the couple was a very poor photograph reproduced in The Era.

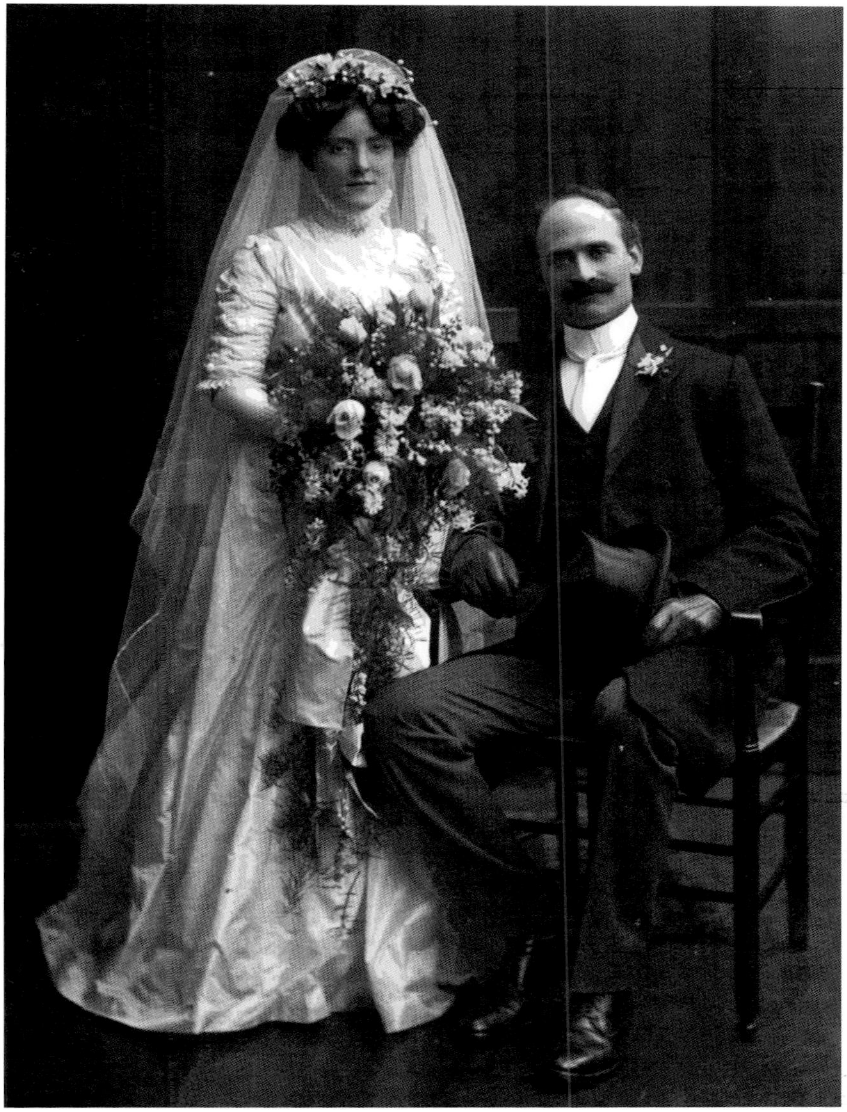

After the Act

On 1st January 1910 the 1909 Kinematograph Act became law and all premises in which film was presented to a paying public audience had to be licensed for that purpose. To obtain such a licence the proprietor of such premises would have to show that safety measures were in place and were properly observed. Bioscope shows would have to obtain a new licence from the local authority each time they were built up – something which made it almost impossible for them to function. The "authorities" might be local government at "borough" or "urban district" level, or county councils, or magistrates.

Premises where films were to be shown regularly on a permanent site were to become what we call "cinemas", but in 1910 there was great uncertainty about what to call them. Popular terms included, "electric theatre" and "picture palace". There was also great uncertainty about whether audiences would come week after week to see such entertainment and many felt it would be wise to hedge one's bets by presenting variety acts in between and alongside the films. Both Irving Bosco and Benjamin Kennedy favoured "cine-variety". (Ben Kennedy's story is told in Chapter Six.)

Some newcomers were attracted to the business of running a cinema – perhaps dreaming that it would be very profitable – at least for a while. Others entered the business because they were already committed to cinematography and its potential entertainment value. Such people came from the travelling bioscope tradition, usually as part of the fairground world; others came from a tradition of presenting films in public halls, in variety theatres and the circus. Irving Bosco was obviously one of the latter. And – as we have already made clear - he was in the vanguard of moving into the cinema business because he had opened The Palace, West Bromwich almost a year before the Kinematograph Act took effect.

We would therefore expect to find Irving Bosco among the pioneers keen to be "up and running" as early as possible in January 1910. On the very first day it was possible – on 1st January 1910 – Irving Bosco obtained a kine licence from Dudley Council to show films at the town's Public Hall, in Wolverhampton Street. This does not mean he had erected a brand new purpose built cinema, nor did it mean it was the first appearance of film in these premises, but it shows how he was "on the ball" and was probably moving into a new stage in his life as a cinema proprietor.

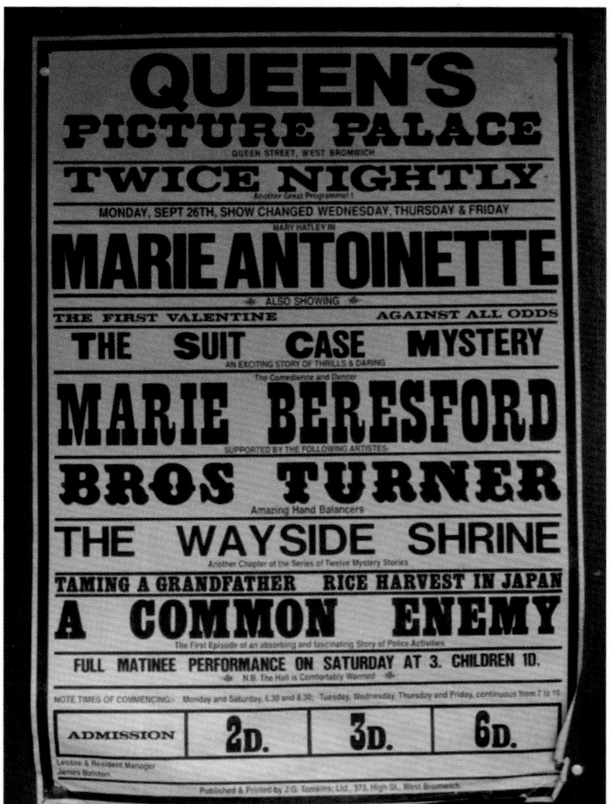

The Public Hall started life as a Mechanics' Institute, built in 1862. Films were certainly shown there before the passing of the Cinematograph Act, but it is not always clear by whom, or even exactly what was being presented. Showmen were careless with phrases like "Animated Pictures" and "Living Pictures" – sometimes this referred to real cinematography, sometimes it just meant that ingenious technology was being applied to what was basically a "magic lantern" type show. For example, from Christmas Eve 1895 onwards, for a short season, the show in the Public Hall was presented by "The Lyric Living Pictures and Grand Variety Company". Before leaping to the conclusion that this might, in part, have been a film show, we should remember that the Lumiere Brothers did not present Britain's first cinematograph show until early in 1896. From the early 1900s onward it is more likely that such shows did include some material on film. In October 1907 and again at the same time in 1908 "20th Century Pictures" ran a season in the Public Hall. This was a company associated with Waller Jeffs, as described above, but what needs repeating here is that Waller Jeff's "right-hand-man" was often Irving Bosco. From Christmas 1909 into the 1910 New Year Professor Wood was presenting a "Musical and Pictorial Combination", but he had decided, by that time, to settle in Bilston. It fell to Irving Bosco, to be the first to present *regular* film-shows in Dudley, at the Public Hall.

Irving Bosco opened the Public Hall as a cinema on 31st January 1910, and his wife, Ducie Saunderson, sang between the films. Irving's stated policy was to "keep one step ahead of Birmingham", and the Public Hall appears to have been a great success. Shows were presented twice nightly and the hall was licensed to accommodate up to eight hundred patrons, a year later quoted as 630! Irving Bosco soon became a well-known local personality and showed the usual showman's interest in raising money for local charities.

It is known that Irving Bosco made his own films, and during the early days at the Public Hall he screened material he had shot on the Priory Fields when Baden Powell had come to inspect local scouts. Unfortunately we have to assume such material, shot on nitrate film, has been lost. On 19th October 1911 he persuaded the

Left: A 1909 advertising bill from Bosco's pioneering "Queens Picture Palace" in West Bromwich – up and running before the 1909 Kinematograph Act came into force. Cine-variety is being presented plus a children's matinee on Saturday afternoon: "The Penny Rush".

Mayor, Dudley's M.P., and the Earl of Dudley, to attend a benefit show. The films shown are not recorded, but again Ducie Saunderson sang for the enthusiastic audience.

Irving Bosco continued to present shows at the Public Hall until sometime in 1919, or possibly the summer of 1920. Films then continued to be shown at the Public Hall by Edwin Griffiths, but in 1922 Griffiths' application for his kine licence was refused and he was told that the premises were not considered suitable for that purpose anymore.

Before we look at how Irving Bosco's cinema empire rapidly expanded, it is worth noting the changes in his personal life that took place at the same time as cinemas were "taking off". Having married Ducie in 1909 we can assume his life was becoming more "settled". Their first child was born in 1910 – William Oliver – and they may have begun looking for a permanent home. They may not have been immediately successful in this as the 1911 census finds the three of them lodging at the Albion Inn in Dudley's Stone Street! Several things about this census record are interesting. Firstly, they describe themselves as the Boscos, the name "Bainton" is not mentioned at all. Secondly, they do not disclose any occupation but The Albion was not far from The Public Hall where Irving was showing films. Their host – the licensee of The Albion was Joe Darby, better known as The Dudley Jumper. Joe had acquired fame with his record-breaking standing jumps, had moved on to present his athletic skills in circuses and as a variety act, and then, in 1901 had become licensee of The Albion.

Entries in the 1911 census also seem to suggest that Irving Bosco had a house at 79 Mornington Road, Smethwick at the time. As we will see, Dudley and Smethwick seemed to become the centre of his activities.

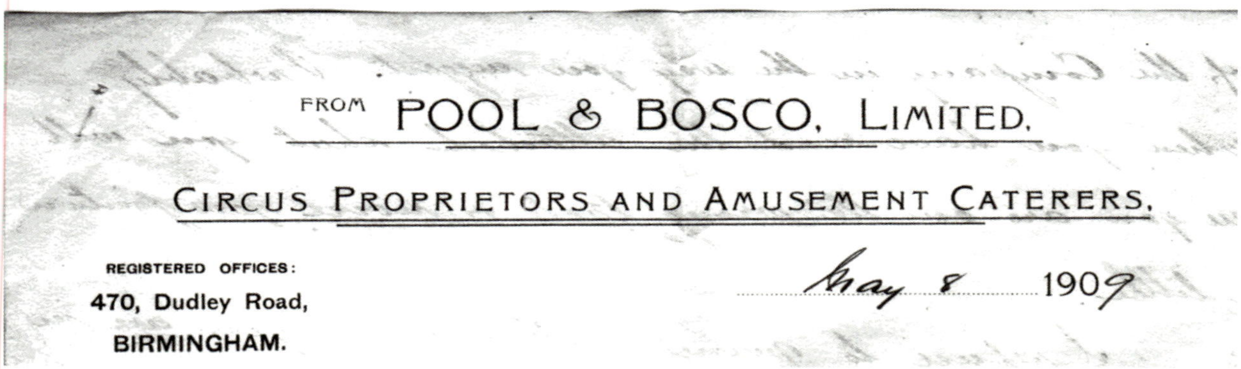

Surviving stationery of 1909 vintage.

Above: Headed notepaper used in 1909 shows the Pool & Bosco partnership spelling "Pool" without the "e" and the mysterious address in Dudley Road, Birmingham.

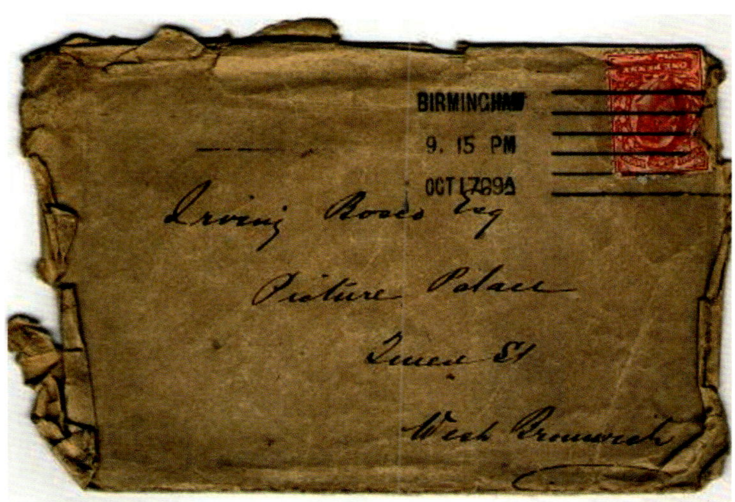

Right: A surviving envelope, used in October 1909, shows Irving received post directly to the Picture Palace in Queen Street, West Bromwich.

Bosco's Pictures

Irving Bosco's success as a cinema proprietor at the Queens Picture House, West Bromwich, and the Public Hall, Dudley, prompted him to plan some brand new purpose built cinemas, although these could not materialize overnight.

His first new cinema to open was The Cape Hill Electric Cinema in Smethwick. It was opened on Monday 19th June 1911 in the presence of the Mayor of Smethwick in the midst of George V's coronation celebrations. The first programme included films of that event. The cinema's advertising included the invitation: "Bring the little ones to see the Coronation", as well as informing everyone the cinema was "The most cosy and comfortable picture house in the Midlands."

The cinema housed an audience of 680 which was modest compared with cinemas built later, and included a "Ladies' tea room" adjacent to the balcony. It was designed by the Dudley architects, Messrs. Gammage & Dickinson, which should not surprise us as Irving Bosco had become quite focused on Dudley. He also used Dudley-based building contractors: Messrs. Oakley & Coulson. (The latter became associated with the Grand Cinema, Kingswinford and may have been introduced to the cinema business by Irving Bosco.) A Mr. Chas. Merrick was put in charge as manager, and the cinema focused solely on film presentation rather than "cine-variety".

In 1912 Irving Bosco took over two existing enterprises to expand his cinema empire. On 8th January 1912 Irving Bosco took control of the Empire, Hall Street, Dudley, and implemented a programme of full time cinema entertainment in a hall which had sometimes presented "variety" and sometimes "cinema variety". The Empire had a troubled past, having opened as a variety theatre in 1903. Ironically, Irving Bosco had obtained a cinematograph licence for the Empire at the beginning of 1910, but seems to have leased the place to a number of people who failed, one after the other, to make it a success. Another interlocking part of this jig-saw is that Arthur Gammage had been the architect of The Empire, and as stated above, undertook the same task at Cape Hill.

On 12th April 1912 he opened The Rink Picture House in Windmill Lane, Smethwick. As its name implied this building had begun life as a corrugated iron skating rink, opened in 1909. At the same time "Bosco's Pictures" were showing films at the Palace Picture House, Alcester Street, Redditch. It is not clear how Irving Bosco came to be showing films in Redditch as this enterprise seems to have been firmly in the hands of the Treadgold family since its inception. It opened in December 1913 in what appears to have been an ex public hall. At the time Mr. R. Treadgold was described by "The Era" as "a pioneer of the cinema business in Redditch", but perhaps Irving Bosco had used it before him? The Alcester Chronicle reports on cine-variety presentations in a venue listed as "The Public Hall, Electric Palace, Redditch" in late 1911. Another possibility is that Irving Bosco leased it from the Treadgolds for a period. It held 450 patrons and provided tip-up seats in both the balcony and ground floor, and the Treadgolds seem to have run it successfully until deciding to sell in November 1926.

1913 was also a busy year, keeping in mind that Pool & Bosco's Circus was still travelling in Ireland during this period. On a personal level Irving Bosco's family grew in that year: Eva Margaret Bainton was born on 20th May 1913. The birth was registered in Dudley. On 18th August 1913 The Harborne Picture House opened in a fairly modest building, but nevertheless one which had been designed by Archibald Hurley Robinson – a Birmingham-based architect who designed a number of local cinemas. One important thing about this cinema was that Irving Bosco invited his old friend Waller Jeffs to manage it – thus ensuring that Waller had a job to do in the post Kinematograph Act age.

When the Great War broke out in 1914 it brought a cinema-building era to a close, but somehow Irving Bosco managed to continue expanding! His last new purpose built cinema was to be bigger than anything he had planned up until that time. Although in Handsworth it was going to be bigger than any cinema in Birmingham! The New Picture House, Villa Cross, opened on Saturday 22nd May 1915 with a ceremony performed by a Mr. Samuel Adkins. The Birmingham Daily Gazette on 24th May reported, *"...the hall which has a capacity of 1,600 is the largest in the city. The front is handsomely embellished in cream and ivory colours, whilst the interior is enriched by fibrous decorations of various figure subjects. Mr. Irving Bosco promised that everything possible would be done to please the inhabitants of Handsworth.* Strangely the report does not mention the large rose-pattern stained glass window that dominated the frontage above the main entrance.

The Picture House, Villa Cross, was designed by C. Sharp-Smith, a Birmingham architect, but apparently using Irving Bosco's Dudley connections, it was built by Mark Round & Sons – a well-known Dudley-based building firm. Mr. L.C. Lax was installed as manager. He was described by the Gazette as *"very well-known in the entertainment world".*

Right: The Empire, Hall Street, Dudley, was opened by Tom Pritchard on 6th May 1903, replacing early semi-permanent circus buildings. It changed hands a number of times until12th April 1912 when Irving Bosco took control. For a time it was Irving Bosco's "HQ". At the end of 1920 it was sold to Mr. Shapeero but in 1928 became part of the Gaumont circuit. It closed in 1940 but the building was not demolished until 1973.

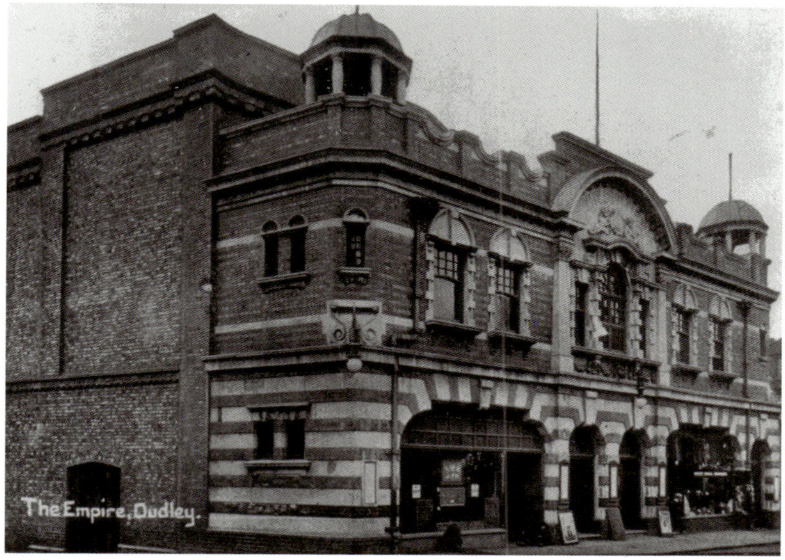

Right. The Harborne Picture Palace was opened by Irving Bosxco on 18th August 1913. Waller Jeffs, with whom Irving had worked in Birmingham's Curzon Hall,became manager of this cinema.

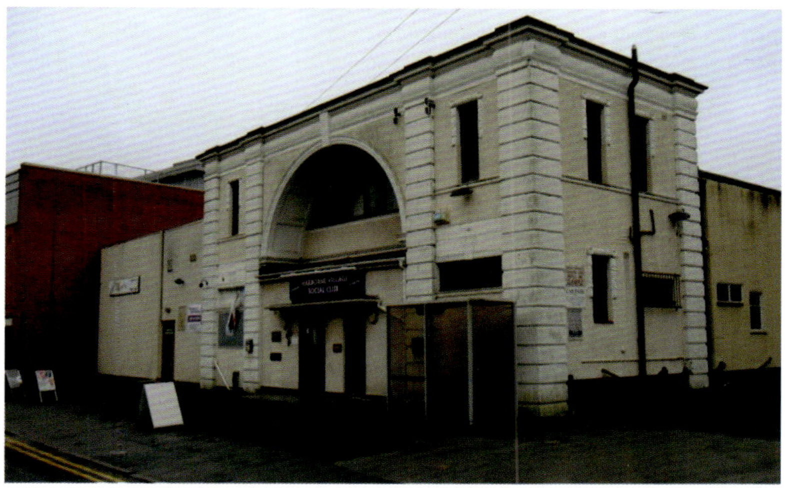

Right: the New Picture House,,Villa Cross, in Aston, was opened by Irving Bosco on 22nd May 1915.The Empire, Dudley, and the two cinemas in Smethwick, plus these two in Birmingham were all sold to Mr. Shapeero in 1920. For a few years Irving Bosco continued to be involved in the cinema business by taking control of The Picture House in Stratford-on-Avon, but then sold that enterprise to the Clifton Circuit. Having been so involved in the early days of cinematography it is interesting to see that Irving had retired from the business even before the arrival of the Talkies.

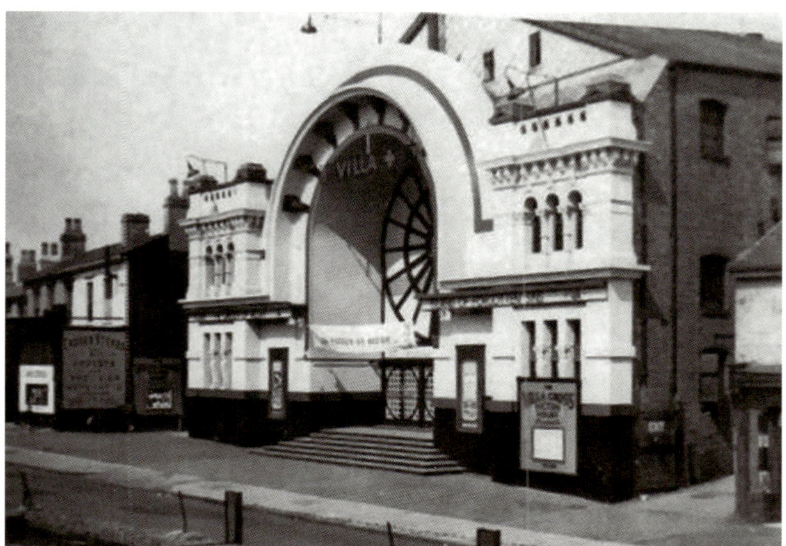

After the Great War

During the First World War, or just after it, Irving Bosco relinquished his interest in the West Bromwich cinema, to Thomas Leach, and he abandoned Dudley's Public Hall. Some cinema pioneers, such as Professor Wood and his son, Thomas, decided to expand after the war, but it seems that Mr. Bosco felt unsure of the industry's future. In October 1920 Kine Weekly reported that he was putting his cinemas up for sale. In a subsequent edition it reported that he certainly did not intend giving his cinemas away but a buyer materialised and Bosco's Pictures Ltd. was wound up at a special general meeting on 17th December 1920.

The man who bought the Empire, Dudley, the Rink and the Cape Hill Electric, and the two Birmingham cinemas was Ezekiel Charles Shapeero of the Record Cinema Circuit based in Nottingham. Although this deal marked the end of Irving Bosco's association with Black Country cinemas, it is interesting to recall what happened next. From the same Mr. Shapeero, and a partner named Mr. Cook, Irving Bosco acquired the Picture House in Stratford-upon-Avon, and installed Waller Jeffs there as the manager. This cinema had opened in 1913 and had developed a few problems that its new owner was quite equal to solving.

To his staff at Stratford Mr. Bosco was always the "Great White Chief' and he regularly visited the cinema on Saturdays to see Waller Jeffs and note how business was going. Very quickly it became apparent that the unreliable electricity supply was the cinema's main problem. A power cut on Whit Monday 1921 while queues waited outside the hall convinced Irving Bosco that there was only one answer: they would generate their own power. A gas generator was installed and the staff trained in its use. A lamp was erected at the top of a flag pole to proclaim their triumph and even during power failures in the mains supply they could announce, "Bosco's Beacon shines nightly!". In 1924 he sold out to the Clifton Circuit, but he made sure that Waller Jeffs' position at the cinema was to be permanently safeguarded.

Below: The wedding of Eva, Irving's daughter, to Alex Willington in 1938. Irving, Waller Jeffs, and Ducie (seated) are to right of the bride.

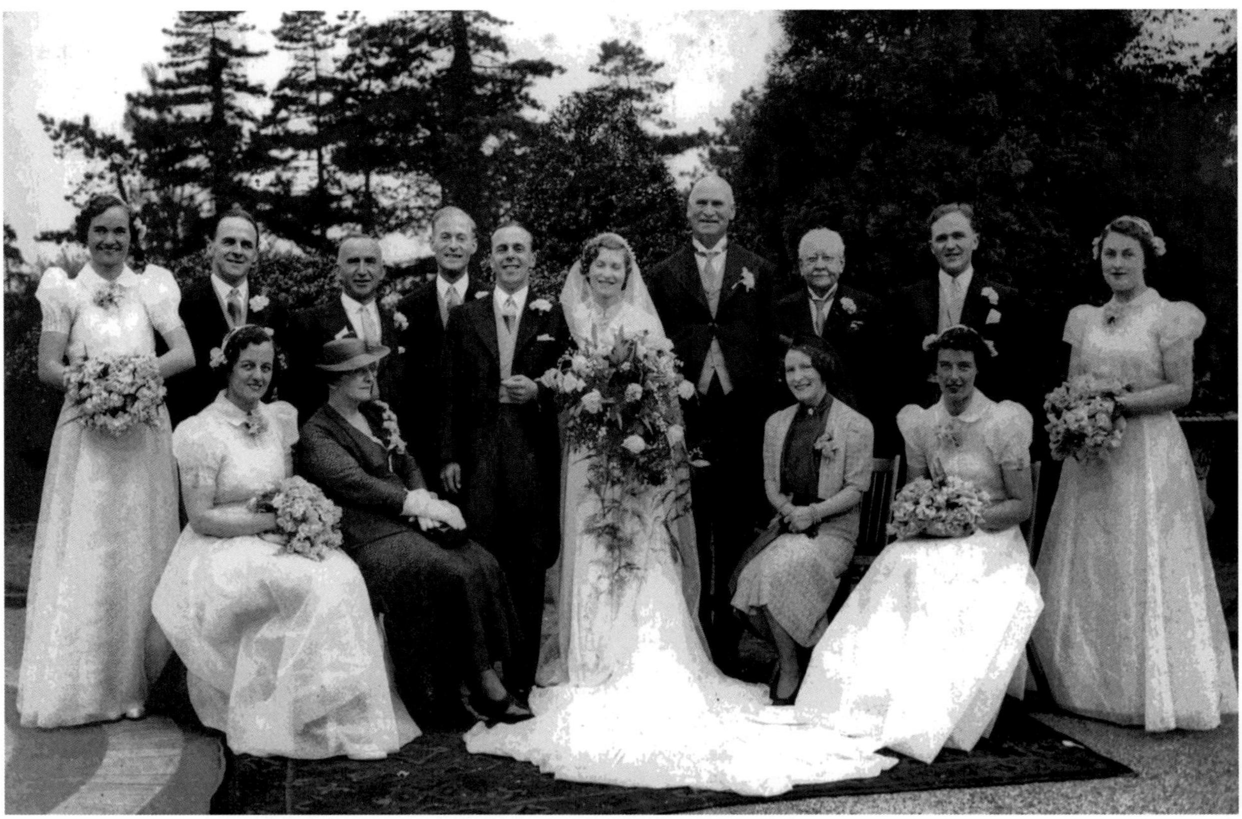

The period from 1920 to 1924 found Irving and Ducie enjoying a social life both in Dudley and Stratford. In Dudley they were treated like royalty. For example in April 1921 Ducie was invited to open a 'sale of work' at the King Street Methodist Church in King Street, Dudley, in the presence of the Mayor and many local dignitaries. Irving was present alongside her and must have enjoyed the speeches that spoke of his pioneering cinema days in Dudley. Apparently Irving had been very generous in his financial support of the "Astley Burgh Holiday Camp for Poor Children" and had supported the work of King Street Methodist Church. In Stratford it appears that the Bosco's were also part of the social scene around the Shakespeare Theatre and the town's literary and social circles. A key figure in this social scene was Marie Corelli who had been one of Britain's best-selling novelists in the late 1880s and into the 1890s. Her interests ranged from preserving Stratford's architectural heritage to Rosicruianism and other occult ideas. However the real reason that the Boscos may have enjoyed her friendship was that her origins embraced being a musician in early variety theatres, and, of course, "Marie Corelli" was not her real name. She died at Stratford in April 1924.

It might be thought that the sale of the Stratford Picture House would be followed by Irving Bosco's retirement, but it seems that he had different ideas. In the Birmingham Daily Gazette of 26th April 1927 we find that Irving Bosco is applying for a music and dancing licence for the Piccadilly Café in Birmingham's New Street. These premises were part of the Piccadilly Arcade that had been created out of a one-time cinema enterprise, but the authorities in Birmingham seem to have been alarmed by the licence application and adjourned making a decision about it on at least two occasions. "The Stage" of 12th May 1927 dismissed Birmingham as a place *"full of censors and public morality folk who find harm where none exists."*

We also know that Irving Bosco maintained his interest in the Cinema Veterans Association. On 3rd December 1929 Irving Bosco and Waller Jeffs, joined by Thomas Wood and his father Joseph Wood, the Bilston-based pioneers, went down to London to attend the association's annual reunion in Holborn. (The Association had been founded in 1921 and invited members from amongst those that had been pioneers in the business before 1903. Later this was modified and later still it was widened to include television pioneers.) Irving Bosco became the CVA's President in 1946.

Considering the fact that Irving Bosco had led such a varied and busy life in the pioneering days of cinema, his life in the 1930s seems to have been fairly quiet. By the 1930s it seems that Irving and Ducie had started to enjoy the idea of retirement. They enjoyed travelling by train and by ship, and while seeing the world, it seems that Irving made 16mm cine films of their travels – a cinema pioneer who ended up making "home movies"! Irving seems to have maintained his connections and interests in the CVA (Cinema Veterans) and the CEA (Cinema Exhibitors Association) but his name rarely appears in the press. In September 1932 he is listed among CVA and CEA members who paid tribute to Bill Blake. Bill had been a cinema pioneer in Bedford and his huge funeral was attended by many people in the cinema business.

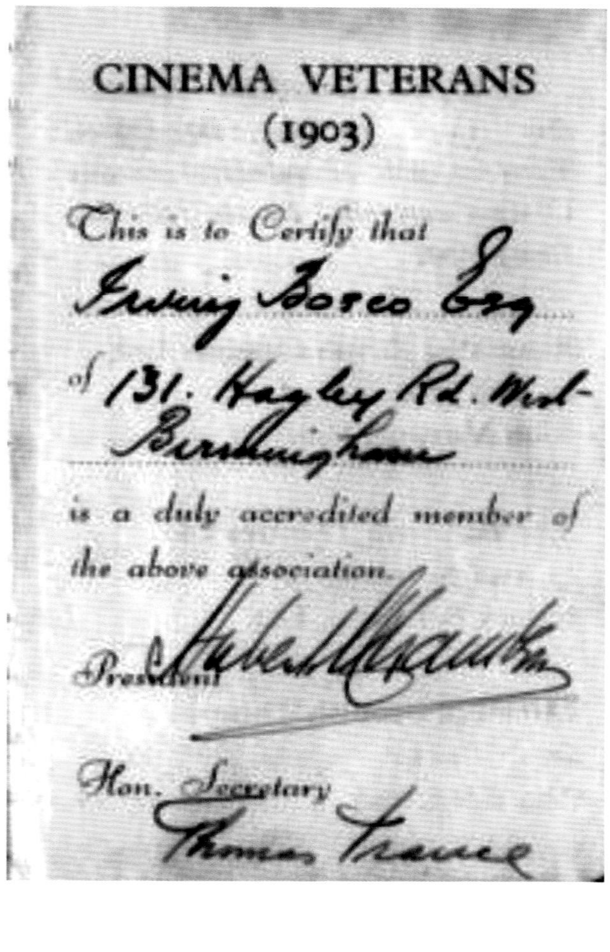

Above: Irving Bosco's membership card of the Cinema Veterans Association, issued when he was living in Hagley Road West in the 1930s.

In "The Stage" of 16th June 1938 Clarkson Rose, the Dudley-born variety artist who made his name as a pantomime dame, wrote about his memories of pioneering showmen of Dudley. He names John Maurice Clement of the Dudley Opera House, and Tom Pritchard of the Dudley Empire and recalls that Irving Bosco opened the town's first cinema. Clarkson describes Irving as "a great showman of those days".

Irving and Ducie had two children: William Oliver, born in 1910 and Eva, born in 1913. Both children had been sent away to boarding school and Eva went on to 'finishing school'. (She hated both!) By the end of the thirties they were moving on to the next stage in their lives: Eva married Alexander Willington on 15th June 1938 and William, by then a solicitor, married Betty Dallaway in late 1940.

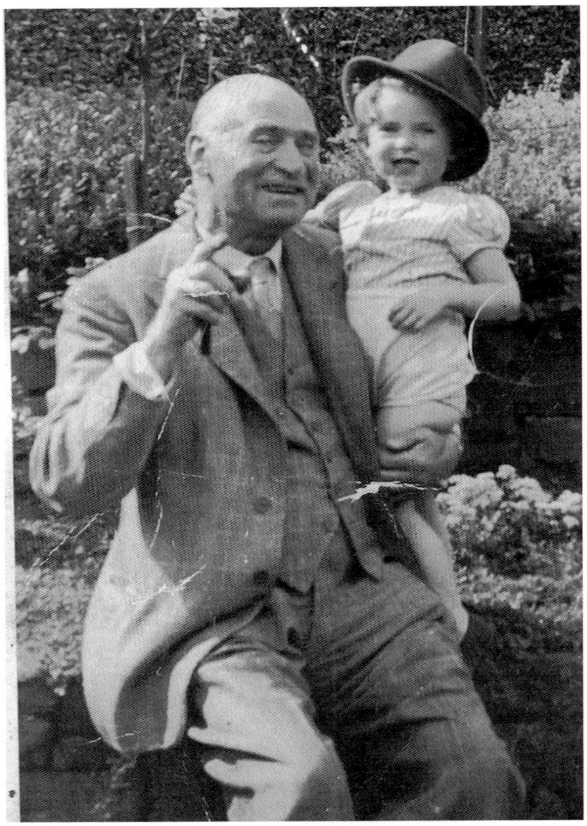

Above: Irving Bosco with his granddaughter, Jill, not long before his decline in heath and subsequent death. (Family photographs in this chapter have been provided by Irving's other grand-daughter, Susan, from the family's archive.)

On 1st July 1941 Irving's old friend, Waller Jeffs died. A number of obituaries of Waller appeared in the press and it seems ironical that when Irving died a few years later his death was barely noticed by the press. Perhaps the realities of the Second World War rather obscured the pioneering cinema activities of days before the First World War?

Irving Bosco died on 12th November 1946 at 342 Lordswood Road, Smethwick. No obituaries appeared in the press and no details of his funeral seem to have survived. It seems likely that it was a modest family affair probably missed by members of the CEA and CVA. Irving's place in history was "fading". It is therefore interesting to note that in 1968 the Birmingham Daily Post published an article on cinema pioneers of Birmingham and failed to even mention Irving Bosco. Eva, his daughter, was incensed, and a few days later, on 28th February 1968 the paper published a letter from her:

"I read with interest the Post's article on 'how cinema came to Birmingham' but wonder why here was no mention of my father, Irving Bosco, who was one of the pioneers of the silent era. He was the owner of several picture houses around Birmingham, at Smethwick, Villa Cross, Handsworth, Harborne and Dudley. He was Waller Jeff's greatest friend, and appointed WJ as his manager at Harborne.

I am sure most of the people you mention in your article would remember Bosco of Bosco's Pictures as he was well-known to everyone in the cinema world. He sold out and retired when the talkies came."

Like many of his fellow-members of the Cinema Veterans Association, Irving Bosco was definitely a great showman. He was a big impressive man with an engaging outgoing personality. He could combine a shrewd business sense with generosity, fairness and a sense of humour. These attributes, plus his continual inventiveness, made him an ideal pioneer of the new medium. He retired before the advent of the talkies, and when he died in 1946, many of the buildings in which he had shown films had disappeared or changed their use. His most lasting monument in the Black Country was the Cape Hill Electric, which survived into the mid-fifties, but in Handsworth the Villa Cross Picture House stood until the mid-1980s. (Bingo operators had even restored the decorative plaster figures that Irving Bosco had made such a feature of the auditorium back in 1915.) The cinema in Harborne still stands today, having been used as a club and has recently suffered a fire..

A Postscript:

Other Members of the Bosco Family

It is interesting to speculate on whether any other Baintons decided to become a Bosco, and what role they may have played in William's busy life. The first to consider is his brother James, maybe only a year or so younger than William. In the above narrative we have come across him as a fellow teenage vocalist appearing with their father Joseph and mentioned in the 1891 census. Later he is briefly mentioned as playing the role of Ring Master when William's circus appeared in Hull in 1905. Later still he is helping William by looking after the Palace Picture House when it opened in West Bromwich in 1909. He seems to have shared Irving's interest in cinematography and in one advertisement in The Era in December 1898 it is James who is seeking engagements for the Excelsior Cinematograph having apparently presented it in for a week at Stourbridge Town Hall.

Additional information comes in a record of James Bainton's marriage to Mary Clark in Newcastle during July 1900, and a year later we find the couple lodging with the "in-laws" in Crook, County Durham, as listed in the 1901 census. Mary's parents, Mary and Alfred Black head the household, and Alfred claims to be a photographer. More interesting is that James claims to be a cinematographer. (From the record of the wedding of 1900 we learn that James had a middle name: "Sheering" which was his mother's maiden name.)

In the 1911 census we find James and Mary Bainton lodging in a house in Lancaster with James claiming to be an "Employer" and working as a "Living Pictures Exhibitor" – suggesting that James did not remain for long at his brother's cinema in West Bromwich, but in fact became the proprietor of one in Lancaster! (They also have three children: Ruby Mary, then nine; Louie, then 6; and Ada Kate, then two.) James and Mary later went into hotel management and returned to Mary's home county of Durham.

Of the other Baintons, the only one who seems to have become connected with show-business was William's sister Frederica Justina Bainton, born in Broughton, Lancs, on 27th February 1882. On 3rd March 1907 she married Edwin Moxon who was part of a three-man acrobatic troupe!

BOSCO'S EMPIRE PICTURES,
HALL STREET, DUDLEY.

MATINEES, MONDAY & SATURDAY, at 3.
MONDAY, TUESDAY & WEDNESDAY NEXT,

SHEPHERD LASSIE
OF ARGYLE.

Featuring Miss Florence Turner. Magnificent film-drama taken in the Highlands of Scotland. The glorious Scottish Scenery forming a distinctive effective setting.

THE MYSTERY OF THE SLEEPING DEATH.

The strange trance into which Harrison, a young millionaire, and Lizzie, a girl of the slums, have fallen, puzzles the physician at the hospital. Amar, a Hindu mystic and hypnotist, is called as a last resort.

THURSDAY, FRIDAY AND SATURDAY,
Daniel Frohman presents the eminent dramatic Star, H. B. WARNER, in the World-famous Drama of Capital and Labour:

THE LOST PARADISE.

LATEST AUTHENTIC WAR PICTURES.

PUBLIC HALL, DUDLEY.

WEEK COMMENCING - JANUARY 4th.
THE GREAT SPORTING DRAMA IN THREE PARTS,

KISSING CUP.

Excitement follows Excitement in the greatest Racing Drama ever produced.

SPY AT BAY.

Or, THE SECRET OF THE EMBASSY.

FULL MATINEE SATURDAY AFTERNOON at 3 o'clock. Doors Open 2.30.

THE KINEMA,
MARKET PLACE, DUDLEY.

MONDAY, TUESDAY AND WEDNESDAY NEXT—

THE FINGER OF FATE.

(Pathe Drama). COMEDIES AND TRAVEL.

THURSDAY, FRIDAY AND SATURDAY,

VICTIMS OF BLACKMAIL.

(Drama). WAR TOPICALS.
CONTINUOUS PERFORMANCE DAILY,
3 until 10.30 p.m.
PRICES :—3d.; 6d.; 1/-.

Adverts from a Dudley Herald of 1915 vintage, while Irving Bosco is showing films at the Empire, Hall Street, and the Public Hall. Meanwhile Ben Kennedy is showing films briefly in "Tthe Kinema" better known after the First World War as The Criterion.

BOSCO'S EMPIRE PICTURES,
HALL STREET, DUDLEY.

MATINEES, MONDAY AND SATURDAY at 3.
WEEK COMMENCING FEBRUARY 22nd.

CAPTAIN SWIFT

From the Famous Novel by C. Haddon Chambers.
THRILLING & SENSATIONAL, Full of Excitement. Magnificently Acted. A gripping Story.

BRAVO KILTIES!

The Picture that has taken London by storm.

THE TREY OF HEARTS.

Every Tuesday.

THE JUNGLE.

By Upton Sinclair.
Produced by the All-Star Feature Corporation, New York. Depicting how Chicago manufacturers, for the greed of gain, cause riot and disorder.

Look out for "BOOTLE'S BABY."

PUBLIC HALL, DUDLEY.

MONDAY, TUESDAY & WEDNESDAY NEXT.

THE GAMBLER'S PENALTY.

SENSATIONAL DRAMA IN 5 PARTS.
Also showing:—KATHLYN. Series 8.

THURSDAY, FRIDAY & SATURDAY.

IN THE SHADOW OF BIG BEN.

Don't miss this grand British Production in four acts.

SATURDAY, FEB. 27th—Grand Pantomime:—
BABES IN THE WOOD.

THE KINEMA
Market Place, Dudley.

MONDAY, FEBRUARY 22nd, AND DURING THE WEEK.

TOMMY ATKINS

By Arthur Shirley and Ben Landeck.
THE GREATEST OF ALL MILITARY DRAMAS.
The Play recently performed at the Lyceum, London, and over 10,000 times throughout the English-Speaking World.

MATINEE, Tuesday and Saturday.
2½ HOURS' ENTERTAINMENT.
Children's Matinee every Saturday at 3 p.m.

DUDLEY MARCH PLEASURE FAIR

FAIR GROUND,

COMMENCING FRIDAY, FEBRUARY 26th, 1915.

P. COLLINS'

GREAT AMALGAMATION OF HIGH-CLASS

AMUSEMENTS.

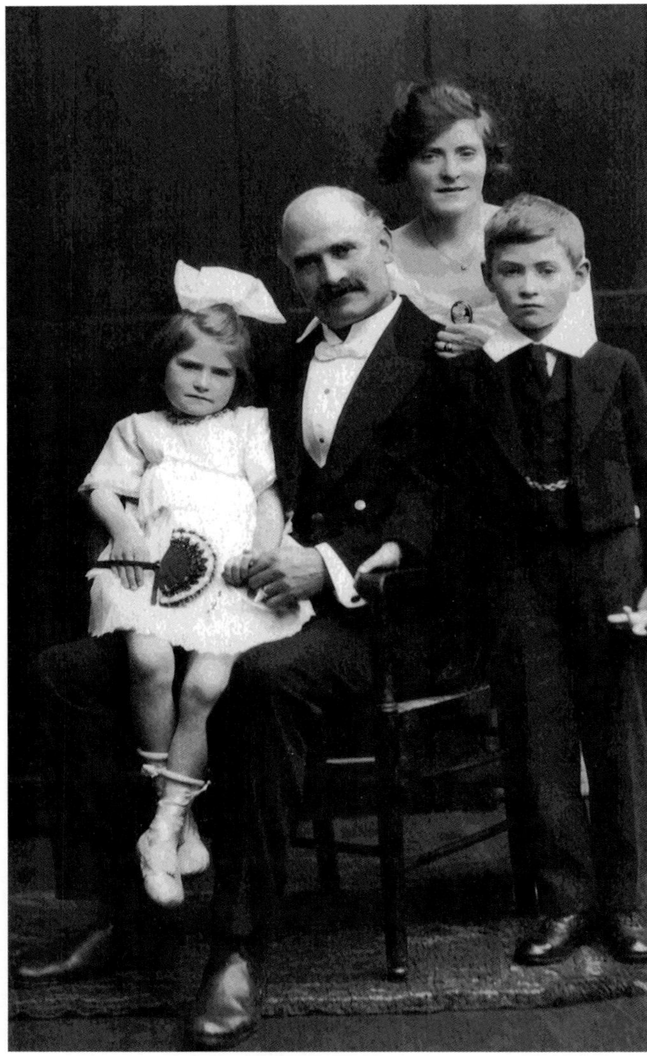

Above: Boscos or Baintons? Irving and Ducie, and their chidren, William and Eva about 1920.

Left: Adverts in the Dudley Herald for 2nd February 1915. A pantomime is coming to the Public Hall and Pat Collins is already publicising has forthcoming March Fair!

Chapter 3

Black Country Bits

JBT

Looking for JBT

It is strange to recall how I once became obsessed with the quest to find out more about a man known to me only by his initials: "J.B.T." It began somewhere in the 1980s following the publication of my book called *"Cinemas of the Black Country"*. In this book I had included descriptions of four cinemas once owned by Patrick Collins – well known fairground showman. Writing about Pat's cinemas, and undertaking the research had stimulated an interest in Pat himself. This was encouraged by people who contacted me after the book's publication to ask why I had wasted my time only concentrating on his cinemas when his real contribution to history had been on the fairground. Slowly, but inevitably I began to become interested in the self-styled "King of Showmen" although he had inhabited a world of which I knew very little – after all I had spent my life watching films, not visiting funfairs!

A biography of Pat Collins had been written in 1959 by E.J. Homeshaw, a Bloxwich-based local historian, and this had been professionally turned into a hand-written book and had been presented to Pat's widow, Clara, to mark the centenary of Pat's birth. This book had "disappeared" but about 1986 I found a type-written copy of the text in Walsall Archives. I studied the text and produced an article about it which was published in The Blackcountryman, the quarterly magazine of the Black Country Society. I concluded that it failed to tell the whole story, but that by then it would be impossible to improve on it. There is nothing like saying that something is "impossible" to set things going. By 1988 I had been joined by a three others, and between us we reckoned we had the skills to attempt writing a proper biography of Pat Collins. In the end only two of us stayed the course, but after three years of intensive work Freda Allen and I published our biography of the great man towards the end of 1991. Those three years of research had led me into new and exciting worlds.

The first exciting world explored was the world of the fairground itself. People who are not born into that world are known as "flatties", and Freda and I were a pair of pretty ignorant flatties. We were made welcome and given a great deal of generous help by the showmen we met, and by enthusiastic fans of the fairground world who had pursued their interest for whole lifetimes. The other world that had to be explored was made up of archives in which we would have to spend hours looking for relevant information. We soon learned that one of the most important sources of information was "The World's Fair" – the weekly newspaper of the fairground scene which had been published every Friday since 1904. At the time the complete set of World's Fairs was to be found at the National Newspaper Collection at Colindale in North London. Many days were spent endlessly devouring the pages of The World's Fair at a desk in Colindale. We consulted many other newspapers but none were as addictive as The World's Fair!

World's Fair is a labyrinth in which an army of "correspondents" chronicle events week by week covering the world of fairs, circuses, and a whole range of amusement-catering and even market-trading, sometimes with the use of supplements. We, the readers, soon became familiar with these correspondents and knew which ones to look out for when it came to collecting information about the life and work of Pat Collins, or whatever might be our chosen interest. World's Fair did not rigorously edit the material published so it is sometimes repetitive and duplicates itself, at other times it fails to report on events, and sometimes it published contradictory material – but that is all part of the fun of reading it.

One World's Fair correspondent that grabbed our attention called himself "J.B.T". His reports appear in the paper during the 1930s and were often entitled "Black Country Bits". Not only do his reports cover a huge variety of activities – fairs, circuses, variety theatres, markets etc., but they also have another intriguing dimension. Frequently, in describing a contemporary 1930s aspect of the local scene, JBT harks back to former "good old days" and he provides us with glimpses of showland as far back as the 1880s. There we were – in the 1980s, reading words set down in the 1930s, recalling scenes and people and events of the 1880s! Now we find ourselves in the twenty first century and the perspective of JBT's writing becomes even more dramatic. If you visited the fair in a place like Tipton, in the heart of the Black Country in 2018, it is not very likely that you would meet anyone who could give you a detailed picture of a similar event a hundred and thirty years ago.

Reading report after report gradually produces a picture of the reporter himself. We can almost see JBT – a man perhaps in his sixties, cycling round the Black Country, visiting markets, fairs, circuses etc., always finding someone he knew well and always finding some excuse to share his reminiscences with us. The greatest mystery of all simply becomes the identity of the man himself – how could I find out about a man known only by his initials? Nobody among local showmen or fairground enthusiasts seemed able to help me identify him.

At some stage I began more systematically collecting his reports and was able to put them in chronological order and this sometimes provided clues about the details of his life, but not everything made sense. Nevertheless his life seemed to have been rich in variety and experience. He often reported that he had some part in the presentation of somebody's show, or had provided the catering that is part of the showland world. For example I learnt that he had sold gingerbread and ice cream at Tipton Wakes in 1887. He sometimes mentioned Kitty whom I assumed was his wife. He recalled that she had appeared as a parader on the front Texas Bill's Wild West show at Willenhall in 1896. ('Texas Bill' was William Shufflebottom – but that's another story!) It also seemed that he and Kitty had worked on the Wall & Hammersley show before it had been acquired by Pat Collins and his wife in 1899. Such matters are totally obscure to someone who has not been lured into a study of the world consisting of these long-vanished stars of the fairground. However, for anyone fascinated by bioscopes, ghost shows, Wild West shows and the smell of gingerbread, JBT is going to be a heroic guide to such past matters. JBT also disclosed that he had worked in local theatrical enterprises such as Douglas Phelps' Alhambra in Dudley Port, and John Maurice Clement's Colisseum in Dudley.

I spent a long time in the early 1990s looking for someone with a surname beginning with "T", plus the appropriate initials, who might be "JBT". On at least one occasion I was certain I had found him only to find that the contender was not the man I was seeking. I eventually wrote an article about this quest and about JBT's writings for the Fairground Mercury – the quarterly magazine of the Fairground Association of Great Britain. Its publication produced no immediate response. However, sometime later Graham Downie, the editor of The Fairground Mercury, was talking to Reg Smith of Charlbury, and the long-sought information was suddenly revealed.

Reg Smith told Graham that JBT was "Joe Bate of Tipton", and that he had toured his native Black Country with a mirrors show known as 'Kitty de Smilo's Show' – named after his Irish wife. This was supported by JBT's own references to his wife in some of the reports, but turned out to be an incorrect interpretation of the facts. So much for all my searches based on the idea that I was looking for a man whose surname began with a "T"!

About the time of Reg Smith's revelation, I was also looking into early days of cinema history and in particular looking at how some of the early bioscope showman reacted to the arrival of the 1910 Kinematograph Act by becoming owners of permanent cinemas. Having already looked at the life of Pat Collins, I was wondering whether he had dabbled in cinema ownership in 1910. Up until then it had seemed that he only became interested in cinema ownership during the First World War facing circumstances when it was a good idea to "diversify". By coincidence JBT had something to say on the subject.

In World's Fair of 13th February 1931 JBT commented on an encounter with Bob Brown. Bob and his family worked for Pat Collins, and JBT wrote:

"....he also painted for Pat Collins, and did up a hall which I obtained and opened for Pat Collins in -

Lichfield – the first permanent cinema in the Cathedral City."

Searching the local paper was not very productive at first, but fellow cinema historian Brian Hornsey, of Stamford, tracked down the local licensing records and found that Seagraves Assembly Rooms in Dan Street, Lichfield, had indeed been converted for use as a cinema. The hall opened on 31st October 1910 as the "Electric Picture Palace", and the licence holder was confirmed as Pat Collins. On 28th October, just before it opened, The Lichfield Mercury revealed that the cinema's manager was Mr. J.D. Bate.

Armed with the information in JBT's contributions to World's Fair, and the new knowledge that he was Joe Bate, and that he had a middle initial "D", the research into his life story could begin. As the research developed it became clear that some of the information in World's Fair was misleading. However Joe's life was amazing and was a story worth telling, as it encompassed such a variety of Black Country entertainment history.

While dealing with census records, electoral rolls, newspaper stories etc., I eventually reached the stage where I felt I needed to see whether any of Joe Bate's descendants were around to help make sense of the story and to fill potential serious gaps in it. I was lucky in that Joe's surname was Bate rather than Bates – there would be fewer threads to follow! In the end I wrote to every "Bate" in the phone book who was still to be found in the Tipton and West Bromwich area - the area at the centre of the story.

I was very lucky in that I received two replies and, as a result, met two of Joe Bite's grandchildren: Leslie Bate and Spencer Bate. They, and their wives, were extremely helpful and provided key pieces of the jig-saw I was trying to complete. Leslie met his grandfather on several key occasions, and still had clear memories of Joe. Spencer's father; Arthur Bate, also played a key part in the way the story unfolded and was able to make a truly amazing contribution to our understanding of Joe's life.

In 1943, shortly before he died, Joe Bate had communicated with Arthur via a hand-written note on a piece of his headed notepaper. Remarkably, not only had this note survived, but the notepaper's design included a "C.V." of Joe's career! It is every biographer's dream to stumble upon a note from the subject himself and to find it contains a neat outline of the life being studied. Such a twist of fate suggests that Joe's life was a story waiting to be written!

Before telling Joe's story, I will attempt to give the reader a flavour of his contributions to World's Fair.

BLACK COUNTRY BITS.

By J.B.T.

We are experiencing what is called an Indian Summer round these parts and attendance at all indoor places have been on the lean side. The local wakes all round have been well attended. At Willenhall Mr. Collins preferred a big array of stuff, also at Blackheath, and the crowds were very big.

Some old-time personalities at Wednesbury Theatre are once more providing variety fare there. Royal Quixottes this week with Sinclair and his Manikin Music Hall are very entertaining. It is quite a change for the local patrons; many have never seen stuff like Sinclair and Rob Roberts are putting on here, and it was pleasing to see the audiences enjoying it.

Aldridge Wakes was held from September 13th to 16th. Mr. Davies attended with some up-to-date rides, and was supported by a host of old and new tenants. Mr. W. Young, the old Midland traveller, was present with some of his stuff, and Mr. Davies says he is an old but "Young" tenant of his. Well, I hope they all did good business. I am informed Old Hill Wakes follow on, also Uttoxeter, both of which are under Mr. W. Davies's control.

During Wednesbury Wakes I was pleased to see Charley Frazer, who had recently come from the Birkenhead Infirmary. He looked exceedingly well and had the greatest praise and respect for the Birkenhead hospital, doctors and nurses.

A typical "Black Country Bits" supplied to World's Fair by JBT describing Pat Collins' fair in Willenhall and William Davies' fair in Aldridge – but in no detail! Plus comments on Wednesbury Hippodrome and people he knew!

Black Country Bits

One of the earliest reports written for World's Fair that I have found dates from 25th July 1931, although JBT is yet to use the title "Black Country Bits". Rather appropriately it describes his personal view of Tipton Wakes. The fair was being presented by Patrick Ross Collins, Pat Collins' son, and was part of his Black Country run of fairs. Most World's Fair reporters would have given us a list of the main riding machines present and named the managers, followed by a list of the sidestalls and caterers. Joe focusses on the shows and uses the event as an excuse to reminisce.

"One of the attractions at Tipton Wakes this year is Proctor's Circus, a concern I have known for many years. It is now thoroughly modernised, with a neat front with two wagons, several others at the sides and back, a couple of motor lorries and a good heavy tent. It provides a show which gives satisfaction at the cheap prices of 3d and 6d.

The next show is Charlie Hickman's, the boxer; I think he has some of the Regan boys on his show. The slot arcade ends the side shows for this year."

In World's Fair for 5th September 1931 there are two items by JBT, one is a report of Oldbury Wakes, the other comments on other matters and uses the heading "Black Country Bits". Even in the former JBT is more concerned with personalities and memories than with naming machines present. However, he does mention Pat Collins' Whale Island Scenic Switchback, which would have been in the no.1 machine position. It was managed by Clara Mullett. Clara, and her siblings, were orphaned in the 1880s and were adopted or "absorbed" by Pat and Flora Collins. She grew up to become manager of Pat's no. 1 machine, and four years after this report was written she became the second Mrs. Collins – and thus of some historical importance. JBT knew her well, as we learn in several of his reports, and he goes on to say:

"I was talking to Miss Mullett about the small old time Wakes and she recalled a pleasant little 'do' at Ocker Hill (a remote part of Tipton that even today is known as 'The Lost City'). *I think that if presented with a nice little machine and a few tenants all these places would be more profitable than over-crowded big places. I do not see why a little lot should not be kept specifically for these little gaffs, and I hope they will be revived and that variety booths will come back again."*

In the chapter below, in which I trace the course of JBT's life, it will become apparent why he makes this point. In a report appearing on 26th December he makes the point yet again – specifically mentioning the ideal location for presenting such an event: Hill Top, between West Bromwich and Wednesbury – a place which had become very close to JBT's heart.

JBT had known Clara Mullet for a long time as made clear in some comments made in January 1936: *"My mind goes back to the good old days when we used to winter in Dudley Street, Birmingham. I was then with Charlie Johnson and his mother, plus Leah Hayes, Annie Russell and Jack Hayes. Young George Russell and myself used to be rollicking about the Smethwick grounds at Grove Lane and Clara Mullett was among us. How the time does go by."*

In his Black Country Bits column of 5th September 1931 he tells us that Pat Collins was one of the first people in Walsall to purchase a motor car. Such a move was not popular in a town devoted to the manufacture of leather saddles for horses – a point not lost on JBT. Pat's big fairs on the wakes grounds of the Black Country were often described by other World's Fair correspondents – some of whom JBT seemed to know, but in finding his own niche for his reports he does provide an antidote for future historians who may have otherwise felt that Pat's monopoly in the area was 100%. As it was, some fairs in the Black Country were still presented by William Davies from Stoke-on -Trent for historical reasons, and JBT's knowledge of "who's who" included tenants of the Davies family as well as the Collins. As always, JBT's work was always very people-centred.

Perhaps because JBT's memories stretched back to 1887 he was able to identify people from times before Pat Collin's grip on the Black Country became so absolute. As already made clear he knew Harry Collet-Humphries, Williams Davies, Mrs. Shepherd etc. but he also spots other showmen appearing in the area at the height of Pat Collins' power. For example he sees George Wallis, the Lancashire showman at the Corbett Hospital Fetes of the mid-1930s. He spotted the Drakeleys at Great Bridge. In Spring 1939 he glimpses Ernest Steel at Blackheath.

Following Flora Collins' death on 8th April 1933, JBT toured the Black Country and spoke to many acquaintances about her virtues and personal qualities. His report, as usual, adds a few personal memories:

"She was a strict, albeit warm hearted person, and would never tolerate rowdiness or vulgarity on the

showground. It was only recently that she gave up being 'on the spot' with the grand show-front which was purchased from Hammersley, known as Wall's Phantoscope. My wife and I worked on that showfront prior to it being taken over by Mrs. Collins at the end of the 1890s."

JBT here is referring to a show that became Pat and Flora's first venture into the world of bioscopes. Flora Collins presented it as a bioscope from 1899 onwards, although in 1908 it was replaced by one of the more modern "Wonderland" shows. The ex-Wall & Hammersley show became even more redundant when the Kinematograph Act came into force at the beginning of 1910. Flora converted the old show into a lion-show and the frontage was found a new semi-permanent home at the Collins' ground in New Brighton around 1930/1.

Following the death of a showman, JBT was sometimes able to supply the kind of information lacking in the brief obituaries that might appear in World's Fair. For example, in July 1933 he writes about Bert Humphries:

"Bert was a well-known Midland lad, the second son of Mr. H. Collett Humphries of Tipton, who was for many years with Pat Collins' staff controlling this area. Bert was a diminutive figure, but always had a smile for everybody. I knew his parents and even his grandparents. They were of the old sturdy stock and used to attend the local markets and wakes: they were, I should think, the pioneers in regard to the short-throw coconut sheets. Bert was in his element when he was working a sheet for his various friends in the Black Country." ("working a sheet" meant presenting a coconut shie.)

As far as JBT was concerned Tipton was the centre of the world and he would always find plenty to say about a fair in Tipton. In July 1933 he wrote as follows:
"Tipton Wakes are well-billed all round this area, and Mr. Collins is presenting a fine array of stuff, some of the latest rides and games and also so the big machine. Many old tenants and new tenants are present and will look for a tidy Wakes as things round here are not too bad. Tipton is one of those places that have made wonderful strides recently. They have created practically a new Tipton – new housing estates and a wonderful parks area. The ground is situated between the old schools and the new schools and the new baths. I can remember the old style Tipton Wakes very well. I attended them with showfolk as far back as 1887. Johnson's Peep Show, Russell's and Hayes' horses, W. Davies, Stocktons, Antill, J.Caddick, Lalloo, Parker's Ghost Show, Wakeman's Theatre, Chittock's Dogs – in fact most of the old school of travellers have attended it. It used to be controlled by Mr. Whitehouse at the Golden Cross Inn adjoining, but for many years Mr. Collins has controlled it."

Some of these people have really disappeared into the mists of history, making us wish that JBT had told us more. I know a little about some of them, such as Joe Caddick and George Russell, but others are complete mysteries. The reference to Wakeman's Theatre is of great interest to anyone investigating the history of 'portable theatres' – the background to the Bennett &Patch story told in Chapter 5 – the link with Tipton is also significant as drawings have been discovered of Wakeman's Theatre when it appeared at Great Bridge.) I would love to know more about the Hayes family, for example. They seem to have strong connections with Dudley, and some worked for Pat Collins. JBT did pause to tell us a little more in 1936 when he visited the Pat Collins ground in Dudley – the "White Nobs" fairground on the corner of Trindle Road and Connaught Road in March. He wrote:

"This was the ground where Jack Hayes ('Deaf 'un') used to winter. Mr. Hayes has been dead some years and his son, Jack, is also now deaf, but has managed machines for Pat Collins at various times and is a good carpenter and now works in the Bloxwich Repair Shops. Daughters, Leah married Cockney Brown and Annie is also married, and they still live in the old horse-drawn style."

This is a reminder that a few showmen still used horses in the mid to late 1930s. The showmens' engines had made large teams of horses redundant in the late 1890s, and most showmen adopted petrol engine vehicles after the First World War, but thanks to JBT we catch glimpses of how one generation of showmen continued in the "old style" for longer than might be imagined.

JBT's reports often remind the reader of links between the worlds of the fairground, circus, theatre, cinema, and markets. Sometimes he chronicles the movement of a fairground from one site to another – as in a report on Darlaston Wakes in August 1933; another time he does the same for market patches – as in a report on Great Bridge . (He claimed his parents and two sisters were married from Great Bridge Wakes.) On another occasion he sets out his history of a theatre and cinema at Dudley Port. In the Summer of 1934 he writes:

"The Alhambra Theatre at Dudley Port is to be demolished. It has served many good purposes, and had many alterations and owners. First I remember it as a Salvation Army hall, then it was a theatre under Mr.

Morton from Cradley Heath. After being used as a skating rink, it was turned into a theatre again by Mr. Phelps of Stourbridge, for whom I managed it temporarily. It later changed to pictures under various owners, and Mr. Pat Collins bought the building. Mr. James Styles had a little time at this place. Then Miles Jervis bought it from Mr. Collins. He has had a tidy do out of it now – a super cinema is to be erected on the site."

Thus in a single paragraph he comprehensively sums up the complicated history of a local theatre referring to a number of names to delight those to whom they are familiar. They may not be familiar to the general reader today, but I have explained them elsewhere; a process which leads into a thousand other stories! The same thing happens when he reports on a visit to Dudley:

"Dudley is a town that used to be good for theatrical stuff, and for circus and variety stars too, and personally I have worked some of the most expensive stars on the stages at the Empire and the Colliseum. At the Colliseum the best was not too good in the mind of Mr. Clements, the owner. There I saw a great actor, O'Toole, and before that I saw Culine's Circus on the same site."

Ironically at the time of writing the Dudley Hippodrome is facing demolition, having not been used as a theatre since 1964. The people making decisions on the Hippodrome's fate are not likely to have any sense of that building's history, let alone understand that it had a predecessor in the form of the Dudley Opera House, and that the man who had the vision to build that – John Maurice Clements – had previously owned a theatre called The Colliseum in Trindle Road. The Colliseum's story would take us back into the world of late nineteenth century circus buildings. And even taking account of that would not give us the whole picture of the theatre history of a place like Dudley because it would ignore the story of The Empire, in Hall Street. JBT knew all these places and had worked in some of them. Their stories also include the lives of Irving Bosco and Ben Kennedy who receive attention in this book. This is the context in which we strive to understand what JBT can tell us about a world that has now so completely vanished.

Having given us a glimpse of the theatrical past of Dudley Port, and Dudley we should not be surprised that JBT can also remind us of Wednesbury's theatre history, wrapped up in his own interests in "billing" and market trading. In a report on his visit to Wednesbury Market in October 1935 he adds: *"Cycling around my usual pitches and seeing many circus bills about announcing that the Bellinis were at Wednesbury, I decided to visit the Wednesbury Hippodrome to see the full show, So on Tuesday night I visited the show, accompanied by Kitty de Smilo, who is also a pal of the Bellinis. We don't often get a chance to go out, and it is such a long time since we saw our friends that we both felt pleasure in going, although it rained hard at the time for our departure."*

On yet another occasion JBT comments of theatre history in Stourbridge. In 1936 he wrote: *"I also visited Stourbridge. The old Alhambra Theatre has disappeared. The original building was Bennett & Patch's travelling booth. They were real showground folk. Later I managed the place, and also had a very popular film star there in her very early days."*

JBT was quite right – the Alhambra had closed in April 1929, and the building was demolished. I think the connection in this case was Douglas Phelps whom JBT first encountered at Dudley Port's Alhambra. Douglas Phelps tried showing films at both venues but had a much longer association with the Stourbridge theatre – lasting up until 1922. I deal with the legendary "Bennett & Patch" in another chapter.

Although not one of his "Black Country Bits", it is worth mentioning another item which appeared in World's Fair as result of what must have been an initiative by Joe Bate. On the front page of the 1st September 1934 edition we are told that Joe Bate Senior died on Monday 27th August 1934 at the age of eighty-one. It adds, *"He was well known in Tipton and was held in high regard for his integrity and reliability both is work and play. He was at one time a much sought – after judge at pigeon races and whippet coursing. His decisions were always regarded as final. In his younger days he had been a good runner and fist fighter."* This does not clarify Joe Bate Snr's relationship with the fairground world, but it may be significant that Joe felt that his father's life was of interest to readers of World's Fair.

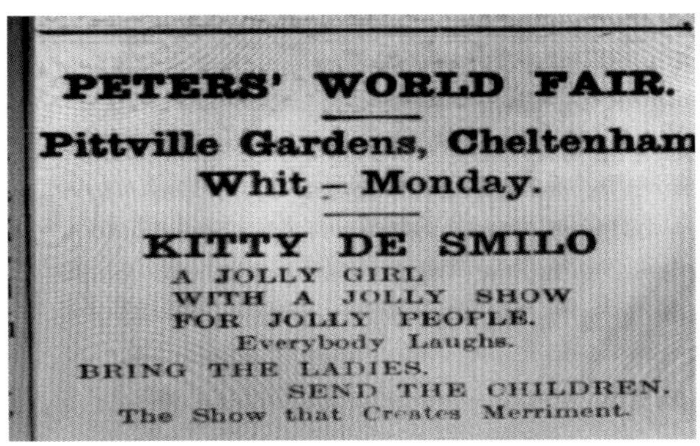
PETERS' WORLD FAIR.

Pittville Gardens, Cheltenham

Whit – Monday.

KITTY DE SMILO

A JOLLY GIRL
WITH A JOLLY SHOW
FOR JOLLY PEOPLE.
Everybody Laughs.
BRING THE LADIES.
SEND THE CHILDREN.
The Show that Creates Merriment.

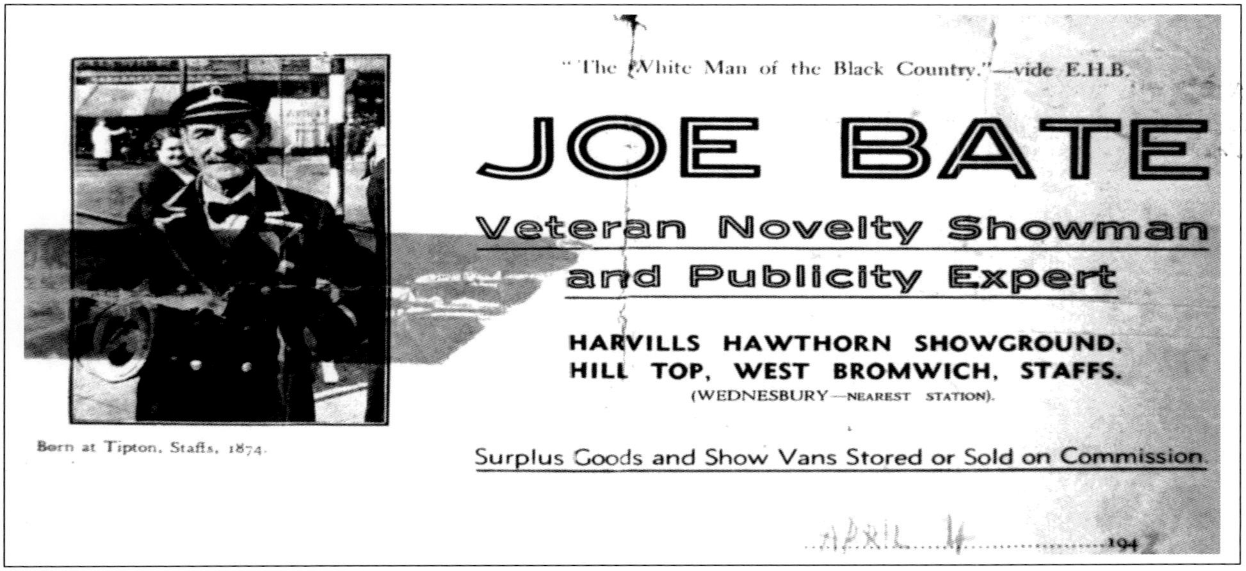
"The White Man of the Black Country."—vide E.H.B.

JOE BATE

Veteran Novelty Showman

and Publicity Expert

HARVILLS HAWTHORN SHOWGROUND,

HILL TOP, WEST BROMWICH, STAFFS.

(WEDNESBURY—NEAREST STATION).

Born at Tipton, Staffs, 1874.

Surplus Goods and Show Vans Stored or Sold on Commission.

APRIL 4 194

Above: Joe Bate's headed notepaper. The left hand side of the notepaper set out his C.V.

The Life and Work of Joe Bate

Josiah Darby Bate was born on 16th December 1874, the son of Joseph Bate and Sarah Jane Bate (nee Evans). His parents were nineteen and eighteen respectively, and Joe later told readers that his parents had got married "from Great Bridge Wakes Ground" – in fact they were married in Dudley just before his birth. He implied that his parents travelled either as showmen or market traders, and we are later told that he was one of seven children – three sons and four daughters.

If his parents were travelling it may account for the fact that Joe appears to have grown up with his maternal grandparents. For example, at the age of six we find him residing with them at 90 Sedgley Road East. The 1881 census tells us that his maternal grandparents were Joseph and Eliza Evans, and that Joseph Snr. was a carpenter. As we would expect, six year old Joe is listed in this census as a "scholar". At the same time Joe's mother and father were living elsewhere in Tipton along with the three children that had followed Joe. His father is identified as an "iron worker" – a term used again in the 1891 census - but this does not mean that he may not have also been part of the fairground business at least on a part-time basis. (Other showmen are some - times listed as "iron workers" or "general labourers" in the census, perhaps because enumerators were more familiar with such occupational labels.)

Six years later, when Joe was a thirteen year-old, it would seem that he had joined the business because he describes the time when he sold ginger bread and ice cream at the Tipton Wakes of 1887. It seems that he joined his friend James Clutterbuck in doing this – the latter coming from a family who presented a "panam" at local fairs. He later said that he and James slept under the 12 foot long stall. (A "panam" is a stall on a fairground devoted to selling sweets.)

A few years after this, when Joe was eighteen, the 1891 census reveals that he was not at his grandparents' home, nor his parents' home. I have not found him to be anywhere else, but this may indicate that he was certainly travelling by then.

Joe's own outline of his career tells us that he travelled with Charley Johnson's Peep Show in 1888, and with Tom Nail's show in 1889. In 1891 he was on tour with H. Humphries' Auction Tent. It would seem that this was a reference to Harry Collett Humphries because he refers to this man in some of his World's Fair reports. Joe writes about him as if we ought to know him, but a twenty-first century reader can be forgiven for never having heard of him. He worked with Sophie Shepherd (1834 – 1915), possibly as manager of her Gondola Switchback – Mrs. Shepherd and her switchback were legends to people like JBT and Southdown, but they are almost unknown today.

In 1892 Joe broadened his experience by touring a whale – or the embalmed remains of one – in a number of Black Country shops, in association with Jack Henri. It seems they hired the show from Harry Collett Humphries. The following year he joined Clown Julian's Circus on their travels. Clown Julian's real name was John Woodrow and, as his showland name implies, he had once been a clown, but in the late 1880s had become proprietor of his own small circus. As with all these names, very little is known about the people themselves today. On leaving Clown Julian he seems to have worked at the People's Palace in Bristol. He was definitely heading south-west.

On 6th May 1893 the prince who eventually became George V married Princess Mary of Tech. Joe Bate was travelling in the West Country with a small un-named circus at the time. The reason he remembered the two things together was that, while travelling through Bath, he met Eva Amanda Ryman. He later recalled that their courtship was brief and mainly conducted by post! They were married on 30th October 1893 at St. Michael's Church in Bath, where Eva had been born on 31st August 1876 – in other words, she was two years younger than Joe. Her parents were Arthur Edwin Ryman and his wife Emma, but her real "claim to fame" seems to have been that her grandfather, Leonard Ryman was, at the time, the last surviving postilion rider of the mail coach era! Once married, Joe seems to have settled in Bath for a while, and tried hawking cough drops – this may account for the fact that his own "CV" says little about his activities in 1894 and 1895

Joe tells us that in 1896 he worked for "Bosco's Show" and for Texas Bill (on tour). At first glance we might guess that "Bosco" was none other than Irving Bosco whose life is also described in this book, but it may be more likely that he travelled with a Leopold Bosco. To find Joe was also working on Texas Bill's show during 1896 is also significant as he later tells us that both he and his wife worked on that show – she was the knife-thrower's "target". Texas Bill was William Shufflebottom and it was a prestigious show on which to work. In his World's Fair writings Joe tells us that both he and Eva also worked on the Wall & Hammersley bioscope show, probably during 1898, just before it was sold to Mrs. Collins.

In later life, when writing in World's Fair, he would describe Kitty Flanaghan as his wife, but during the 1890s and on into the 1900s he was very much the husband of Eva and it appears that they travelled together while they had their children – all the children being born in different places. At the turn of the century it seems that he worked in theatres rather than fairground shows. He mentions the Theatre Royal, Smethwick, in 1897; the Theatre Royal, Exeter, for the pantomime of 1898, the New Cross Empire, London, in 1900 and then the Hippodrome Merthyr in 1901. What was his role in these theatres? – it seems that his work was that of the "bill poster".

In April 1901 when the census took place Joe and Eva were to be found at 21 Garden Row, Merthyr Tydfil and he described himself as "Circus Bill Poster". Joe and Eva are in their mid-twenties and have had two children: Florence and Lily. Florence was born in Smethwick, Birmingham, in 1898 and Lily was born in Exeter towards the end of 1899.

Joe continues his "CV" covering the early 1900s by telling us that he worked in 1902 with various travelling menageries such as Sedgwick's and Purchase's, and with Henry Studt, based in Cardiff and John Studt, based in Swansea. It seems that he also ran his own side shows at the time. The South Wales connection is reflected in the fact that his first son, Cecil Darby Bate, was born in the summer of 1902 in Tonypandy.

His Black Country connections are revived in 1903 because he claims that he worked for the Empire Theatre in Hall Street, Dudley during 1903. The Empire opened in May of that year under the ownership of Tom Pritchard. Tom only stayed at The Empire for two years, moving in 1905 to the management of the Palace, Oldbury. Joe also lists the Palace, Oldbury, as one of his employers so it could be that the connection was Tom Pritchard. Although not listed in his "CV" we learn from Joe's writings in World's Fair (See World's Fair of 18th August 1934.) that he also worked with Douglas Phelps at the Alhambra Theatre at Dudley Port. I think we have to assume that Joe's work was always in the business of "billing" the shows, rather than anything in the theatre itself. "Billing" was an important way of publicising a theatre's shows and often involved asking shop-keepers to display a bill (or advert) in return for a pass.

If the 1901 census return, completed in Merthyr Tydfil, and the birth of Cecil in South Wales suggest his life was centred in that area at the turn of the century, then working for theatres in the Black Country suggests a return to his home area about 1903. This view is supported by the fact that his daughter Winifred Kate was born in Tipton in Spring 1905 and his son Leonard was born in Oldbury in Spring 1907. To what extent Joe was ever in one place for long is reflected by the fact that he also seems to have worked for Scott's Circus during that period, and in 1910 became involved with Pat Collins venture into the cinema business in Lichfield.

His "Black Country period" seems to be followed by a "Hinckley/Nuneaton" period. Sure enough we find him living at 22 Regent Street, Hinckley, in the 1911 Census. He describes himself as "Advertising contractor and poster writer" but it is interesting to find that his wife, Eva, describes herself as "assistant in window cleaning business", and they have a lodger with them named William Forest who describes himself as a "window cleaner". Window cleaning may have been an important contribution to the household income in the years running up to the First World War – hence the wording of the World's Fair caption to a photograph of 1914 vintage which I will describe in a moment. Joe no doubt felt it more important to maintain his showland endeavours, thus during that period he claims to have also worked with Pat Collins and toured his own "novelty show". Joe's son Arthur was born in Hinckley in 1912.

In the 14th February 1914 edition of World's Fair a photograph of Joe Bate is prominently displayed on the front page with an informative caption: *"Mr. Joe Bate is a well-known, experienced, tactful, and energetic worker, well versed in variety and picture management, and a smart gentlemanly agent or doorsman. He has also been with Bosco, run duff shows of his own, and had a regular varied career. He is now co-partner in the local concern known as Bate Brothers, Bill Posting and Window Cleaning Co., Hinckley."* – a wonderful summary of Joe's career up until this time.

The First World War and after

The outbreak of war may have led Joe Bate and his family to forsake the Hinckley base and move back to the Black Country. His own account of his activities tells us that he worked at the Olympia, West Bromwich from 1915 to 1918. The Olympia was a wonderful corrugated iron building erected at the Carters Green end of West Bromwich High Street, having opened as the "New Hippodrome" in 1906. In 1914 it was acquired by Ben Kennedy, apparently to obtain theatre and kine licences

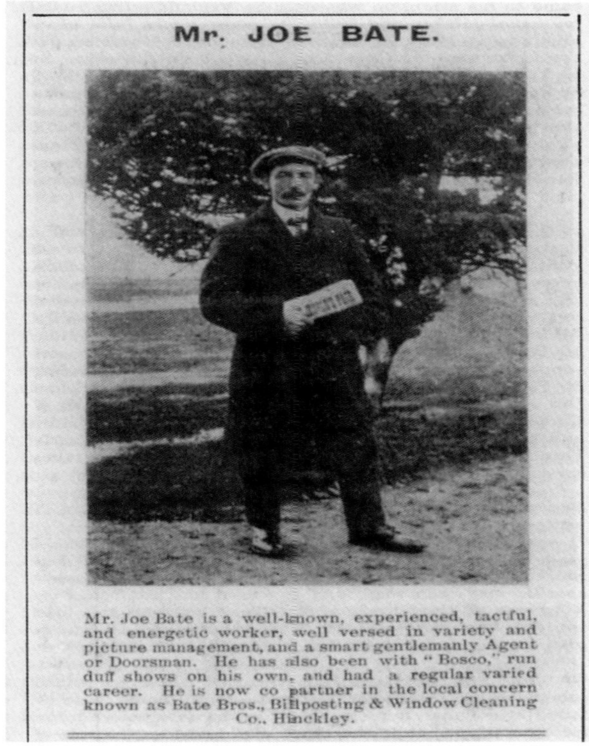
MR. JOE BATE.

Mr. Joe Bate is a well-known, experienced, tactful, and energetic worker, well versed in variety and picture management, and a smart gentlemanly Agent or Doorsman. He has also been with "Bosco," run duff shows on his own, and had a regular varied career. He is now co partner in the local concern known as Bate Bros., Billposting & Window Cleaning Co., Hinckley.

Above: Joe Bate as he appeared on the front page of World's Fair during 1914. He dressed smartly and clutched the World's Fair for the occasion.

that could be transferred to the Empire he was building close to the other end of West Bromwich High Street. When the Empire did open he leased the Olympia to others and then took back control of it in the early twenties. It seems likely therefore that Ben Kennedy was not involved with the Olympia at the time Joe Bate was working there, nevertheless I am sure the paths of Joe and Ben would have crossed. Joe was probably undertaking billing for the Olympia, and maybe assisted in the projection room.

Working at the Olympia seems to have led to the family settling in West Bromwich, but as we can see from Joe's life up to this time, he was bound to get itchy feet as soon as the war was over. When life returned to normal Joe was drawn back into presenting a fairground show and doing anything else that came up such as billing for various circuses. He seems to have joined with Kate Flanaghan in presenting a mirror show using the name "Kitty de Smilo". Kate has always been something of a mystery character but we now know that she was born in Northampton on 16th January 1895, the daughter of Stephen and Fanny Flanagan. (Sometimes the name is spelt Flanagan, sometimes Flanaghan!) Members of her family, with whom she was living during the First World War, were associated with the boot and shoe trade of Northampton but Joe always wrote about her in World's Fair as if she was an older woman who had paraded for Texas Bill in Willenhall in 1896, and had come from Ireland! As we will see later, Kate herself provided confusing biographical information.

Joe's presentation of the Kitty de Smilo show seems to have been well organised and it seems that Joe bought a petrol vehicle to pull their living van and equipment from place to place. At the same time he bought a "bucking broncho" juvenile ride which he could present alongside the mirror show. From 1920 onwards we can trace some of Joe's movements from advertisements he placed in local newspapers to promote the Kitty de Smilo show. He tells prospective customers that Kitty is the "Mary Pickford of the fairgrounds" and refers to the mirror show as "The Laugh and Grow Fat Show". He also claimed the show had been visited by a Princess, but this royal figure is never identified. Luckily a photograph of the show has survived.

The advertisements appearing through the 1920s record visits to Gloucester, Banbury, Lichfield, Reading, Kettering, Northampton, Cheltenham, Yeovil and Trowbridge. Often they appeared at small local fetes, carnivals and gymkhanas, but at Lichfield they appeared at the Bower with Pat Collins, and at Banbury they were with Thurstons. At least on one occasion Joe's "Rodeo Horse" earns a mention as well as the Mirror Show. However, Joe never did one thing when it was possible to do several things, so we also find that he was trying to establish a site at Stourport on the River Severn. In World's Fair of 30th April 1921 he advertised "space to let" on this site. (Possibly the Kitty de Smilo show was permanently built up on that site in 1921, but was off on its travels again in 1922.)

Below: The Kitty-de-Smilo mirror show with Kitty seated on the right, and Joe peeping round the showfront on the left.
(Photo: Stephen Smith Collection)

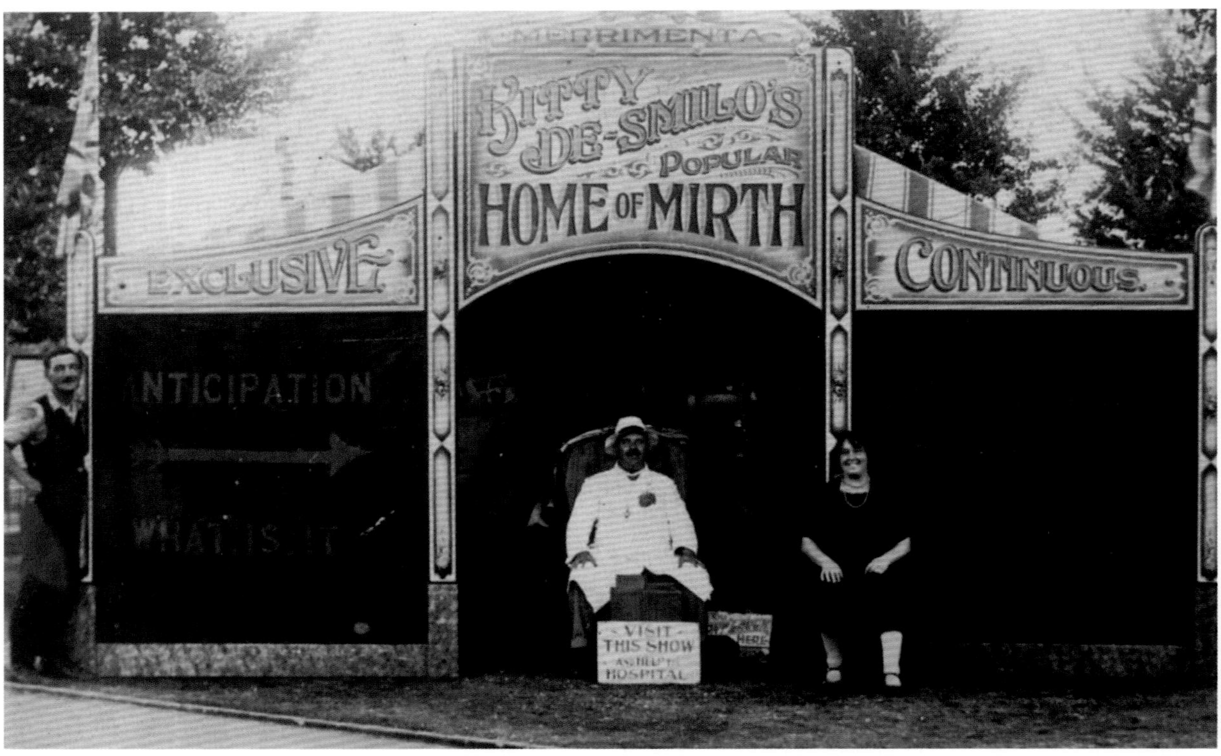

Off to Harvills Hawthorn

The "Kitty de Smilo" years seem to come to an end as the decade closes. In 1929 Joe Bate suddenly appears on the electoral role of West Bromwich by moving into Number 3, Harvills Hawthorn as a lodger with Harry and Elizabeth Roberts. At the same time Kate Flanaghan is registered as living in a caravan on waste ground at Harvills Hawthorn. This poetically named location is a small hamlet at Hill Top, half way between West Bromwich and Wednesbury, at the junction of the road leading down to Great Bridge. At Great Bridge Market Place Kate took on a sweet stall.

The Electoral Rolls help us see what happened next. In 1930 we see that Cecil and Gladys Bate join Joe at No.3. Harvills Hawthorn and from 1931 onwards Joe and Kate are listed as living in the caravan on the wasteland at Harvills Hawthorn. Joe's son Cecil (24th June 1902 – 4th April 1972) was the only child to really follow his father into the business. He also joined the circus world and did some clowning; later he worked for Pat Collins and spent some time as the driver of Pat's engine, "Goliath". To many people he was known as Jack Bate. He and his wife, Gladys, moved to Reform Street in West Bromwich, but perhaps he was able to join his father for that year in Harvills Hawthorn as they shared an interest in the fairground world. The rest of the family, including Eva, obviously felt estranged from Joe as he had effectively abandoned them.

As usual Joe remained alert to any new opportunities. At one stage in the early 1930s it looked as if he was hoping to turn the ground at Harvills Hawthorn into a potential fairground. In World's Fair of 26th December 1931 he wrote: *"H. Bailey's Circus intended to look in at Hill Top, but the route was altered, and it went to Gornal. This little place seems very popular. I believe it is one of the most prosperous places around here.* (Did he mean Hill Top or Gornal?)

At Hill Top we are promised a good outfit by a well-known Lincolnshire and Derbyshire traveller. Only a small lot, but I think by the time these notes are read he will be making a tidy fiddle, and if the weather keeps kind, he is sure to have plenty of kiddies throughout the holiday."

In the same issue Joe comments on the arrival of the first coin-operated slot machines arriving in High Street premises in West Bromwich and Dudley. Writing these notes for the World's Fair obviously provided Joe with a new opportunity to feel busy and well-occupied in the business and were probably very important to him. As the 1930s progressed his heath seemed to decline. Cecil Bate's son, Leslie, born in 1930, remembers going to Harvills Hawthorn to see his grandfather. He remembers him as a tall imposing figure with a bristling moustache. At the time Joe still had some swings but most of the mirror show had been sold, although there were still a few mirrors packed away in a shed. We know from his headed notepaper of the time that he was still looking for business and called himself: Veteran Novelty Showman and Publicity Expert" as well as offering to wheel and deal with "goods" and show vans!

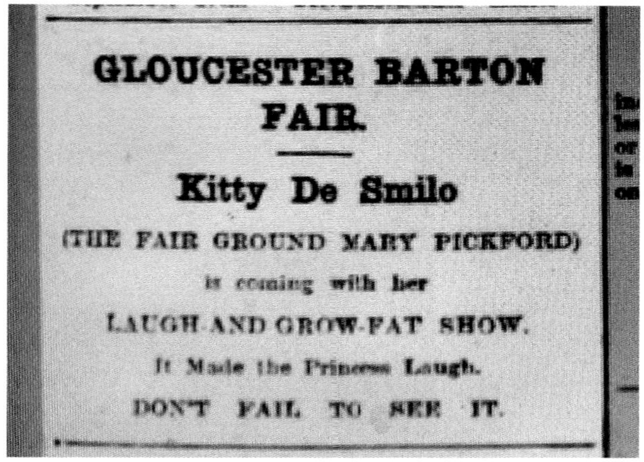

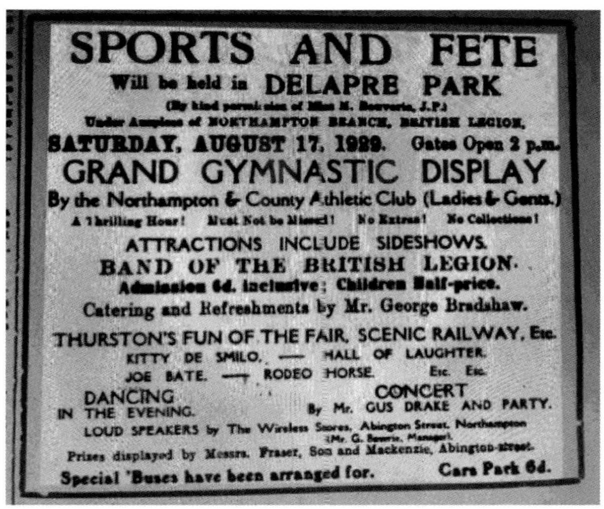

Above: Advertisements in local papers sometimes reveal the travels of Joe and the Kitty-de-Smilo show.

The August 1929 advert for the event in Delapre Park, Northampton actually mention's Joe's "Rodeo Horse"!

A Sad Final Act

For the nation the thirties ended in the outbreak of the Second World War, but on an individual personal level for Joe Bate life looked grim as the war started, as he was finding it increasingly difficult to earn a living. He wrote his last report for World's Fair in November 1939. Then, on his sixty seventh birthday, on 16th December 1941 he suffered a stroke. Even World's Fair informed showland that Joe was not well and would appreciate any help that could be offered, and perhaps readers could write to him to cheer him up. The suggestion was made in January 1942 and was repeated in April. Amazingly, in June 1942 the paper announced he was "out and about again after six months of illness", but I think life remained difficult as he battled with lack of mobility, depression and a minimal income.

In April 1943 he tried to contact his family, in particular hoping to see his youngest son, Arthur. He wrote a note to Arthur, but Arthur refused to accept it. By a twist of fate Arthur's wife kept the note and passed it on to their son Spencer who showed it to me in the early 1990s! Unfortunately matters grew worse and by the end of 1943 Joe was admitted to Burntwood Hospital.

Joe died in Burntwood Hospital on 20th January 1945. His death certificate correctly described his occupation: "Showman". Poor Eva put an announcement in the Midland Chronicle:

"BATE: Died January 20th, Josiah Bate, Harvills Hawthorn, Hill Top, husband of Mrs. E Bate, 10 Young Street, West Bromwich."

No local paper printed an obituary but World's Fair gave his death front page attention on 27th January 1945: *"Travellers in general, and showmen of the old school, will regret to hear of the death of Mr. Joe Bate, West Bromwich, which occurred last Saturday after a short illness following a stroke.*
At one time Joe Bate and his 'Kitty de Smilo' show were well known throughout the country, but his connection with showland had stretched back over fifty years. He had filled various positions in theatres, circuses, and side shows, and was for a time publicity man for fairground amusement caterers. He acted as one of World's Fair correspondents in the Midlands for many years, his feature being known as 'Black Country Bits'. Much sympathy will be felt for his widow, who is 69 years old and in straightened circumstances."

A week later Southdown wrote in World's Fair saying: *"It is with great regret that I read in last week's World's Fair of the passing of the old time showman, Joe Bate, whom I had known for quite a long time, and whom I last met when he was carrying out publicity work for the late Alderman Pat Collins."*

Eva Bate, Joe's wife, died in 1960 without making any public record of her life and work. She once said that she had worked in the theatre and had dressed Vesta Tilly so probably had an interesting life long before having to take up a nomadic life for a while with Joe, and being mother to their six children.

Meanwhile Kitty continued to live in West Bromwich and had several jobs including working for West Bromwich Corporation as a lavatory attendant. She died in June 1949 and was given a great deal of attention by the Birmingham Daily Gazette who interviewed a Mr. Arthur Woodhouse about her life. Because the Gazette's story is slightly bizarre it is worth quoting some of it: The story begins on the front page and is headlined: *"Mary Pickford of the Fairground: Kitty was a toast of the stage."*

Kitty Flanaghan, the West Bromwich Corporation attendant is dead. Why is that news? Because Kate was the toast of the variety stage – a girl who loved wearing beautiful clothes and jewels – a lovely girl who became 'The Mary Pickford of the Fairgrounds'. Her then stage name was Kitty de Smilo. This is Kitty's story, with interpolations by Arthur Woodhouse, who knew her twenty years ago, and with whom she has lodged for the last six weeks. Kitty came to England from Ireland aged thirteen, in 1907. She got a job as a dancer with Mr. Joe Bate' travelling fair.

Her friendship with Mr. Bate flourished and for years she travelled the country as a variety artist under the name 'Kitty de Smilo'."

Mr. Woodhouse confessed that he had first met her when she was running a sweet stall in Great Bridge Market in 1929, adding, *"She had hit hard times and lived alone in a caravan at Hill Top for many years."* It was Mr. Woodhouse who had apparently found her dead, guarded by her two pet terriers and their puppies. His concluding words were, "We'll miss her in these parts."

This newspaper story must have annoyed the Bate family at the time, but is even more remarkable now for its inaccuracies and misunderstandings, not forgetting the crime of confusing "Bate" with "Bates". Perhaps Kitty and Joe jointly decided to create the legend that she came from Ireland, along with the claims that she appeared on various late 19th century fairground shows.

And After All That…

As already made clear, I first encountered JBT and "Black Country Bits" while researching the life of Pat Collins at the end of 1980s. I then "mispent" several years looking for someone with a surname beginning with "T". I wrote an article for the Fairground Mercury about JBT's writings while still not knowing who he was. Indirectly that led to finding out that he was "Joe Bate of Tipton", and following that discovery I was able to start piecing the story together. Just before the publication of *"Fairs & Circuses in the Black Country"* in 1994 I made contact with two of Joe's grandsons and learnt much more – particularly as the result of seeing Joe's "CV" printed on his headed notepaper.

Returning to Joe Bate's story in the second decade of the twenty-first century, more detail has been added as a result of further research – some of which has been the result of new research resources becoming available via the Internet. Meanwhile what could happen if I returned to the pages of World's Fair?

After all this, it has now become clear that Joe Bate provided the outline story of his life at least twice within the pages of World's Fair, but, of course, I missed them because they were not about a man with a surname beginning with "T".

Ironically Joe appeared twice on the front page of World's Fair without me realising it! One occasion was in 1914 while he was still based in Hinckley. The second occasion was on 25th July 1925 in the midst of his time spent travelling the "Kitty de Smilo" show. On this second occasion he obviously captured the imagination of someone writing for World's Fair and a lengthy item appeared on page 13 of the paper headlined: "The Varieties of a Showman's Life". Unfortunately this item appears anonymously, but may have been generated from an outline supplied by Joe himself.

Below: A very grainy photograph provides us with a wonderful image of Joe and Kitty setting off on tour with the "La Smilo" show – from a photo reproduced in World's Fair.

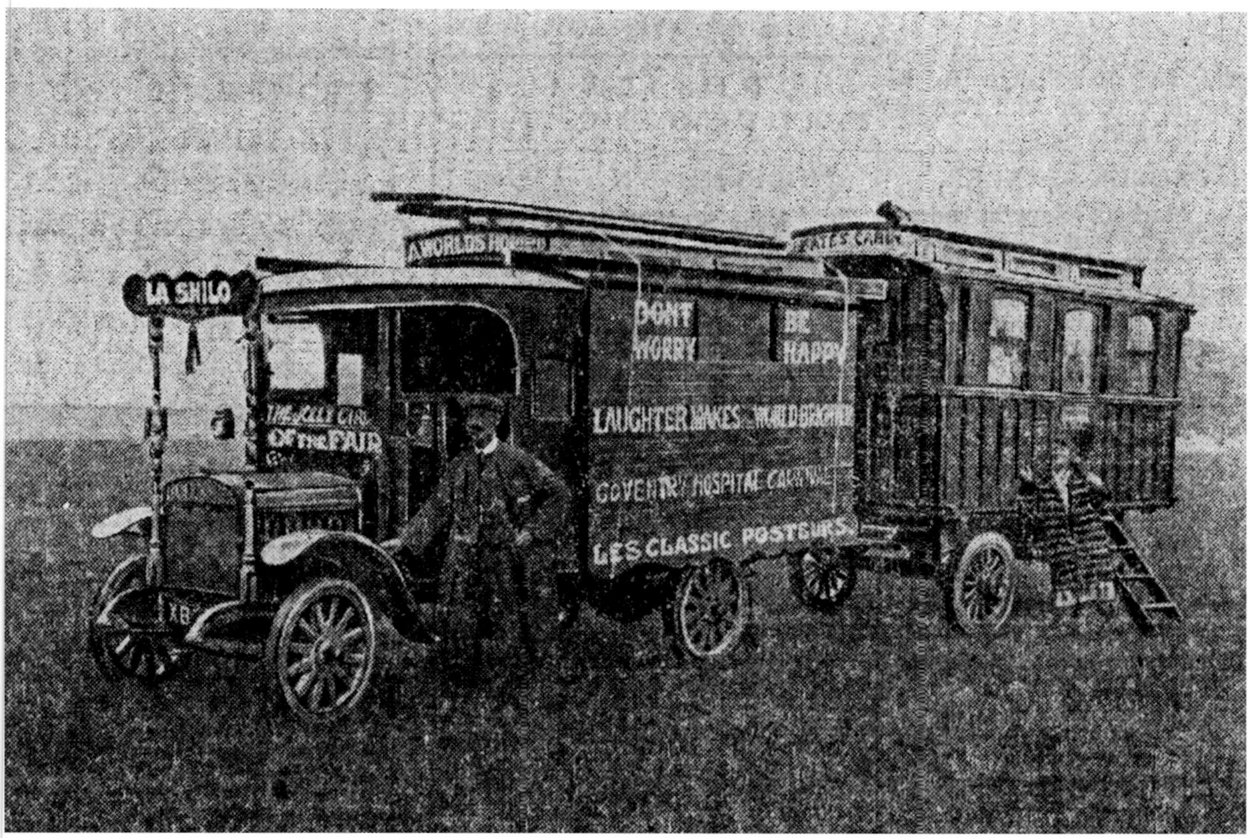

After praising the turn-out of Joe's transport and show it moves into biographical mode and goes back to the beginnings of the story at the Tipton Wakes of 1887. Much of the detail provided in this account has been integrated with the above narrative, but overwhelmingly it presents a picture of a restless figure who seldom stayed in one place for very long, summed up in the sentence, "Joe has tried to settle several times but he could not."

The article concludes: *"Up to the present date this gives us a brief idea of the varied and precarious life of a showman, which is always full of grit and go, overcoming all sorts of difficulties, facing and struggling through hard times. Mr. Joe Bate has three sons and three daughters but none care to follow the precarious calling of Showlife, so Joe has not overcrowded the fairgrounds in any form, but is popular in most of them."*

(The writer was possibly ignorant of Joe's son, Cecil's, participation in the fairground world as a driver for Pat Collins.)

The other occasion in which Joe's biography was covered in World's Fair came six years later when Joe had "settled" after all. In Worlds Fair of 7th March 1931 there is a headline proclaiming, *"Joe Bate 'settles down'"* and subtitled, *"But still entertains the kiddies"*.

The article goes on to say:

"The retirement of a showman is a curious thing. Consider Joe Bate who has been on the road for forty years. He says he has 'settled down' only in the sense that he stays in one place. He lives at Hill Top, West Bromwich, in the caravan that has served him for so long, and he spends his time providing all sorts of entertainment for the kiddies of the district. His heart is in the work he has known all his life.

Born in Tipton, fifty six years ago, he had his own show in 1892, and joined the travelling circus in the following year as a musical clown. In this capacity he travelled all over England, Wales and part of Scotland and came into contact with many famous show people of bygone days – good old Dan Leno, the inimitable Vesta Tilley, who once nursed his baby daughter – and the temperamental Violet Friend who used to sack him every night when he was the manager of a theatre of which she was part-owner.

After extensive touring he has come back to the district of his birth. Although he was born in a house, you can wager he will die in a caravan."

Below: Kitty and her show.

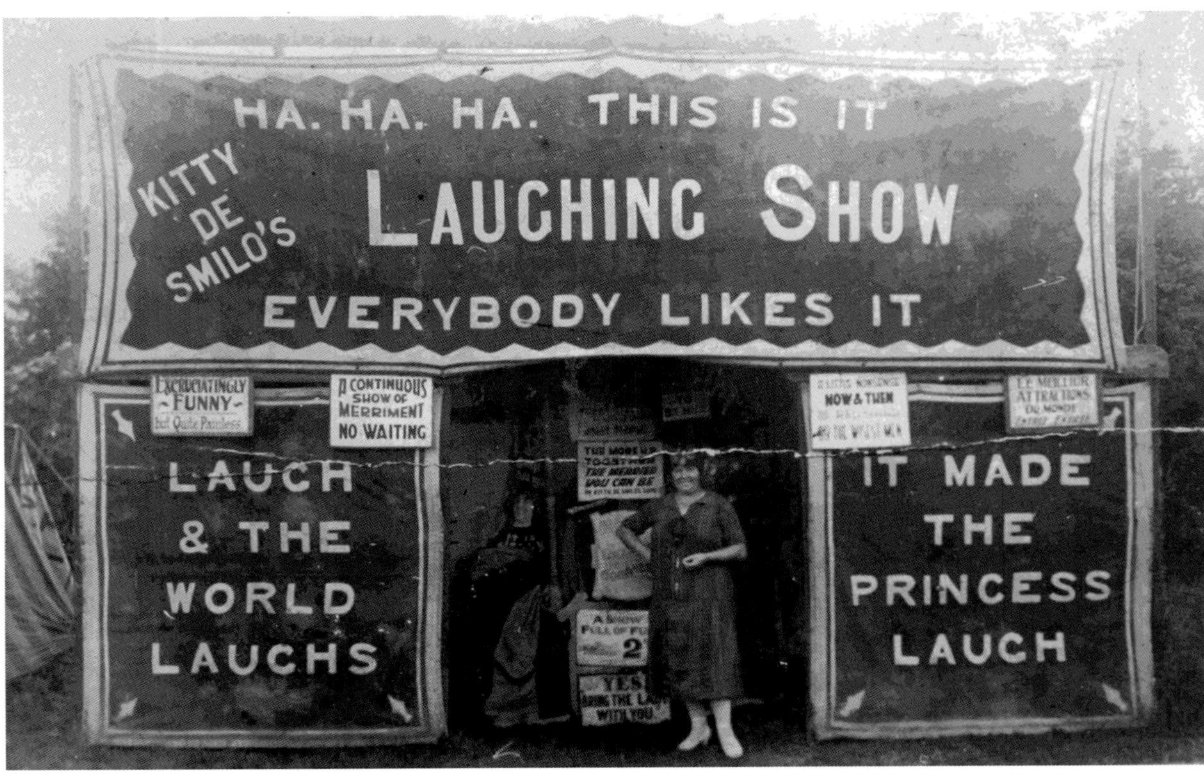

Chapter 4

More than a few long shots

Southdown

Southdown: The Fairground Chronicler

One might have thought that my obsession with the identity and life story of JBT was enough to sustain my interest in such things, but when reading those pages of old World's Fairs, one notices that JBT was not the only correspondent from the West Midlands to chronicle the local fairground and circus on a fairly regular basis. Even before JBT's reports begin, and long after they cease, another writer with a mysterious non-de-plume was producing work in the same vein. I refer to "Southdown".

Southdown's work has some similarities with JBT's: it often includes reminiscences that take the reader back to far-off times, and if often has a slightly quirky view of the world it describes. The texts describe fairs, circuses, variety theatre, carnivals, flower shows and fetes. The memories recalled often involve bioscope shows, marionettes and turn-of -the -century personalities. The writer also frequently offers his opinions and gives advice!

One thing that becomes obvious as one reads the Southdown contributions to World's Fair: the writer seems to live some kind of dual existence – one based on Cannock and the other based on the Sussex coast!

The latter obviously led to the non-de-plume. The name, "Southdown", immediately made me think of the Brighton-based bus company and my own childhood memories of buses painted in a luxurious livery of two tone green. When he writes about his South Coast travels it convinced me that he must have been a bus conductor, on the other hand some of his reminiscences made feel he had been a projectionist. It was easy to become interested in finding out who he was and how his life had gone.

It didn't take too long to put two and two together and work out that his real name was Arthur Sellman, and when not calling himself "Southdown", he was sometimes "APS" and sometimes Arthur Fay. I guess I knew all that at least twenty years ago but that is where I remained stuck. I did talk to other fairground enthusiasts, including one or two who had corresponded with Arthur Sellman many years ago, but they were unable to tell much more about him. (The enthusiasts include the late Fred Richardson whom I knew quite well. He had corresponded with Arthur and exchanged Christmas cards etc., and was convinced that they had met – but could not recall anything!) All this added to the sense of mystery surrounding him, and increased my curiosity. I often wondered what Arthur Sellman looked like, and how various elements of his life, as revealed in his writings, tied together.

Over the years small snippets of information emerged which enabled me to record some details of his life, for example his birth was located in the Somerset House indexes, and his date and place of death were revealed, but I did not know whether he had ever married let alone had any children. I produced an article for Platform, the quarterly magazine of the Fairground Society, in which I assembled everything I knew at the time and presented extracts from some his World's Fair writing. It was serialised over three issues of the magazine and lived in hope that it would stimulate a readers to share any information they might have, and might produce some more clues that would help create a biography. However, the articles produced no response.

A sudden leap forward was made when it became possible to look at the 1939 mini census via the Internet. Arthur was listed at a Cannock address and suddenly it was revealed that he had married and that he had a daughter. A quick look through the death indexes revealed that his widow, Elizabeth, died in Hove in 1991. This new information made me feel that there was still some hope that one day more biographical information about Southdown might emerge.

Once embarked on this project, I contacted the Brighton & Hove Argus and asked if any its readers could help me locate and contact any descendants of Arthur or Elizabeth Sellman. I did this without any great hope of success, but luckily my request in The Argus was spotted by Laura King. Laura is the daughter of Margaret Gunn-King who is Arthur's cousin. With the help of these contacts I was soon in touch with Arthur's grand-daughters: Jenny and Susan! A meeting was arranged with Jenny who had become custodian of a "Southdown Archive". To actually see a photograph of Arthur after years of wondering who he was and whether I would ever have an idea of what he looked like was a magical moment.

The Family Tree:

Arthur Sellman = Mary Margaret Cope (married 1890)
(1866 – 1900) (4th July 1865 – 1941)

Arthur Percival Sellman "SOUTHDOWN"
b. 1st April 1891
d. 18th October 1970
married Elizabeth Evans on 11th Nov 1917
b. 1897, d.1991

Amy Violet Sellman
b. 28th May 1897
d. March 1988
married John Williams

Margaret Doreen Sellman
b. 24th March 1920, d. August 2006
Doreen married Ray Harris on 26th Feb 1944

Barbara Mary (b.26th Jan 1934)

Jenny Harris
b. May 1947

Susan Harris
b. Sept. 1948

Right: Arthur Sellman, known to readers of World's Fair as "Southdown". His grand-daughters remember him in a brown suit and spotted tie! All the family photographs in this chapter have been made available by Jenny Hall who has maintained an archive relating to her grandfather's life.

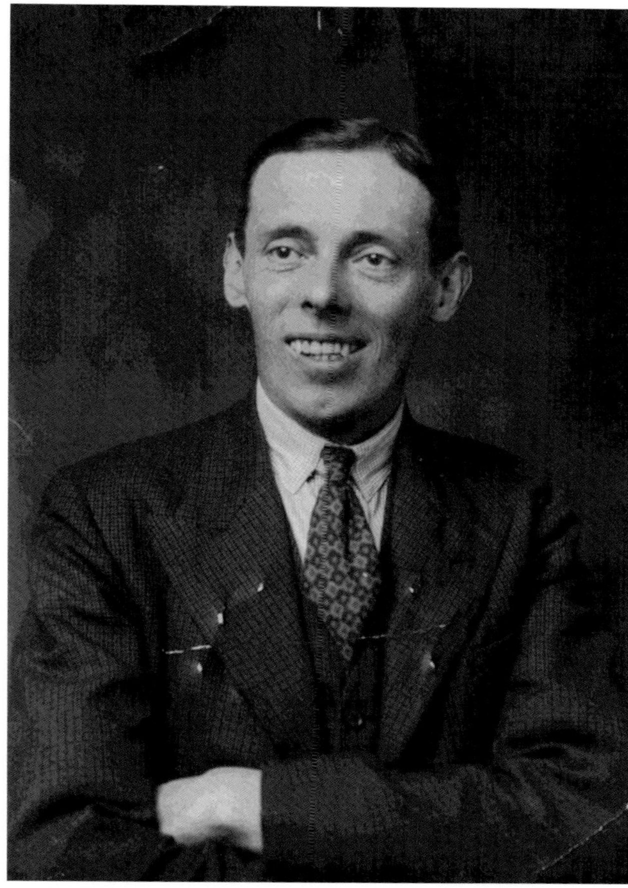

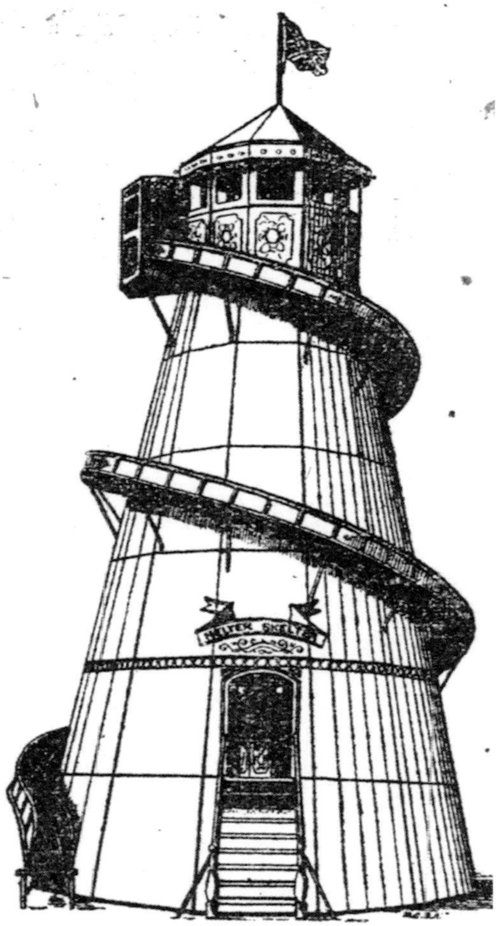

A poor quality picture of Arthur as a young lad. It is interesting in the context of this book as Arthur was later able to use memories from his early life to pass on first hand observations based on what he had seen in the 1890s and early 1900s. He must have developed his interest in showland at an early age.

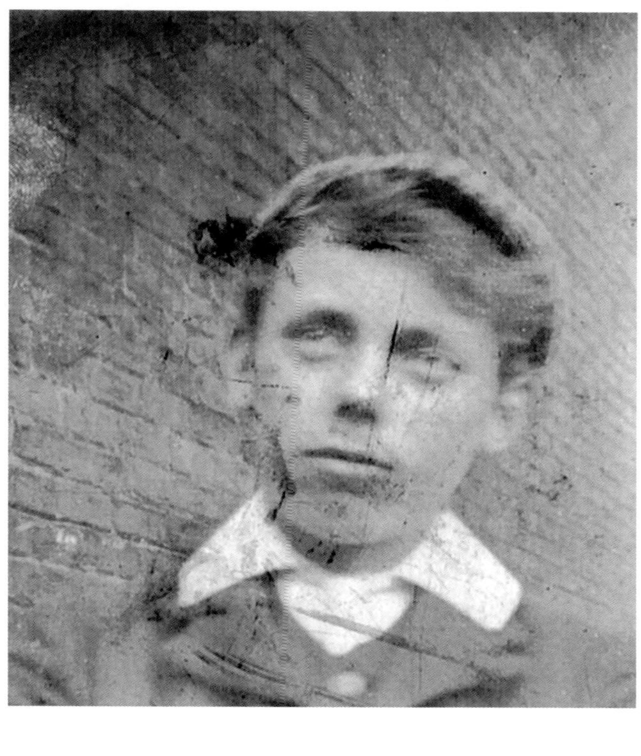

The Biography:

Southdown's story begins in the small Staffordshire town of Cannock. Cannock was more or less equidistant from Walsall, Wolverhampton, Lichfield and Stafford and developed as a market town like its neighbours. Industry came in the mid nineteenth century onwards as a result of exploiting the mineral resources: coal, for industrial and domestic use, and clay, for brick and tile manufacture. The iron-trades were represented by modest edge-tool manufacturing. The canals, and then the railways, put Cannock "on the map", and made it accessible, although it had traditionally enjoyed proximity to the old Roman Road route from London to Chester (The "A5").

Arthur Sellman had the good fortune to be born just before the compilation of the 1891 Census and thus is immortalised at the age of "five days old" in that document. He was born on 1st April 1891 at 28 Mill Street, Cannock. His father, also named Arthur claimed to have been born in Cannock, and Mary claimed to have come from Penkridge, a few miles from Cannock. (Arthur Snr. had married Mary Ann Cope in 1890 – a year before young Arthur's birth.) Arthur Snr. states his occupation to be "Undertaker's Assistant" in the 1891 census which leads us to think he was related to the Sellman family that became well-known funeral directors in the town of Cannock. Arthur Snr was the son of Joseph and Sarah Ann Sellman. Joseph stated in the 1881 census that he was a "Cab Proprietor and Undertaker". The link with the funeral directing business is interesting as the family firm is still operating today. On the firm's website we are told it was founded by an Alfred John Sellman in 1870. Unfortunately I have not been able to locate Alfred John Sellman in the census records or substantiate a connection with Arthur's family – his father's occupation as stated in the 1881 census seems the only suggestion of a link.

Every story needs an exciting twist at the very beginning and in this case we find that the young Arthur is actually listed as "Alonzo" – a name that possibly suggested an interesting future. Also listed as residents of the 28 Mill Street household are Lizzie Sellman, Arthur Senior's sister, and also Lucy Cope, his sister-in-law, who later plays an important part in our story. The use of the name "Alonzo" is so far unexplained. It is the kind of name that might have been encountered in a show or a circus but there is no evidence to suggest that Arthur's parents were interested in such things. Family tradition has it that Arthur's interest in "show-business" was not encouraged.

Arthur was born with a mal-formed foot and an unsuccessful operation on this resulted in a "club foot" which gave him a pronounced limp for the rest of his life. He was self-conscious about this, did not like it mentioned, and did what he could to ignore it. It certainly did not prevent him walking great distances in pursuit of his interests.

Arthurs' father died in the Spring of 1900 in his early thirties. It appears that this was followed by the family moving to 214 Price Street in Cannock, to some rooms that may have been above a wine shop. Therefore we find them at this address in the 1901 Census, Arthur and his mother having been joined by Arthur's sister Amy, who had been born in the Spring of 1897. Arthur is "Percival Arthur" as all signs of "Alonzo" have disappeared! His first names appear in different order in different records, but we know he wasn't very fond of the name "Percival". Two doors away from the Sellmans in 1901 we find twenty six year old Alfred Sellman and his wife Sarah. Alfred is listed as a "coachman and public worker", with the word "groom" crossed out, but this proximity of the two Sellman households may be another indication of a relationship between Arthur's family and the family of Cannock based funeral directors. In the 1900s it seems that Arthur began working with the horses of the funeral business. At the same time he was developing interests that would shape the rest of his life. The 1896 Staffordshire Kelly's Directory lists two Sellmans in its business register covering Cannock: John Sellman who is a "cab proprietor and hairdresser", and Joseph Sellman who is "Cab proprietor and Undertaker".

It seems that Arthur was fond of his sister Amy and he wrote to her regularly once their lives went in different directions. Amy stayed in Cannock and married a local collier: John Williams, early in 1919. Their daughter, Barbara, is alive at the time of writing and still lives in the area.

So – Arthur and Amy grew up in Cannock in the 1890s and on into the twentieth century. It is a good idea to remember that Arthur was only nine in 1900 – this is important when we look at the way his writings later explore memories of the shows, and fairground rides etc. of that period. Shows had once been the major attraction of fairs, hence the people who populate the fairground are called "showmen", but from the 1870s onwards riding machines had become the dominant feature of the fair, supported by games in the side stalls and round stalls. The shows enjoyed a complicated ancestry which takes us back to the days of "portable theatres", travelling menageries, waxworks and peep-shows. Now, in the twenty-first century, is it is difficult to imagine the impact of entertainment such as the Ghost Shows of the 1880s, even if we happen to have heard of them, but Arthur grew up at a time when "shows" were still popular. As Arthur Sellman grows up a new kind of show emerges: the "bioscope".

Cinematography, the art of projecting a moving image on a large screen before an audience, became a reality in late 1895 when invented and demonstrated by the Lumiere Brothers in Paris. They came to London in February 1896 and introduced this new technological wonder to an English audience. During the next few months British inventors duplicated the Lumiere Brothers' success, and almost immediately British showmen began to see its possibilities. At the "World's Fair" at The Agricultural Hall, Islington, in January 1897 Randall Williams, an ex Ghost Show proprietor, demonstrated that cinematography could thrive in the form of a fairground show. The following month his show opened at Kings Lynn Mart – the fair usually considered to be the one which opens the British travelling fairground season. At first no-one was sure what to call this new show but later they became generically known as "bioscopes". Just over a century later there are few devoted historians whose aim is to preserve what can be found out about these shows. Their history is not very well documented, so imagine how interesting it might be to come across the writings of people like Arthur Sellman who was around at the time.

Riding equipment on fairgrounds had developed enormously in the second half of the nineteenth century and large machines were steam-powered. Then came "electricity", first to provide light and then provide power as the 1890s progressed. Arthur was also a witness to this, and everything he witnessed had to be within the possibilities imposed by growing up in Cannock, and within the financial constraints of the world in he which grew up. Sometimes the list of the shows that Arthur seemed to recall looks too vast to be feasible, nor do we wholly understand what drew him to them, but nevertheless his encyclopaedic knowledge cannot fail to impress us.

Walsall-based Pat Collins was the foremost showman in the area in the 1890s and 1900s, and Arthur saw his machines and bioscope shows in Cannock, and sometimes in other towns such as Wolverhampton. The Cannock Chase towns were also much visited by other bioscopes, circuses, and shows. Arthur seemed to know everyone involved, and by his teens may have assisted them in any way he could, although he never claims to have been regularly employed by them. Let us look at the way in which information about the shows can be interwoven into our quest to understand the world in which Arthur grows up.

In Arthur Sellman's book, "Bioscope Shows and Their Engines", published in 1966, he writes: *"I remember a cinematograph show known as Mrs. C. Weir's Electric Chronograph Empire being in Chadsmoor in 1906. The high winds prevented the show from opening one night because it was found quite impossible to get the canvass roof off the booth. The two following evenings, with high winds still continuing, the exhibition opened, but minus the top canvas, and managed to get two full houses. The only trouble was, quite a lot of smoke came from the traction engine that stood alongside the show, generating electric light, and was blown across the moving picture, which somewhat obscured the view."*

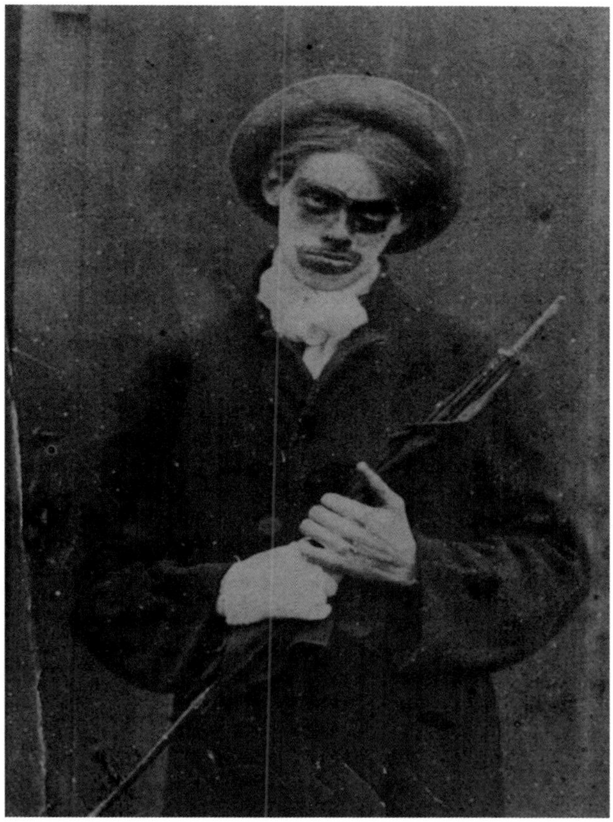

Young Arthur Sellman as "Arty", the clown. Unfortunately we do not know if Arthur, as seen here, is just "dressing-up" or whether he was making an early appearance in a professional show, as suggested by his description in the 1911 census.

Mrs. Weir was based at Burton-on-Trent and had been involved with bioscope shows since they began in 1897. Records exist of her appearance at the Lichfield Bower Fair of 1905, an indication that she regularly ventured into this part of Staffordshire. The engine mentioned by Arthur was "The Major", a Burrell engine supplied to Mrs. Weir in 1906. When she gave up the bioscope the engine was sold to Pat Collins and she "diversified" into other areas of fairground work. Arthur was fifteen when this event took place in Chadsmoor, just down the road from his home in Cannock. Clara Weir had lost her husband, Luke, in 1897 and was thus travelling in her own name. She died in Burton as late as 1929.

Having written about high winds, Arthur Sellman is reminded of a memory of Annie Holland's "Palace of Light". He recalls a rough night in February 1912 when the show had stood in the football field in Hednesford:

"The show was in total darkness and I was in conversation with one of Mrs. Holland's sons near the entrance to the ground. Suddenly a sheet of flame shot high into the air from the rear of the show booth, and we saw the canvas ablaze. Fanned by the high wind, the flames soon spread along the entire roof of the show, with blazing pieces of the canvas falling into the auditorium to ignite the inside linings, the seats and the massive gold carved work that formed the proscenium surrounding the screen. On the ground not a drop of water was to be found, but in a matter of moments, men, women and children were racing with buckets, baths and bowls from the row of small houses standing opposite. Meanwhile the fire brigade had been summoned, but all to no avail, and in twenty minutes the show booth was burned almost to the ground.

It was only through Mr. Rowland Barton, the proprietor of the nearby rolling skating rink, that the show's ornate front and beautiful Gavioli organ were saved. I lost quite a lot of personal belongings including a new fur-lined overcoat and the whole contents of a travelling hamper. The cause of the fire was thought to be a spark of burning soot from the traction engine's chimney..."

Annie Holland (1844 – 1924), like Clara Weir, was a widow, but bioscope operation must have been in her genes as she was the sister of Captain Payne who also presented an impressive bioscope show. She was assisted by her sons, one of which was the show's projectionist – perhaps suggesting that Arthur was not with the show on that occasion in that capacity. This fire was not the end of her career as the show's remains were taken to Messrs Orton, Sons and Spooner at Burton-on-Trent and were added to parts of Edwin Lawrence's show to create a new one.

Below: Annie Holland's "Palace of Light", which burnt down on 10th February 1912 at Hednesford. Arthur lost some of his belongings as a result of the fire suggesting that he may have been travelling with the show. (Stephen Smith Collection)

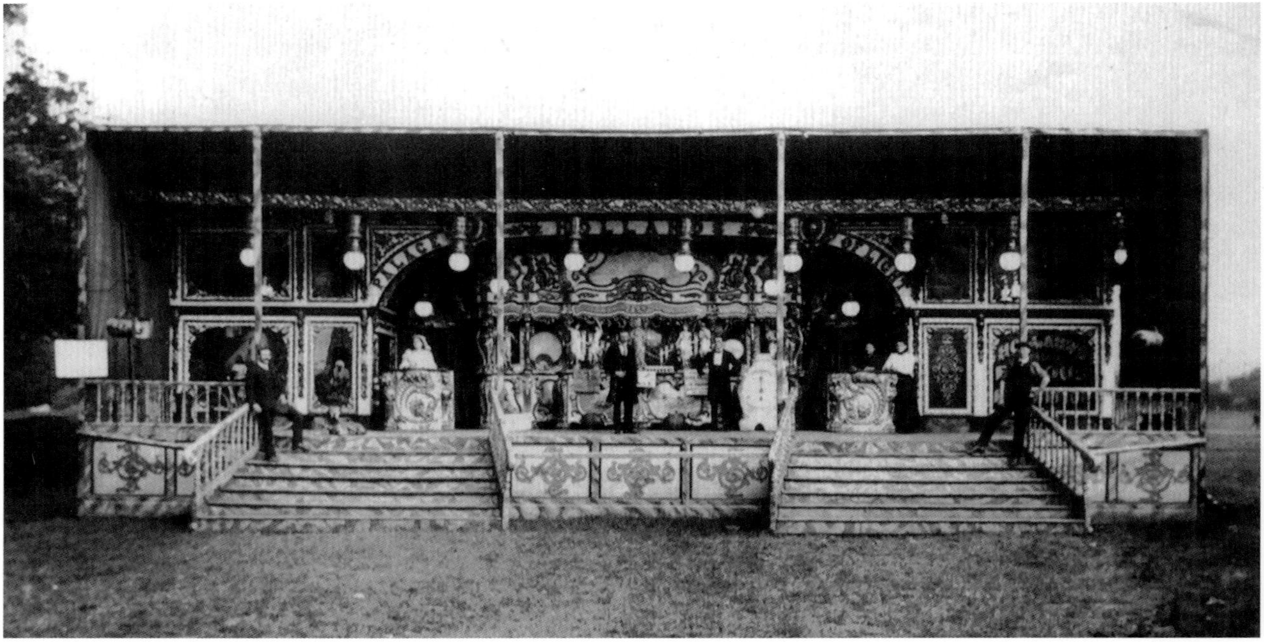

Arthur Sellman also provides an un-dated account of seeing Pat Collins' first "Wonderland" show: *"I first saw this show when it was on a visit to Wolverhampton, in St. Peter's Square. On the front, standing in the centre of the stage was a large carved and gilded clock with wooden figures. Mounted on top of which was a large card printed with the words 'Collins' next Electrical Fireworks Display' with the hand set for a time when the big arc lamps hanging from the front rail of the show would be switched off and thousands of coloured lamps set round the massive carved work adorning the front would be brought into play."*

Later we will look at how many of these memories contributed to his writing which regularly appeared in "World's Fair", even if at the time he did not aspire to be a writer. In his teens he may have aspired to become a projectionist, or even more ambitiously to become an artist appearing in a show. A photograph exists of him as a fourteen-year-old made up as "Arty" the clown – was this just "dressing up" or was he taking part in a show? There is one reference to him being the "lecturer" in a bioscope show, introducing the films to an exuberant audience, but such a role demands a confidence that Arthur may not have possessed.

In the 1911 Census, the twenty-year-old Arthur Sellman appears in lodgings in Rugby, claiming his occupation is "circus artiste". A surviving postcard written to his mother a month later was posted from Metheringham, near Gainsborough, in Lincolnshire. Is this proof that he was travelling with a show during that period? It looks as if he was back in Cannock in 1912 because we know of his encounter with Annie Holland's show described above, and he appears in a family photo of 1912 vintage. Years later D. Taylor writes in the World's Fair about Arthur's life in the period just before the First World War, as part of a tribute to him after his death. He says, *"As a young man Arthur travelled the fairgrounds widely... He was also connected with the circus and did much advance work. He was engaged in puppet and marionette shows, in connection with which he made his own figures. At the outbreak of the 1914 war Arthur was entertaining the troops in Norfolk."*

Below: Edwin Lawrence's "King of Humanities" show as it was in 1904. It had been used for marionette shows, cinematograph presentation and variety acts. Most of the show was destroyed in a road accident is September 1906 but its replacement later provided parts for rebuilding Annie Holland's show in 1912.

(Collection of Stephen Smith)

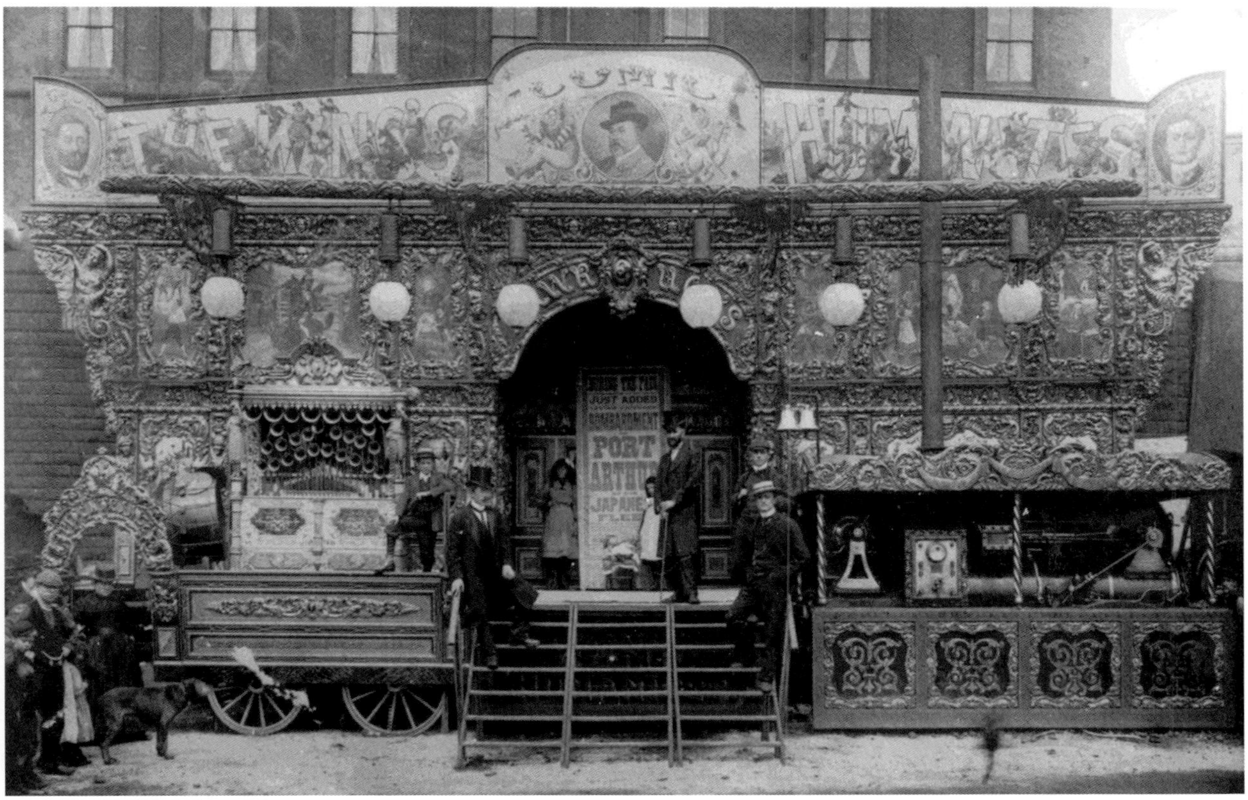

The First World War and after

Arthur's disability seemed to exclude him from joining the services during the First World War. At that time or soon afterwards he appears to have managed the Variety Cinema in Rugeley, and, most importantly he gets married. (The Variety Cinema in Rugeley may have been Johnson's portable theatre that had "settled" in Rugeley according to Southdown in some comments made in Worlds Fair on.)

On 11th November 1917 Arthur married Elizabeth Evans at St. Luke's Church, Cannock. He was 26, she was 20, and she came from Lancashire. On the marriage certificate Arthur is described as a "cinematograph operator". The Lancashire connection may indicate that Arthur was working there at the time and this theory is supported by the fact that when their daughter Margaret Doreen is born on 24th March 1920 their address is 27 Rydal Street, Newton-in-Makerfield, near Warrington, and Arthur's occupation is again described as "Bioscope operator at cinema".

The cinema in which Arthur was working as a projectionist was probably the Hippodrome – opened by Harry Kemp in November 1910. It was a wood and corrugated iron structure of the type erected by ex-bioscope proprietors after the Kinematograph Act had come into force. (See "A Few Long Shots" of 10th October 1931.) The building was destroyed by fire on the afternoon of 29th August 1929, and was not rebuilt. The next important step in Arthur's story, of which we have any evidence, is the family's move to Brighton.

This must have happened by the early or mid-1920s and was possibly the result of several factors. Firstly, Arthur's cousin Lucy Cope had already moved to Brighton and therefore Arthur may have been familiar with the town. Secondly, Arthur and Elizabeth were anxious to send their daughter to private school and there may have been one in Brighton (Ellington House) which they liked. Arthur was always very protective of his daughter, and possibly had not enjoyed his own contact with schooling in the public sector. And lastly of course there is the question of earning a living. This was solved by Arthur finding a job at The Princes in Brighton. He was involved in both projection and management at this cinema, and probably stayed there for up to thirteen years. At some point during these times Arthur became a regular contributor to World's Fair, the weekly newspaper of the fairground and circus world.

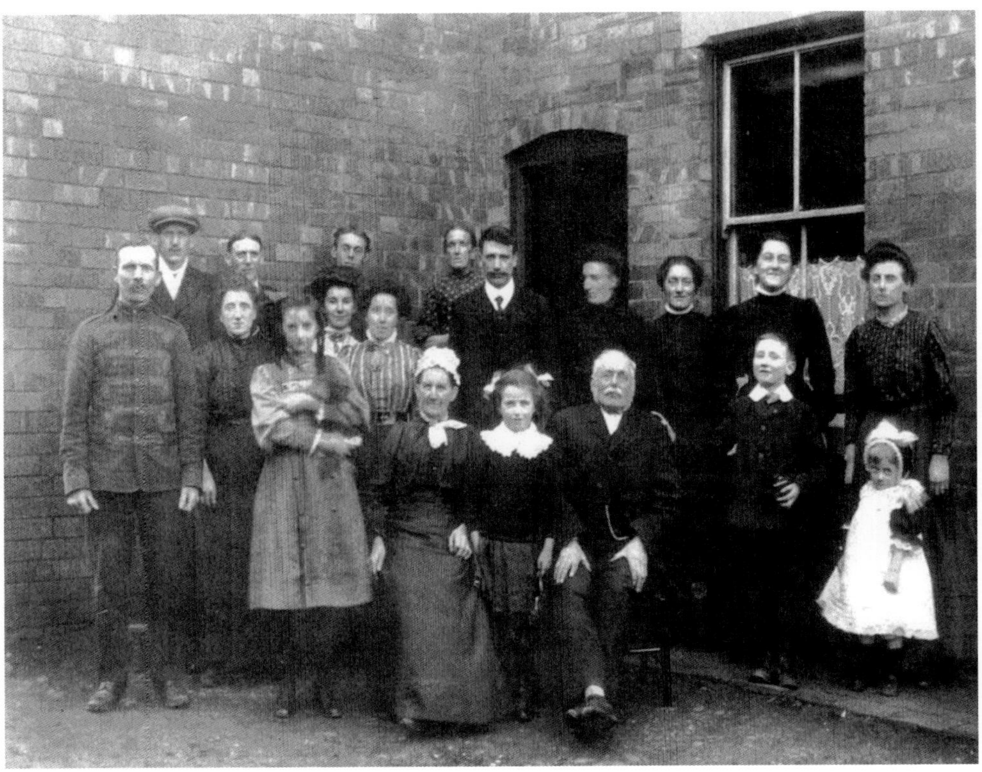

The Sellman Family in Mill Street, Cannock in 1912. Arthur is third from the left in the back row. Arthur's mother, Mary is fourth from right, centre row. Arthur's father, Joseph, is not in the picture but his parents dominate the front row. In the centre is Gwennie Sellman who later ran the famous Cannock funeral business and on the right is Lucy Cope who led the way to Brighton!

Arthur becomes a contributor to Worlds Fair

In its obituary for Arthur Sellman, the World's Fair suggested that he had been writing for the paper since 1914 and had used various aliases: "King Pole", "Scout", "APS" and "Southdown". This made me look back through copies of World's Fair to find evidence of this. I have not yet found any articles written by "King Pole". As a king pole is used to hold up the Big Top, it would seem such articles might have been concerned with circus matters, but the only references to the circus world that I have seen from the pen of Arthur Sellman came in the post-1930 period under his regular title: "A Few Long Shots".

Reading many copies of "World's Fair" induces a kind of blindness so I would only tentatively suggest that I have found Arthur's first contribution. In the paper issued on 8th December 1923 an article appears entitled "Progress and Change" by "APS". Until I find something earlier, I will consider this to be his debut. It takes about two and a half columns to discuss the outline of twentieth century fairground history and offer some general inconclusive thoughts on the current state of affairs. Rather sadly I have to admit it is not a very audacious start to his journalistic career, but it does establish what we can expect from Arthur in subsequent articles, and some features of his writing can be explained. For example: World's Fair paid by the column inch therefore there was no incentive to be concise – rambling was financially rewarded. Secondly it was difficult to avoid treading on the toes of other contributors. Someone was already reporting on West Midlands fairs (W.S. Sorrell) and some contributors such as Harry Wilding and H.M Jay had been writing for the paper for a long time and had their own subject areas "sewn-up".

Obviously Arthur's article was satisfactory as far as the editor of World's Fair was concerned and as 1924 unfolded we see a steady stream of articles appearing. On 19th January 1924 he wrote about the importance of advertising and this becomes one of his most repeated themes, a week later he wrote about those who "dabbled" with the fairground world and therefore were not properly "professional". On 23rd February he contributes a very general overview of the previous year, headed simply, "1923", concluding that the absence of "shows" is to be regretted. All these articles are credited to "APS". Interestingly the articles are more or less repeated in early 1925, but this time credited to "Southdown".

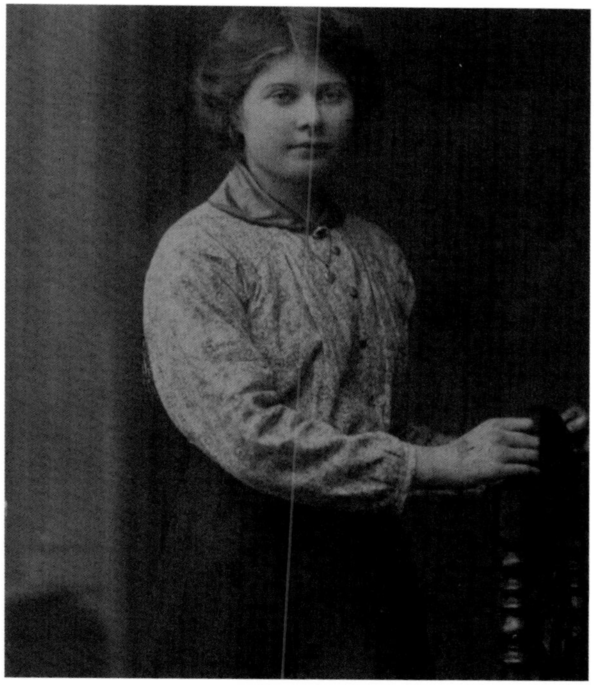

Above: Elizabeth Evans, whom Arthur married in November 1917. She later became his proof-reader! Below: The Princes Cinema, Brighton, where Arthur worked for thirteen years. (CTA Archives)

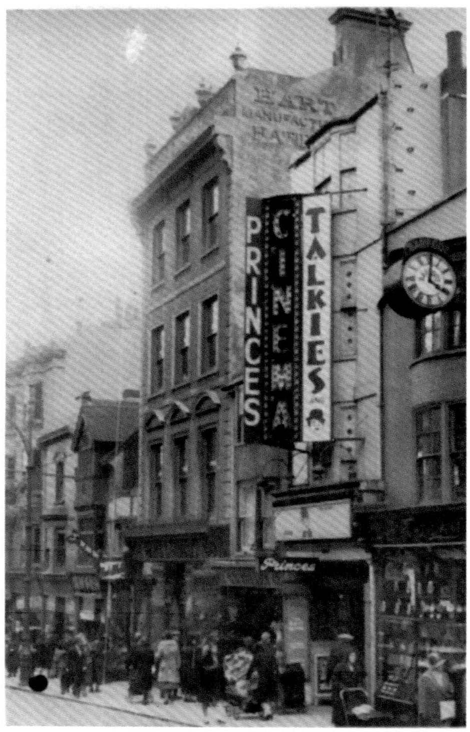

I think Arthur's writing is at its best when he is passing on experience and information rather than offering large doses of advice and opinion. Like "JBT", he becomes really interesting when he provides a living link to a past that is now beyond our living memory. Both men actually knew the shows and riding equipment we can only know as names, some photographs and a few facts. It is interesting therefore to see Arthur listing his "top one hundred shows of all time" in an article published 0n 28th February 1925, still credited to "APS". His list is as follows: Mrs. A. Holland's 'Palace of Light', Pat Collins' 'Wonderland', Edwin Lawrence's show, Mrs. Biddall's 'Ghost Illusion', Horace Holloway's 'Ghost Show', Wall's 'Ghost Show', Hayes' 'Ghost Show', the bioscopes of James Crighton, Randall Williams, Sophie Shepherd, Charles Farrell and Captain Payne, at which point he gives up, simply adding, *"I could go on...."*

We have to remind ourselves that Arthur was born in 1891 and was therefore possibly too young to have seen all these shows in operation, particularly when appearing as 'Ghost Shows'. However his writings seem to show that as a teenager he became well acquainted with the bioscopes. Eventually he must have realised that it was worth putting some of this experience into words and hence the subject matter of his two later books. But back in the 1920s, when memories would have been fresher, he generally filled his columns with opinions!

On 14th March 1925 he bemoans the Government's lack of showmanship in the way in which the six week Wembley Empire Exhibition Fair was presented, and suggests that cheap rail travel should have made it accessible from the provinces. On 21st March 1925 he tells us, "Showland must have a man at the wheel at Westminster", and praises the work done by Pat Collins during his two year sojourn as an MP. The following week he reviews traffic laws and defends the steam traction engine. In the midst of all this discussion of contemporary issues, his love of the past occasionally bursts through. On 18th April 1925 he tells us, *"Any new and novel ride is, in my own opinion, of no use without a large organ and plenty of light, and carved work – and these things have been conspicuous by their absence on almost every new ride that has come out in recent times."*

A reader named Mr. Haithwaite commented on this and suggested the "Hey Day" was just such a new ride, but Arthur did not respond. (The Hey Day itself went to a permanent site at Belle Vue.) Occasionally Arthur does use his column to respond to things that have happened or been said. For example 0n 16th May 1925 he counters some criticisms he had encountered of the recent fair in Lincoln. Then it's back to endless reminders that it pays to advertise. Later in the year he is advising readers of the dates of local flower shows! (Some of these were of particular interest to Arthur – e.g. in July he discusses the forthcoming flower show in Cannock which the Pat Collins fair will attend.

It is also in July 1925 that Arthur seems to first use the pseudonym "Scout", but I have no idea why that is so. It heads an article on the problems arising from allowing "traders" onto the fairground. He uses the name "Scout" once again in August complaining that there is not enough variety to be found on recent fairgrounds.

Otherwise he continues to be "APS" – when not concerned with Cannock, and when he feels ready to admit to being in Brighton – for example in July 1925 he admits to watching Jack Dempsey boxing in Brighton and finds himself thinking that Dempsey should appear on a fairground boxing booth. For the rest of 1925 all three pen names are used, covering topics such as the need for fairs to clean up after themselves, and a plea that all equipment needed to be bright and clean: not exactly riveting stuff!

Around 1930 Arthur seems to acquire more confidence in his contributions to Worlds Fair, and it was about then that he seems to have identified being a 'journalist' as his occupation. His contributions became weekly and he presents them under the heading "A Few Long Shots" – a heading that he will use for three decades! The vagueness of this title suited the fact that he would write on a huge variety of topics, rather than being a correspondent covering a well-defined region. A number of World's Fair correspondents start to write more reflectively at that time; the paper starts regularly printing a column highlighting the news of twenty years earlier, and even the editor, Frank Mellor, produces a few reminiscence-based items.

This is where Arthur's writing comes into its own, when he uses his recollections to take the reader back to matters already fading from memory. For example, on 5th January 1931 Edwin Lawrence died at Swadlincote. Arthur comments on the news and goes on to say: *"I have had many a chat with Mr. Lawrence and was once his guest for a whole week. As I write I have before me a photograph of his once famous show – Lawrence's Empire Theatre".* He goes on to recall the winter of 1912/13 when the show was presented at Sheffield and was then sold to Annie Holland. Mostly his article is about the arrival of the talkies and the fact that he has noticed many cinemas have put up a notice saying: "Silence please – Talkies"!

A Few Long Shots

In January 1931 Frank Mellor, the editor of World's Fair decided to hold a gathering of World's Fair correspondents, after consulting Arthur Sellman and Edward Graves, the paper's circus correspondent. It was to be held on Monday 19th January at the World's Fair event at the Royal Agricultural Hall, Islington, and would begin with everyone being invited to the afternoon performance of the circus, and that would followed by a formal dinner, with printed menu and a series of toasts. Arthur travelled up to London by train and was met by a fellow correspondent at Victoria and together they made their way to Islington. It seems to have been regarded as a great success although one or two correspondents had to apologise for their absence, including Harry Wilding from Birmingham who was perhaps still embarrassed by his failure to buy John Swallow's elephants. (See the Broncho Bill story.) Possibly Arthur met John Swallow while at the circus, but he does not subsequently mention it. Several speeches were made and it looks as if Arthur was able to thank everyone for their presence and to suggest it should become an annual event.

In his column Arthur writes: *In my opinion it was a wonderful gathering, and that's to say all I met there were a real regular lot of fellows. And as for our chief, he was on fine form.* He returned to the subject on several occasions over the following weeks! Meanwhile Southdown returns to some of his memories, writing at the end of January, *"I can well remember the late Mrs. Weir's big show which toured the Midland counties presenting talking pictures well over twenty years ago at 3d, 2d and 1d for children. The show was called Mrs. C. Weir's Electric Chronograph Empire, and used Gaumont equipment. The trouble was the maintenance of synchronisation between disc and film. The pictures were projected on a translucent screen, permitting the gramophone to talk through the picture. Pictures were mainly of well-known Music Hall stars like Henry Lauder singing 'She is ma' Daisy'. Of course the voice reproduction was not as clear as it is today."*

The Talkies were proving so popular at that time we can hardly be surprised that Southdown discussed them on many occasions, particularly as he had been connected with projecting films himself. There were other new technologies that he found difficult to appreciate, for example discussing recorded music played on the fairground via loudspeakers; he usually reached the conclusion that the fairground organ was the most appropriate way to fill a fairground with a suitable sound.

Another way in which Southdown could start to reminisce and pass on his memories arose when he started to muse on a photograph from his collection. For example, in February 1931 he looks at some pictures, taken at Nottingham Goose Fair before the War, of Pat Collins' No.1 Scenic (The Gordon Bennett Motors) and the No.2 Scenic. He reserves his full appreciation for the No.3 Scenic: *"I recall seeing Pat Collins' new electrically driven No.3 Scenic at Ilkeston. The machine was known as "It" and carried a flag from its centre pole with just those two letters on it. Sure enough it had one of the nicest waterfalls that was ever put on a machine of this class. The decoration was superb with rounding boards painted in the jungle style. It also had a superb organ which was very much responsible for the ride's popularity. I believe Miss Clara Mullett was in charge of the machine and I will take this opportunity of congratulating her on the excellent manner in which she has always presented the enterprise under her management."*

World's Fair readers do write in to Southdown for opinions on such subjects, promoting further recollections, such as those of 30th May 1931: *"A correspondent asks if I can recall one of Pat Collins' famous machines – The Racing Cockerels? I can well remember the machine. It was a sectional set of cockerels and one of the most elaborate machines of its type. It was extensively carved and gilded. It had a beautifully designed centre drum which consisted of carved and gilded heads. The rounding boards, cornice and droppers were amongst the best seen on nay fairground. I believe the lettering read: 'P.Collins, Walsall, Grand Electric Racing Cockerels', the lettering itself was superb, and it had a splendid organ. The last time I saw this famous ride was at Blackheath, having seen it before at Bloxwich, West Bromwich, Oldbury, Wednesbury, Walsall, Burslem and Hanley, and other towns."*

He also takes note of the fact that his fellow correspondent, "Kingsley", writes about Mr. Payne who had once presented a popular portable theatre all over the Midlands. This leads to some correspondence with readers. Southdown adds, *"I saw Payne's Theatre at Rugeley, in the yard of the Shovel Inn, some twenty five years ago when it was one of the finest shows travelling".* He goes on to list the shows of that time which included Holloways (Still running in 1931), Summerville's, Alf Peasnal's, Weight's, Hayes', Johnson's and Bowcott's. Later, in May 1931 he writes about Burnett's Military Exhibition which he saw in Cannock around 1900. He recalls that it stood alongside Kayes' Grand Start Menagerie, Wall's Ghost Illusion, Albert Powell's Peep Show, and John Catrell's show.

He thinks Buff Bill was there, which was probably correct as Buff Bill was Richard Kayes who founded a large fairground dynasty of that name. On another occasion he writes about a photograph of Hull Fair in which sixteen shows stand side by side and this leads into a lament for vanished shows. Maybe even Southdown could not realise how really "vanished" the world of portable theatres and shows would become to those of us inhabiting the twenty-first century!

Sometime Southdown does stumble across genuine news. For example, in March 1931 he comes across work taking place on the construction of a new amusement park in Brighton – *"right on the prom, opposite the new aquarium"*. He interviewed someone from the management of South Coast Entertainments Ltd and was able write about it. Later he went so see the Great Carmo's "Shrine of Mystery" show at a Brighton theatre. He lists all the acts in this show, including a young Max Wall – "the boy with obedient feet" – and re-runs the story of the Great Carmo's crisis of 1930 when his circus tent was destroyed twice in one week while in Birmingham – once destroyed by snow, and then by fire.

Through the 1930s Arthur's writings become prolific and deal with a bewildering number and variety of topics – some of them will be described in the section below. There is a "south coast" bias to what he writes but other parts of the country, particularly the West Midlands, do continue to receive his attention. For some of this time Arthur was not in full-time employment, and was certainly never "well off", but his enthusiasm for his pet interests never waned. At the same time Arthur was a family man, and regularly took Elizabeth and their daughter Doreen to the Hippodrome in Brighton.

When Doreen was ten she found herself at Bramber Castle where Arthur was involved in an exhibition featuring wolves – Doreen helped by selling the tickets. At this event she met Vera and Ray Harris who were performing in Henderson's Circus. Arthur was already acquainted with their father: Frank Harris. The Harris family and the Sellman family became great friends and Doreen and Ray eventually became man and wife. Frank's memories could be used as further material for Arthur's items in World's Fair.

Back in the West Midlands we know that Arthur visited Harry Wilding in Chadsmoor, a village almost adjacent to Cannock, in 1934. The meeting prompted a long article in World's Fair about Harry Wilding and his "Champion Marionette Show". Arthur could provide his own memories of this travelling theatre going back to the 1890s, and the interview provides a lot more information. I also wonder if it kindled Arthur's own interest in marionettes. Could he have even bought one or more of Wilding's puppets? It seems that by the end of the 1930s Arthur was seriously working on putting together a marionette show.

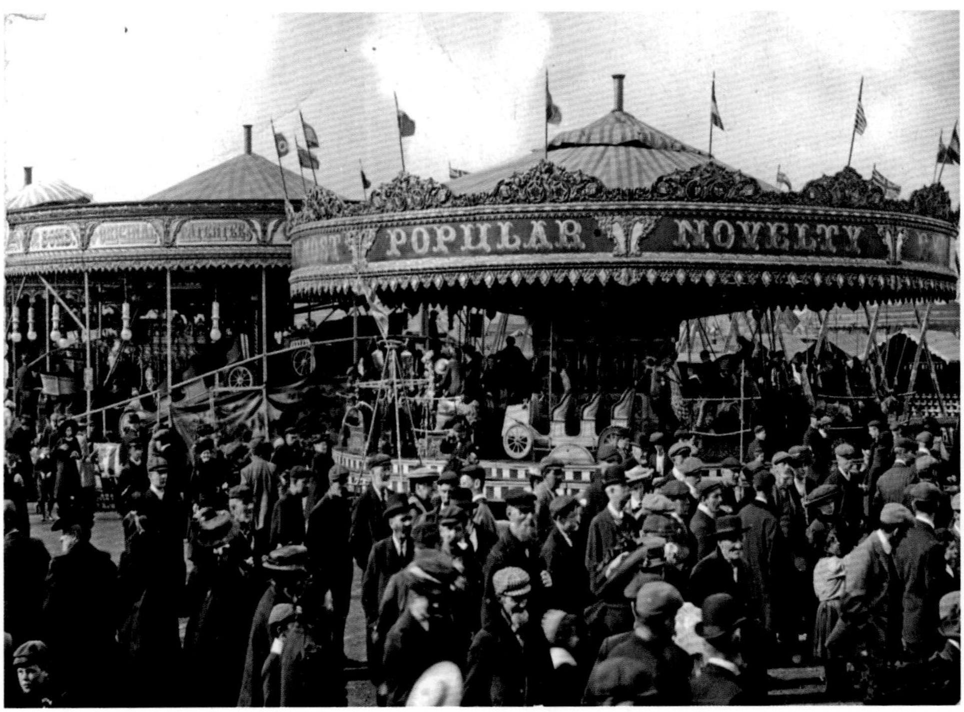

Left: Pat Collins' "Cockerels" surrounded by the crowds at Hull Fair. Arthur recalled admiring this machine at various Black Country locations and happily reminisces about it in World's Fair of 30th May 1931.

(Stephen Smith Collection)

The Second World War.

When the Second World War looked imminent Arthur Sellman decided his wife and family would be safer living away from Brighton on the South Coast. Arthur and Elizabeth went back to Cannock to live near his sister. The quick census taken in 1939 just before the outbreak of war found the Sellmans lodging with Frank and Gwendoline Lees at 30 Price Street, Cannock. (Frank Lees was in the funeral business, as was Hannah Sellman next door at No. 28. (Arthur and Elizabeth may also have lived for some time in sister Amy's home at 33 Girton Road.) In giving an account of his work in this census, Arthur described himself as, "Journalist, partly incapacitated". This phrase gives us a clear picture of how Arthur saw himself. Writing for Worlds Fair had virtually been his only regular income through the 1930s.

Southdown's writings had always focussed on both the South Coast and the West Midlands, but with the move back to wartime Cannock, his work definitely became centred on that town, at least for a while. For example, in April 1943 he comments on Pat Collin's Blackout Fair coming to Cannock – built up on the Brookfield Ground. Shortly afterwards he sees Paulo's Circus on the same site and notes John Swallow's elephants and their part in the show. They were still doing one-night stands and were off to Stafford the next day. He notices how many of the sites used by fairs and circuses in the Cannock area have houses built on them by then. When he returns to the Brookfield site later he finds the Blackout Fair has not moved on, it has simply been dismantled. *"Everything is being repainted in preparation for Easter"*, he writes, *"and the tackle looks as good as it did in pre-war days."* Few writers have recorded the life and times of Pat Collins' Blackout Fairs so this now has some interest. Pat, in his eighties, was determined not to let the war bring his fair to a halt and had two blackout fairs on the road by that time, staffed by elderly members of his workforce and women who were also working twelve hour shifts in munitions work.

Strange as it may seem fairs and circuses did unexpectedly enjoy a surge in business while the war was on, supported by policies like "holidays at home" and "business as usual". Southdown's observations reveal some of the many things that were going on. For example he spots Arthur Joel's Circus on the Big Top site in Birmingham, and a host of other small makeshift circuses appearing across the Midlands. Within a month he sees both the Francis Brothers and Ernest Steel presenting small fairs in Hednesford, and he notes changes to Pat Collins' amusements in Sutton Park. He watches Ringling's Circus and Menagerie in Cannock, and Rosaire's in Shifnal and Walsall. As usual he was surprisingly mobile, but as far as I know he always used public transport.

As the war went on Southdown seems to have roved even further afield from Cannock and reports on things he has seen all over the place. One day he might catch a matinee performance of Robert Gandey's Circus in Halifax, the next he sees Atlas Circus in Wolverhampton, in Brickklin Street, on a site just vacated by Pat Collins' blackout fair!

In December 1943 Pat Collins died and the whole of showland stopped to note the fact. Pages of World's Fair were devoted to epitaphs and details of the huge funeral. I have no idea of whether Arthur attended the funeral but like everyone else he wanted to write about Pat in World's Fair, even when everything had already been said. On 18th December 1943 he writes: *"The passing of Alderman Pat Collins has removed one of the greatest showmen of all time.... My earliest recollections of him go back over forty years to the days when he used to go tober-hunting in a smart gig coupled to a high-stepping cob.... His two organ-fronted cinematograph shows ranked second to none in the kingdom.... I was in Walsall Town Hall in 1922 on the eve of the General Election for the final meeting before he was elected as the town's MP, and we all joined a torch-lit parade in his support."*

But, of course, Southdown's "Long Shots" are interesting not because of comments on the major figures of showland history, but because he was able to write about lesser-known figures. In July 1943 he had commented on the death of John Cordwell – a name now only recognised by enthusiasts of obscure fairground history. *"Nearly forty years ago John Cordwell's Electric Lifeograph was a popular show on many grounds. Mr. Cordwell was among the first showmen to take moving pictures of subjects like the miners leaving the pit. This I well remember as a great draw for his show. He had an engine called "The New King", and had some very good paraders".* (Paraders were the girls who danced on the small stage incorporated into the show-front to draw people to the show.)

One never knows where Arthur's work is likely to pop up! In the Skegness Standard of 11th October 1944, the paper's regular, columnist assuming the name "Old Salt", used his "Skegness Topics" column to discuss the world of bioscopes. This was prompted by something

Arthur had written in World's Fair in which he recalled memories of Edwin Lawrence's bioscope show in Skegness: *"It was a four week visit and was doing badly. In 1910 he* (Edwin Lawrence) *closed it and in the winter of that year it stood on the Cattle Market at Sheffield."* From our point of view it is fascinating to think that Arthur had visited Skegness in 1910, but "Old Salt" was more interested in the mention of Lawrence's show as he had no such memories. (He claimed that bioscope shows had been presented in Skegness by one Fred Clements, who later developed cinema interests in the town.)

The Second World War had several repercussions for the Sellman family. They had to move their furniture into store to cope with the return to Cannock. Eventually they could not keep up the payments involved and they lost everything – another indication of the fragility of Arthur's finances while he focussed on being a journalist. Arthur's daughter Doreen had left school way back in 1934 and had worked in a sweet shop in Brighton called "the Candy Box". In Cannock Doreen found a job at Perks' grocery shop and later worked at GKN's factory on war work. In 1940 she started to write to Ray Harris who was serving with the 7th Armoured Division, better known as "The Desert Rats".

Doreen's pen-friendship developed into romance and in December 1942 Ray suggested they should become engaged to be married. He was still in North Africa, and as well as combat duties had been busy providing entertainment for his fellow troops. His duties took him up through Italy, until, on reaching Naples he was able to sail back to Britain. A wedding opportunity was determined by when Ray could take leave, but on 26th February 1944 Arthur was able to "give away" his daughter Doreen to Lance Corporal Ray Harris at St. Peter's Church in the Preston area of Brighton. After the wedding Ray had to return to his unit to prepare for D Day. It would be the end of 1945 before their life together in Brighton could properly begin. Arthur and Elizabeth also returned permanently to Brighton once the war was truly over – moving into Clifton Street. Arthur continued to write for World's Fair and dreamed of putting on marionette shows.

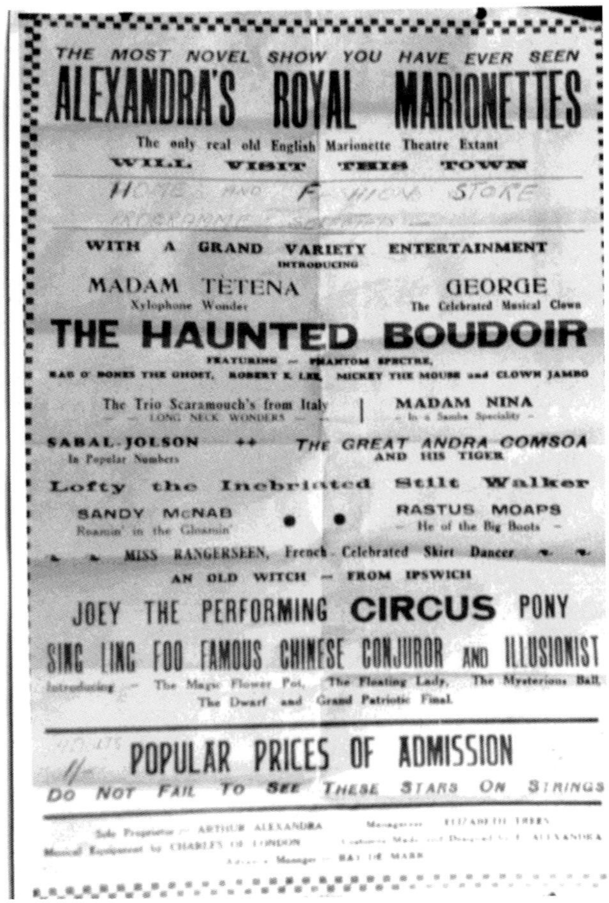

Left: An advertisement for Arthur Sellman's post war venture into the world of marionette shows. The names of the "artistes" were all references to family names, and Arthur's wife, Elizabeth, made all the costumes. Elizabeth also joined Arthur with operating the puppets.
It seems that Arthur may have bought some puppets from Harry Wilding. He met the latter living in semi-retirement at Chadsmoor near Cannock.

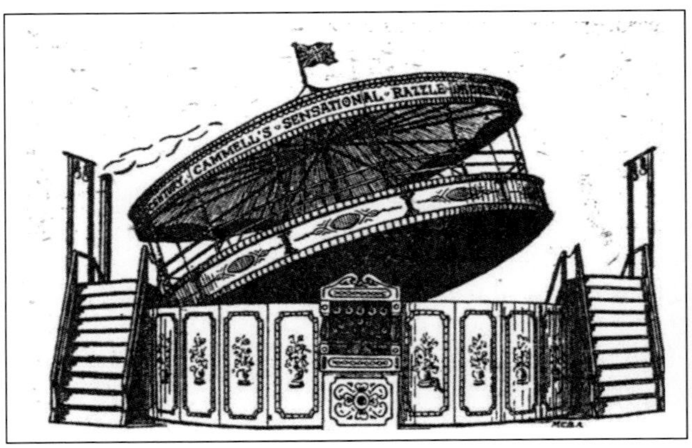

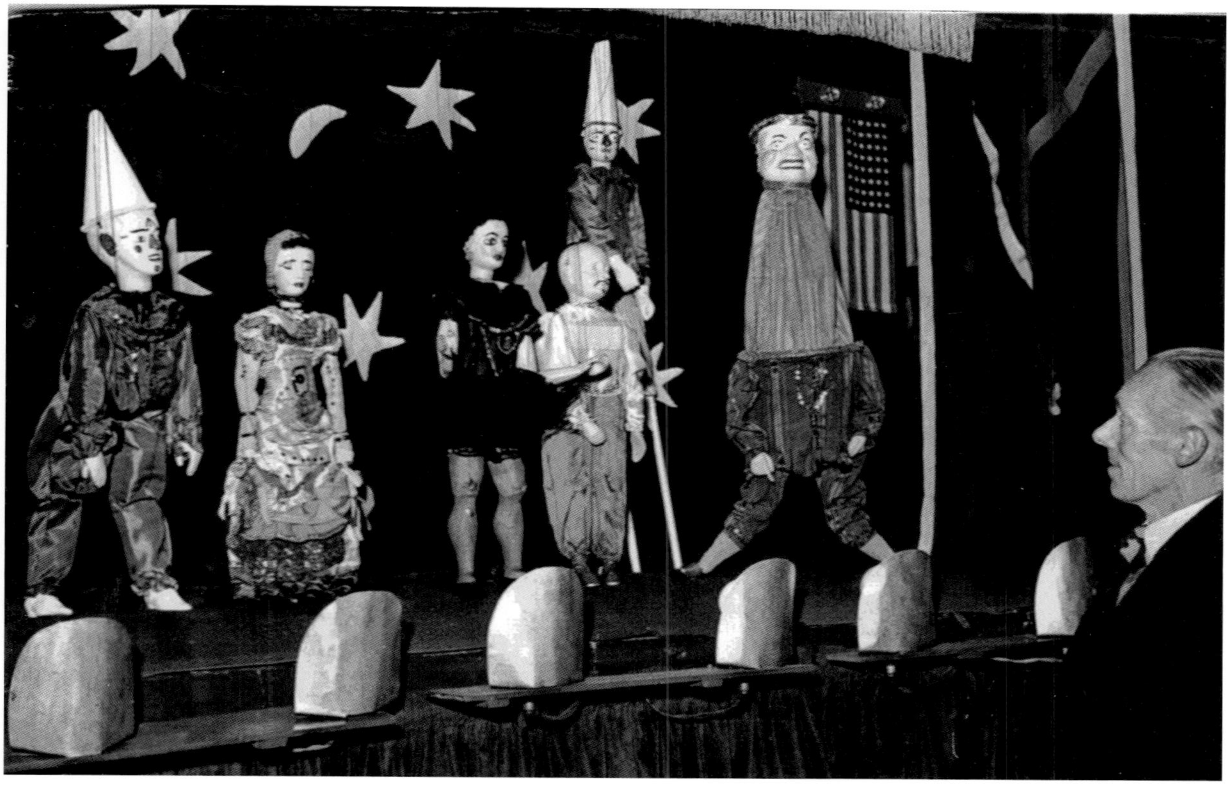

Above: Arthur and his marionettes and home-made stage.

After the War

As life returned to normal there was no lessening of Arthur's interest in fairs and circuses, and his regularly writing for World's Fair continued. He also returned to his ambition to create a marionette theatre, building the show in cramped conditions in his flat. He built and equipped the stage, and he and Elizabeth worked on the puppets themselves. As stated above some of these may have been Harry Wilding's puppets and were already very old. Arthur repainted their faces and repaired the strings. Elizabeth assisted Arthur in putting on the puppet shows, providing accompaniment with recorded music.

Several venues were found on the South Coast where the marionette show could be presented, for example in Driscoll's Stores in Hove. He may have even taken the show further afield and presented it under canvas for a short season. A poster survives to tell us about Alexandra's Royal Marionettes and we are supplied with a list all the people involved in the management and presentation of the shoe – all of which were "stage-names" for Arthur and Elizabeth!

Family associates also kept Arthur busy in the post-war period. The Harris family were now connected to the Sellmans by Doreen's wartime marriage to Ray Harris. Ray's sister Vera had a son called Peter who today can recall being taken by Arthur to watch the build-up of the Big Top when the circus came to town. Doreen and Ray's daughters, Jenny and Susan, preferred walks in the park with Grandad, but were also taken to see various shows. As I have mentioned above, Ray's father, Frank Harris had long been a friend of Arthur and in the post-war years Arthur would regularly go round to see Frank to share news found in World's Fair and to discuss the movement of fairs and circuses. Frank's sight had deteriorated and much appreciated these visits, and of course, the memories that emerged from their conversations led to further topics that could be mentioned in World's Fair. (E.g. In July 1958 Southdown reports on an interview with Mr. Francis Harris who looks back seventy years to recall his memories of Wadbrook's Ghost Show.)

Eventually Jenny realised the "symmetry" of having two grandfathers with showland backgrounds, and the link to her father's skills as an entertainer. She uses this symmetry as a starting point in a book she wrote about her father, Ray Harris. ("A Desert Rat Entertains" by Jenny Hall, Pen Press, 2013.) Family connection even determined where the Sellmans would live. When Ray and Doreen moved to Hove, Arthur and Elizabeth left Clifton Street and moved into Doreen's former flat at 3 Albert Road.

Anyone who accompanied Arthur on his travels knew that he would converse with everyone, and had friends all over the place. Son-in-law Ray worked at Harrington's Coach Works after the war and became friends with a work colleague named Dennis Parsley. One day Dennis happened to say that the one person he would really love to meet was a World's Fair correspondent named 'Southdown'. "He's my father-in-law", exclaimed Ray! Dennis was a member of the Fairground Society and later made a model of a showman's caravan for Arthur. The Fairground Society was formed in 1962 and a photograph of many of the founder members was taken, posed in front of Bottons' Gallopers, later during that year. Arthur joined in signing a copy of the photograph and corresponded with some of his fellow members.

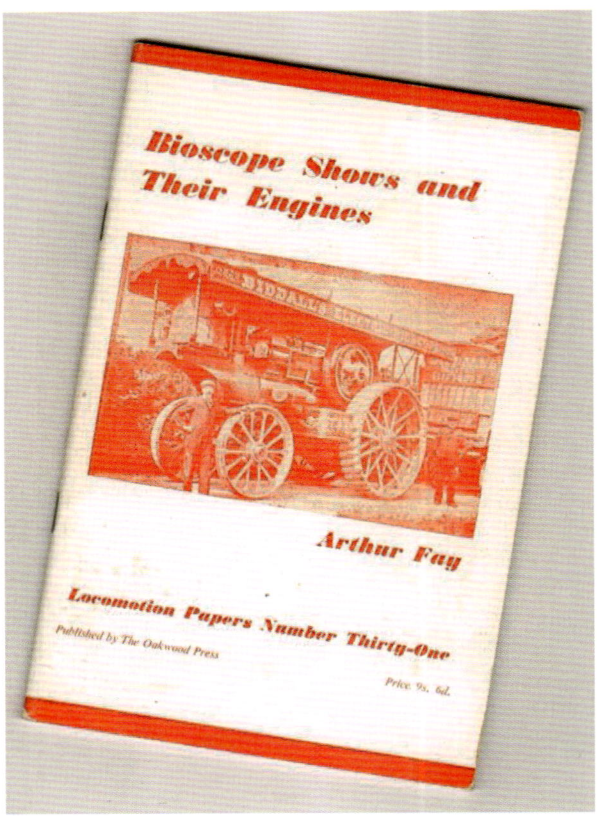

Arthur was good at keeping in touch with people. One such person was Professor Pat Cullen, a well-known palmist, and another was Horace Riddler who was better known as "The Great Omi" – the most tattooed man on Earth. The Great Omi came from Hailsham and had himself tattooed in all-over Zebra-like stripes. Omi, and his wife, known as Omette, presented themselves in a show at a number of fairs in Sussex. When Arthur was less able to travel around he relied on his network of contacts to keep him informed.

Arthur also enjoyed going down to the Brighton "junk market" where he would buy various vases and ornaments. He would paint these in very bright "circus" colours, and with copious quantities of gold paint. They were then given away as presents or added to the clutter he collected and stored at home. At the end of life he wrote copious instructions about how such things were to be found new homes.

By the 1960s he was becoming increasingly frail and was suffering from the effects of rheumatoid arthritis. The result was that he set about writing two books. The first, entitled "Bioscope Shows and Their Engines", was published by Oakwood Press in 1966 as a small paperback in the "Locomotive Papers" series. Arthur was very pleased when his book was given a brief mention in the Daily Telegraph on 25th March 1966. As a matter of interest, the book's author uses the name "Arthur Fay" – another pen name to add to the list.

Oakwood Press was a small independent enterprise run by Robert Kidner who had quite a cultivated interest in minority-interest subjects. Arthur did not live to see his second book published and left instructions stating that World's Fair should take it on or even serialise it in the paper. They passed it on to someone else who took it to Robert Kidner. It was published by Oakwood Press in 1975 as "Travelling Shows and Roundabouts". This time the author was clearly identified as Arthur Sellman.

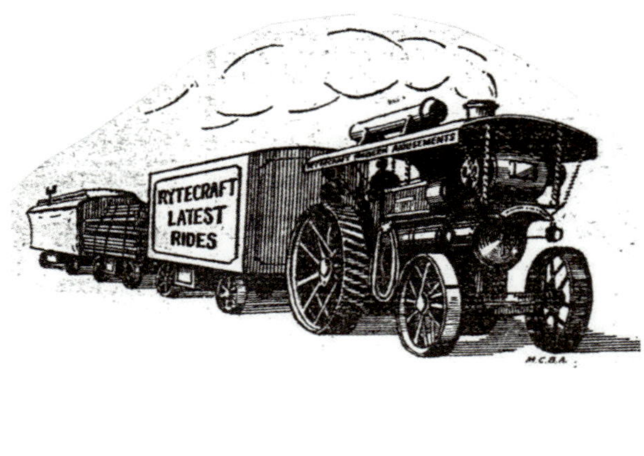

The post-war Long Shots

Arthur sustained his writing for World's Fair during the post-war years and continued to cover an amazing variety of content. As before, items covered things he saw in the Midlands, and of course, the South Coast. His memories of what he had seen in the 1890s and 1900s were now more distant, but it did not take much to send him back to them! Let's look at an example from 1st October 1955:

"A Few Long Shots" includes a description of the variety show at the London Palladium as well as comments of the loss of winter fairs on a site outside Clapham Junction station! His main topic is about "Loades' Model Circus" which he had found built up inside the Show Boat at the Festival Gardens in Battersea Park. Taking in some of the other attractions in the Show Boat leads Southdown into one of his classic reveries in which he transports the reader back to a much earlier time, and draws heavily on his own memories:

Other comments concern Lord George Sanger's Circus in Crawley and Tunbridge Wells, and an end of pier show in Morecambe featuring The Starlights".

A week later Southdown comments on the closure of the Odeon, Broadstairs, and the success of the Margate Trades Exhibition, but it seems that the start of the Back End always encouraged him to make a return visit to his roots in and around the Black Country and Cannock Chase. We learn that he passed through Birmingham on the Wednesday prior to the opening of the Onion Fair. He called at the Serpentine Ground and was immediately excited to see "The Leader" lifting parts of the Waltzer into place. Pat Collins' Foster showman's engine was still at work. Pat's widow, Clara Collins, had made a point of preserving some of the engines despite the general post-war trends.

He also mentions conversations that he had with various showmen including a 'Mr. Dobson' who was able to discuss over fifty years of travelling in the area – including memories of the Onion Fair when it had been held on The Pleck. The fair had last been held on The Pleck in 1909 so it is interesting to wonder which 'Mr. Dobson' was doing the reminiscing. (It could have been John Dobson {1904-1960}.) Southdown also had a long chat with Tommy Allen, and spent time looking for fairground organs. In the end he was rewarded with the sighting of just one organ – an instrument attached to the front of Tom Norman's Palladium Show. To a large extent Arthur was writing with confidence that these names of people and places meant something to his readers.

We learn that Southdown then had to travel from Birmingham to Walsall by train. From the carriage window, as the train passed through Perry Bar, he noticed some packing trucks belonging to J.P. Collins parked at the Greyhound Stadium. The true enthusiast misses nothing! Why should this resonate with me – looking at all this half a century later? Well, J.P.Collins' waltzer did become a legendary ride and was managed by his son Kevin – who – in the 1990s was running a launderette at the end of the road in which I lived.

He then comments on a variety show being presented at the Plaza Theatre in West Bromwich – a few months later the theatre would close to be reincarnated as a cinema. (Alert readers will realise that the theatre played a part in the story of Ben Kennedy and his descendants, as told in Chapter Six.) He even notices that the Wolverhampton Arts Society were organising a meeting on "The Creation of a Marionette", by Waldo and Muriel Lanchester. (This may seem obscure but the Lanchesters were famous puppeteers in their day – it's still possible to look them up on the Internet!) For some reason he draws the reader's attention to a cutting he has found from the Cannock Advertiser for 26th September 1931 – the cutting concerned a farewell visit made to Cannock by Bostock & Wombwell's Menagerie. Once again his links to the Cannock area and his love of the old shows assert themselves.

Although I had been drawn into the fairground world in the 1980s, I must admit that Arthur's work would have been wasted on me before that time. However, having become interested in Pat Collins, and then other local showmen, Arthur's words actually make up for a history that I "missed". For example, I never knew Pat Collins' permanent amusements at Sutton Park, and totally missed the attempt to create such a facility at Chasewater. In the World's Fair of 26th September 1959 Arthur had dealt with all these things:

Arthur describes a visit to the Crystal Palace Amusement Park in Sutton Park, Sutton Coldfield. He felt the amusements on offer were varied and "up to a standard" as one would expect of a Pat Collins enterprise. He specifically mentions the Scenic Railway, the Monte Carlo Rally, a waltzer and dodgem, the Speedway Ark and the 'Grand National' Steeplechasers, and the miniature railway, plus an arcade, a juvenile roundabout, a row of games, the overboats, and a set of swings. He adds that it costs 3d to gain admission to the park, but there is no extra charge to enter the Crystal Palace Grounds. On leaving the ground he noted the huge hoardings announcing the imminence of the Onion Fair – the Pat Collins' empire's flagship event held towards the end of September a few miles away in Aston.

The amusement park at Chasewater – seven miles from Sutton Park – had also opened for its first season in 1959. It had been developed by William Bagnall who had previously looked after the Crystal Palace ground for the Pat Collins organisation. He had persuaded some of the tenants at Sutton to follow him to the remote windy shores of the lake at Chasewater. Arthur lists the attractions he found at Chasewater and was positive about the place: .... *"A wonderful job has been accomplished. The attractions include a set of dodgems, an Autodrome, a set of park swings, a Ghost Train, a set of Flying Chairs, a Monte Carlo Rally, a Speedway Ark, juvenile roundabouts, and a long row of games with uniform fascias. The amusements are nicely laid out on level ground with a hard surface, and the site is reached from the main entrance by way of a newly made road."*

Reflecting his divided loyalties between the West Midlands and the South Coast, he comments on shows coming to the end of their seasons in Margate and Cliftonville as well as anticipating Christmas shows in Birmingham and Coventry.

By the early 1960s Arthur was now writing his "Long Shots" in his seventies. He seems to write less from first-hand experience and begins to rely on readers sending him accounts of the fairs he once knew well. In The World's Fair of 16th October 1961, for example, he is grateful to a reader who has attended the Burton on Trent Statutes Fair at the beginning of October. This was another important event in the Pat Collins calendar and was still well attended, and on this occasion enjoyed good weather. *"Alas, adds my correspondent, there were no big organ-front shows or Scenic Railways in evidence: their places were taken by such popular machines as Hurricane Jets and Ark Speedways."*

Southdown's main topic was the imminent demolition of the Theatre Royal in Bilston. He gives an account of the history of the theatre and reminds readers that Bilston had once been regularly visited by the portable theatre provided by Messrs Bennett & Patch – thus taking readers back to events of the 1850s and providing a link with another chapter of this book! He concludes with an interesting comment:

"Yet another famous old portable theatre to visit Bilston was Bowcott's, whose descendants, I am given to understand, established a printing works in the district and carried out quite a lot of contracts for both theatres and cinemas".

Bowcotts did indeed establish a printing business, in nearby Wednesbury, and produced a great deal of material for fairs, circuses, cinemas and theatres. For years they kept huge archives of their work but unfortunately all this was lost in a fire. This is the only reference I have ever come across to the effect that the family were once more directly involved in the world of travelling entertainment. Once again Southdown leaves us wishing he had told us more!

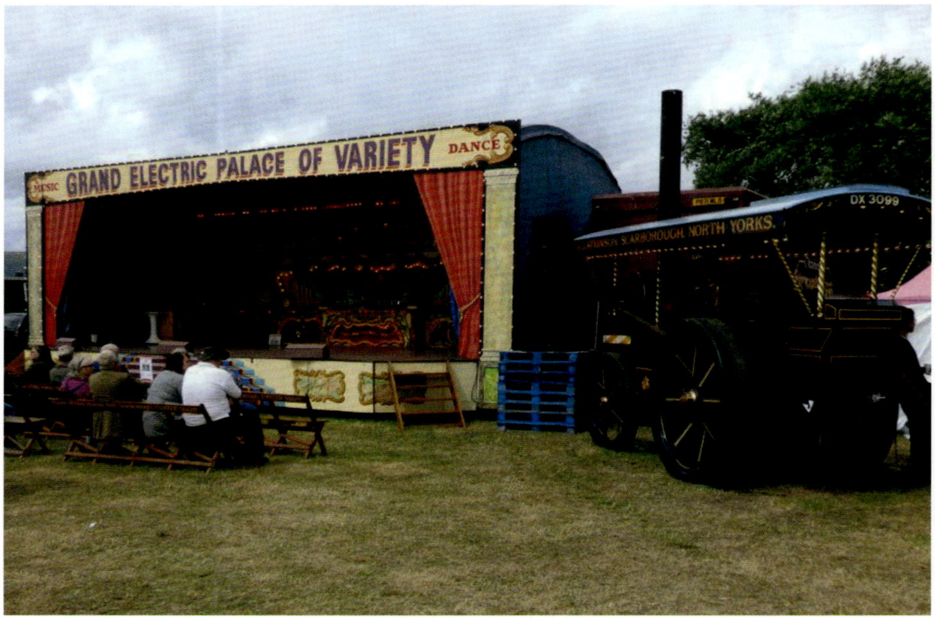

Sometimes at contemporary steam rallies there is an attempt to re-create the traditions of the shows that Arthur Sellman loved. Left: "The Grand Electric Palace of Variety" at Welland, 2017.

At Hollycombe Working Steam Museum, a replica "bioscope show" has been created – illustrated on the back cover.

The Last Chapter

While writing his two books, in his seventies, Arthur still maintained his life-long interests – his love of all entertainment never diminished. He used his tape-recorder to fill the flat with what he called "thrilling music" while he sorted out his collection of photographs and prepared his "Instructions" regarding the disposal of everything after his death. He completed these instructions and signed them on 15th September 1969.

Arthur's instructions included the sale of two albums of photographs of bioscopes. Possibly they still exist.

Arthur Sellman died in Brighton General Hospital on 18th October 1970 and his death certificate described his occupation as "Variety Artist (retired)". Shortly before his death he had told Doreen, "I have done everything I've wanted to do. I have had a wonderful life." On 24th October World's Fair told its readers of Arthur's death describing him as, "...the oldest of our contributors."

World's Fair went on to describe Arthur:

"Acknowledged to be one of the greatest authorities on all aspects of show business, he was the author of "Bioscope Shows and Their Engines", and wrote a weekly column for this paper under the pen-name 'Southdown'. It reflected the extent and depth of his vast experience of show business, and drew a large volume of correspondence from old artistes (many of whom were mentioned in his writings), and students. When the World's Fair celebrated its Golden Jubilee issue in 1954, Mr. Sellman contributed a lengthy illustrated article on the history of the cinema which had its origins in the travelling shows of the fairgrounds. He enjoyed the confidence of three successive editors of this paper and will be missed by countless friends throughout the country."

Arthur's funeral took place on Friday 23rd October and an impressive service was held at St. Luke's Church, Prestonville, Brighton, conducted by Rev. Towne who was described as "a friend of the family". As well as the family, many others came to pay their last respects. D. Taylor came to represent the "World's Fair"; Dennis Parsley represented the Fairground Society. Professor Pat Culleen, the palmist, and "The Great Omani" were among his friends present. Ironically that week's edition of The World's Fair came out on the day of the funeral – reporting Arthur's death and apologising of not being able to inform readers of the funeral in advance.

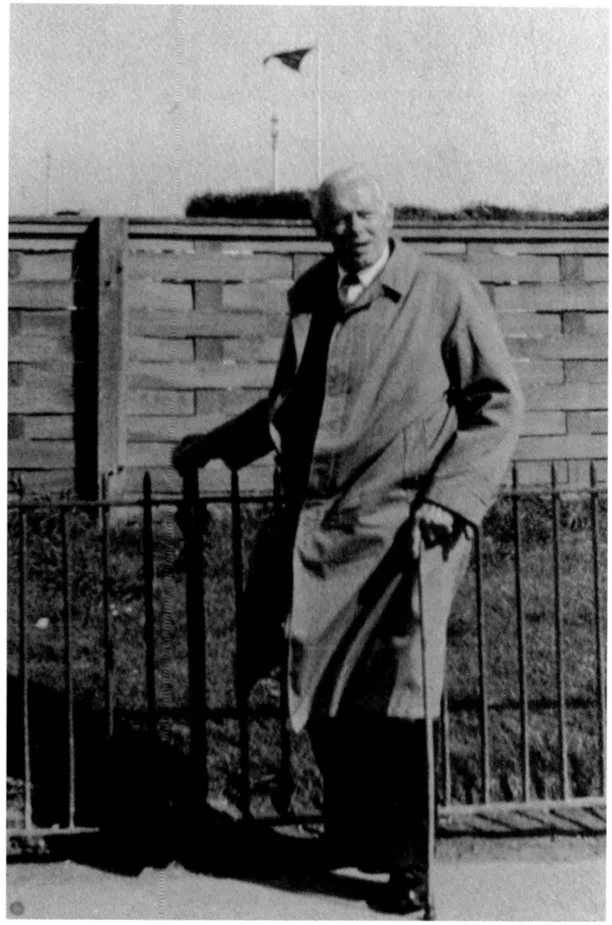

Above: Arthur Sellman at Hove in August 1967.

Epilogue

In the World's Fair of 7th November 1970 D.Taylor wrote a report of Arthur's funeral and provided his own obituary saying, *"A native of Cannock, as a young man Arthur travelled the fairgrounds widely, as a projectionist and lecturer on the early bioscope shows, with such firms as Hollands, Crichton's, Pat Collins, and others. He was later engaged in puppet and marionette shows, in connection with which he made his own figures. At the outbreak of the 1914 war Arthur was entertaining the troops in Norfolk. He was also connected with the circus and did much advance work. He later turned his attention to the permanent cinemas and at Rugeley he managed the Variety Cinema. He later proceeded to The Pavilion, Earlstown, in Scotland, and from there to the Princes Theatre in Brighton, which he managed for some 13 years. He was a correspondent for World's Fair for over fifty years.*

He had a natural flair for writing, and a few years ago published a very interesting book on the history of bioscopes under the pen-name of 'Arthur Fay'. A man of vast experience and of a kindly nature, he will be sadly missed. In the words of his old friend, Professor Pat Cullen, 'Arthur will always be remembered with true affection.'"

I think Mr. Taylor drew on his own memories of Arthur, and what may have been said in a eulogy at the funeral which would have been drawn from the family's memories. As can be seen it differs in one or two details from the narrative provided here, but never the less adds to the mixture of facts, minor mysteries, and legends now surrounding Southdown. Despite all his writing activity, it does not seem that Arthur found time to sit down and write his autobiography – perhaps never quite realising how useful this would have been given his first-hand experience of many aspects of showland history of which we only have an incomplete picture.

As already mentioned, Arthur left instructions about the disposal of his collection. For example his photograph collection was sold, and puppets had to be found a new home. The text of his second book also awaited publication. It was eventually published by Oakwood Press in 1975 as "Travelling Shows and Roundabouts" – again set out in the format of Oakwood's "Locomotion Papers" – often described as monographs.

It was reviewed in World's Fair by Peter Barnes who made sure that Elizabeth Sellman received a copy. She wrote to thank him and he replied, *"I am glad you liked my write-up of your husband's book. I thoroughly enjoyed reading it and shall keep it always. There was something about the style of his writing which conveyed not just the facts of the subject he was describing, but the essential feelings of those involved. It is a rare gift."*

When I spoke to Robert Kidner about the publication of Arthur's books he was particularly vague about how the second one had come about and with whom he had dealt, but it is ironic that only following his death did Arthur's work appear under his real name. And it is only now that we begin to appreciate the content and style of Arthur's work. The quality that Peter Barnes tried to identify way back in 1975 was perhaps the result of the enthusiasm that Arthur brought to his task of writing about things that many people would have found obscure.

When we look back at the early days of the Fairground Society it is obvious that many enthusiasts were motivated by their love of fairground organs, showmen's engines, and vintage rides. As time has passed a greater sense has developed of the need to chronicle fairground history, and a need to collect data which will later acquire a historical value. In this respect an interest in the fairground and circus world is now more sophisticated than it was in Arthur's day and this has led to the need to "rediscover" his work.

Arthur's widow, Elizabeth, died in Hove in 1991 – twenty one years after Arthur's death. In that time it seems that no one approached her to talk about Arthur's life, or even to hear an account of her own contribution towards his endeavours. We know now that she assisted him in his puppetry and was his loyal proof-reader of all that he wrote. Arthur's daughter, Doreen Harris died at Lewes in August 2006, but her daughters, Jenny and Susan are alive today to provide us with first-hand memories of their grandfather. Jenny has written: "Arthur usually wore a brown suit and spotted tie. Despite his handicap, he had a rather aristocratic bearing. Tall with prominent cheek-bones, he exuded an empathy, warmth and enthusiasm which touched everyone he met. He was a very kind person and took an interest in all. His love of entertainment never diminished."

It is in words like these that we can now appreciate Arthur Sellman as more than just a long lost writer of obscure recollections published in World's Fair under an assumed name. He now appears as a very real person who has given us a remarkable legacy.

Below: The model showman's van made for Arthur by Dennis Parsley.

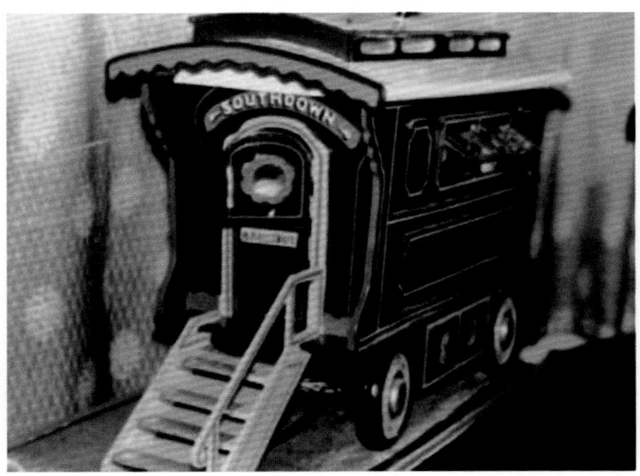

An example of Arthur's writing:

The Portable Theatre

By "APS", published in World's Fair, 30th November 1935.

A few wagon loads of large and square wooden shutters, numerous poles of various lengths, a quantity of seat planks and their supports, scene-painted canvas wrapped round longer rollers and some nailed and glued upon framework, a collections of ropes and pulleys, various stage properties, three or four open coke-fire grates, a quantity of drapery, travelling baskets, rolls of carpeting, and a mass of other things – meet these on the highway and you would know that a portable theatre was shifting its quarters.

Soon after the wagons had reached their destination the work of building up would commence. Men would start hacking up the ground, digging narrow holes wherein to erect uprights. While some erected the framework, others built a gallery at one end, and at the other a stage, and so bit by bit it progressed. After an adornment of the interior by draping the walls with some material and giving a covering to the best seats, and a sawdust carpet to the whole show, the building-up was at an end. Forty years ago such scenes as I have described were common in towns which had manufacturing, mineral and agricultural interests.

Unquestionably among the most popular theatres to tour the country were those of the Holloways, William and Horace, both of whom could trace their family's association with the travelling theatre for over a hundred years. It was in 1905 that Mr. William Holloway had one of his best shows. This was a spacious building known as the New Empire Theatre. The interior which was illuminated by gas throughout comprised a gallery, pit and stalls, and a very well equipped stage with an abundance of artistically painted scenery that was adaptable for each and every piece presented. Draped with thick inside lings and kept warm by the aid of three big coke fires in winter time, William Holloway's booth always presented a cosy appearance and at all times a good company, hence the theatre's long run of popularity.

Doubtless there will be some of my readers who will recall Mr. W Henderson, an actor of outstanding ability, who for a long time played the heavy leads with Mr.W. Holloways's company. Then there was our old friend Mr. Will Bradley, who was succeeded by Bert Fox. Others were Will Collins, Rose Holloway, Mr. & Mrs. Lea and Mrs. Wallace, Mr. Holloway Jnr, Mrs. W. Holloway, and by no means least, Mr. William Holloway himself who always played the leading comedy parts. No portable theatre proprietor worked harder than Mr. Holloway, of stout build and genial disposition, he not only took part in the nightly dramas, but in the daytime was nearly always affecting repairs to his theatre. At Christmas he worked doubly hard for it was always the custom to produce a pantomime. For this special dresses would be made and new scenery and effects introduced.

The length of stay in a town or village varied according to the importance of the place, but usually three months was the time for which the necessary licence would be taken out. For many years Mr. William Holloway's show was a popular feature on the Green Hill, at Lichfield Bower. On such occasions the show had a front built on to it that carried a fine trumpet organ, and a good parade was had as an outside attraction.

Mr. Horace Holloway had been the proprietor of several fine booths during his long career, perhaps the finest being the Prince of Wales Theatre, which was among the most elaborate of its kind. In this theatre, in the early days of cinema, Mr. Holloway introduced, in addition to the usual dramas and farces, varieties and sketches, moving pictures for all for the one inclusive admission charge. It proved no easy matter as the construction of a portable theatre was unsuited for projection purposes. The problem was eventually solved by projecting the pictures from an aperture in the side of the tent, although this slightly distorted the picture.

Below: William Holloway's "Empire Theatre" built up for its appearance at the Lichfileld Bower Fair about 1903.

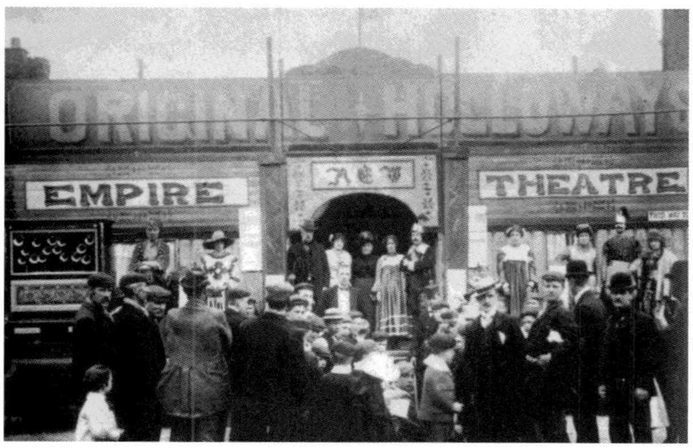

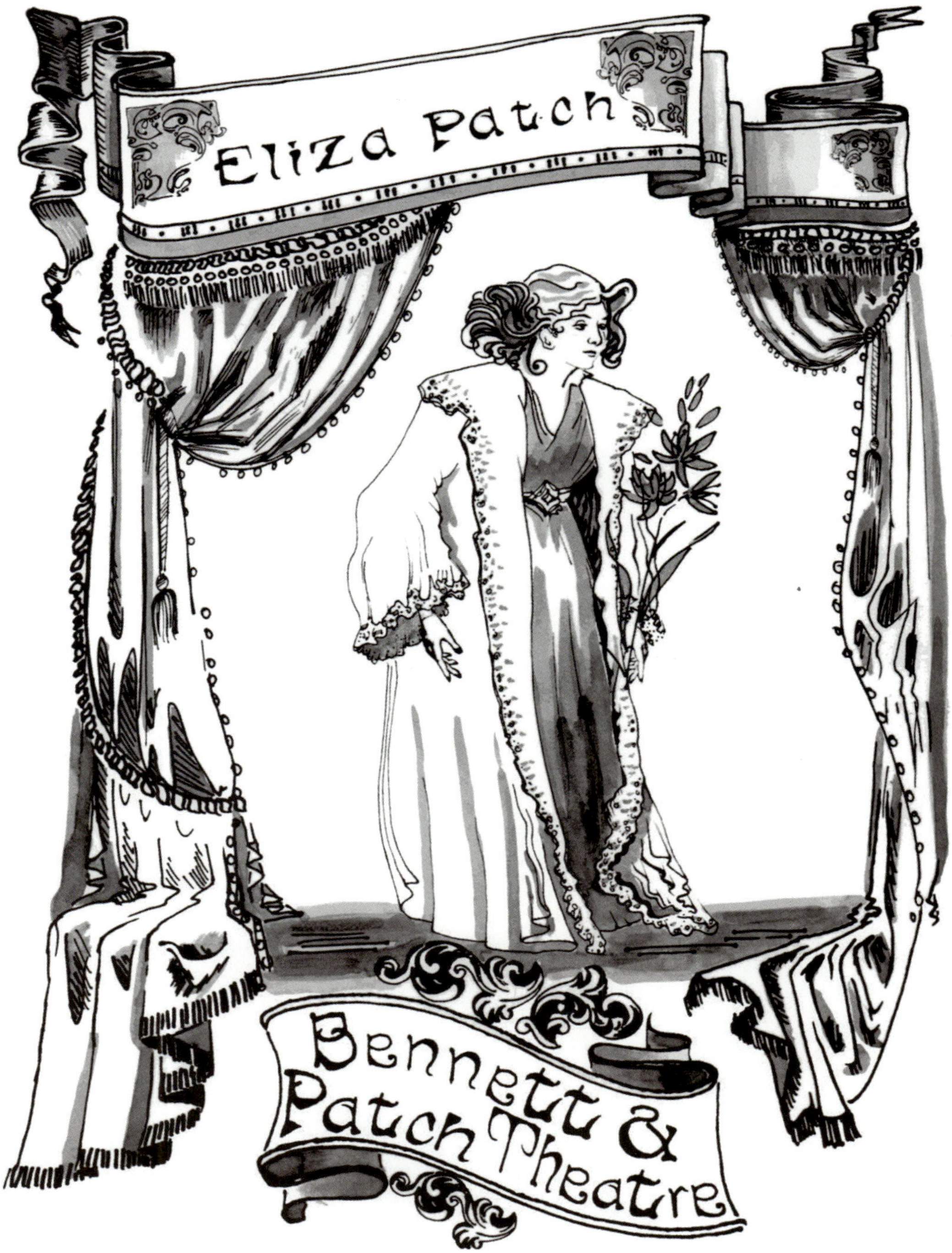
Eliza Patch
Bennett & Patch Theatre

how they only returned in a very restricted way following the Restoration. Once I started looking into it, I realised that "legitimate theatre" was limited at one time to simply two or three stages in London. Eventually provincial Britain was served by "Theatres Royal" but their spread was slow and did not keep up with the urbanisation that followed the Industrial Revolution. I also knew that some kind of theatre existed at a grass roots level – that "fit-up" companies travelled from town to town and put on plays in whatever halls existed. What took me totally by surprise was that there was another kind of theatrical experience from fairly early in the nineteenth century onwards – presented by people who erected temporary buildings and then took them with them to the next place – the "portables".

The second surprise came once I started trying to answer the question: Who were Bennett & Patch? It was not a male double-act as I had once thought – it turns out to be a father and daughter or a husband and wife. At the centre of the story stands Eliza Bennett. But even after trying to unravel some of the details of Eliza's story we are still left with the mystery of which Bennett and which Patch is being named in that partnership: "Bennett & Patch"?

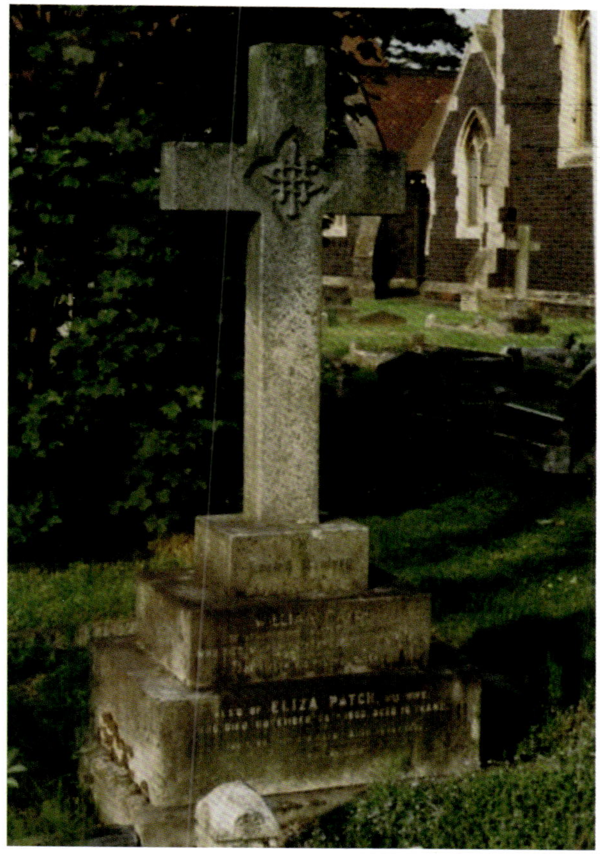

Right: Eliza's grave

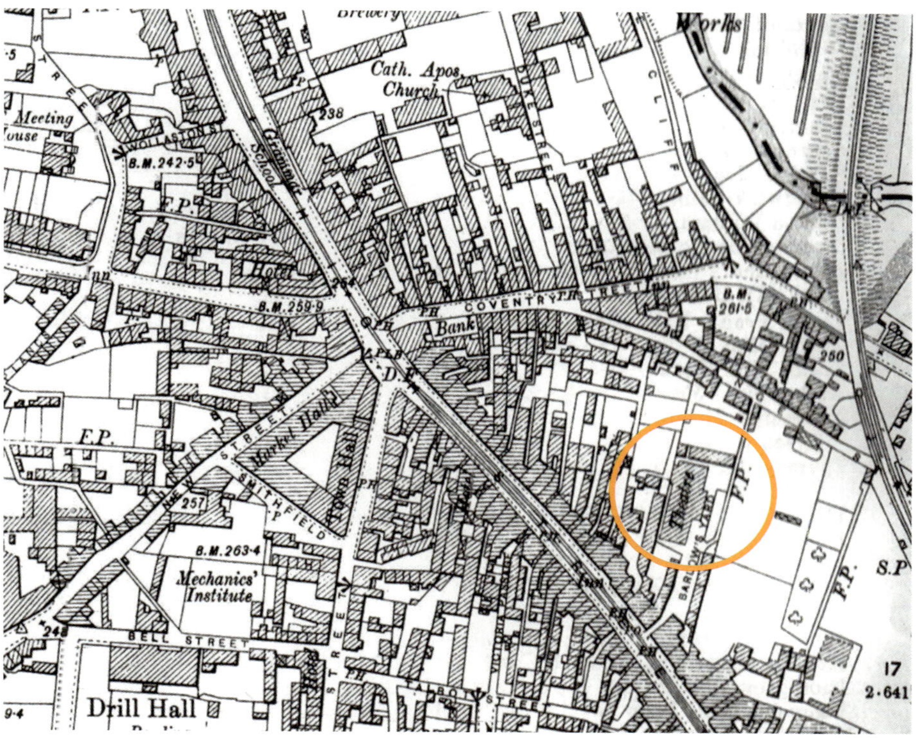

Right: This small section of the 'Alan Godfrey' map of central Stourbridge of the 1900s shows the location of Eliza Patch's Alhambra Theatre in Barlows Yard quite clearly. Tram tracks occupy the High Street as it heads south from the Market Hall and Town Hall – passing the "entry" into Barlows Yard.
The letters "PH" printed over the tram tracks indicates the location of "The Coach & Horses"- owned by William Patch, passing to Eliza and then to her nephew, William.

The Bennett Tree

Edward Bennett (c1801 – c.1880) = Elizabeth

Eliza Bennett = William Patch
(married 1844)
(1824 – 1900) (c.1823 - 1895)

William Edward Bennett = Mary Jane Humpherson
(married 1864)
(1836 – 1911) (1846 – 1907)

William Edward Bennett
c.1866 – 1927
Married Mary Ethel Tangue in 1900

Henry George Dudley Bennett*
c.1866 - 1918

Isobel Bennett
July 1870 – ?
Married WGR Sprague (1863 – 1933)

*Henry George Dudley Bennett, known as Harry, married twice.

1. He married Annie Maria Whittem (1869 –8th Dec 1893) in 1891
   (They had one child: Guy Whittem Bennett)
2. He married Florence Laura Aronson (1872 – 1947) in 1897.
   (They had two sons: Cecil Harry Andrew Bennett and Wilfred George Dudley Bennett (23rd Sept 1900 – 1984.) and a daughter: Marjorie.

Notes:
William and Mary Jane also had a daughter, Amy Eliza, born 1865, died 20th Sept.1898. On 12th Jan. 1882 Amy married Charles Machin – a London theatre proprietor, who was briefly in partnership with the Bennetts. They had four children. Amy died on 20th Sept. 1898

Isobel Katherine Bennett married WGR Sprague in Spring 1900 in Lambeth.
They had a daughter, Amy Ida (born 1899, and two sons: Sidney William (born 1905) and George Drummond (1907 - 1997)
By 1911 they had settled at Tankerton on the North Kent coast.

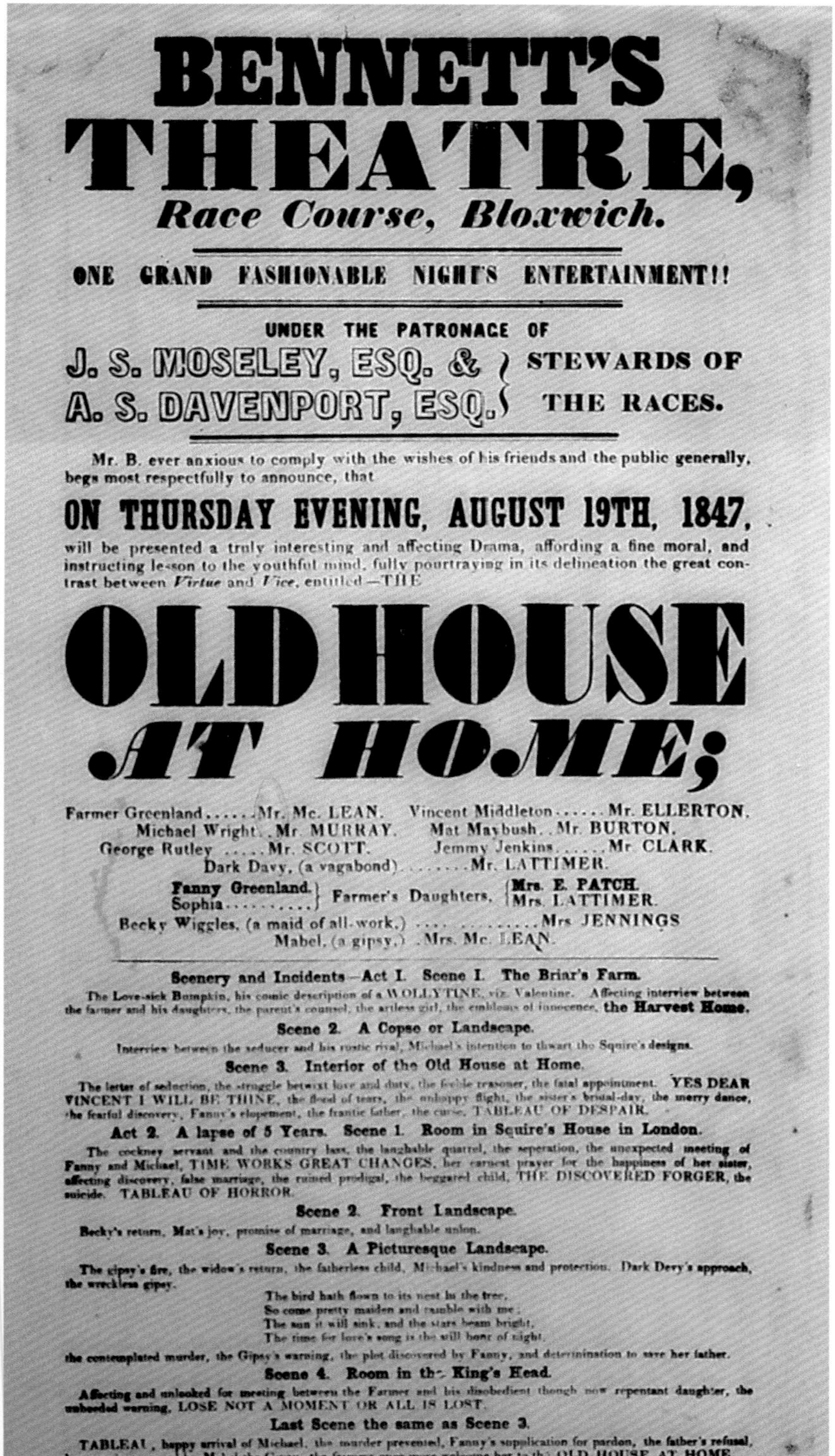

BENNETT'S
THEATRE,
Race Course, Bloxwich.

ONE GRAND FASHIONABLE NIGHT'S ENTERTAINMENT!!

UNDER THE PATRONAGE OF
J. S. MOSELEY, ESQ. & } STEWARDS OF
A. S. DAVENPORT, ESQ. } THE RACES.

Mr. B. ever anxious to comply with the wishes of his friends and the public generally, begs most respectfully to announce, that

ON THURSDAY EVENING, AUGUST 19TH, 1847,

will be presented a truly interesting and affecting Drama, affording a fine moral, and instructing lesson to the youthful mind, fully pourtraying in its delineation the great contrast between *Virtue* and *Vice*, entitled—THE

OLD HOUSE
AT HOME;

Farmer Greenland......Mr. Mc. LEAN. Vincent Middleton......Mr. ELLERTON.
Michael Wright..Mr. MURRAY. Mat Maybush..Mr. BURTON.
George Rutley ......Mr. SCOTT. Jemmy Jenkins......Mr. CLARK.
Dark Davy, (a vagabond)........Mr. LATTIMER.
Fanny Greenland. } Farmer's Daughters. { **Mrs. E. PATCH.**
Sophia.......... } { Mrs. LATTIMER.
Becky Wiggles, (a maid of all-work.) ....Mrs JENNINGS
Mabel, (a gipsy.) ..Mrs. Mc. LEAN.

Scenery and Incidents—Act I. Scene I. The Briar's Farm.

The Love-sick Bumpkin, his comic description of a WOLLYTINE, viz. Valentine. Affecting interview between the farmer and his daughters, the parent's counsel, the artless girl, the emblems of innocence, **the Harvest Home.**

Scene 2. A Copse or Landscape.

Interview between the seducer and his rustic rival, Michael's intention to thwart the Squire's designs.

Scene 3. Interior of the Old House at Home.

The letter of seduction, the struggle betwixt love and duty, the feeble reasoner, the fatal appointment. YES DEAR VINCENT I WILL BE THINE, the flood of tears, the unhappy flight, the sister's bridal-day, the merry dance, the fearful discovery, Fanny's elopement, the frantic father, the curse, TABLEAU OF DESPAIR.

Act 2. A lapse of 5 Years. Scene 1. Room in Squire's House in London.

The cockney servant and the country lass, the laughable quarrel, the seperation, the unexpected meeting of Fanny and Michael, TIME WORKS GREAT CHANGES, her earnest prayer for the happiness of her sister, affecting discovery, false marriage, the ruined prodigal, the beggared child, THE DISCOVERED FORGER, the suicide. TABLEAU OF HORROR.

Scene 2. Front Landscape.

Becky's return, Mat's joy, promise of marriage, and laughable union.

Scene 3. A Picturesque Landscape.

The gipsy's fire, the widow's return, the fatherless child, Michael's kindness and protection. Dark Davy's approach, the wreckless gipsy.

The bird hath flown to its nest in the tree,
So come pretty maiden and ramble with me;
The sun it will sink, and the stars beam bright,
The time for love's song is the still hour of night,

the contemplated murder, the Gipsy's warning, the plot discovered by Fanny, and determination to save her father.

Scene 4. Room in the King's Head.

Affecting and unlooked for meeting between the Farmer and his disobedient though now repentant daughter, the unheeded warning, LOSE NOT A MOMENT OR ALL IS LOST.

Last Scene the same as Scene 3.

TABLEAU, happy arrival of Michael, the murder prevented, Fanny's supplication for pardon, the father's refusal, her marriage proved by Mabel the Gipsy, the farmers once more welcome her to the OLD HOUSE AT HOME.

Left: A bill produced for Bennett'sTheatre's appearance at the Blaoxwich Races of August 1847 – three years after Eliza's marriage to William Patch. The wording implies that it is still being presented by her father, not just by the heading but by the fact that the text claims, "Mr.B. ever anxious to comply with the wishes of his friends and the public generally, respectfully wishes to present this affecting drama which contrasts Virtue and Vice…"

Eliza is referred to as "Mrs. Patch" and is playing the heroine, Fanny Greenland. Her name appears in bold type, reflecting the fact that she is the star of the show.

Mr. & Mrs Lattimer are also appearing in the show. Sometimes the Lattimers and the Bennetts each presented separate shows, as recorded in a report of the Tipton Wakes of 1855. Mrs. Jennings also appears and may be from another family associated with portable theatres of the mid 19th Century.

Portable theatres of the mid-nineteenth century relied on the posting of "theatre bills" as their main means of advertising. Such advertising was very ephemeral and we are fortunate that a few examples survive.

Endings and Beginnings

On Sunday 2nd December 1900 the Rev. George Gilbanks, the first vicar of St. James', Wollaston, on the outskirts of Stourbridge, conducted a very well attended funeral. He had come to the church when it first opened in 1860, had become well-known locally, and was deeply involved with the local community and seemed to know everybody and everything that went on. All funerals are important, but maybe some seem more significant than others! There was a definite sense in the air that he had to say something to mark the significance of this funeral. The sheer size of the crowd emphasized this. He needed a phrase to describe the deceased, and rising to the occasion as he spoke at the graveside, he proclaimed the deceased would never be forgotten. I am sure everyone present agreed with him, and with those words Eliza Patch was lowered into a grave – a grave already occupied by her late husband, William Patch.
The day before the funeral, the local newspaper, the County Express, had published a tribute to Eliza as follows:

"The news of the death of Mrs. Patch, of Stourbridge, will be received with regret by many people in an exceedingly wide area, for the name has been prominently before the public for more than half a century. As proprietress of the Alhambra Theatre, she has catered for the amusement of the district for more years than most people will care to recollect, and before the building became permanently settled in Stourbridge, no institution in the Black Country was better known than Bennett & Patch's travelling theatre, whose wardrobe was reputed to be worth £2000.

In many ways she was a wonderful woman... In her younger days she made a considerable reputation as a Shakespearean actress, and though she had not acted professionally for the last twenty years, she has appeared occasionally in benefits and charity performances, her last appearance being as the Player Queen in Hamlet upon the occasion of Mr. Herman Vezin's visit to Stourbridge some years ago.

As well as being a successful young actress, we pay tribute to her ability to run a complex and successful business. It is remarkable that she ran her theatrical enterprise for as long as she did. Her health had been ailing for some time, and an accident in February seems to have broken up her strong constitution, and she gradually became worse.

She always upheld the best traditions of her profession in being ready to assist charity, and, besides helping in public matters, her private charities were many, though perhaps known to only a few."

This report was one of the few printed accounts of Eliza Patch's life and achievement, and goes on to include information I will reveal as we try to assemble Eliza's life story. The report's tone, and its details, certainly reinforced the phrase used by Rev. Gillbanks at her graveside – that she would "never be forgotten".

Even though Eliza now seems forgotten after all, the words of the County Express and Rev. Gillbanks make it clear that she was appreciated at the time and her local fame should have guaranteed that someone would eventually try to tell her story. The problem is that in trying to tell the story over a century later means that

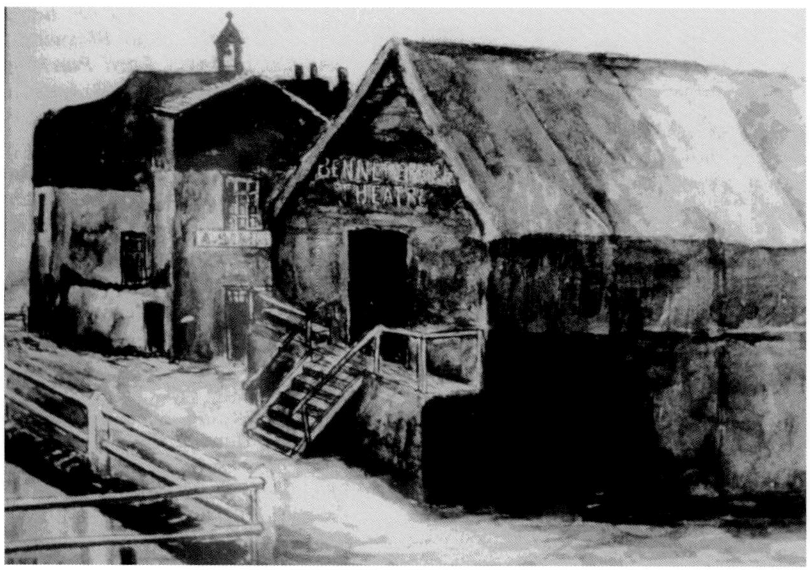

Right: Bennett & Patch's Theatre built up at the Walsall Races - a pen and ink drawing by Billy Meikle of Walsall. This rare and remarkable picture shows the construction of a typical portable theatre with its wooden panelled sides and the canvas tilt stretched over an "A" frame to form the roof. Steps and shallow stage form the frontage. The front. carries the name: Bennett & Patch's Theatre.
Behind the theatre we see the back of the race course grandstand.. (Walsall Archives)

some of the details are "lost", and are now too distant to be unveiled.

We really know very little about Eliza's early life, and so far no picture or photograph has been found of her. It seems that she was born in Dudley in 1824. An Eliza Bennett was baptised at St. Thomas' Church in Dudley on 28th March 1824 – a time when the church, now known as "Top Church", was a relatively new building, and the surrounding town was beginning to expand. Her mother was Elizabeth Bennett, and her father, Edward, was at least on the way to becoming involved in the theatrical world – although there is nothing to suggest this in the information surrounding that baptism, nor in the first census which took place seven years later. The County Express of 1st December 1900 had no hesitation in saying, *"Her father, Mr. Bennett, was a well-known theatre proprietor in his day, so the whole of her long life was spent in a theatrical atmosphere."* Alas, we have no written or printed records from the 1830s and early 1840s to explain her progress into the theatrical world.

During her teens, say between 1834 and 1844 Eliza must have travelled with her father and gained her reputation as an actress. Unfortunately there is no documentation of this and it is difficult to imagine what a travelling theatre was like at the time – perhaps yet to evolve into the temporary buildings used from the 1850s onwards. Nothing seems to be known about Edward Bennett – in particular it is not clear whether he was related or not to other Bennetts of the time who were taking part in the theatre business – e.g. James Bennett who was associated with early theatre history in Wolverhampton, or Henry Bennett who was lessee of the Theatre Royal in Worcester during the 1840s, and there was a Mr. Bennett to be found in Coventry.

In1836 Eliza was joined by a brother: William Edward Bennett. William also became part of the theatrical world. He was born in Longton, near The Potteries, and this may be evidence of the family's travels in the 1830s.

A key event in our story, and one that is documented, occurred in 1844 when a twenty year old Eliza Bennett married William Patch in the parish church at Bromsgrove, on 23rd July. Bromsgrove was linked to Dudley by a turnpike road and both towns had strong association with the nail trade. (In 1842 striking nailers in Dudley had pushed a tub of nails to Bromsgrove to plead for better pay, or a better price for their nails!) Bromsgrove also had an important fair that is known to have hosted travelling theatres and the shows that came later in the nineteenth century. It is entirely likely therefore that a travelling theatre business, operated by a Dudley family, would have been found in Bromsgrove. The bridegroom also came from an interesting background.

William Patch was born in the early 1820s in Exeter, where his father and grandfather had been hop and wine merchants. He also had an uncle who had been a mayor and benefactor of Exeter. (William's year of birth is something of a mystery as he seems to have given a variety of inconsistent "ages" when providing census information.) He had been educated with a view to entering the church, but seems to have joined the family business for a while. His life took a significant turn when a huge whale was stranded and died on a beach near Plymouth! At first a local company was formed who were going to somehow make money out of the whale, but this failed and William Patched stepped in to purchase it. William had the whale gutted and embalmed and set out to turn into the centre-piece of a travelling show. In this way he entered show business with a portable whale, mounted on a set of articulated and coupled wagons 120 ft. long. Visitors were able to walk through the skeleton and body of the whale and study pictures explaining what could be seen. It was an immense success and William travelled far and wide with his whale show for several years. Later he joked that he was the only man who had lived off one fish for so long!

All this may seem strange, but the last travelling whale show toured the Black Country as recently as the 1950s and those that witnessed it admitted that the corpse of the whale did eventually become the worse for wear and rather smelly. Perhaps that helps to explain why William Patch may have been keen to relinquish his whale and join the travelling theatre world.

Family historians would be amused to find that the registration of Eliza's marriage was spectacularly non-communicative. Neither Eliza, nor William, stated their ages - simply choosing to put "of age". This might have been to disguise the fact that Eliza was not "of age" as she was only twenty. They also both decided to describe themselves as "servants", and the occupation of both fathers is simply recorded as "traveller" – nobody used words like "actor", "showman" or "theatre proprietor", let alone "whale exhibitor".

During the first ten years of Eliza's and William's marriage we once again encounter a lack of documentation to enable anyone to describe their progress, but the late 1840s and early 1850s seem to have been a time when portable theatres "took off". Names such as Latimer, Wardaugh, Holloway, and

Jennings do seem to establish themselves, and appear in occasional reports in local papers. The emergence of the portables during this period can be linked to the simultaneous emerging importance of "amusements" as opposed to "trade" in the world of markets and fairs. The amusements on offer included swing boats and early riding equipment ("merry-go-rounds" etc.) but also included shows such as menageries, dioramas, and the theatres. In 1855 Messrs Bennett & Patch are often appearing alongside Wombwell's Menagerie, for example.

In the Birmingham Journal of 29th September 1855 a contributor supplies a story of a court case in Wednesbury in which Edward Bennett, Elizabeth Bennett, Eliza Patch and William Patch face charges of assaulting John Latimer, *"the much respected manager of the Mammoth Theatre"* and John Campbell, one of his actors. Neither Elizabeth, nor Eliza, appeared in court to answer the charges, but the case was dismissed for lack of evidence anyway. It would seem that when travelling theatres operated alongside each other competition could be fierce, but we also have examples where they co-operated and appeared in each other's shows! For example – at the Bloxwich Races of August 1847 Bennett's Theatre had presented a play featuring Eliza, Mrs. Latimer and Mrs. Jennings.

In the 1851 Census we find a list of "Travellers attending Stourbridge Fair asleep in their vans". Eliza and William are in the company of John Patch, William's father, and several other families are listed – some of whom could have been appearing in the theatre, others perhaps presenting other amusements. Once again this suggests that the portable theatre was generally built up as part of a fair. As the 1850s progressed it could be that the portables started travelling more independently and looked for sites in towns where they could open on a fully licensed basis. In this case it could be significant that the census found Bennett & Patch in Stourbridge because the town eventually plays a large part in this story, particularly as a "case study" of how travelling theatres sometimes became "permanent".

Below: Barlow's Yard, Stourbridge, in the late 1880s, looking towards the back of buildings in the High Street. Here we catch a glimpse of Bennett & Patch's Alhambra Theatre then operating as a permanent theatre. Horizontal lap-boarding now seems to clad the structure. On the right stands Eliza Patch' carriage.
(Dudley Archives & LHS)

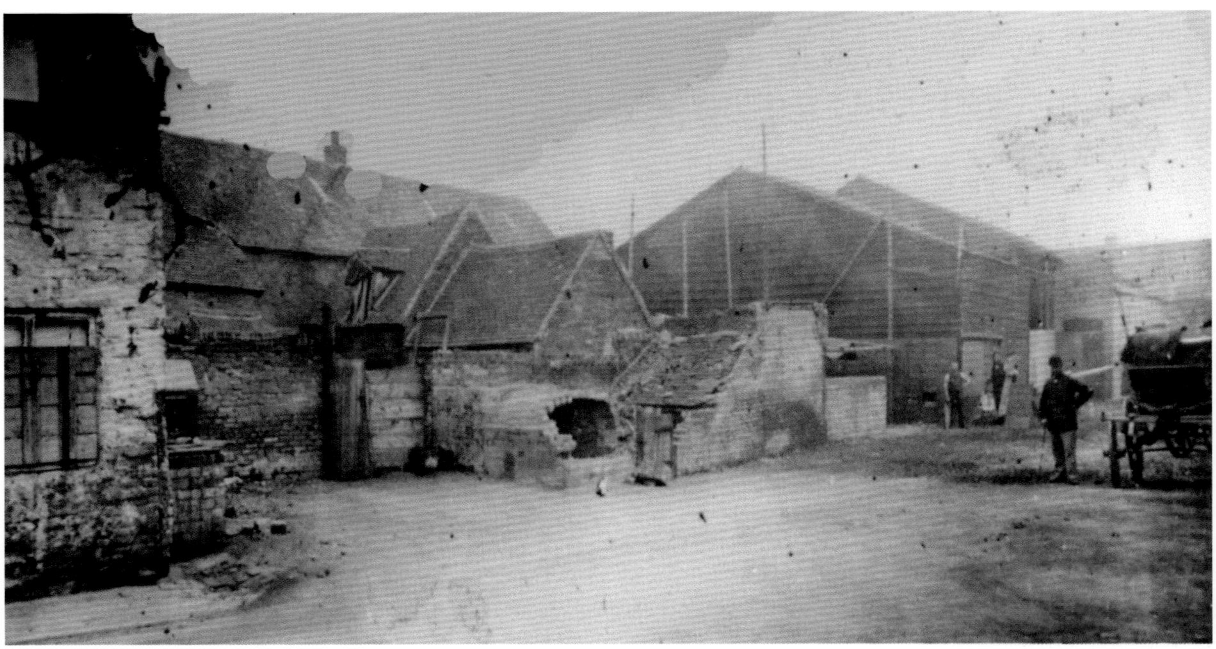

On the Record at last.

From 1855 onwards it easier to find some surviving documentation to give us a glimpse of the activities of Messrs Bennett &Patch. This does not mean we can find detailed descriptive accounts of their movements, but it does mean that brief reports and advertisements begin to appear in The Era and there are occasional mentions in local newspapers. In the Spring of 1855 The Era mentions Messrs. Bennett & Patch several times in relation to their success in Bilston. This must have been in the theatre in the market place found neatly marked on an 1850s map of the town. The earliest report appears in April and the last in August suggesting quite a lengthy stay, while reports after that month record Bennett & Patch appearing in Tipton, Darlaston and Wednesbury. From all the fragments of information from The Era and local papers we can collect some information about Bennett & Patch's activities within the Black Country and occasional reference to travels to more distant parts – such as appearances at the Nottingham Goose Fair. The following section of this chapter will look at their Black Country activities town by town; meanwhile we will look at how their lives progressed and some of the general issues that can be discussed.

While the Bennetts and Patches were touring around the Black Country in the late 1850s, 1860s and 1870s there were other developments taking place. Eliza's brother William, born in 1836, seems to have gone into the theatre business but, soon showed a degree of independence. The 1861 census reveals that as a twenty-five-year old he was boarding in Halesowen with a couple of "comedians", identifying himself as a "musician". At the same time his parents, Edward and Elizabeth Bennett are "Living and sleeping in their vans" on Bilston Market Patch.

On 1st February 1864 William, Eliza's brother, married Mary Jane Humpherson at St. Peter's & St. Paul's Church in Aston. (A few decades later this church was popular with showmen as a result of its proximity to the Serpentine Ground used by Pat Collins for his annual "Onion Fair" and two other fairs, but seems to have been chosen by the couple as they were residing in Duddeston at the time.) William gave his occupation as "Musician" which was consistent with his statement in the 1861 census. The nineteen year old Mary Jane was the daughter of George Humpherson of Bewdley. The Humphersons had established the Horn Works in Bewdley. Her father was present at the wedding so we must assume he was happy to see her marry into a theatrical family.

If "Bennett & Patch" was a partnership between Eliza's brother and husband it would be interesting to learn at what point William gave up travelling and working independently as a musician, and joined the family business.

In the 1871 census we find the two families both occupying living vans in Barlow's Yard in Stourbridge. William and Eliza Patch are joined by a couple of "theatricals", and William and Mary Bennett are with their children: four-year-old twins, William and Harry, and four-month old Isabel. Their sister Amy was staying with her grandparents, the Humphersons, in Bewdley at the time. Also present, as a visitor, was Eliza Humpherson – William's sister-in-law. It would seem that Edward and Elizabeth, the previous generation, were in a caravan in Queen Street, West Bromwich, another town favoured by the Bennetts.
One source later suggested that 1873 was the year in which Eliza and her brother William formally separated their activities – adding to the picture we have of Eliza and William Patch becoming increasingly settled in Stourbridge and brother William still travelling.

The owner of Barlow's Yard, in Stourbridge, died in 1865 and his death was followed by legal proceedings before his estate could be sold. It seems that the Patches purchased the yard and the adjoining properties on the High Street, including the Coach & Horses inn, having previously leased land from Mrs. Pilsbury – the daughter of Mr. Barlow. Gradually they rebuilt the Coach & Horses and the adjoining properties and William Patch became licensee of the inn. It is difficult to follow the developments and refurbishments in and around the theatre in the yard, but gradually it became more "permanent". In the 1881 census William Patch lists himself as "Licensed Victualler" at the Coach & Horses and although the theatre is not mentioned it can be noted that among the people living in the property are sixteen year old Amy, listed as a musician, and fourteen-year-old Harry who is listed as an actor. Harry, listed as "nephew" was obviously one of the twins born to William and Mary. (Amy was Eliza's niece, and Harry's older sister.)

Eliza's father, Edward Bennett died about 1880 – just as the traditions of the travelling theatrical world were becoming a thing of the past and the permanent theatre was about to become the norm. (There is a death of an Edward Bennett recorded at Stourbridge in the last quarter of 1880s which would appear to be the death of Eliza's father, but it does not seem to have been noticed by the local press.)

During the 1880s Eliza "retired" from the acting side of the business, and there is also evidence that William's health declined, although we also know that he was active in local "civic" affairs for a time. By the time we reach the 1891 census neither William, nor Eliza, claim an occupation, despite the fact that they were still running the theatre in Barlow's Yard. A George Sykes is acting as manager of the Coach & Horses. Meanwhile Eliza's brother William, and his family are now firmly based in Coventry, where William is a theatre proprietor and manager. His son Harry is "musical director" and his daughter Isobel, now twenty, is an actress.

William Patch died at the end of March 1895 in the Coach & Horses. The County Express provided a reasonably detailed account of his life, concluding, "Mr. Patch's career has not been devoid of its spice and romance". The account focussed on the travelling whale show rather than giving us a clear account of the portable theatres but it had positive things to say about the theatre in Stourbridge. His funeral took place on 3rd April and he was buried in Wollaston churchyard, following a service conducted by Rev. Gillbanks. Members of the family mentioned in this story attended the event – including William Bennet (Eliza's brother) and his twin sons Harry and William.

William's death left Eliza with the task of running the theatre in Stourbridge on her own, although she was by then in her seventies. The Stourbridge Kellys Directory of 1896 informed readers that the theatre had been entirely rebuilt in the md 1890s, and to some extent it advertised more regularly in the local press enabling us to see a record of the shows appearing there. It would seem that the theatre remained firmly in Eliza's control. Although Eliza's health also declined, it was an accident in February 1900, when she broke her hip, which seemed to precipitate the final chapter in her career. She decided to retire and to sell the theatre. She found a customer in the shape of Douglas Phelps, an actor who had appeared in the theatre in September 1898, and who had positive ideas about how programming at the theatre could be improved.

Her retirement was brief. On Wednesday 28th November 1900 Eliza died at the Coach & Horses, and an obituary appeared in the Country Express on 1st December. The words of this obituary were repeated in The Era, The Stage and other papers. The Staffordshire and Worcestershire Advertiser &Herald produced its own text which included the following words:

"Mrs. Patch managed the Alhambra with consummate skill and it is strong testimony to her keen business capacity and indomitable energy that for a long period she never required the assistance of an acting manager. She was a clever woman of excellent judgement and much force of character."

The funeral took place at St. James' Church Wollaston at 1.00.pm on Sunday 2nd December. As explained at the beginning of this chapter, Rev. Gillbanks addressed the mourners at the graveside before she was buried alongside William Patch. Her oak coffin was carried to the grave by Messrs R and J Heathcote, Henry Sanders, Squire Baker, W. Platt and George North. The Heathcotes were member of the Alhambra Theatre's small orchestra, and George North was the son of the funeral director William North, who was also present. Other members of the orchestra and actors who had appeared at the theatre also attended, but were not named in the local paper's report. The chief mourners were Eliza's brother, William, and his thirty three-year-old twin sons, Dr. William Bennett of Birmingham, and Mr. Harry Dudley Bennett who was managing a theatre in London at the time. Douglas Phelps and his wife, the new proprietors of the theatre, were also present. Despite the "never will be forgotten" words of Rev. Gillbanks, I do not think Eliza's death and funeral were more widely reported in the Black Country – already the portable theatre world of which she had been a part was slipping into the past.

ALHAMBRA THEATRE, STOURBRIDGE

Proprietress & Manageress: Mrs. Patch

SATURDAY April 8th. Last night of "THE GOMBEENS GOLD" also the startling Drama of "ROBERT MACAIRE" or "The Roadside Inn"

MONDAY April 17th, Messrs Rose and Hertie

Farewell visit of "MY SWEETHEART" Tony, Mr. Frank Hertie, Tina, Miss Lizzie Boone

MONDAY April 24th, the great Drama of the Day entitled "THE DARK CONTINENT".

Time and Prices as usual. No Smoking allowed.

The South Staffordshire Advertiser, 8th April 1893

AHAMBRA THEATRE,
STOURBRIDGE
Proprietress…… Mrs. Patch
For Six Nights only, commencing December 6th.
The renowned actor
Mr. HENRY LORAINE.
The popular and accomplished Artiste
Miss EDITH KINGSLEY,
supported by a
Powerful Dramatic Company
On Monday and Tuesday 6th and 7th.
Will be produced the great
Sensational Drama
In a Prologue and Three Acts entitled,
"THE FACE IN THE
MOONLIGHT."
On Wednesday and Thursday December 8th and 9th
will be produced the great Play entitled
"THE GAMESTER"

On Friday Evening December 10th
will be acted
Shakespeare's sublime Five Act Tragedy
"HAMLET"

On Saturday Evening December 11th
Grand popular Entertainment, the beautiful play
"INGOMAR, THE SON OF THE
WILDERNESS"
To conclude with the great
Sensational Drama,
Entitled, "THE DUKE'S MOTTO."
To be followed by
"Miss HARDING'S UMPIRE"
THE DANITES COMPANY
for Christmas
With New and Original Effects,
"MULDOON'S PICNIC", "BLACK
FLAG"
"STOWAWAY", and other Novelties
Times and Prices as Usual
SCENES, DRESSES
all requisites for amateur and
other Performances to LET or HIRE.

The following year produced another census and from that we learn that William Bennett, Eliza's brother, continued the run the theatre in Coventry. Harry, his son, was with William in Coventry at the time of the census along with his wife Florence and son Guy. Eliza's other nephew, William, continued to work in Birmingham as a consultant and later had two children: Mary and Anthony. It might therefore be possible that their descendants are alive today and it would be intriguing to find out if anyone is working on their family history and discovering that they are descended from Eliza. Someone might even have a photograph of her.

There are two "unresolved issues". Firstly, how many portable theatres did Bennet & Patch use? Did William Bennett use an entirely separate one? To what extent could a temporary "portable" turn into a permanent theatre as seems to have happened in Stourbridge, and to a lesser extent in New Hall Street Dudley? On some occasions was a portable theatre left on site while Bennet & Patch moved to another, and was such a building ever then leased to another company for a short season?

Secondly: What is the precise meaning of the title "Bennett & Patch"? Obviously from a twenty first century point of view it would be nice to imagine that the partnership was between Eliza Bennett and her husband William Patch – a husband and wife team in which Eliza was the star of the show. However, it is much more likely that "Bennet and Patch" describes a partnership between William Patch and either Eliza's father or her brother.

THEATRE ROYAL.—We observe that Messrs. Bennett & Patch, proprietors of the Theatre Royal, are to commence with the "Poor of London" on Saturday evening first, and remain during the ensuing week. As this company has hitherto been well patronised, no doubt, from the attractive programme which has been issued, they will receive bumper houses.

Newspaper cuttings: Above: Stourbridge 1868, Below: Brierley Hill, 1874.

THE THEATRE. — Messrs Bennett and Patch's new Theatre opened with a powerful company for the first time to a crowded house on Saturday night last. The plays ar every good, and the entertainment throughout are full of fun and amusement. We hope Messrs Bennett and Patch, who have been so long known as caterers for the amusement of the public, will not have cause to regret their visit to Brierley Hill. Numerous novelties are in preparation.

Bennett & Patch's Black Country Theatres

(This chapter is provided for readers who wish to study a particular theatre or location without having to disentangle the information from the historical narrative in the previous section.)

Dudley

Our search for the Bennett & Patch theatres starts in Dudley because that is where Eliza was born and it is where she may first have appeared on stage – with her father Edward Bennett. "T.B"'s words in a Dudley Herald of 1889 hark back to a theatre appearing in Dudley Market Place "fifty years ago". Unfortunately we have no records going back to the late 1840s, but we can find references to Bennett & Path's presence in Dudley in The Era in 1855, 1856, 1859, 1860, 1867, 1868, 1871 and 1880. Records are brief, few and far between, and sometimes ambiguous, and sometimes it is not clear whether a theatre is being run by Eliza and William Patch, or by William Bennett, Eliza's brother! References in the local press, the Dudley Herald, are also few and far between and ambiguous.

The Era of 15th April 1855 tells readers that Bennett & Patch opened for a short season in Dudley on 31st March and states: *"We understand that it is the manager's intention to erect a permanent theatre in this town which will be in readiness for the ensuing winter."* We hear no more of this until the 21st December 1856 edition mentions that they have built their new theatre and applied for a licence on 17th of that month. Apparently decisions were deferred. Meanwhile the town's Garrick Club used it to present the play "Still Waters Run Deep" to raise money for building the proposed Mechanic's Institute in Wolverhampton Street. (This play was written in 1855 by Tom Taylor – only a year before Dudley's Garrick Club wanted to perform it.)

In March 1858 we learn that the Dudley Garrick Club have once again rented "*the new theatre in New Hall Street*" to present their own amateur production of "Othello". This may be the confirmation we are looking for that Bennett & Patch eventually built up their theatre in New Hall Street, and from then onwards that would be their usual venue when open in Dudley for short seasons. Some years later the Year Book published by E Blocksidge included a photograph of premises in Dudley Market place in which we can see an entry marked: "Entry leading to Bennet & Patch's theatre."

An isolated reference in The Era of 5th May 1872 says that Bennett & Patch were open again in Dudley.

When we come to 1880 the Dudley Herald does cover Bennett & Patch's season in this theatre – opening on Monday 9th February and running through to Easter Saturday on 27th March. It was usual to present the same play on Monday and Tuesday night and then change the programme every night through to Saturday – readers of the Herald are told to see local bills for more details, but unfortunately for us samples of such bills do not seem to have survived. We do know that Eliza made her debut for the season on 12th February, appearing in a play called "The Eviction".

At the end of that 1880 season the Dudley Herald did provide an over-view of its success, saying:

"The season has been marked with a vast improvement of the class of pieces produced at this theatre. Mr. Bennett has endeavoured to keep pace with the wants of modern play-goers and gives excellent representations of various London and provincial pieces – especially "The Seven Sins", "Velvet and Gags", "Lady Clancarty" and Shakespeare's plays, not forgetting "L'Assomoir" adapted by William Bennett from Zola's novel. Everything reflects credit on Mr. Bennett and his manager Mr. J. Dwyer."

William Bennett presented another season in 1881 – leaving us to wonder if the building stayed in place or was moved to other venues for short seasons. One problem was that local authorities were reluctant to issue theatre licences for long periods, and most portables preferred to open for short periods at local fairs where apparently such licences were not sought.

When William Bennett returned to present the 1881 season, his efforts were again applauded by the Dudley Herald. It was a season in which the theatre had to cope with competition from entertainment in the Public Hall, visiting circuses and an appearance of Pepper's Ghost – the optical illusion show that took Britain by storm in the 1880s.

The 1881 season in Dudley also provided an opportunity for Amy Bennett, William's teenage daughter, to appear on stage. She joined a "well known tragedian", Mr. T.C. King in a presentations of "Othello" and "William Tell". (Amy was born in 1865 and was named Amy Eliza, after her aunt.)

In the following years the Dudley Herald does not mention the theatre, leaving us to wonder if it continued to be used or was pulled down and rebuilt elsewhere.

Edwin Blocksidge 1847 – 1909) produced his annual Dudley Almamac from 1886 onwards. He was not any a printer, lithographer, and painted but he was also a keen local historian. In 1914 he reproduced this rare 1850s photograph given to him by G.T. Owen, son of the John Owen who owned the wine shop in the centre of the picture. He then added the explanations printed below the picture – including the reference to the entry, next to John Owen's shop, which provided access to Bennett & Patch's Theatre in a yard off New Hall Street. These shops, overlooking the market were demolished c.1860.
(Dudley Archives & LHC)

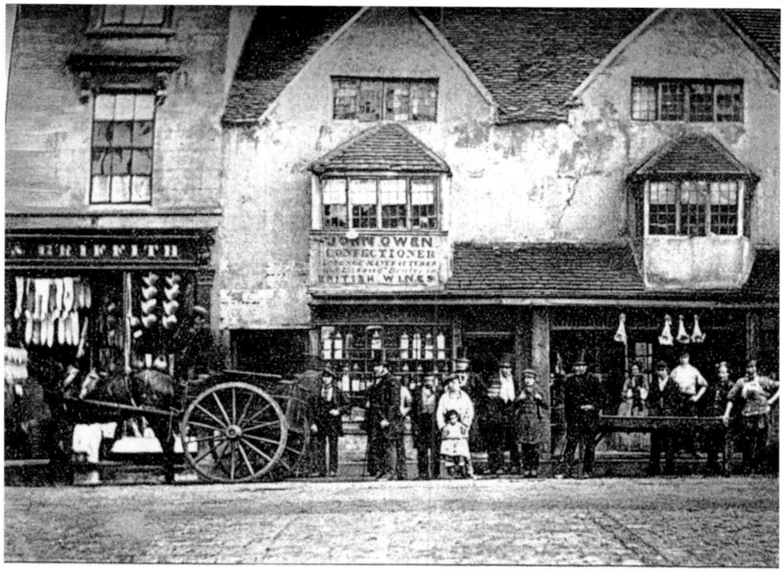

A. Griffith, Draper, &c., (now Hunt & Hunt). | Private Entrance to Bennett and Patches' Theatre, New Hall St. | John Owen, father of the present G. T. Owen. | William Self, butcher.

Bilston

We have already noted Bennett & Patch's presence in Bilston. The Era of 10th August 1855 mentions the closure of the theatre in Bilston after a two week season, suggesting that the company was setting off for a new theatre in Dudley. The Era of September 1856 also comments on short season during that year, and mentions a particular appearance of Eliza Patch in "The Stranger". However a much later source makes a much stronger case for regarding Bilston as an important place in this saga. After Eliza's death the The Staffordshire and Worcestershire Advertiser and Herald claimed: *"Her first permanent theatre was at Bilston, which opened in 1852. It was there that Montagu Williams played Macbeth to Mrs. Patch's Lady Macbeth."* (Obviously we should not be taken in by the word "permanent" in this reference.

Five years later The Era of 1st April 1860 tells readers that Bennett & Patch are celebrating Lord Ward's elevation to the title of Earl of Dudley both in Dudley and Bilston and children are being admitted free to the celebrations!

In the 1861 census we find Edward & Elizabeth Bennett "asleep in their van" in Bilston Market Place perhaps indicating that the whole family had to be involved in running the theatres if they were open in more than one location. It is not clear where Eliza and William were at the time. In July 1866 the Bilston theatre is described as "to let".

When Walter Edwin opened in Bilston Market Place in 1874 a report implied that it had been some years since Bennett & Patch had been seen in that location.

Willenhall

In The Era of 11th May 1856 there is an amusing reference to Willenhall:
"Willenhall: Our unusually dull town has recently been enlivened by the presence of a very respectable company of comedians under the management of Messrs. Bennett & Patch."

Tipton

A brief reference to Bennett & Patch's theatre appearing at Tipton Wakes belongs to the period when the theatre was being built up as part of fairs and wakes rather than opening independently. Its appearance at Tipton suggests that they built up at many other local fairs, most of which will be undocumented.

West Bromwich

The Era of 9th July 1865 informs readers that Messrs. Bennett & Patch applied at the Police Court for a licence and intended building a permanent theatre in that town. Apparently they had previously had a twelve month licence in West Bromwich – presumably using a more temporary building. No precise locations are mentioned. A further reference is not found until November 1872 when The Era reports:

West Bromwich: Royal Alhambra Theatre (Proprietors Messrs. Bennett & Patch). This place has been reopened with The Miser of Atherstone & Kenilworth". The appearance of Mr. Jas Matthews, Mr.T. Davenport and Mrs. Bourne (old favourites) was the signal for prolonged cheering. The characters throughout were well sustained. The audience has been good."

Having ignored West Bromwich for several years The Era then features Bennett & Patch's presence every week for the next few weeks and carries an advertisement on 8th December 1872:
Wanted: for Bennett &Patch's Theatre, West Bromwich: A useful couple, Gentleman for responsible business, and Lady to play leading business occasionally; also a Single Young Man. Those used to Portable Theatre. Must be sober and respectable. Permanent situation in buildings seven months in the year."

Reports of activities in West Bromwich continue through to 29th December 1872 when the pantomime "Mother Red Cap, or Little Bo Peep" is being presented. *("The pantomime abounds with local hits and good scenic effects")*. It seems that the theatre was built up on a site in Queen Street, and was soon to be challenged by theatrical presentations at The Royal Exchange in Walsall Street – an enterprise that eventually became the town's permanent "Theatre Royal".

Wednesbury

When Wednesbury's Theatre Royal opened in February 1892 the Wednesbury Herald commissioned local historian Frederick Hackwood to write a memoir about theatre in the town. He recalled early touring companies and the fact that Latimers' Theatre and Bennett & Patch's tended to turn up at the Wakes. He tells us that Bennett & Patch built up in High Bullen using "the greater part of the highway". On one occasion Bennett & Patch were prosecuted for blocking the highway! Hackwood reckons all this came to an end in 1873 when the wakes were "banned".

Walsall and Bloxwich

Bennett & Patch built up their portable theatre to appear alongside the annual horse races in both Walsall and Bloxwich in the 1840s, usually during September. The racecourse in Walsall was remarkably close to the town centre, and was to be found on the "Town Meadows" – an area now occupied by a Homebase car park! Considering the fact that any visual record of the existence of Bennett & Patch's portable theatres is as rare as the proverbial hens' teeth, we should be very grateful to Billy Meikle of Walsall. He was a local historian and an artist – the archive of his work is now invaluable to anyone interested in Walsall's past. Fortunately for us Billy painted a picture of Bennett & Patch's theatre!

Brierley Hill

Annual horse races were a feature of life in several Black Country towns and were often accompanied in the mid nineteenth century by entertainment and amusements. Evidence survives describing such activities in Brierley Hill, and several references are to be found in which a number of portable theatre companies use an area called "The Old Boiler Yard". This was close to a five-ways crossroad at the western end of Brierley Hill's High Street and is currently buried beneath a small shopping area called the Moor Centre.

Theatres appearing on this ground included Holloway's, Latimer's "Mammoth Theatre", and Bennett & Patch's. In February 1881 the Brierley Hill Advertiser records that they were applying for a licence so perhaps Bennet & Patch used the ground at other times of the year and left 'Raceweek' to others. The Advertiser also printed the local history based recollections of Walter Clulow and in an item printed in March 1914 he makes a specific reference to Bennett & Patch coming to Brierley Hill.

The site was used for some years by a building called "The Palace Theatre" which opened in 1914 and was often also used as a cinema. Its footprint may have been that once occupied by visiting portables!

Stourbridge

Although there have been sightings of Bennett & Patch's theatre at many other towns, in, around and beyond, the Black Country – the most important place in the story is Stourbridge.

Eliza herself seemed to suggest that the enterprise had been coming to Stourbridge since the mid-1850s, probably at a time when they usually accompanied the fair. In those far off days fairs were relatively little organised, controlled or regulated, but that was soon to change, and those changes may have led to the portables taking on a more independent style of travel. Certainly, in the 1871 census, we find them in Stourbridge, but without any mention of the fair being there simultaneously.

Although Bennett & Patch may have come to Barlow's Yard in Stourbridge regularly from the1850s onwards there is plenty of evidence of other shows also visiting the same ground. Making matters a bit more permanent in Stourbridge seems to follow a decision to purchase property in the High Street at the front of the yard. This included the Coach & Horses inn. When the 1881 census was taken Eliza and William are residing in the Coach and Horses and William is calling himself a "licensed victualler".

Records and references are intermittent and even more confusing is the continual inter-changeability of names – sometimes the Theatre Royal, sometimes the Alhambra, and sometimes with the word "New" in front of either of those. There are occasions when Eliza seems to be mounting the shows; there are other occasions when it is being used by touring companies. There are also references to improving the theatre. For example, The Era of 14th September 1889 contains an "artistes wanted" advertisement explaining that the theatre was reopening after a closure at Whitsun in which time a new larger stage has been installed, and the front of house refurbished.

One of the most likely interpretation of the evidence is that the most dramatic rebuilding of the theatre was in 1894 or 1895 and by that time its presence was definitely "permanent" and was sticking to the name "Alhambra". A Kelly's Directory of 1896 describes the theatre as "entirely rebuilt" and enlarged to accommodate 2000 patrons! By this time Eliza was a widow and facing the realities of growing old, but she soldiered on until 1900 when the theatre was sold to Douglas Phelps. The theatre survived until April 1929.

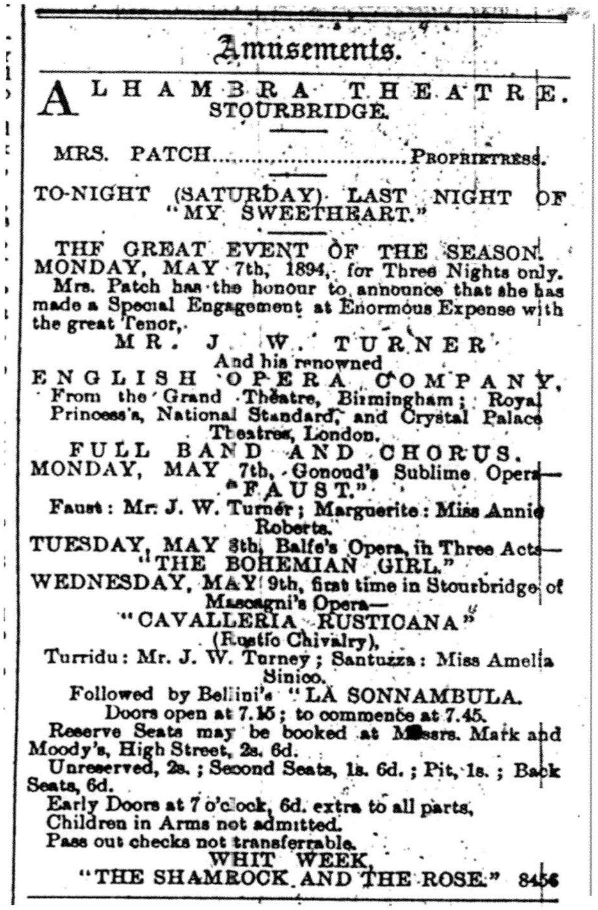

Amusements.

ALHAMBRA THEATRE. STOURBRIDGE.

MRS. PATCH.................................PROPRIETRESS.

TO-NIGHT (SATURDAY) LAST NIGHT OF "MY SWEETHEART."

THE GREAT EVENT OF THE SEASON. MONDAY, MAY 7th, 1894, for Three Nights only. Mrs. Patch has the honour to announce that she has made a Special Engagement at Enormous Expense with the great Tenor,

MR. J. W. TURNER

And his renowned

ENGLISH OPERA COMPANY,

From the Grand Theatre, Birmingham; Royal Princess's, National Standard, and Crystal Palace Theatres, London.

FULL BAND AND CHORUS.

MONDAY, MAY 7th, Gonoud's Sublime Opera— "FAUST."

Faust: Mr. J. W. Turner; Marguerite: Miss Annie Roberts.

TUESDAY, MAY 8th, Balfe's Opera, in Three Acts— "THE BOHEMIAN GIRL."

WEDNESDAY, MAY 9th, first time in Stourbridge of Mascagni's Opera— "CAVALLERIA RUSTICANA" (Rustic Chivalry).

Turridu: Mr. J. W. Turney; Santuzza: Miss Amelia Sinico.

Followed by Bellini's "LA SONNAMBULA.

Doors open at 7.15; to commence at 7.45.

Reserve Seats may be booked at Messrs. Mark and Moody's, High Street, 2s. 6d.

Unreserved, 2s.; Second Seats, 1s. 6d.; Pit, 1s.; Back Seats, 6d.

Early Doors at 7 o'clock, 6d. extra to all parts.

Children in Arms not admitted.

Pass out checks not transferrable.

WHIT WEEK, "THE SHAMROCK AND THE ROSE." 8456

Above: An advertisement from a Stourbridge County Express of 1894.Note that tickets can be obtained from Mark & Moody's shop in the High Street – they were publishers of the County Express. Note that during this week of opera, "Children in Arms not admitted." Also note that even the Alhambra ran an "early doors" policy for those who wished to arrive early.

"My Sweetheart", mentioned at the top of this advert, was presented the following week at The Coliseum – John Maurice Clement's theatre in Dudley.

This advertisement is reproduced as it appeared in the paper – and has not been "re-set" as in the examples shown earlier in this chapter.

Postscript:

What happened to William Bennett?

When Eliza's brother William died in 1911 The Coventry Herald of 24th April 1911 provided a life story as part of an obituary – filling in more background information and helping us understand how William's life can be compared and contrasted with Eliza's story.

Mr. Bennett came from a theatrical family, his father, who died at the age of 88, having during the greater part of his life, carried on the business of theatrical proprietor. He was born in Longton and was baptised at Dudley Parish church where his uncle was organist, and was educated at a boarding school in Dudley. When his education was finished he joined his father. At that time – more than sixty years ago – there were few buildings in permanent occupation as a theatre as there are now. Theatrical companies travelled the country in summer months, performing in towns in the winter months.

When a boy Mr. Bennett frequently accompanied the baggage in journeys from district to district, the travelling often being at night. Mr. Bennett's father had a standard theatre at Stourbridge and others at Bilston and West Bromwich, and appeared at the Great Fair in Coventry on their travels. Mr Bennett never acted. When he grew to manhood he made advance arrangements for his father and sometimes led the orchestra. He was a skilful player on the cornet, cello and violin. Once at a place where Wombwell's Menagerie was exhibiting next door their orchestra played music William Bennet specially composed for them. He could also recite Shakespeare's works from beginning to end.

Coventry people who have scarcely reached middle age remember Bennett & Patch performing at the fair in Pool Meadow. Patch was the son-in-law of the elder Mr. Bennett. The ground usually occupied by the theatre was on the Cox Street side of Pool Meadow, and the theatre was a great attraction, though it had its rivals. Messrs Bennett & Patch had a repertoire of 100 plays and Mr. Montagu Williams, the well-known London magistrate was once with them, and he mentions in his reminiscences that he acted with Mrs. Patch.

Sixty years ago Mr. Bennett's father built a theatre on the site of Addison Road station in London. It was intended for the entertainment of visitors to the Great

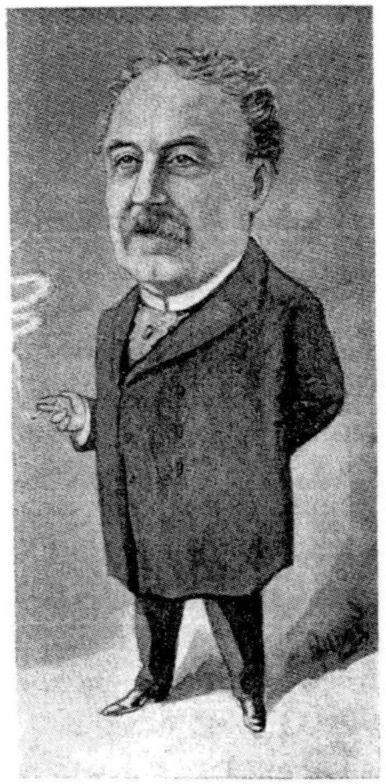

CARTOON No. 6.– Mr. WM. BENNETT.

Mr. Bennett, who died last year, was perhaps the best known theatrical manager in the Kingdom, partly on account of his age and partly owing to his early career as touring theatrical proprietor. Sixty years ago when, on leaving school he accompanied his father throughout the whole of the Midland Counties, he acquired that extensive knowledge of persons and places of which he had such interesting recollections, and which he was so pleased to relate. There are few middle aged Coventry citizens who cannot remember the annual visit to the Great Fair of Bennett and Patch's Theatre, when Mr. Bennett was a young man and manager in advance for his father ; and Mr. Patch, who was his brother-in-law—the latter having married his only sister, who was many years his senior. The old stock companies included men and women who possessed a repertoire of sometimes a hundred plays, and regularly produced a different one every night of their visit. Instead of being content with three or four towns in the Black Country, where he had permanent buildings in which to pass the winter, Mr. Bennett entered into new enterprises at Coventry, Clapham, Balham, Burton, etc. There is scarcely a theatre of any distinction in any part of the United Kingdom Mr. Bennett had not visited, and hardly a proprietor or manager to whom he was not personally known.

Although no picture of Eliza Bennett has been found, we do have this cartoon picture of her brother, William – published in the Coventry Herald.

Exhibition of 1851. It was not a successful venture and was taken down before the Exhibition closed.

Mr. Bennett's father died about 33 years ago at a time when there was a development towards theatres being erected in larger towns for longer periods. Mr. Bennett erected play houses at Dudley, Darlaston, West Bromwich, Bilston, Stourbridge, and Kidderminster. These he kept open for part of the year as theatres and they were rented for the remainder of the year by other people… sometimes even by the Salvation Army.

The Britannia Music Hall was Mr. Bennett's first purchase in Coventry. It was erected on the site of the Royal Exchange by James Eaves, a local auctioneer.

Later Mr. Bennett sold the building to the Co-operative Society. After buying the Britannia he bought the old theatre in Smithford Street, which twenty two years ago was superseded by the Opera House in Hales Street. The old Smithfield Street theatre prospered under the control of Mr. Bennett and well-known actors appeared there.

There were people who prophesied that the Opera House would not be a success as it was thought not to enjoy a central enough position – but they were wrong. The Opera House opened on 25th March 1889 with a production of Midsummer Night's Dream featuring F.R. Benson, the Shakespearean actor. Mr Bennett made a brief speech on the opening night, and was heartily received.

Some years ago Mr. Bennett bought the Coventry Corn Exchange building, now occupied as The Empire Theatre, and at different times he was the owner of the theatre at Leamington Spa, and part owner of theatres at Clapham and Balham.

Although we can regard this as a fairly thorough account of William's life it is worth going through it in a bit more detail – just to put as much information "on the record" as possible - although this is probably the best account of his early life that we are likely to encounter.

Just as Eliza's marriage to William Patch in 1844 was a significant moment in her life, I think we would have to say the same was true for William. Early in 1864 he married Jane Mary Humpherson at Aston. She was born in 1846 and grew up in Bewdley. William and Mary had four children, starting with Amy, who was born in 1865.The twins, Henry George Dudley Bennett (known as Harry) and William Edward Bennett were born in 1867, and their sister Isobel was born in 1870. All four were born in Bewdley, Mary Jane's original home, suggesting that if she and William were leading a nomadic life she might have returned "home" to deliver her children.

We know from the above account that William's travels with the portable theatre took him to Coventry, and it was there that he decided to adopt a more settled existence. His first "permanent" theatrical venture in Coventry was at the Britannia Music Hall, followed by the Theatre Royal off Smithford Street. The latter was in a fairly poor state when he took it over – having been a barn-like structure converted to occasional theatre use early in the nineteenth century. Other characters who had leased it at one time or another was another Mr. Bennett – Henry Bennett (1791 – 1868) – usually associated with the Theatre Royal in Worcester. (The theatre had been created by Sir Skears Rew, one-time Mayor of Coventry, and had opened at Easter 1819. Henry Bennett ran the place from 1830 to 1851 in which time it became "The Royal", and in the years that followed it was leased and managed by a variety of people, all detailed in Ted Bottle's book: "Coventry's Forgotten Theatre".)

William Bennett, on taking control in September 1880, spent some money in improving the Theatre Royal and revived its fortunes but knew that the licensing authorities were never very keen to renew its licence – making him decide that he should build a brand new purpose built theatre. According to the Coventry Herald of 25th November 1887 he had announced his intention of building an Opera House in Hales Street. Plans for such a building were not approved until April 1888 but on 14th September of that year the Herald was able to report that ground had been broken on the site and the foundations were about to be laid. The architects were Messrs Essex & Nichol, and Mr. C. Gray Hill was going to build it at accost of £4000. It was scheduled to open in 1889 – by which time William Bennett had abandoned his use of the Theatre Royal.

As stated above the Opera House, Coventry, opened on 25th March 1889 with Midsummer Night's Dream but it wasn't going to be tied to opera and Shakespeare. On 8th May 1889 the Coventry Times reported:

"We are getting used to processions through the city nowadays. The circus has done a great deal for us in this direction during the past few months... But on Monday morning came the best show I have yet seen. First in an open carriage came the proprietor of the Opera House, Mr. William Bennett, accompanied by a cornet player. Then, at a slow march and regular intervals, came Crocker's Sixteen Performing Horses bearing coloured head-dresses and numerous bells, and led by uniformed attendants. They were followed by two dainty little ponies and then Professor Crocker himself in a light gig."

In February 1891 the Coventry Herald told its readers that William Bennet had bought the theatre in Leamington and a year later it seems that William had taken control of the Theatre Royal in Kidderminster. At the latter he installed his son Harry as "General Manager" while leaving the supervision of the theatre to James Moore whom we also encounter in the account of Ben Kennedy's progress in another chapter. This may have only lasted a few years because by 1897 it was under the control of Mrs. Alice G. Carte. By that time

William had decided to extend his operations to London!

Forming a "consortium" with Harry and Charles Machin, William Bennett managed to open The Shakespeare Theatre on 16th November 1896 in Clapham, on a site next door to the Town Hall, a few yards from Clapham Junction – Britain's busiest railway station! It was quite a large theatre, with a capacity of 1,205 patrons and remained in use as a theatre until becoming a cinema in 1923, long after its association with the Bennetts. It was bomb damaged in the Second World Was and demolished completely in 1957 – the site now being occupied by an office block called "Shakespeare House". The architect of this theatre had been William George Robert Sprague who William then employed to design a new theatre in Coventry.

When the Shakespeare Theatre in Clapham opened Harry moved down to London to manage it. Meanwhile Coventry had become permanent "home" to William and Mary Jane Bennett and they lived at 33 Hertford Place. A new theatre was being planned in Coventry and was to be called the "New Grand Theatre of Variety". However, all did not proceed to plan regarding this project and construction stalled. Meanwhile William had bought the old Corn Exchange for about £16,000 and Mr. Sprague produced plans for its rebuilding and conversion into a theatre suitable for straight drama – leaving variety to the Opera House. The project would have involved building a new "corn exchange" facility – possibly on the site of The Royal – while The Grand was built. However, all these plans came to nothing. (Bennett sold the old Corn Exchange in 1906.)

Meanwhile William's activities in South London continued. William and Harry joined Mr. Sprague in forming a consortium to build The Royal Duchess Theatre, Balham, with the intention of opening it in 1899. It was a large theatre built in grand Renaissance style and was designed to accommodate 2500 patrons. Mr. Sprague drew the plans and decided to incorporate a theatre organ into the theatre's features. The theatre opened on 18th September 1899 with Hayden Coffin in "the Geisha", all of this being reported in the pages of The Era.

The Royal Duchess Theatre quickly adopted a variety programme and introduced some "moving pictures" from about 1908 onwards, and became a full time cinema in 1912 by which time it was in other hands. It closed after serious bomb damage during the Second World War and its remains were demolished in the 1960s.

William's use of William Robert George Sprague as his architect had interesting consequences. On 30th April 1900 Mr. Sprague married William's daughter, Isobel, at St. Saviour's Church in Camberwell, an event duly reported in The Era. William Sprague had been born in Australia, but his mother, Dolores Drummond, was an actress and was keen to resume her career in Britain. They came to London in 1874 and William grew up with an interest in theatre architecture, rather than acting. He worked for four years with the legendary Frank Matcham, but soon showed he had ideas of his own and a love of the Renaissance style. While working with William Bennett he was hailed as London's youngest theatre architect, and designed a number of well-known theatres… all a million miles in style from his wife's grandmother's portables. William G.R. Sprague had been married before, having married a Mary Jane Beer in 1890s, but that marriage had ended in divorce in 1898.

As the 1900s progressed William and Mary Jane Bennett must have sat back and been pleased with the progress they had made. He was running theatres in Coventry and Leamington Spa, and with Harry's help he was running the two London area theatres – in Clapham and Balham. Things had begun to slow down with the plans to build another theatre in Coventry having stalled. All three surviving children were married and the twins, William and Harry had found careers in medicine and the theatre business. The first sign of any cloud being on the horizon emerged in 1903 when Mary Jane Bennett became ill. It was an illness that lasted for four years and she died on 16th August 1907 at the age of 61. She was buried at Coventry Cemetery.

William Bennett died on 26th April 1911, aged 76, at the family home in Hertford Place. He had been seriously ill for about six weeks. A large funeral took place at 9.45.am on Sunday 30th April with a service conducted by Rev. Saunderson followed by burial at Coventry Cemetery, where his coffin was carried by members of the Opera House orchestra. It was attended by his children and their partners and by grandchildren, theatre staff, and people from the theatrical world and the community of Coventry.

Harry Bennett

William's death did not quite end the Bennett's association with the theatrical world, as William's son, Harry was still in the business. Henry George Dudley Bennett and his twin brother William had been born in 1866 in Bewdley. As we have seen, he worked alongside his father in expanding the theatrical empire – particularly in relation to the London theatres, but he had also played a part in managing the Leamington theatre. Towards the end of 1902 he set off on his own by buying the St. Georges Hall in Burton-on-Trent, and transformed it into the "New Opera House", capable of accommodating two thousand patrons. A cinema licence was obtained in 1910 to cover occasional use of film in variety shows, but the building eventually became a full-time cinema in 1930 long after any connection with the Bennetts.

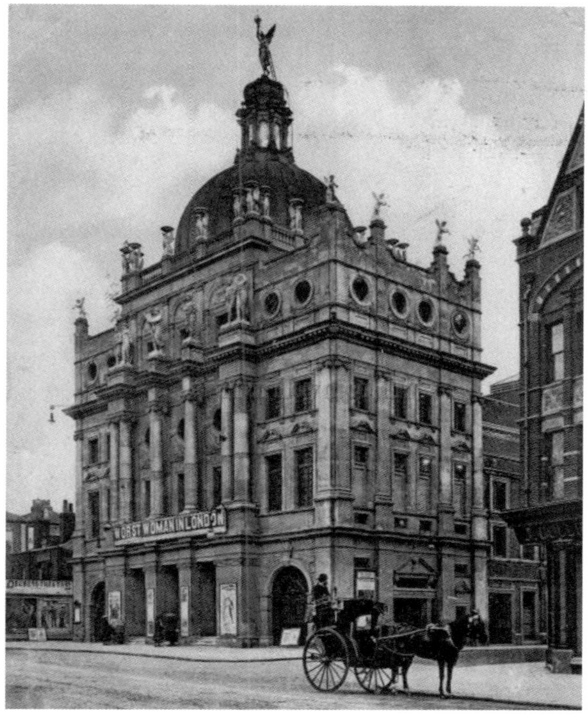

Above: a postcard view of The Duchess Theatre, Balham. opened in 1899, and built by William and Harry Bennett, working in partnership with the architect, William Sprague, who joined the family by marrying Isobel Bennett. William's theatres in London were on a very different scale to his sister's little wooden theatre in Stourbridge!

Harry Bennett married Annie Maria Whittem, a twenty-two year old farmer's daughter on 17th July 1891 at St. Paul's Church, Leamington Spa. Harry was managing the Leamington Spa theatre at the time. They had a son, Guy Whittem Bennett. However, Annie Maria died in 1893, at the age of twenty four.

Harry married for a second time four years later. His second wife was Florence Laura Aronson, and they married at St. Martins in the Fields near Trafalgar Square in London on 7th October 1897. I believe that Harry and Laura had two sons: Cecil Harry Andrew and Wilfred George Dudley. The latter was born 23rd September 1900 and he died in 1984. If he had children they could still be alive today.

Harry died towards the end of 1918 at Meriden, aged fifty two. His death brought the Bennett family's association with the theatre world to an end. As no image of Eliza Patch seems to have survived in any local archive, it is always tempting to wonder if such a picture is still to be found in any family photographs hidden away by a descendant of Eliza's nephews. As stated above, it could be that Harry Bennett's grandchildren are still alive. The other line one could follow is that of Isobel – Harry's sister. In the 1891 census she is nineteen years old, living with her parents in Coventry and listed as an "actress". We have already noted that she married William G.R. Sprague – the architect, and sometime business partner, associated with William Bennetts' London theatres. They married in 1900, in Lambeth and their children were old enough to attend William Bennett's funeral in 1911. Isobel's grandchildren could be alive today. All these strands provide a hope that Eliza is not quite forgotten.

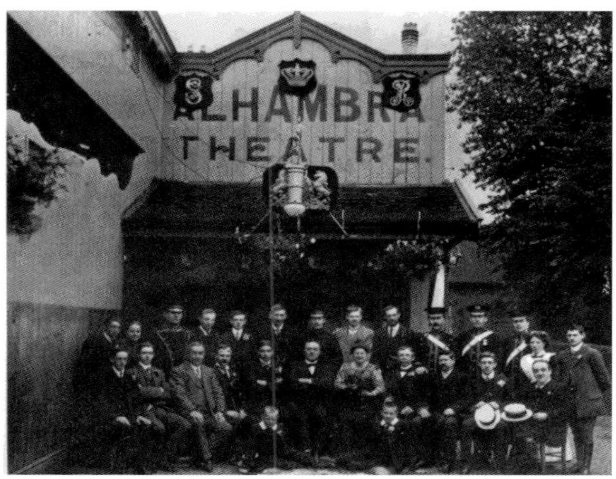

Above: The Alhambra, Stourbridge continued to exist after Eliza Patch's retirement – as described on the next page.

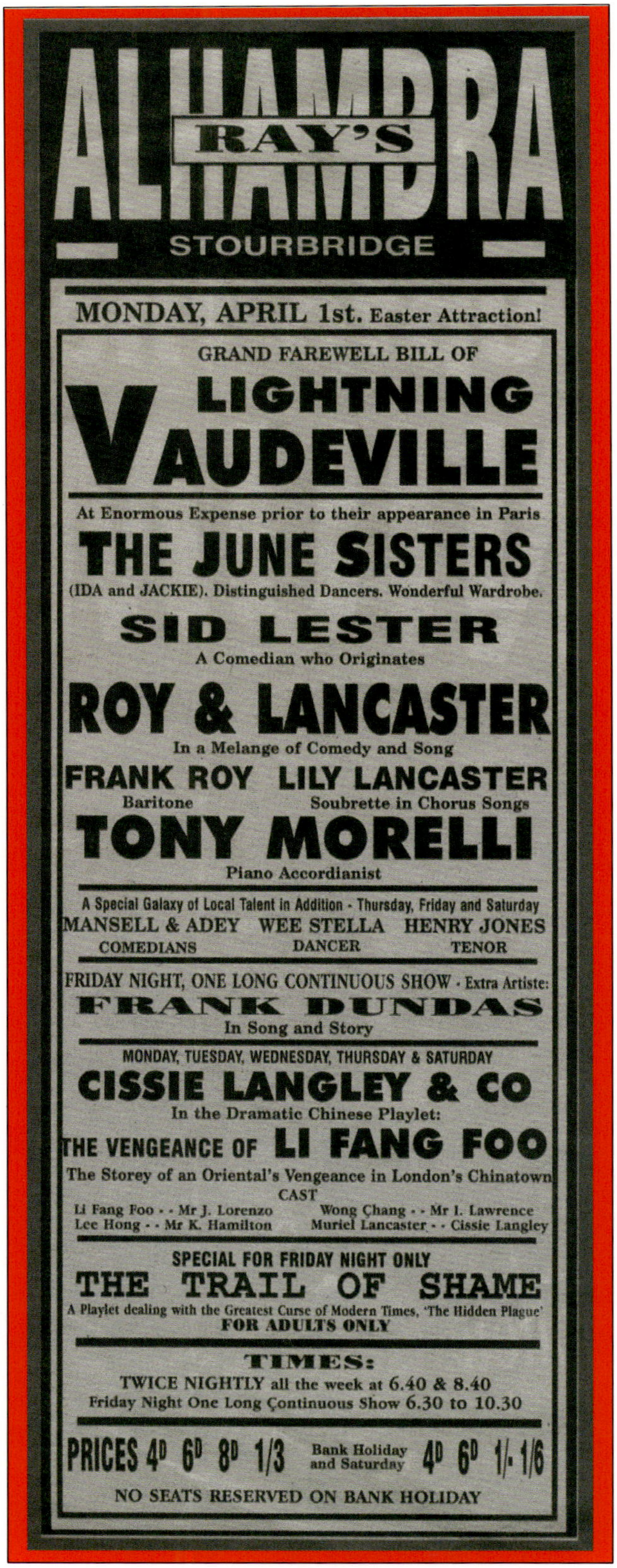

What Happened to the Alhambra?

Douglas Phelps first appeared at Mrs. Patch's Alhambra Theatre in a production of "They All Love Jack" in September 1898. Maude Lynton played the "charming heroine". In 1900 the couple returned to take over as proprietors of the Alhambra – enabling Eliza Patch to enjoy a short retirement. Douglas Phelps went on stage on 2nd April 1900 to tell the audience that he would maintain the high standards that they associated with Eliza Patch's regime.

Douglas Phelps' first production at the Alhambra was "The Devil's Mane", described as "powerful drama". It was soon followed by refurbishment of the theatre which included installing some plush tip-up seats, gas lighting and a new second entrance. In October 1903 a week of entertainment on film was provided by "Edison & Barnum's Electric Animated Pictures" – the business run by none other than Ben Kennedy as described in the next chapter!

By 1909 Mr. Phelps was experimenting with "cine-variety", and the Alhambra was quick to obtain a Kine Licence in 1910 and for the next decade cinematography and live theatre filled the Alhambra. Douglas briefly explored other venues for showing films, including "The Empire" in Duke Street, Stourbridge and the Alhambra, Dudley Port.

The Phelps ran the Alhambra very much as a family affair – Maude, Douglas's wife played a managerial role until their twenty-year-old son, John Phelps took over in 1919.

In 1922 Douglas Phelps sold the Alhambra to George Ray and it gradually phased out the films and returned to a focus on stage entertainment. George Ray kept the old wooden theatre going until a final show on 6th April 1929 – defeated by the imminent arrival of the "talkies" in the new Central Cinema nearby. The building was demolished in 1932.

Left: Poster for the last show to be presented at the Alhambra, Stourbridge, almost thirty years after the death of Eliza Patch.

Chapter 6

The Man Who Built the Hippodrome

Ben Kennedy

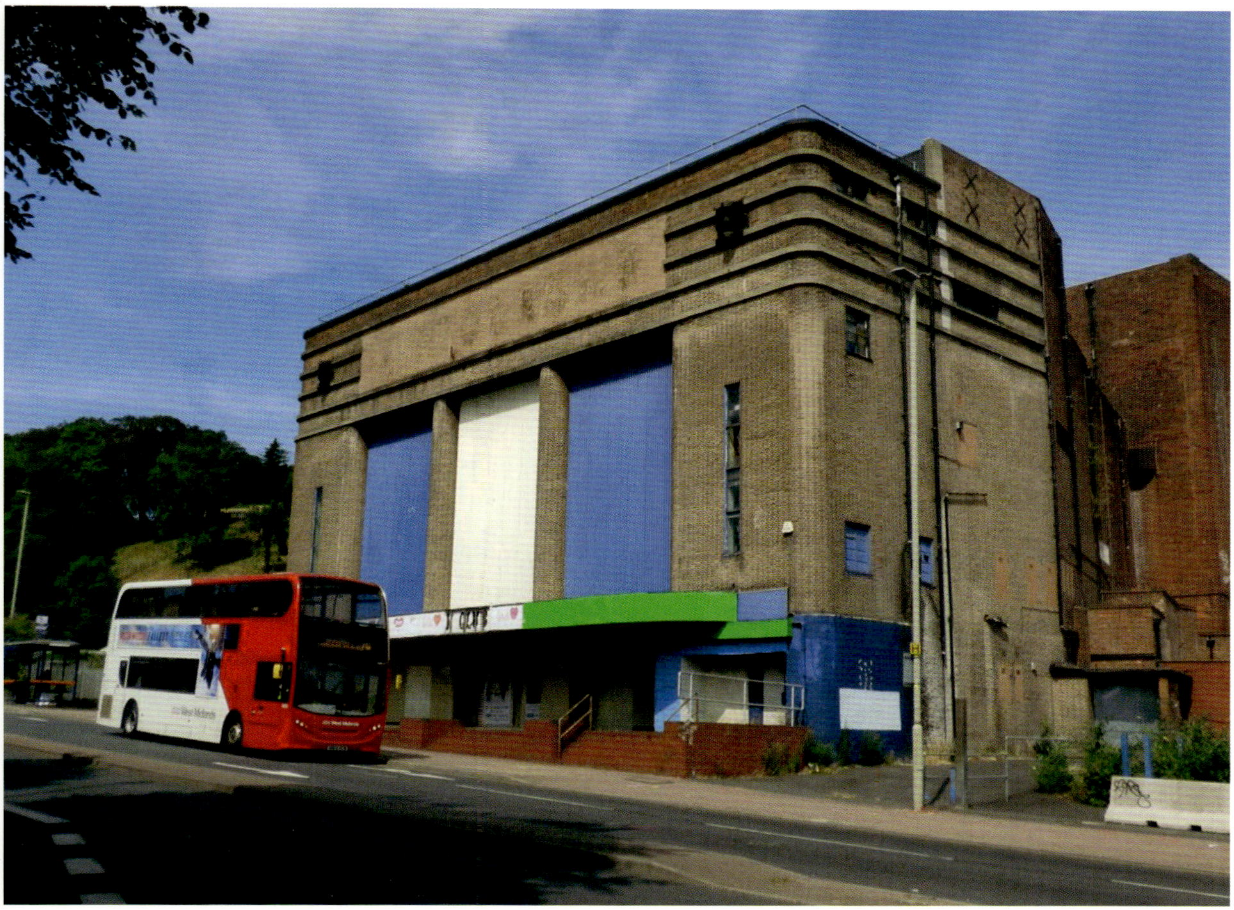

At the time of writing this book, in 2018, the huge brick edifice that was once the Dudley Hippodrome still dominates the gateway to the town of Dudley. Shorn of its details that once made it a striking building, it awaits its fate – the demolition of a grand theatre, and monument to its builder: Benjamin Kennedy, who died four months after its opening.

Who's Who for the Kennedys

Robert (b. c. 1821 in Possen, Germany) d.1901 & Clara (b.c. 1845 in Munich) **BERNHARD**

Auguste (b. c.1860)

Benjamin BERNHARD (1866 – 1939)
Known as **BEN KENNEDY**

Isador (5th Aug. 1868 – 8th June 1947)
Known as Harry Kennedy

Ben's first marriage:
Benjamin Bernhard = Theresa Levy (1872 - 1916). They marry on 8th June 1892. They separated about 1900/01 and divorced in 1915.

Ben's second marriage:
Benjamin Bernhard = Catherine Louisa Harriette Bradford (1880 - 11th July 1929).
They marry on 11th July 1917.

Ben's third marriage:
Benjamin Bernhard Kennedy = Annie Cora Stanton (1898 – 1983).
They marry on 23rd April 1931

Ben Kennedy's children and grandchildren:

Robert Bernhard Kennedy, known as Bob: Born 19th October 1907. Died 3rd December 1989.
Bob married Joyce Alexander Harris in 1930 and they had two children: David (born 1933) and Jane (born 1935). Bob and Joyce divorced in 1956.
Later Bob married Beryl Stephens (1917 – 2016), in 1957. Beryl had one son by her first marriage.

Audrey Clara Kennedy: Born17th Oct. 1909. Audrey did participate in the family business in the sense that she ran the bars in the Hippodrome, having acquired experience of running pubs (Eg: The Bush Head Hotel, Wellington). She married Frank Ferriday and had a son, Brett, but later divorced. Died in 1980 in Gloucestershire. (Sometimes also used the name Clarice.)

Maurice Kennedy: Born 18th February 1911. Died 19th October 1962.
Maurice married Vera Penfold, known as Penny, in 1936. They had two daughters: Elizabeth (born in 1938) and Diane (born in 1942).

Derek Kennedy: Born 27th April1921.

Alan Kennedy: Born 26th October 1922.

Cecil Kennedy: Born 6th March 1925.

Bryan Kennedy: Born December 1928.

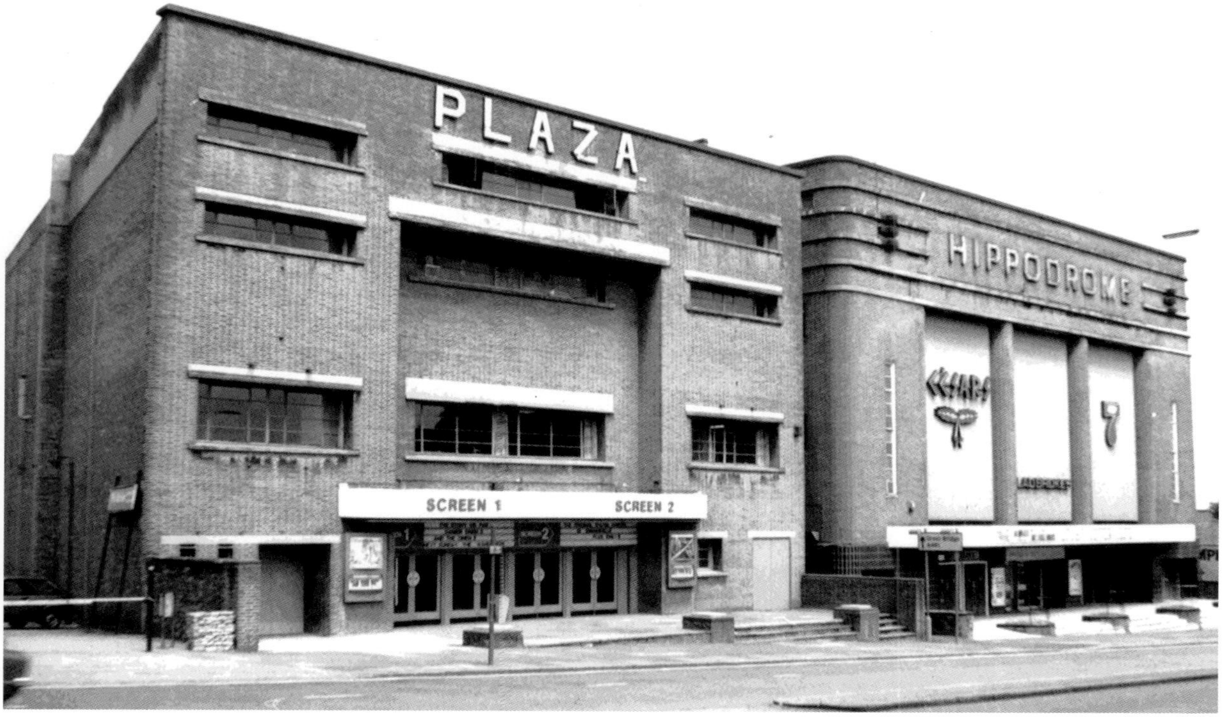

Above: Castle Hill, Dudley, in the 1970s. The Plaza was opened by Ben Kennedy in 1936 and was still showing films, on two screens, when this picture was taken. The Hippodrome was then Cesar's Palace in which Ladbrooks experimented with "variety" and Bingo.

Discovering Ben

Having been parachuted into the Black Country in the Autumn of 1962 as an ignorant eighteen-year-old from the London/Essex border I set about exploring my new home. I had landed in the Eve Hill area of Dudley and from then on Dudley was the centre of the Universe. The only "Kennedy" I knew of at the time happened to be the President of the United States of America.

I soon discovered the Odeon and Plaza cinemas on Castle Hill, and took in the great brick monolithic presence of the Hippodrome. The theatre sometimes seemed to be shut and at other times was putting on a series of "strip-shows" with titles featuring titillating puns like "Strip, Strip Ahoy! – the Great Navel Revue". As a rather serious and possibly priggish lad I dismissed these shows as being unworthy of my attention and never crossed the Hippodrome's threshold. Now, of course, I regret that because not only did I miss the opportunity to have first-hand experience of a piece of entertainment history, but I also denied myself the chance of seeing the architectural splendours of the place while still in use as a theatre.

If I asked anyone about the Hippodrome I was told, "It's something to do with the Kennedys." However, that answer meant nothing to me and I failed to investigate the matter any further. When it came to entertainment, I was hooked on the cinema. There were some interesting aspects of the world of theatre but I had my work cut out simply keeping up with the cinema. Even when my interest in theatre began to widen, it took me a time to become interested in the buildings themselves and the question of who had developed them.

At some stage of my developing interest in local theatres and cinemas I came across a little brown paperback book dealing with the history of the Theatre Royal, West Bromwich. I think it cost £1, and upon inspection turned out to be written by Fred Bennett who had once been Chief Reporter on the Midland Chronicle. The book contained no date of publication and in fact did not make very clear use of dates in telling its story, but it was still a marvellous introduction to a great list of names and turbulent history. However, among the names and the "turbulence", I came across the name "Kennedy" once again. (The book was written after Maurice Kennedy's death in 1962, and within the time that Bob Kennedy was working for Harry Secombe which was between 1960 and 1989.)

Fred Bennett seems to have been impressed by Ben Kennedy and wrote: *"He was a colourful personality and a born showman who owned 18 theatres and music halls at the peak of his career in 1922."* However, he did not feel it necessary to really investigate Ben's story. Instead Fred Bennett gives us a mix of various legends:

"A Polish American, Mr. Kennedy sold newspapers in America as a lad. His ambition was to enter show business and he joined Barnum and Bailey's Circus, where he must have gained invaluable experience. He came to Britain with a travelling waxworks, and as he could not afford lodgings he used to sleep in a coffin which in the daytime housed the effigy of Napoleon."

At the end of the 1970s I was moved to write a book about the Black Country's cinemas and soon discovered that films had often been shown in theatres. Some theatres had eventually become cinemas and in one case a building mainly used as cinema spent its later-life as a theatre. There was also an obvious over-lap in the architectural side of the story, and therefore it was difficult to be interested in just one and not the other. Although "Cinemas of the Black Country", published in the Autumn of 1982, tried to focus only on cinemas – as the title implied, I did feel guilty about ignoring so much theatre history! Eventually I was able to remedy this by producing two volumes – one on cinemas (again!) and one on theatres.

While researching and writing "Cinemas of the Black Country", I once again found myself having to look at the biographies of the people who populated the story. This led to my first investigation of the life and achievements of Ben Kennedy. When my research widened to include theatres for a second foray into entertainment history I found myself trying to make sense of his biography all over again, and to look at the lives of his sons; Bob and Maurice.

Throughout all this activity I think I can say that Ben Kennedy remained a fairly shadowy figure! Even when I met and interviewed Ken Shepherd in January 1993 I still felt that Ben was barely taking shape in my imagination. Ken had been associated with the Hippodrome from his teenage years right through to a long period of stage management at the theatre. However, this had brought him into close contact with Bob and Maurice Kennedy rather than their late father.

Once I had seen the opening brochure produced in 1939 for the Dudley Hippodrome I was able – at last – to put a face to a name, for the brochure included a picture of Ben Kennedy. Even now it still seems quite an enigmatic portrait, one notable feature being the horse-shoe shaped tie pin that Ben is wearing on his tie. Many years later I found a very grainy newspaper photograph in the Midland Chronicle of Ben at the time of the opening of the Empire, West Bromwich. Once again we see him wearing the same tie-pin. The text in the paper suggests that it may not have been a contemporary photograph, but it does mention the tie-pin, telling us that it was his "lucky horseshoe" and that it had been a twenty-first birthday present from his father.

When making a second attempt to learn more about Ben Kennedy I was very keen to actually meet a "Kennedy". I finally achieved this when I met David Kennedy at his home in Romsley in 2010. David was Ben's grandson but Ben had died when David was only six so maybe I could not expect him to have clear coherent memories of Grandad! Ben's oldest son, Bob, had married Joyce Harris on 12th April 1930. Their son, born in 1933, was David – the gentleman I was able to meet. I also later corresponded with his sister, Jane. It was the nearest I came to making contact with anyone genealogically close to Ben Kennedy. I later enjoyed a long distance telephone call to Beryl Stephens in Sydney – Bob Kennedy's second wife - but their life together came long after Ben's death so she had an interesting story to tell about Bob Kennedy but not Ben. It seemed that every time I tried to find out more about Ben I found myself sidetracked into the story of the generation that followed him.

Just as this book was reaching its final stages of production I was able to make contact with Elizabeth (also known as Penny) the daughter of Maurice Kennedy. Her generous assistance has provided more images of Ben, and an archive of material relating to his various enterprises going back to his time with "Edison" and his own early bioscope and theatre ventures, some of which were a result of his partnership with James Moore. Some of the paperwork reveals Ben as a real "showman" – using his own likeness and name to promote the businesses in a way that had not been previously appreciated.

Ben: The Reluctant Furrier

It seems that no-one sat down with Ben Kennedy at any stage of his life and attempted to come up with a definitive biography of the man. Writers like Fred Bennett, who produced a history of the Theatre Royal, West Bromwich, were impressed by Ben Kennedy and wrote the colourful account of his life quoted above. However, I have never seen any evidence to suggest he was a Polish American who started his working life by selling newspapers!

A slightly different biography was provided in Blocksidge's Dudley Almanac for 1940 – looking back at the deaths of local people in 1939.The writer tells us that Ben Kennedy was.... *"Born in London, a son of a furrier, Mr. Kennedy was intended by his father to go into the fur business, but young Kennedy thought differently. At the age of thirteen, he ran away and joined a travelling waxworks show, with which he spent three years. His bed while with this concern was a coffin in which an effigy of Napoleon lay by day...."*

Interestingly, the account gives a better picture of Ben's background but it still returns to the story of Napoleon's coffin – as told later by Fred Bennett. Can any of this be sorted out? What follows is an attempt to put together a more realistic account of Ben Kennedy's life.

Ben Kennedy was born in London in 1866, apparently the son of Robert and Clara Bernhard, both born in Germany. I have not yet located the family in the 1871 census but in the 1881 Census we find the family at 7, Ashwin Street, West Hackney and fifteen year old Benjamin is endearingly listed as "Benny"! (His place of birth is listed as Holborn.) His fifty nine year old father is described as a furrier. Ben is also described as a furrier and therefore seems to be following his father's footsteps rather than running away to be part of a show. In the 1881 census we learn that he has a brother, Isador, who was then twelve, and a sister named Auguste, then twenty three.

The story about leaving home at the age of thirteen, and even the identity of his brother, is mysterious. In the 1891 Census we again find twenty-three year old Benjamin Bernhard living with his parents and brother, Isador, at 5 Ashwin Street, Hackney. (Auguste is not listed, and Ben should be 25 rather than 23!) Ben still seems at the time to be a furrier, like his father and brother. Perhaps things were about to change.

In the opening brochure produced for the Dudley Hippodrome in 1939 it states that Ben Kennedy was managing the Colosseum, Dalston, near Hackney in 1890 but there is nothing in that 1891 census return to indicate that any more than there is any hint of having run away to join a travelling waxworks! The Colosseum Dalston had opened about 1886 as a circus building, adopting the name Colosseum the following year. It is possible that Ben was introduced to the entertainment world via this theatre, or was connected with it later, but once again we are short of facts on which to base the story.

The information gleaned from the 1881 and 1891 census returns are the only documentation that we have, but if we try to reconcile such information with the more romantic stories told by the Dudley Almanac and Fred Bennett, the story could go like this: If Ben had run away to join the waxworks at the age of thirteen, that would have happened about 1879. Although allegedly with the show for three years, his father, hoping that he would return to the fur business, would have filled in the1881 census form in Ben's absence. Similarly we can imagine the record provided by the 1881was simply wishful thinking on his father's part and that really Ben was working at the Colosseum in Dalston, and was already in show business. Whatever really happened, it seems to be the events of the 1890s that put Ben firmly on the road to the entertainment world.

Below: Ben Kennedy: the portrait used in the brochure produced to mark the opening of the Hippodrome.

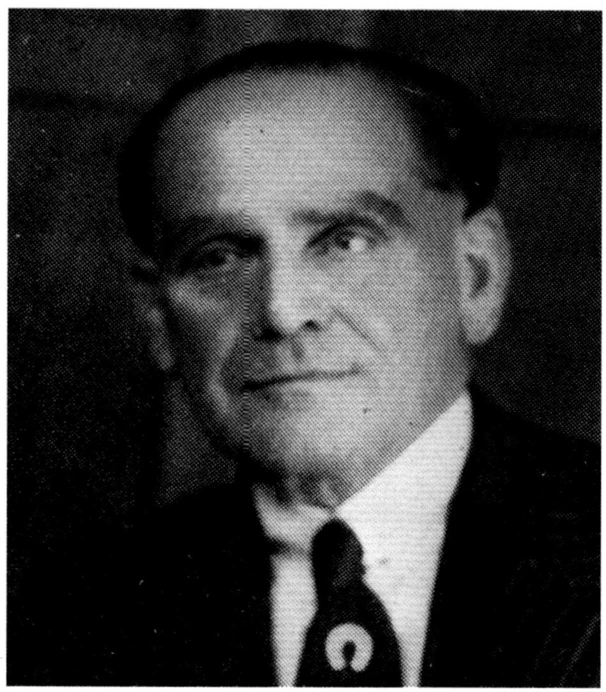

Out of the Shadows

The 1890s has to be the key decade in which young Ben turns his back on becoming a furrier, like his father, and sets out to have some of the experiences attributed to him in a world of travelling waxworks, shows, bioscopes and variety theatres. Maybe he even becomes a "Kennedy".

On the 8th June 1892 the twenty-six-year-old Benjamin Bernhard married a Theresa Levy at the Great Synagogue situated in Aldgate. This building was the third synagogue to occupy the site but was destroyed in an air raid in May 1941.) It has not been possible to find out much about Theresa, but she may have been responsible for encouraging him to take up a show business career. On the marriage certificate she is not given an occupation, but we do learn that her father, Mort Levy, was a clothier. Ben describes himself as a "master furrier" continuing to give us the impression that his show business career has not yet taken-off.

We know that Theresa later described both of them as "variety artistes", but we can only guess that their career began soon after their marriage. The earliest proof of this to be found so far is a brief mention in The Surrey Comet of 4th August 1894. Kingston's Excursions were appearing for three days at the Albany Hall, Kingston and for two nights at the Conservative Hall, Molesey. The show included a "Grand Minstrel Variety Show" and Ben Kennedy is specifically mentioned as being part of that show. This is also the earliest use found of the name "Ben Kennedy"

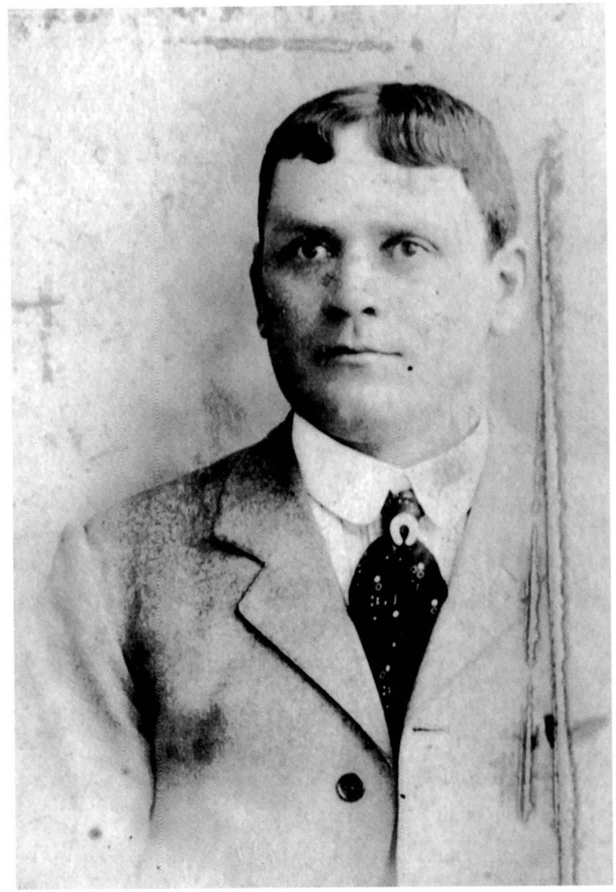

Above: A portrait of the young Ben Kennedy – seen, as always, with his horseshoe tiepin which was said to have been a twenty-first birthday present from his father. This photograph survives in the collection of Elizabeth Shepherd-Barron, daughter of Maurice Kennedy.

"Kingston's Excursions" was a travelling diorama show. Such shows were quite different to the "magic lantern" shows that were popular at the same time. The dioramas presented a series of giant scenic 'backcloths' before the audience, rather than a projected picture. Usually a narrator, or lecturer, would provide a commentary and the show was enlivened by the inclusion of variety acts. The most famous shows of this sort were "Hamilton's Excursions" and "Pooles' Miriorama", both of which were known to visit the Black Country. "Kingston's Excursions" seems to have been so called because the show was presented by a Mr. H. Kingston. And in this case the minstrel show was almost given equally billing with the dioramas.

During 1894 and on into 1895 "Kingston's Excursions" seem to have maintained a popular tour, taking in places like Watford, High Wycombe, Luton, Banbury, and Northampton. They earn a brief mention in the local papers as they progress and sometimes Ben Kennedy is mentioned. Sometimes Miss Theresa Lacy – "Tyrolian and Ballad Vocalist" is mentioned. Ben was also part of an act called "The Three Ks": Kennedy, Kingston & Kenway providing knockabout comedy. Early in 1896 shows are presented in Kent at places like Broadstairs and Canterbury. At the latter an advertisement for the show lists Ben Kennedy and Theresa Lacy together as "Black and White Burlesque Artistes". After that we seem to lose track of "Kingston's Excursions", however on 3rd June 1897 The Stage reports that Ben Kennedy's Minstrel Troupe was fulfilling an engagement at the Farnborough North Camp Theatre, suggesting that Ben and his troupe continued to travel independently.

According to an obituary in the Dudley Herald, Ben went into 'theatre management' in the 1890s and ran the new Colisseum theatre at Dalston, North London, from about 1893 to 1896. (The Colisseum, Dalston, was built in Kingsland Road in 1886 and had started life as a circus building, but had then been rebuilt along the lines of a variety theatre, opening in this form on 25th July 1898. As a variety theatre it ran until 1919 when it was rebuilt again and became a cinema, opening on 6th December 1920. It was acquired by the Gaumont circuit in 1927 and lasted as a cinema until 19th November 1960. It later acquired some fame as the home of the Four Aces Club – associated with the development of Reggae in Britain! However, despite all its history it was demolished in 2007.) If the Dudley Herald's dates are correct Ben's association with the Colisseum would clash with his work with Kingston's Excursions so this remains to be sorted out. Possibly he managed it for a time after 1898.

By the end of the 1890s Ben Kennedy had acquired experience of variety theatre and minstrel shows, and possibly some experience of theatre management. The few accounts we have of his life also include reference to the world of cinematography: the new entertainment medium that swept the country at the end of the 1890s.In looking at Irving Bosco's life we have been able to illustrate the fact that early films were presented in several different contexts: the bioscope world associated with the fairground, secondly the public hall presentation, and thirdly the use of film as just another "act" within a circus or variety show. Ben Kennedy seems to have become involved in the second and third categories of film presentation.

At some stage he joined Edison's Animated Photo Company and played some part in travelling their early cinematograph shows throughout Britain and then on the Continent – possibly even followed by a stint in the USA. It is said that he returned to the UK in 1902 to manage the Olympia, Newcastle on Tyne, for the "Edison Company". He is impossible to find in the 1901 Census which lends support to the idea that he may have been in America at the time, but the "American Connection" may simply be the result of his association with the Edison Animated Photo Company. The latter was a British company established a Mr. A.D. Thomas from Devon! However its name was deliberately chosen to suggest an American connection.

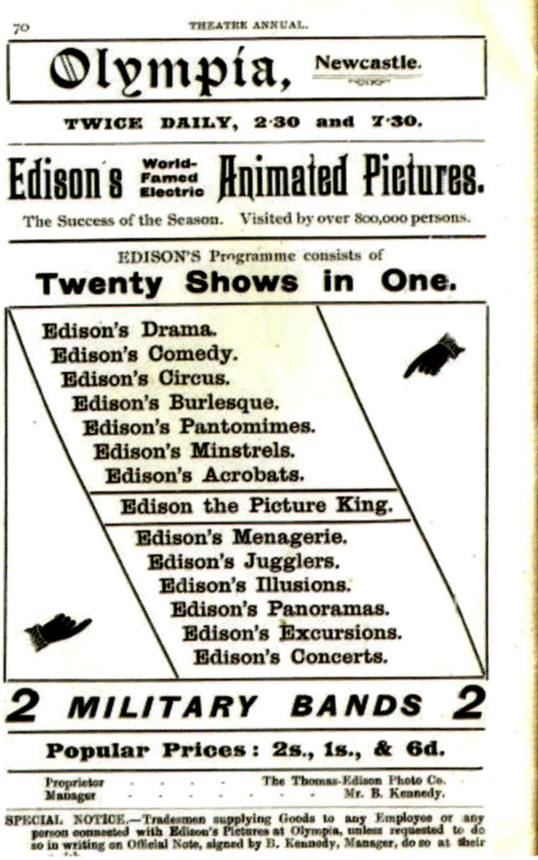

THEATRE ANNUAL. 71

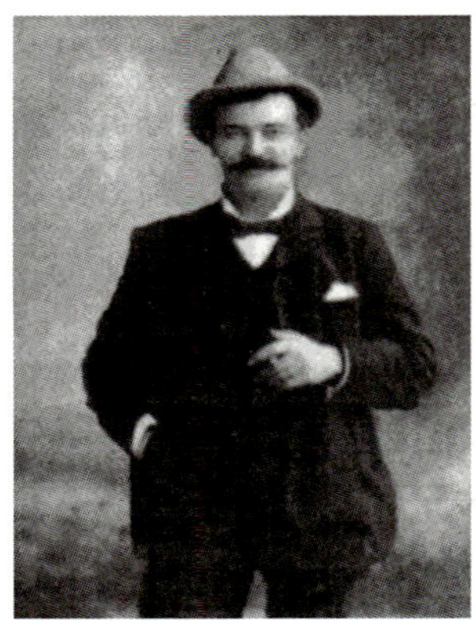

Mr. A. D. THOMAS

Mr. A.D. Thomas whose brilliant exhibition of Animate Pictures at Olympia has been the talk of the city and surrounding district for many months past, may be said to stand alone in this particular entertainment. Nothing comes amiss to him, and no expense is spared to secure the best and most novel results. With an army of operators at command, he has scoured this country and the Continent to provide new and interesting pictures for the millions of patrons, and it must be remembered that this is no slight task, for at the present time he has between 20 and 30 exhibitions in various cities in the Kingdom. To control such a number of enterprises speaks volumes for the energy and ability of the man, and if his success has been great it has been well deserved. We are to be afforded an extended opportunity of witnessing the show, which remains for some time longer, but with plenty of novelties added from time to time.

A SHOW WITH A REPUTATION.

The History of the World from Day to Day.

THIS IS THE ORIGINAL SHOW
FROM
St. James's Hall, Manchester.
Albert Hall, Nottingham.
Great Curzon Hall, Birmingham.
Colston Hall, Bristol.
Albert Hall, Sheffield.
Olympia, Newcastle-on-Tyne.
St. George's Hall, Bradford.
Colosseum, Leeds.
St. George's Hall, Liverpool.
Great St. James's Hall, London,

And all the Principal Theatres in the United Kingdom.

Grand Concert Company of Star Artistes.

8th Year of Continuous Tour

EDISCOPE
AND
BARNUM'S
WORLD-FAMED ELECTRIC
ANIMATED PICTURES.

KENNEDY'S ENTERPRISES:
Kennedy's Komiks.
The Moore-Kennedy Panto, "Dick Whittington."

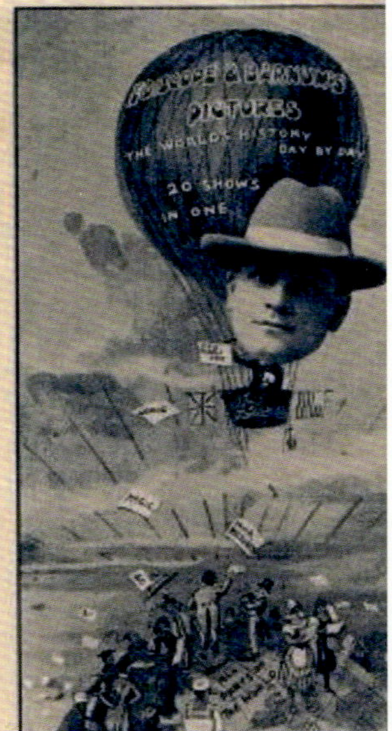

Proprietor: J. B. Kennedy.

Has been given with Enormous Success in the Principal Cities and Towns of Great Britain, and has received the Highest Encomiums from Press and Public.

The following (among others) have honoured Ediscope & Barnum's Pictures with their patronage:—

THE RIGHT HON. JOSEPH CHAMBERLAIN, M.P.
LIEUT.-COL. STURGESS, 5th Northumberlands.
COLONEL GORDON, C.V.O., Royal Scots.
THE COLONELS COMMANDING H.M. REGIMENTS at Lancaster, Oldham, Bury, Ashton-under-Lyne, Newcastle, Bury St. Edmunds, Norwich, Leicester, Nottingham, Derby, Northampton, Shrewsbury, Chester, &c.
THE MAYORS, ALDERMEN, AND COUNCILLORS of Bradford, Halifax, Huddersfield, Darlington, South Shields, Derby, Stockton-on-Tees, West Hartlepool, Oldham, Newcastle, Norwich, Bury, Middlesborough, Shrewsbury, Carlisle, Bury St. Edmunds, Northampton, Lancaster, &c.
MEMBERS OF PARLIAMENT representing the following Constituencies: Bradford, Derby, Newcastle, Bury St Edmunds, Stockton-on-Tees, South Shields, West Hartlepool; and many other influential Gentry.

Theatres visited, booked and re-booked by Ediscope & Barnum's, include:

Park Palace Theatre, and Paddington Theatre, Liverpool.
Carlton Theatre, Birmingham.
Queen's Theatre, Longton.
Opera House & Theatre Royal, Kidderminster.
Arthur Jefferson, Esq.'s Theatres.
Carlton & Duckworth's Theatres.
Ilkeston. Stafford. Chesterfield.
Farnworth. Warrington.
Worcester.
Theatre Royal, Merthyr Tydvil.
Pooles Bros.' Theatres.
Crewe. Manchester.
Newcastle-on-Tyne.
Burton-on-Trent. Bolton.
Morton Powell's Theatr.s.
West Bromwich. Derby.
Oldham Colosseum.
Prince of Wales, Mexborough.
Grand, Doncaster.
Her Majesty's, Walsall.
Prince of Wales, Nuneaton.

BANKERS:
Capital and Counties Bank.

Address: This Week ____________

Next Week ____________

____________ 190

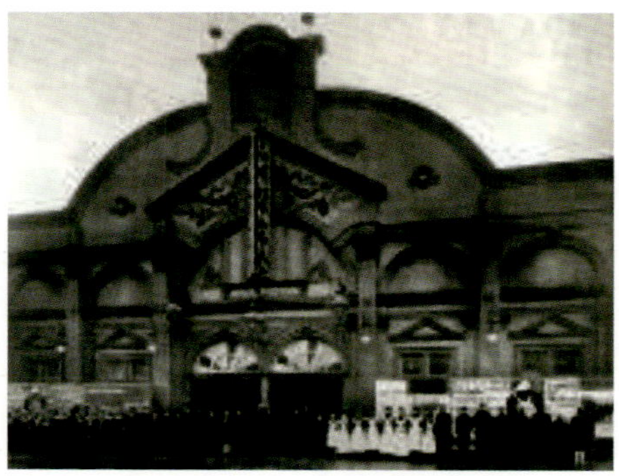

Previous page: Two pages of a "Theatre Annual", c.1900 containing notes on A. D. Thomas and identifying Ben as his manager at the Olympia, Newcastle, presenting Edison's Animated Pictures. This page: Ben's own headed notepaper, from the time of his partnership with J.T. Moore and the presentation of both his "Komiks" and the "Ediscope & Barnum's Animated Pictures". Note the use of his own likeness and the huge quantity of information provided! Above: The Olympia, Newcastle.

Wherever it was that Ben had been initiated into the world of early cinematography, it certainly must have led him to be one of the exponents of "cine variety" – the mixing of screen entertainment with live acts – almost with the intention of pleasing the audience with one or the other – if not both!

Into the Limelight

If Ben Kennedy was transferring his attention to cinematography at the turn of the century, it may have led to the parting of the ways between Ben and his wife Theresa, who presumably continued to pursue a career in "variety". It also seems likely that Ben Kennedy was forging connections with the West Midlands as the twentieth century got underway. By 1901 Ben and Theresa were leading separate lives. He continued to send Theresa an allowance, but for a time she had no idea of where he was living.

Below: The Hippodrome, Carters Green, a hymn to the use of corrugated iron, managed and /or leased by Ben Kennedy between 1911 and 1914.

Early in the 1900s Ben Kennedy was living at "The Beeches" in Warley in the Black Country. His new partner was Catherine Louisa Bradford, who had also been a variety artiste. The Beeches was a fairly isolated house in the Bristnall Fields area of Warley – then a very small hamlet in a rural part of the Black Country. Warley is now part of Sandwell, as are West Bromwich and Smethwick where Ben later had homes. It is not clear how Ben met Louisa but as they were both in the theatrical world we can probably assume that is how they met. Catherine Louisa was born in 1881, in Brentford, Middlesex. Her father, Robert Foster Bradford, was a junior official in the Post Office, and on occasions young Bob Kennedy, her son, (see below) added the name "Foster" to his list of names!

From the beginning of the twentieth century Ben seems to have settled in the Black Country and was moving on into the next stage of his career. In 1903 Ben established "Kennedy's Comics" - a comedy troupe that was on the road for the next seven years.

His first authenticated association with Dudley comes in 1904 when his "Comics" were presented for six weeks at the Dudley Opera House in the June/July of that year. A year later we find a report of "Kennedy's Komiks"

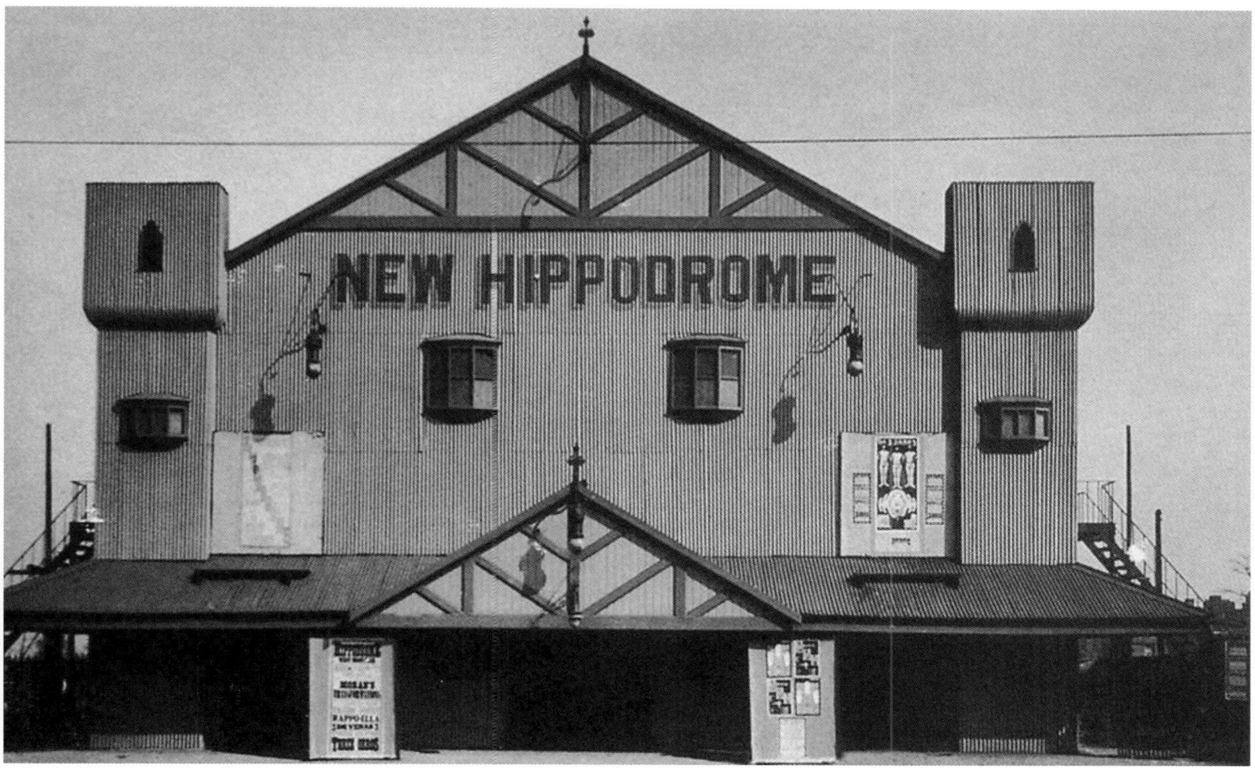

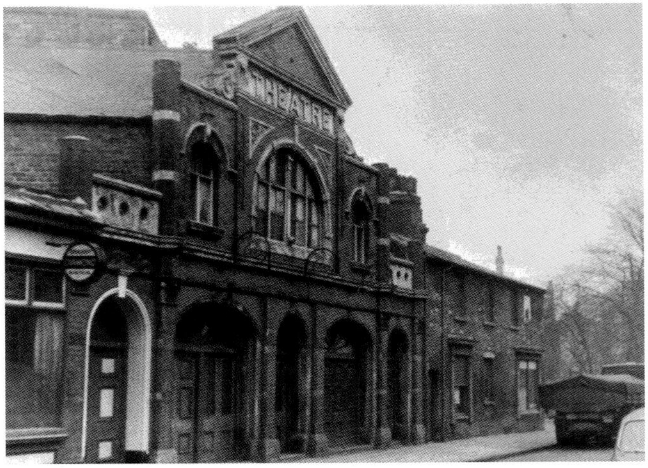

Left: The Theatre Royal. West Bromwich. The theatre grew out of local music hall and became The Royal in 1879 when this entrance was provided. It had a chequered history, but played a part in Ben Kennedy's progress – both as the place where he met up with James Moore, created "Kennedy's Komiks", and, eventually, as part of his own empire. (Photo: Chris Medley)

appearing at the Theatre Royal, West Bromwich. The report states: *"A crowded house assembled here on Monday night for the opening of the summer season, and gave a hearty welcome to Kennedy's Komiks. Some excellent animated pictures added to the success of the performance."* He seems on this occasion to have met James Moore, who described himself as 'Manager and Proprietor' at the Theatre Royal, and the two men established a friendship and occasional business partnerships. James Page Moore (1862 – 1953) was a theatre proprietor and impresario only a few years older than Ben.

James Page Moore had a long association with the Kidderminster Opera House, a base from which he awaited "opportunities" in Birmingham and the Black Country. He took over the Theatre Royal in West Bromwich in August 1894 which suffered a disastrous fire just over a year later. From the reports of the fire we learn that James Moore organised travelling shows from the Theatre Royal, some of whose sets and props were destroyed in the fire. He then set about establishing separate temporary arrangements while organising the rebuilding of the Royal, which opened in its new form on 26th August 1896. At the turn of the century cinematography was also a feature of shows at the Theatre Royal. Either this, or the travelling shows based at The Royal, may have brought James Moore and Ben Kennedy together.

"Kennedy's Kommics" (another new spelling) were featured in the pantomime at West Bromwich's Theatre Royal in early 1906 and they then toured local theatres under the control of this new partnership. James Moore actually announced a retirement from the Theatre Royal in 1906, but it seems that this was to enable him to spend more time on his partnership with Ben Kennedy, and for the two of them to venture into Birmingham.

James Moore later returned to control of The Theatre Royal in 1915, leased it for a while to someone else and then bought the lease back again for two years. What happened in 1917 will be explained below. (In 1901 James Moore had been living in Legge Street, West Bromwich but by the time of the 1911 census he had moved to Acocks Green in Birmingham, where he lived with his wife Gertrude and his son and daughter. His twenty year old son, Harry, is described as a cinematograph operator.)

Meanwhile, Messrs Moore & Kennedy had turned their attention to Birmingham, and in 1907 started presenting the city's first regular film shows at the Kings Hall. (Ben Kennedy took over "Edison & Barnum Animated Pictures", and presented films beneath this banner at several locations including the Drill Hall, Bilston, right next door to the Theatre Royal, but please see the comments made above about the fact that this company had nothing to do with either Edison or Barnum!) The Kings Hall, Birmingham, was in the Old Square, next door to the Grand Theatre. It had first been known as The Central Hall, but Messrs Moore & Kennedy carried out extensive alterations and changed the name. Variety acts and film were presented alongside each other for a time, but by 1911, the Kings Hall was only showing films. It closed in 1927 and then was used intermittently for a variety of activities until closing completely as far as "show business" was concerned in 1932.

The Kennedy family seems to have moved from Warley to West Bromwich at about the time of joining forces with James Moore, and Ben's son, Bob, was born at 39 Rookery Road on 19th October 1907, followed by Clara Audrey in 1910 and then Maurice on 18th February 1911. Bob's and Maurice's second name was Bernhard according to the 1911 census, presumably in memory of Ben's original surname, and for reasons clarified below.

At the time of Maurice's birth in 1911, Ben was living at Leighton House, John Street, Smethwick. Ben's work, and therefore his life-style was not very "home centred", and we should not be very surprised to encounter frequent changes of address.

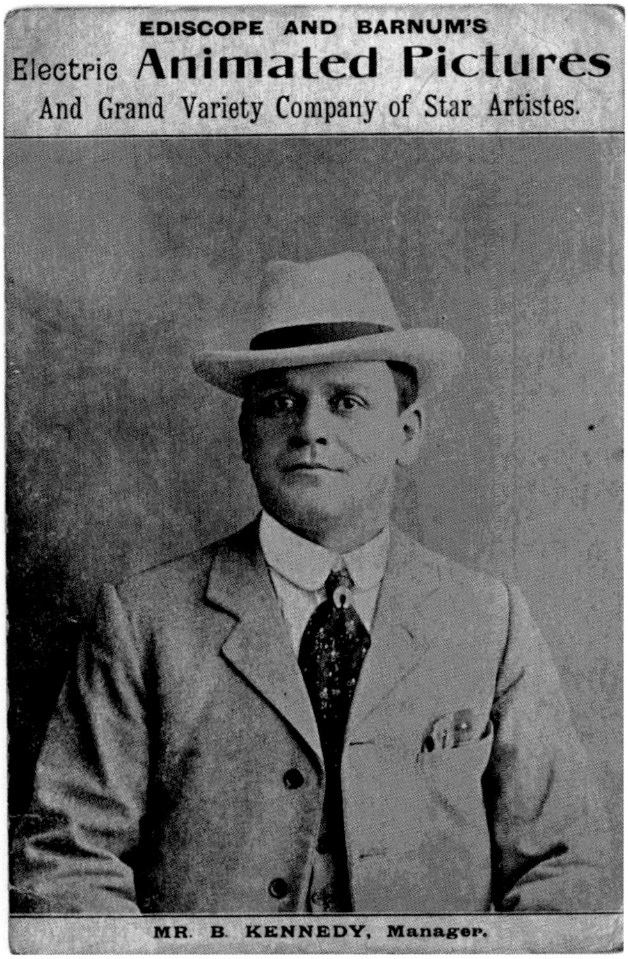

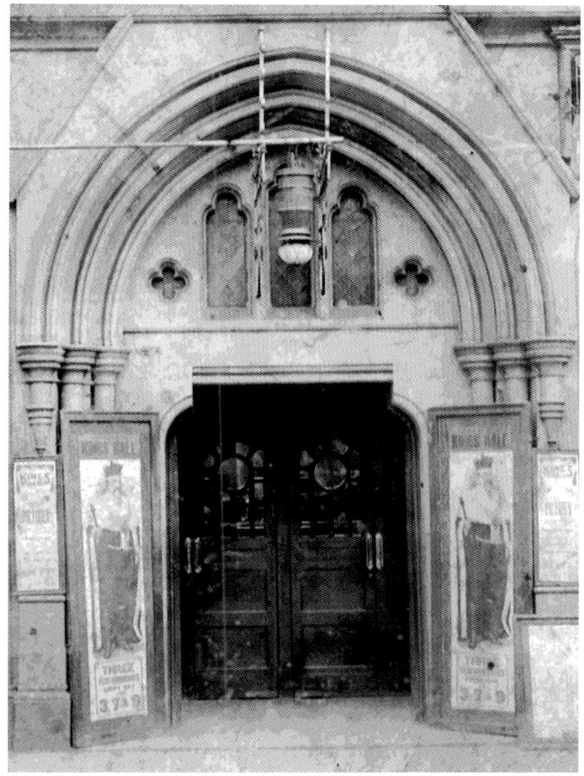

Above: The entrance to the Kings Hall, Birmingham soon after Ben Kennedy and James Moore started presenting "cine-variety on the premises in 1907.

The postcard below shows the building itself and the likenesses of Ben and James Moore inside horse-shoe frames. It clearly states that programmes include vaudeville acts and "electric pictures"

Above: Ben Kennedy, with jaunty hat and good luck horseshoe tiepin, presents himself on this postcard as manager of "Ediscope & Barnum's Electric Animated Pictures" during the period when he settled in the West Bromwich/Smethwick area, joined up with James Moore at The Theatre Royal West Bromwich and developed his repertoire of "cine-variety".(All the images used in this section of the chapter come from the archive now preserved by Ben's grand-daughter.)

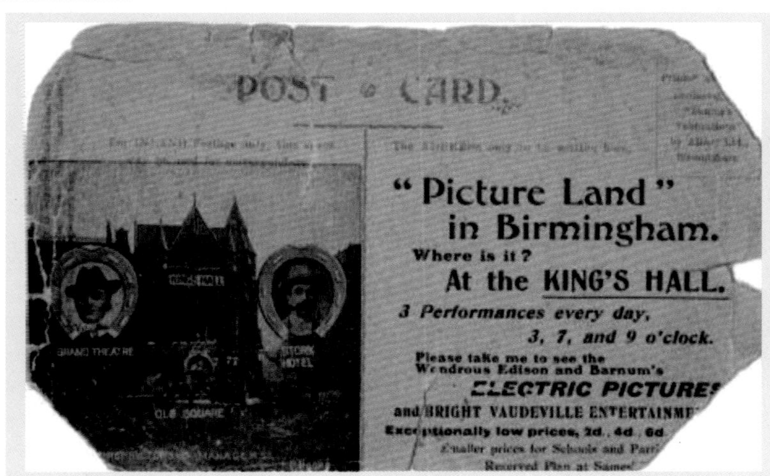

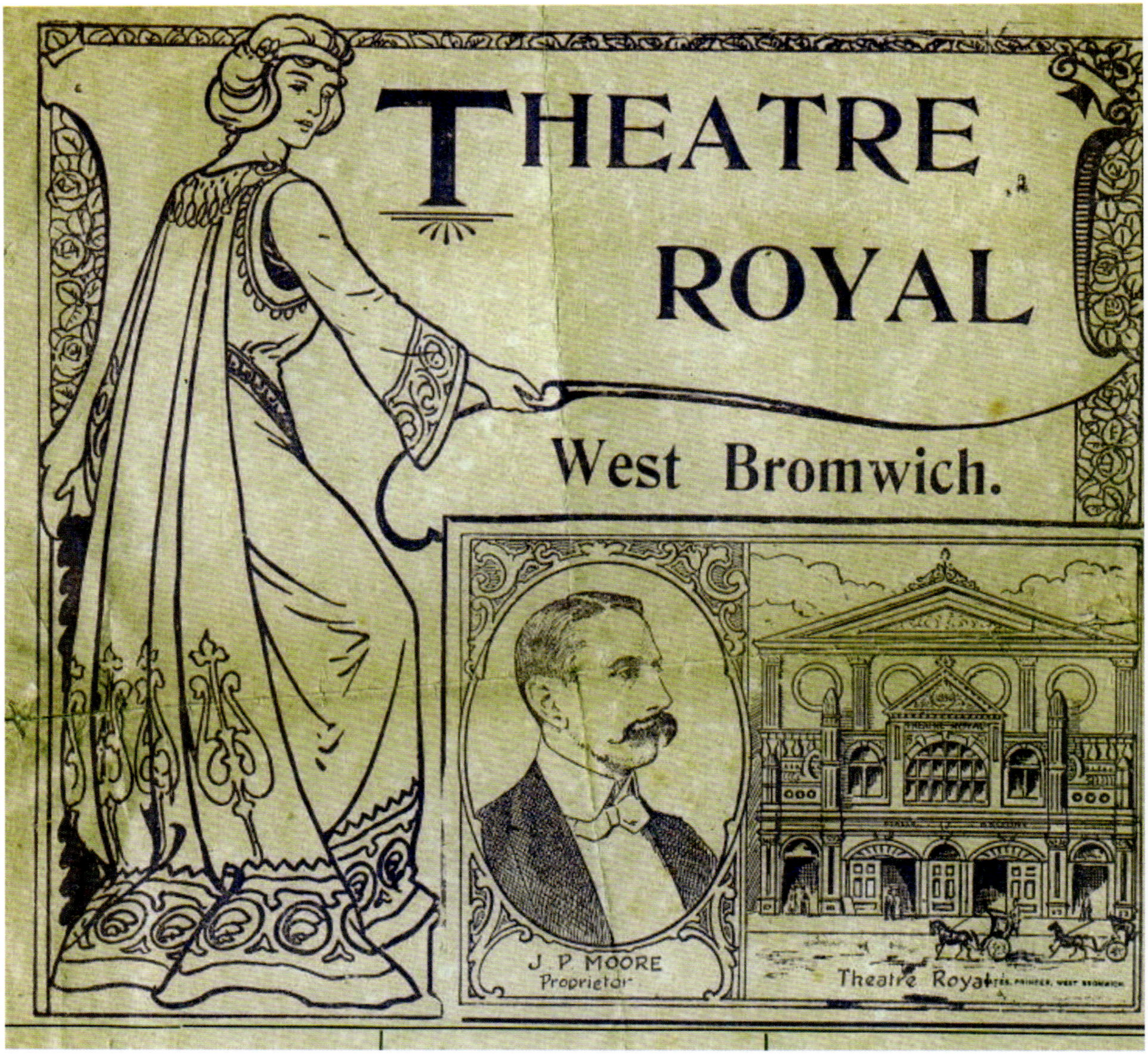

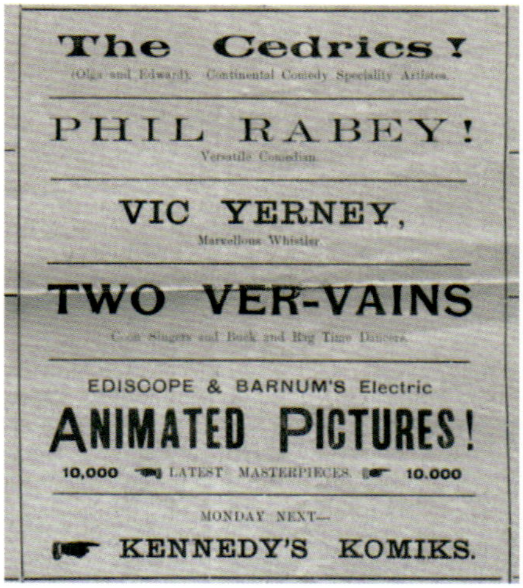

The Cedrics!
(Olga and Edward). Continental Comedy Speciality Artistes.

PHIL RABEY!
Versatile Comedian.

VIC YERNEY,
Marvellous Whistler.

TWO VER-VAINS

EDISCOPE & BARNUM'S Electric
ANIMATED PICTURES!
10,000 LATEST MASTERPIECES. 10,000

MONDAY NEXT—
KENNEDY'S KOMIKS.

Above: The central panel of a programmed produced for the Theatre Royal, West Bromwich in 1906 includes a likeness of James Moore and a drawing of the theatre's frontage that makes it look more impressive than in the photograph on page 138.

Left: The programme includes many advertisements for local businesses and a small panel listing the entertainment being provided. As expected this includes some variety acts and films still presented under the banner of "Ediscope & Barnum's Animated Pictures" and the appearance of "Kennedy's Komiks". It has not been possible to individually identify the members of Ben's comedy troupe.

Busy Times

The years from 1910 until the First World War were a very busy period in Ben Kennedy's life – creating a complex jig-saw of activities that has been fairly difficult to follow. It was also a frenzied period in the history of show business as a result of the passing of the Kinematograph Act. Films posed a threat to live theatre, but even the future of film as an entertainment medium could not be guaranteed.

Before we try to untangle all of Ben's activities let us return to his private life as revealed by the Census of April 1911. The Census tells us that 45 year old Benjamin Bernhard Kennedy was living at 35 John Street, Smethwick, and identified himself as a "theatre manager". He is living with 30 year old Louisa Kennedy who describes herself as his wife, and they had three children: Robert (aged 3), Clara (aged 1), and the one month old "Morris". (Names are frequently mis-spelt in early Census returns!) They enjoyed the service of two servants.

The 1911 Census was the first time we found William Bainton referring to himself as Irving Bosco in official records, and similarly it is the first time we find Benjamin Bernhard using the surname Kennedy.

Technically Ben was still married to Theresa, but to all intents and purposes he had created a Kennedy family and adopted the Black Country as "home". Both Robert and Clara are shown in the 1911 Census to have been born in Handsworth while the baby Maurice is said to be born in Smethwick. I think this means that up until 1910 the family lived in Rookery Road, but then moved to John Street, Smethwick. While everyone in the 1911 census is "Bernhard Kennedy", it is interesting to note on Robert's 1907 birth certificate that his name is given as "Robert Bradford Bernhard" –"Bradford" being his mother's surname. (Louisa may have had a sense of humour regarding names as she describes herself as "Lulu" on Robert's birth certificate.) At other times he included the name "Foster" – another name inherited from his mother's family.

When Kennedy's Kommics ceased travelling in 1910, Ben seems to have thrown himself into a massive wave of theatre-building activity - perhaps following great success at the Kings Hall in Birmingham. He used that name again when taking over the 'Public Hall' in Wednesbury in the September of 1909. This troubled building had precariously been a theatre and then a Salvation Army citadel, but in Ben's hands it settled down to cine-variety until full-time film-presentation became the order of the day. It is interesting to note that he installed Charles Pindar as manager of this Wednesbury enterprise. Mr. Charles Pindar was another

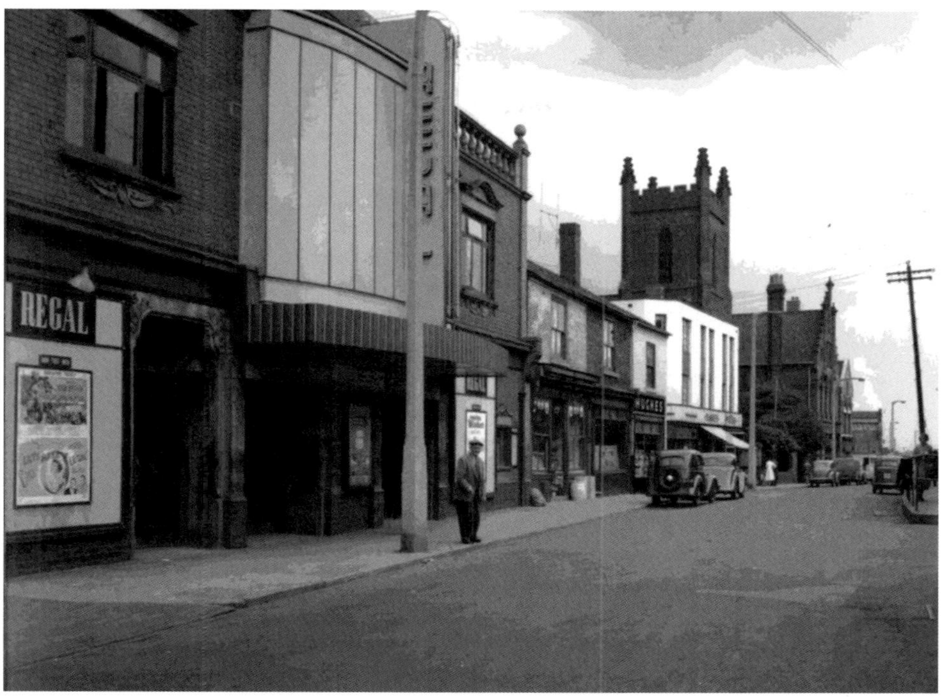

Right: The Market Hall, Owen Street, Tipton, was converted by Ben Kennedy into "The Tivoli" in 1910 for showing films and then "Cine-variety. Although Ben did not keep it for long, it survived as a cinema until 1960, for many years known as The Regal and then The Regent.
(Bill Bawden)

pioneer from the early days of cinematography, and indeed, like Irving Bosco, became a member of the Cinema Veterans Association.

As a result of presenting "cine-variety" at Wednesbury's Kings Hall from the autumn of 1909 onwards, Ben Kennedy joins Irving Bosco as a pioneer of cinema in the Black Country in the year *before* the Kinematograph Act came into force.

In May 1910 Ben Kennedy was granted permission to convert the Market Hall in Owen Street, Tipton, into the Tivoli, while at the same time work began on building the Empire, Smethwick - not a conversion but a purpose built theatre, and therefore an important step forward in Ben's progress in show business. A company was formed to build the Empire with Ben as Managing Director and W.H. Adams as company secretary. A theatre already existed in Smethwick, in Rolfe Street, but Ben seemed confident about providing another. He engaged an architect, Mr. G. Bowden, to design a building that would also comply with the requirements of the Kinematograph Act, as well as having fairly generous stage facilities. It would hold about 1500 patrons and its 64ft frontage, facing St. Pauls Road, was created in the "Free Renaissance" style. It was built by John Dallow & Sons. Mr. Bowden also drew up some plans for improving the Tivoli in Tipton including the installation of a raked floor. (Installing a raked, or sloping, floor was a good way of making a "public hall" type venue immediately seem more theatrical.)

The Empire opened on Monday 5th September 1910 with the Mayor of Smethwick and several local councillors in attendance. They were treated to an entertainment that embraced film and live variety acts. It seems that Ben installed his brother as manager of the theatre. (We last encountered Ben's brother in the 1891 census and have no idea whether he had also ventured into show business or if coming to the Empire was his introduction to it. Isador Bernhard now seemed to be known as Harry Kennedy – or did Ben have two brothers?) The Empire Smethwick seems to have become "Head Office" for Ben's activities.

The Kinematograph Act seems to have inspired Ben Kennedy to invest in the presentation of "cine-variety" in a number of places. One such place was to be found in Oldbury. It was a hall built behind The White Swan public house in Church Street and had been used as a "music hall" in the days when entertainment often supported the sale of alcohol. The hall was the property of a local brewery and a number of people leased it for brief periods. Sometime in 1910 Ben obtained a Kine licence for the hall and opened it as another "Tivoli".

Presenting cine-variety could have its problems. In November Ben Kennedy hit the headlines in the Midland Chronicle when it was clear he was going to be prosecuted for illegally presenting a drama at the Tivoli without a theatre licence. The case was heard at Oldbury Police Court and a policeman gave evidence he had collected at the Tivoli on 22nd October. He had seen a performance of a play called "Cinderella". Not only was Ben Kennedy in the dock, but also Mr. Levaine, whose company had presented the show, and all the cast!

The Defence argued that Mr. Kennedy possessed a licence for singing and dancing, and a kine licence. He had no need of a theatre license because he was presenting "variety", not a play. "Cinderella" was not a play – it was a short variety act – a "simple burlesque lampooning the famous pantomime". The policeman did not agree. He told magistrates that the show had lasted for more than an hour and had included an interval. In his opinion it could not be described a mere "sketch".

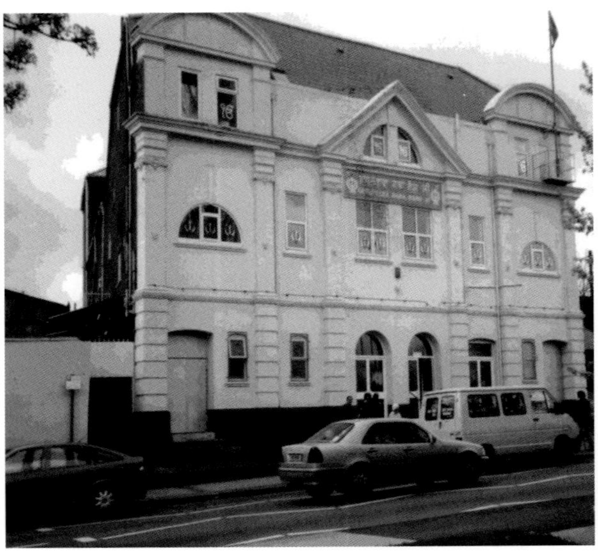

Left: The Empire, Smethwick, opened on 5th September 1910 with a programme of "cine-variety", but within ten years Ben had parted with it, despite briefly becoming Ben's "HQ". At one stage brother Harry managed it. For years it became a DIY shop but now enjoys life as a Sikh gurdwara – as seen here in this 2015 photo taken by Bob Broadfield.

The magistrates agreed, found everyone involved guilty and started to give out sentences. Ben Kennedy was fined £3 plus £2. 2s. costs, Mr. Levaine was fined £2 plus £1.11s costs. The entire cast was then about to be fined when the court was told that Ben Kennedy would be paying everyone's fines for them. The magistrates then decided to waive further fines provided Mr. Kennedy agreed to some further costs. It does seem that Ben Kennedy continued to present shows at The Tivoli, Oldbury. There were plenty of opportunities to explore elsewhere.

In 1911 Ben Kennedy opened the Coliseum Bearwood. Once again it was designed by Mr. Bowden and was purpose built for "cine-variety". For years I have searched unsuccessfully to identify the opening date of the Coliseum – such is the difficulty of finding out things to do with Ben Kennedy. However, an advertisement was inserted in The Stage for 2nd March 1911 by Dr. Walford Bodie who had just appeared at the Empire. It is a letter of commendation from Ben Kennedy in which he mentions the imminent opening of the Coliseum so we must conclude the theatre opened in February or March 1911.

Easter Monday, 12th April 1912 saw Ben opening the Hippodrome, Cannock, a building apparently started by others, but completed as part of the expanding Kennedy empire. The opening of Cannock's Hippodrome earns a mention in The Stage of 11th April 1912 where we learn that artistes who had appeared at the Smethwick Empire were specifically retained to open the Hippodrome; namely John F. Franklin's Western Girls (singing and dancing), plus Jack Watt (comedian). The local paper wrote, *"Mr. Kennedy promises capital entertainment in the future."*

In the case of the Hippodrome, Cannock, Ben only ran the theatre until the Autumn of 1914 before leasing it to someone else. It seems likely that he retained an interest in the freehold of the building because in the early 1920s he resumed control of the shows at the Hippodrome, selling both the freehold and the theatre licence to Roland Barton in 1923. (Roland Barton was already the proprietor of the Electric Palace in nearby Hednesford.) All this is a reminder that the person who ran a theatre was not necessarily the owner of the fabric of the building. Ben's progress is a mixture of building purpose built theatres, sometimes in partnership with others, and taking leases on existing buildings.

In 1912 Ben Kennedy leased The Gaiety Theatre in Coleshill Street, Birmingham; this building had a distinguished theatrical history going back to 1846 and was at one time known as Holders Music Hall. It had acquired the name Gaiety in 1886 when Charles Barnard became involved. It ran into trouble after becoming a public company, but fortunately Ben was able to revive its fortunes for a few years from 1912 onwards. Ben Kennedy brought a number of well-known people to the Gaiety including Gracie Fields, and in 1916 engaged Horatio Bottomley to appear to

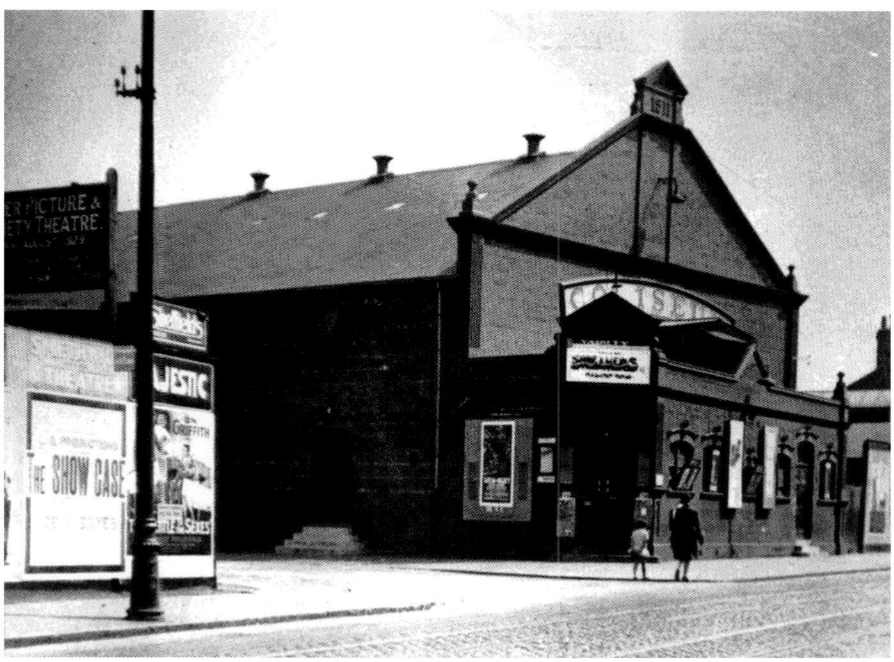

Right: The Coliseum, Bearwood, opened by Ben Kennedy in the Spring of 1911. (Photographed in 1929)

The Coliseum was sold to Edward Hewitson, the Smethwick-based cinema magnate in 1917 and was closed when Hewitson opened the Windsor, on the site on the left of Dunsford Road, in September 1930. (S. Smith, Sandwell Archives)

give a nightly commentary on the progress of the war. Mr. Bottomley is alleged to have earned £250 a week for this task. The Gaiety closed in 1920. This is not quite the end of the story as the building had another life as The Gaiety Picture House and was still part of the Kennedy estate when Ben died in 1939. It closed as a cinema in 1969.

Expansion continued. In some cases this amounted to taking on short leases for places like the Olympia Wordsley (1913). He also seems to have become involved with efforts being taken to reopen The Criterion, Dudley. This had been a small music hall established at the back of the Criterion public house in High Street Dudley. It had almost completely concentrated on showing films calling itself the Criterion Electric Theatre from 27th February 1911 onwards. It floundered but reopened in late 1913 with Ben's help, but by 1915 was taken over by Sidney Bray who was responsible for demolishing the pub and building a much bigger and better Criterion, opening in late 1923.

In other cases Ben Kennedy undertook the building of brand new purpose built theatres like the Empire, West Bromwich (1914). The latter provides a good example of how leases and theatre-building went hand in hand. In 1911 Ben Kennedy had taken a lease on a corrugated iron theatre built at Carters Green – sometimes known as the Olympia, sometimes known as The Hippodrome. It seems this was just a "holding operation" while he

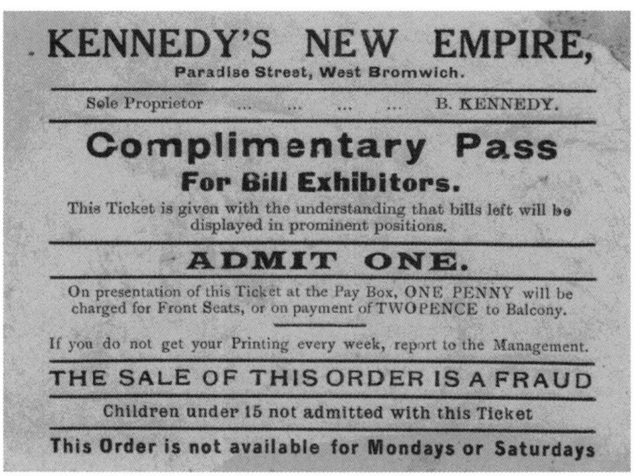
KENNEDY'S NEW EMPIRE,
Paradise Street, West Bromwich.
Sole Proprietor ... ... B. KENNEDY.
Complimentary Pass
For Bill Exhibitors.
This Ticket is given with the understanding that bills left will be displayed in prominent positions.
ADMIT ONE.
On presentation of this Ticket at the Pay Box, ONE PENNY will be charged for Front Seats, or on payment of TWOPENCE to Balcony.
If you do not get your Printing every week, report to the Management.
THE SALE OF THIS ORDER IS A FRAUD
Children under 15 not admitted with this Ticket
This Order is not available for Mondays or Saturdays

Above: An example of a "pass" given to a local shopkeeper in return for displaying a "bill", or advertisement for the week's show. Using "bills" in this way was inherited from the 19th Century – and was replaced by advertising in the local press.

built The Empire because when the latter opened he withdrew from The Olympia, although he did take it on again briefly when it was struggling in the early twenties! The Olympia was one of the Kennedy enterprises managed for a time by Harry Kennedy, Ben's brother. (Although it is not clear how Ben's brother became involved with the growing Kennedy empire, or even when he too adopted the surname "Kennedy", there is evidence of his success in the business. For example, an item in The Stage for 27th January 1910 mentions that staff at the Kings Theatre, Hanley, up in the Potteries, had a collection and bought him a silver cigar case when he left to take over management of one of the Birmingham enterprises.)

On 15th May 1914 The Midland Chronicle told its readers: *"There is no more up to date amusement caterer than Mr. B. Kennedy. When this gentleman added the Hippodrome* (Carters Green) *and the Gaiety* (Birmingham) *to his list of nine halls in the Black Country, prophets declared that he would have his hands full for a considerable period, but by genuine hard work and sound judgement he quickly transformed both places into paying and profitable concerns. His tenancy of the Olympia* (i.e. The Hippodrome, Carters Green) *expires on 30th May and the new theatre is rising like an Aladdin's place in Paradise Street and will open on Whit Monday."*

The Empire was being built by Messrs John Dallow & Sons who had built the Smethwick Empire, but this time the architects were Messrs. Wood & Kenrick. It did indeed open on 1st June 1914 with a programme that used film and variety acts. Ben Kennedy ran the place until 1927 when it was leased to C.D. Cinemas. In this case it returned to the Kennedy fold in 1936 and plays another part in the Kennedy story. (Revealed later in this chapter.)

In the period running up to the First World War we can catch a glimpse of Ben Kennedy's progress in the pages of The Era and The Stage, usually under the heading "Next Week's Calls". "The Kennedy Circuit" is often listed and the lists themselves work as a reminder of just how may theatres Ben could be running at one time, both in the Black Country and beyond.

Altogether in that frantic five-year period running up to the First World War, Ben controlled at least thirteen halls at one time or another - all dabbling in a mixture of film and variety act presentation. Some ventures were far from the main Birmingham and Black Country axis. For example, his interests included the Kings Theatre, Hanley; the Hippodrome, Ilkeston; and the Anglesey Hall, Burton on Trent.

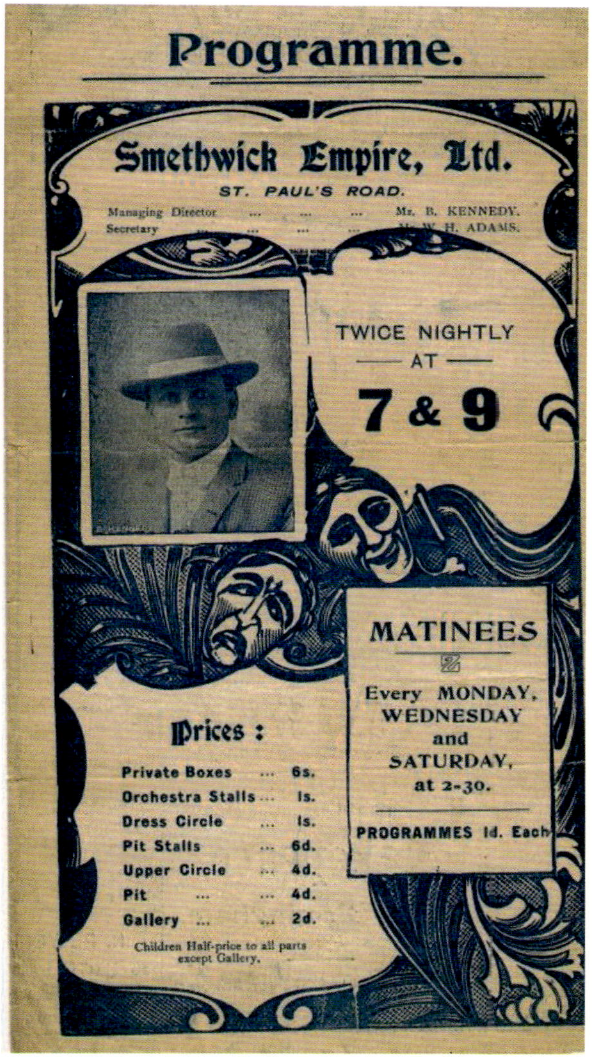

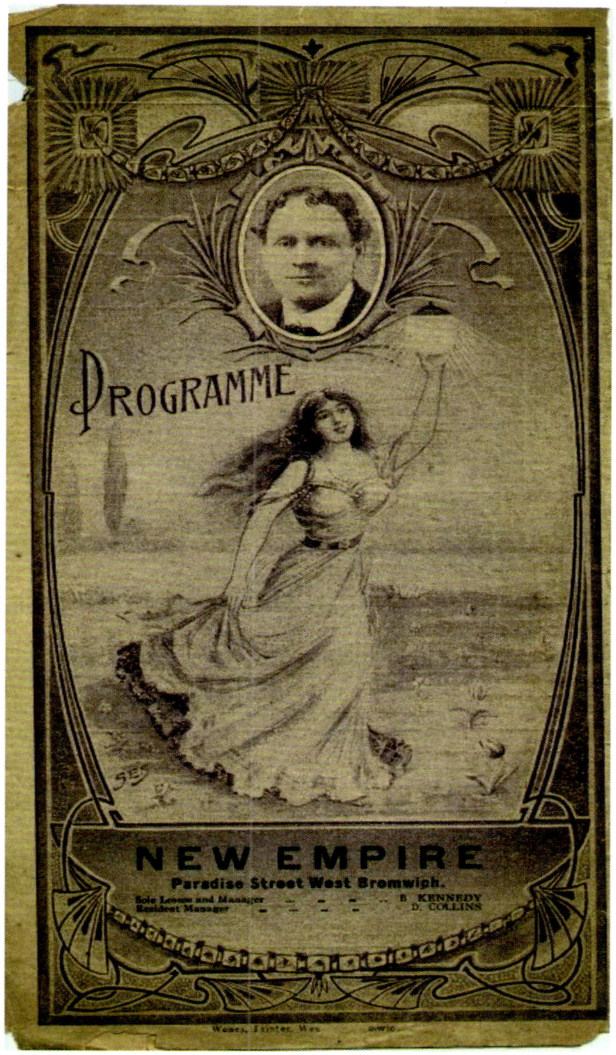

THE KENNEDYTOUR

Bearwood Coliseum (rehearsal 5) – Witty Witty Walton, Harry Hutin, and Dorothy Vetch.
Burton Anglesey Hal l (rehearsal 5) – Company as booked.
Darlaston Queens (rehearsal 5) – Capita, Katie Moro and Charley Drew.
Semthwick Empire (rehearsal 12) – Ella Blair and Bowery Boys and Girls, Violette Proctor, Bert Lytton, Alf Grady, Barbende and the Byrons.
Tipton Tivoli (rehearsal 5) – Keno and Rene, Lillie Hales and Kail Stern
Wednesbury Kings (rehearsal 12) - Katcourt, Stanley's War Scenes, Nora Doone, and Empire Quartet of Glee Singers.

Above left: A programme from the Empire, Smethwick for 16th January 1911, identifying Ben as "Managing Director" and W.H. Adams, as "Secretary"

Above right: A programme from the N ew Empire, West Bromwich for 28th June 1915, identifying Ben as Sole Lessee and Manager, and D. Collins as "Resident Manager".

Left: "The Kennedy Tour" as advertised in The Era in 1911, providing us with a mention of the Anglesey Hall, Burton, The Queens, Darlaston, The Kings, Wednesbury, and Tivoli, Tipton, as well as the Coliseum, Bearwood and Empire, Smethwick.

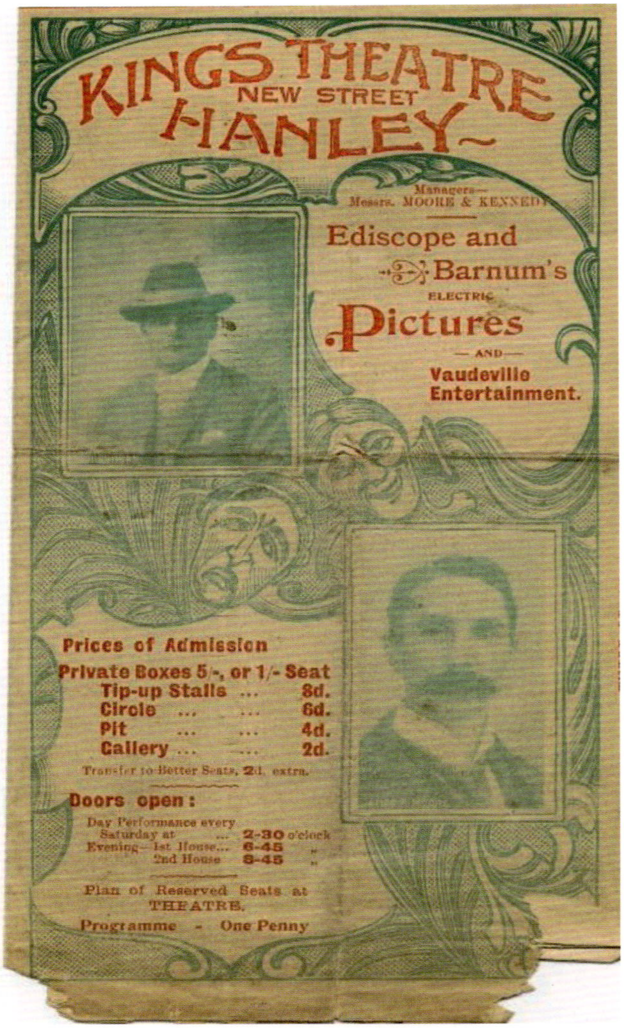

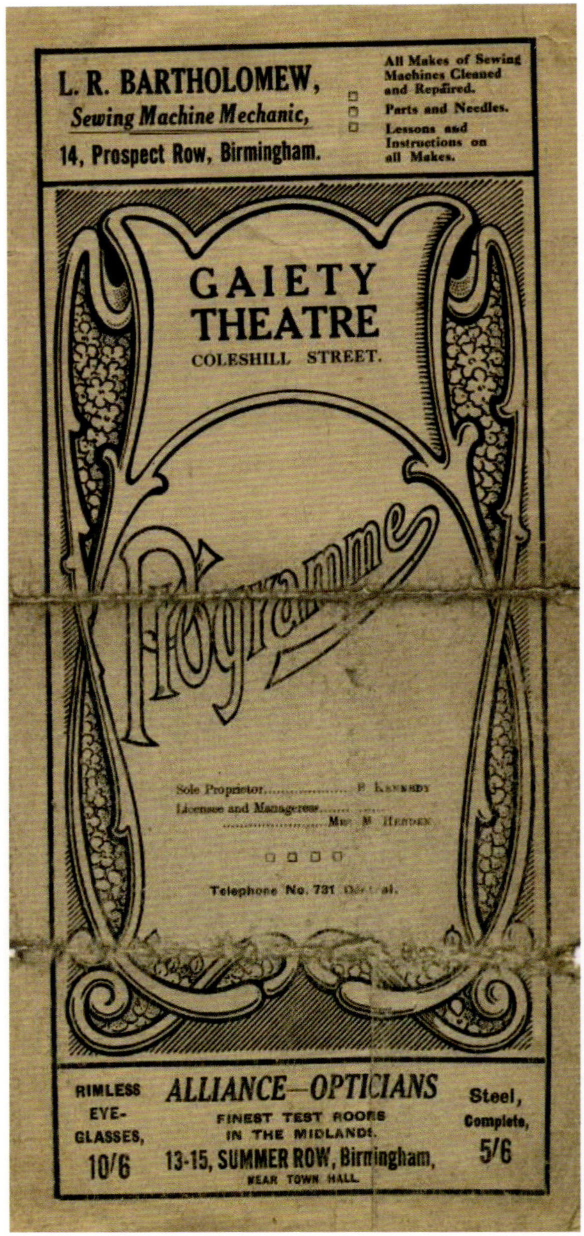

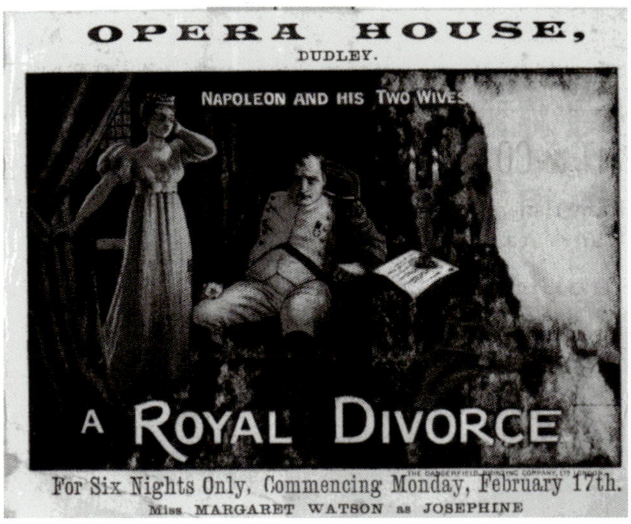

Above left: Programme for the Kings Theatre, Hanley, for 30th November 1908, featuring likenesses of Ben Kennedy and James Moore

Above right: Programme for the Gaiety for 3rd November 1919, identifying Ben Kennedy as proprietor and Mrs. M. Hebden as manageress.

Perhaps Ben Kennedy booked a play for the Opera House featuring Napoleon to remind him of his waxworks day!

The Home Front

The outbreak of war in 1914 created a moratorium on any new cinema building so we should not be surprised to find that Ben Kennedy's progress slowed down. Towards the end of the war we find Ben disposing of some of his enterprises like the Tivoli in Owen Street, Tipton. In other cases Ben resumed control of enterprises that had been in other hands. For example, he took over the Hippodrome Cannock for a brief period before disposing of it completely. At the Theatre Royal, West Bromwich James Moore decided not to renew his lease in 1917. Despite having control of the Empire in central West Bromwich, Ben decided to return to the Theatre Royal and in fact ran it for the rest of the theatre's life. (His sons closed the Theatre Royal in 1940 - a year after Ben's death.)

Ben seems to have had doubts about continuing his interests in Smethwick as the war went on. The key figure in Smethwick was Edward Hewitson, who, as a twenty-three year old, had come to the town from Middlesborough to take on the management of Charles Barnard's Theatre royal in Rolfe Street in 1897. Mr. Hewitson soon took an interest in films and by 1911 was thinking of becoming the local cinema magnate. His first step was to show films in the Town Hall under the name "Pictureland". This proceeded in 1912 while he built his "Princes Hall" cinema nearby. During the second half of the Great War he took over the Coliseum, and possibly set his sights on the Smethwick Empire. However, about 1917 Ben Kennedy leased the Smethwick Empire to Messrs. Black & Hicks who continued to present cine-variety. Edward Hewitson took it over from them in 1924 and from then on it concentrated on being a cinema.

In Ben's personal life the wartime period also saw a few matters sorted out. His wife, Theresa, decided to petition for divorce. The petition was heard in July 1915 and the judge was told that they had parted in 1901. She wanted the marriage dissolved on grounds of desertion and misconduct. No defence was offered and the judge issued a decree nisi. There were some further complications when it became clear that Theresa had withheld some information from the court, but nevertheless the divorce closed that chapter in Ben's life. (Theresa died towards the end of 1916 in Hackney.)

On 11th July 1917 thirty seven year old Catherine Louisa Harriette Bradford and fifty year old Ben, who was using his real surname – Bernhard – were married, having been together for sixteen years. Ben described

THE NEW EMPIRE, WEST BROMWICH.

DESCRIPTION OF BUILDING.

There is no more up-to-date and enterprising amusement caterer than Mr. B. Kennedy. When this gentleman added the old Hippodrome, West Bromwich (re-named "Olympia"), and subsequently the Birmingham Gaiety to his list of nine halls in the

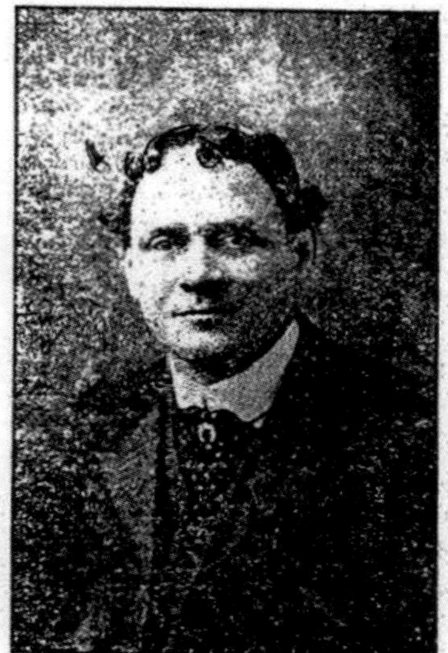

MR. B. KENNEDY.

Black Country prophets declared that he would have his hands full for a considerable period, but by genuine hard work and sound judgment he quickly transformed both places into paying and profitable concerns. His tenancy of "Olympia" expires on the 30th of this month, and the new theatre which is rising like Aladdin's Palace in Paradise Street, he hopes to declare open to the public on Whit-Monday.

A few particulars regarding this important addition to West Bromwich will be of interest to all our readers.

When the Empire, West Bromwich, was opened on 1st June 1914, the Midland Chronicle provided this information for its readers – and provided us with an early portrait of Ben Kennedy. (He was forty eight at the time.) Once again we see him wearing his "lucky horseshoe tie-pin – allegedly a 21st present from his father.

himself as a widower and "variety artist" which was a little modest considering all the theatres he had built or leased! At the time the couple were living at 124 Holyhead Road, Handsworth, and therefore married at the parish church which was St. James's, which was just off the Holyhead Road. The Vicar, Reverend Thomas Lane, conducted the service and four witnesses signed the register. Two of the witnesses appear in this account of Ben's life. One was Annie Cora Stanton, whom he later marries, and the other was Charles Lyons who died in a motor cycle accident described in the next section!

The Roaring Twenties

Some of the pre-war ventures were sold or abandoned at the end of the First World War, but a key event took place in October 1920 when Ben took over the Opera House in Dudley, followed ten years later by the acquisition of the Scala - 'next door.' In acquiring the Dudley Opera House, and gradually making it the centre of his empire, Ben was making a very clear move towards the Black Country, as opposed to Birmingham. The Opera House itself had been an ambitious dream of a Dudley man named John Maurice Clement (1840 – 1912). After John Clement's death in 1912 the theatre was owned by Ernest Davies, sometimes running the venue himself and sometimes leasing it to others.

On Friday 1st October 1920 a gathering and dinner had been organised in the Station Hotel to say goodbye to Ernest Davies and to thank him for his successful eight year stewardship of the Opera House. The Mayor of Dudley (Councillor Adshead) was there and a number of Dudley people. Presentations were made to Ernest Davies, his wife and his daughter and speeches were made praising him for the way he had managed the theatre, along with Edward Baring who had acted as "Chairman" of the Board of Directors of the Dudley Opera House Company. Interestingly Ben Kennedy was also a guest and he was given a toast and received the good wishes of the assembly. Ben then made a short speech and the report of this in the Dudley Herald is one of the few examples found when Ben is actually quoted! Ben claimed that he did not know how to express his feelings in the circumstances, but he was very glad to be present and to hear what was said about Mr. Davies. *"It is a great pleasure to be amongst such people – such as the good people I have met in Dudley in the last few days. I will do my best to deserve their good wishes."*

Apparently shows had been booked up until the March of 1921 so there was a very smooth transition to Ben Kennedy's regime. However, from that moment onwards the theatre's advertisements made it clear that Ben was the "sole proprietor", and he immediately instituted a few changes. He put on the shows on a "twice nightly" basis and announced that he would be putting on Monday afternoon matinees.

When the Opera House was purchased by Ben Kennedy the County Express of 2nd October 1920 stated: *"On Monday next the Opera House passes into the ownership of Mr. Ben Kennedy. Mr. Kennedy is no stranger to Dudley as he will be remembered for his various pantomimes produced by Percy Victor, who has been associated with Mr. Kennedy in all his enterprises as booking agent and producer".*

This reference to Percy Victor is one of the few clues we are given to the necessity of having a "management team" when it came to running all Ben's enterprises. It looks as if Louisa may have helped run the Opera House for a time as the Empire Smethwick still housed Ben's "head office" for at least two years. Fred Rothery-Ellis was installed as Ben's manager on the spot. Another proof of Louisa's involvement comes from the story of an event in April 1921. Louisa was working very late one evening at the Opera House and accepted a lift home in the motor-cycle side car belonging to a Mr. Lyons. By this time the Kennedys were living at Highland Lodge, Holyhead Road, Handsworth. On their way through Oldbury the motor-cycle was involved in an accident. Mr. Lyons was killed, Louisa was injured but survived.

As we look for "Kennedy Circuit" items in The Era and The Stage we can see that many of the small Black Country venues had been "dropped", and by the end of 1920 Ben was concentrating on Dudley Opera House, the Hippodrome Cannock, The Gaiety in Birmingham plus three enterprises in West Bromwich: The Olympia, Carters Green, The Empire and the Theatre Royal.

Ben had four more sons during the 1920s, the mother in each case being Annie Stanton. Derek was born on 27 April 1921, Alan was born on 26th October 1922, Cecil was born on 6th March 1925 and Bryan was born in 1928. As far as it is known they were all registered with the name Bernhard but used the surname Kennedy. Alan Kennedy went straight into the family's theatre business on leaving school at thirteen in 1935. He worked as a "lime boy", looking after some of the stage lighting, at the Theatre Royal, West Bromwich and was, in effect, managing the place when it closed in 1940. After the War he worked as stage manager at the Plaza, West Bromwich. Later in life he looked after a pub near Bromyard. Bryan also had something to do with the theatrical world and in the 1950s he looked after two cinemas in Hednesford for Kennedy Theatres.

For most of the 1920s Ben Kennedy focussed on running the Empire and Theatre Royal West Bromwich and the Opera House, Dudley. His sons Bob and Maurice came into the business in the following decade. The Stage of 22nd September 1927 mentions that the Head Office of the "Kennedy Circuit" had moved to the Theatre Royal, West Bromwich which is a reminder that during that year Ben leased the Empire, West Bromwich, to CD Cinemas. The lease passed to ABC cinemas in 1929 and then returned to the Kennedy fold in 1936!

Life changed again in the summer of 1929 following the death of Louisa Kennedy at the age of forty nine. She died in the presence of her son Bob at 65 Sutton Road. Erdington

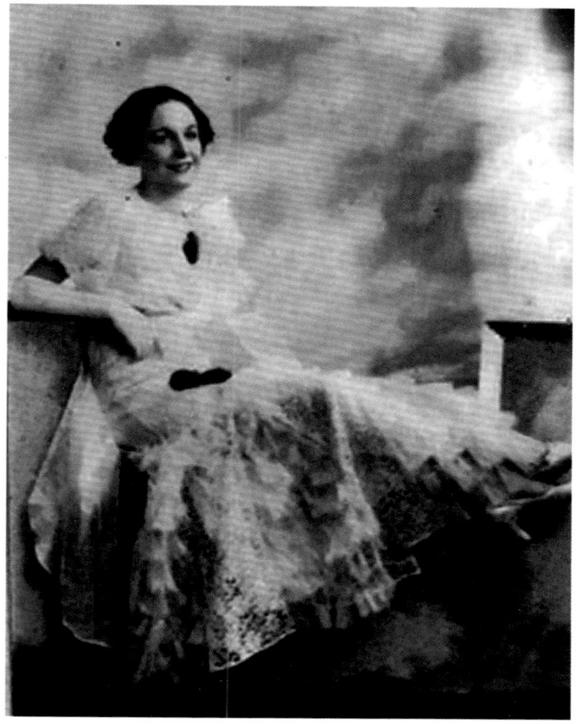

Right: The "Mystery picture"! This photograph meant something to Bob Kennedy, Ben's first son. When Bob died in 1989 it was inherited by his second wife, Beryl. She took it with her to Australia, and when she died it passed to her son by her first marriage. It is believed to be a picture of Louisa Kennedy. In part, it is reproduced here as a reminder of the scarcity of any photographs of Ben and his family.

Below: The Dudley Opera House, opened in 1889 and acquired by Ben Kennedy in 1920.

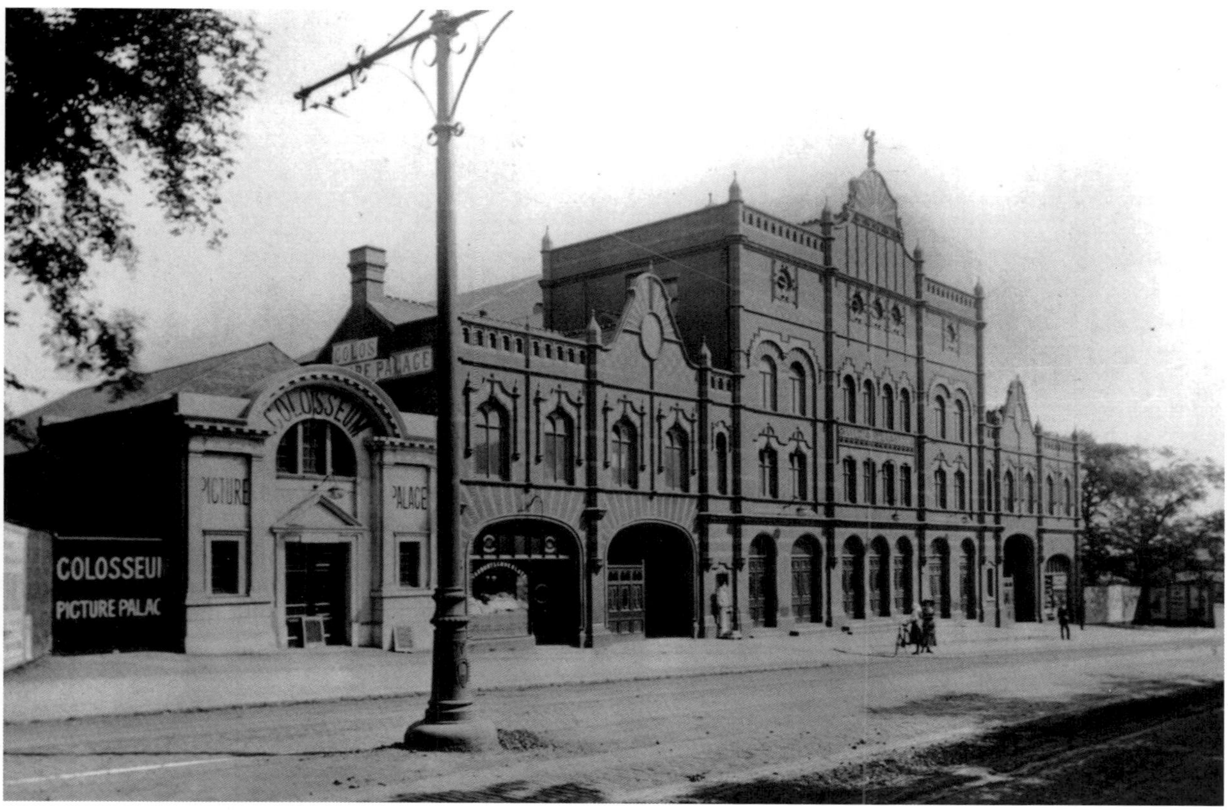

The 1930s

The 1930s begin with Ben enjoying a presence in Dudley and West Bromwich. His interests in Dudley now include the Palais de Danse – a dance hall established in the old Mechanics Institute building in Wolverhampton Street which had also been used by Irving Bosco as a cinema for several years! On stage at the Palais de Danse were "Maurice Kennedy and His Revellers".

The Opera House enjoyed considerable refurbishment in the summer of 1931 and when it reopened Ben Kennedy advertised it as "the cosiest theatre in the Midlands". Next door to the Opera House was a small cinema that had begun life on 24th December 1910 as The Colosseum, promoted by John Maurice Clement, the proprietor of the Opera House. Perhaps Ben had his eye on it during the 1920s, but he was not able to buy it until 1931. By then it was called The Scala, but it seems Ben had other ideas. When he was ready he closed it, pulled it down and replaced it with a brand new cinema.

This new-build venture was to be known as The Plaza, and it opened as such on 28th May 1936 with "Top Hat", starring Fred Astaire and Ginger Rogers. His new cinema was designed by Archibald Hurley Robinson in a modern functional style – all part of the 1930s transformation of Dudley's Castle Hill. It seems that Ben Kennedy was able to entertain civic guests on the opening night, but some may have noticed that his health was beginning to fail. He installed his son Maurice as manager, with Bob running the Opera House and booking films for the new cinema.

Ben's private life saw some changes at the beginning of the 1930s when he married for the third time. He married Annie Cora Stanton on 23rd April 1931, at Bromsgrove Registry Office. On this occasion sixty two year old Ben quite clearly describes himself as a "theatre proprietor", and interestingly calls himself Benjamin Bernhard Kennedy – as result of which Annie becomes "Mrs. Kennedy". Annie described herself as a "housekeeper". Ben's three weddings follow an interesting sequence from synagogue in London, to Handsworth Anglican Parish Church, to a Registry Office. The reason Ben and Annie are married in Bromsgrove Registry Office is that Hagley, where Ben was then living, came under the jurisdiction of Bromsgrove.

After Louisa's death he seems to have moved to Hagley, and after his marriage to Annie he seems to have moved again to Bourneville House, Bridgnorth Road, Wollaston. After the opening of the Plaza in May 1936 it must have seemed that he had begun his retirement with his sons left to run the business. However, one more episode in his life was about to unfold.

On the evening of Saturday 31st October 1936, or rather in the early hours of Sunday morning, someone noticed smoke rising from the Opera House. The Fire Brigade was summoned, but the fire had taken hold and by 7.30.am the Opera House was a smouldering ruin. Bob and Maurice Kennedy had helped the firemen tackle the blaze by taking them to the roof of the Plaza from which to train their hoses, but Ben was away in Weston Super Mare whilst all this was happening.

What happened following the destruction of the Dudley Opera House is still one of the amazing details of the Kennedy story. A decision was made to build a brand new theatre to replace the Opera House on the same site on Castle Hill. We will never know how this decision was made – was it a decision led by Bob and Maurice, Ben's sons? Was it a decision made by Ben himself? What was it going to be like to build a large first class provincial theatre in the late 1930s? How does all this fit in with the changing face of Castle Hill? The Kennedys had opened the new Plaza in May 1936, the Opera House burned down at the end of October of the same year. Meanwhile Oscar Deutsch was planning and then building his new Odeon cinema on the other side of the road. It opened on 28th July 1937. Dudley Zoo, with its famous modern entrance right next to the Plaza had opened on 18th May 1937.

The Kennedys did not drag their feet. Archibald Hurley Robinson, who had designed The Plaza, was quickly engaged to draw up plans for the new theatre. These were submitted to Dudley Council for approval on 4th May 1937 – at which point it was still going to be called "The Dudley Opera House". A.J. Crump, a local builder, began work on the new theatre on 23rd August 1937 – ten months after the fire, and one month after the Odeon had opened. The Hippodrome, as it was going to be called, was not only going to be the best and most up-to-date theatre in the West Midlands – it also had to outshine everything else on Castle Hill. It took sixteen months to build the Hippodrome, and in the tradition of such ventures, it was only just finished in time for its opening.

In November 1938 advance tickets went on sale, from a box office established in the Plaza, for the opening concert and the forthcoming pantomime. The Hippodrome was to open on Monday 19th December 1938, with a civic reception at the Station Hotel, and

Dudley Opera House

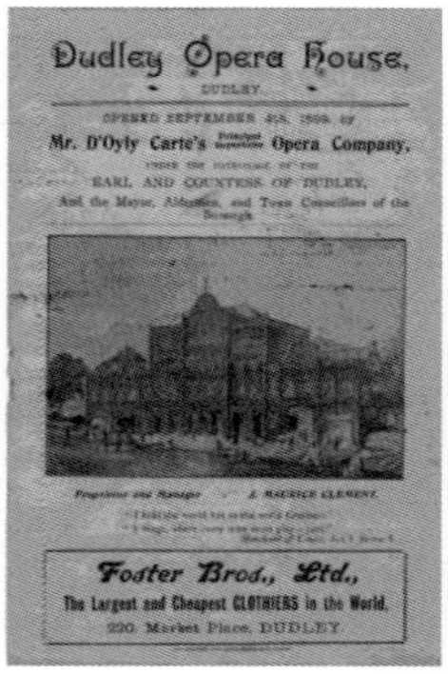

The first programme Issued at the opening of the Opera House

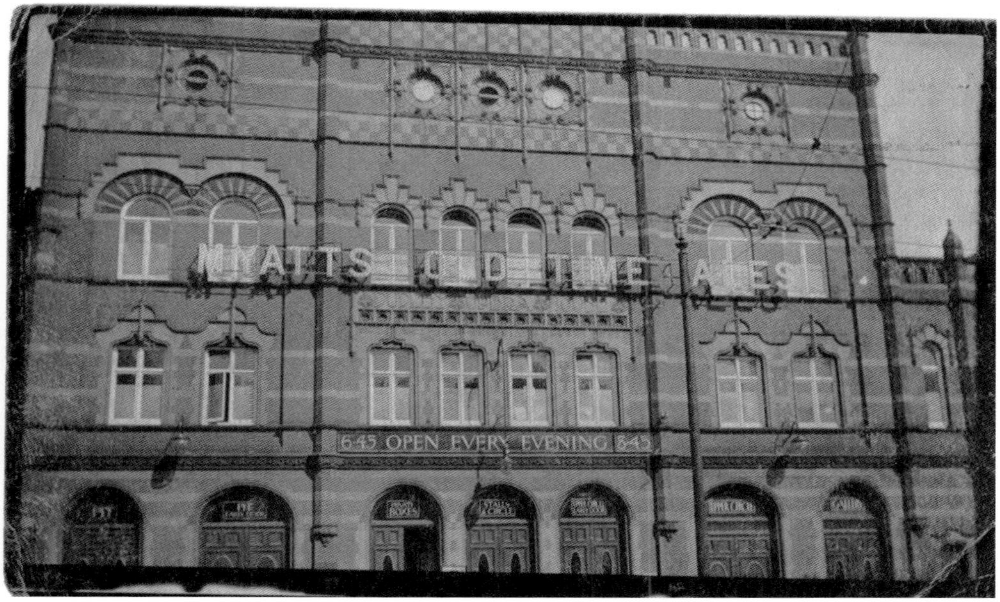

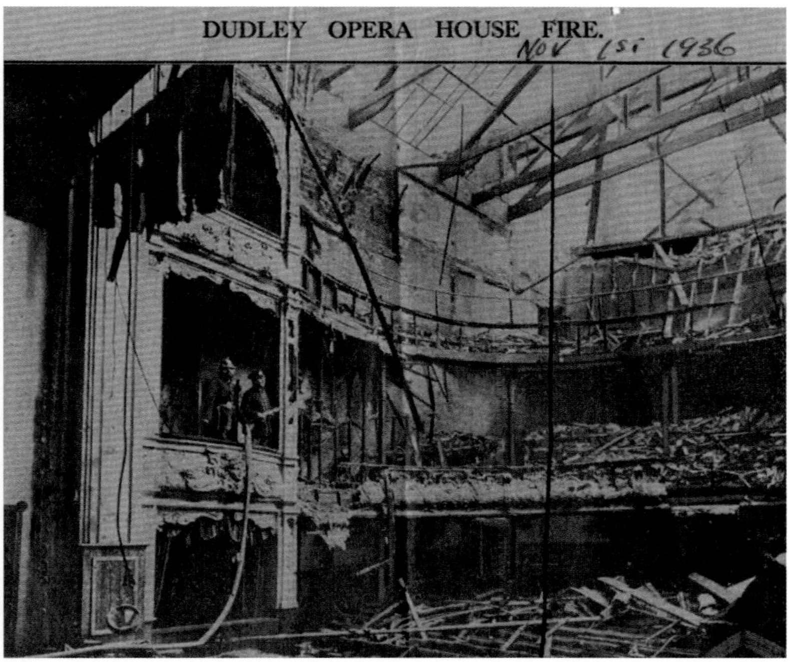

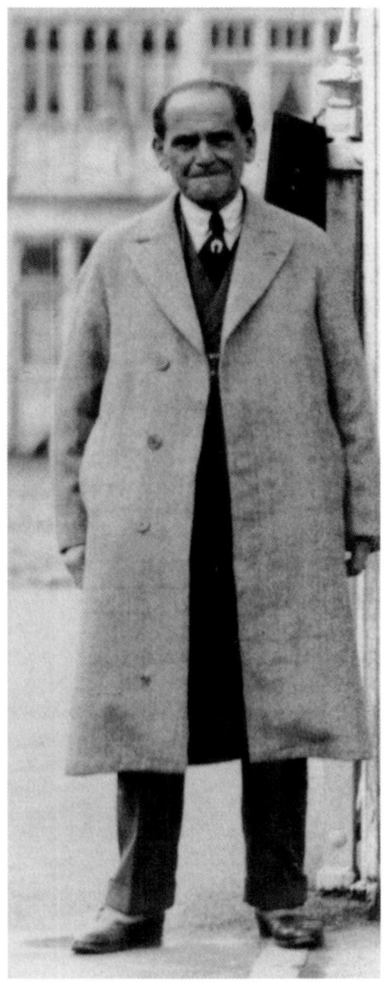

Above (Top): An unusual view of Dudley Opera House – usually seen in three quarter views looking up Castle Hill. This picture was found in the surviving family archive and possible shows the building after 1920 – once acquired by Ben Kennedy.
Above: A newspaper photograph of the Opera House after the fire on 1st November 1936 from a cutting in the same collection.
Right: Ben Kennedy photographed sometime in the mid 1930s, still wearing his horse-shoe tie pin – quite a contrast to the pictures of him as a young man used to illustrate this chapter.

Right: The Dudley Hippodrome under construction in 1938.
Built by the Dudley firm of A.J.Crump it used local steel and locally made bricks. The steelwork supporting the two stages of the huge balcony can be seen clearly – producing the interior seen on the next page.

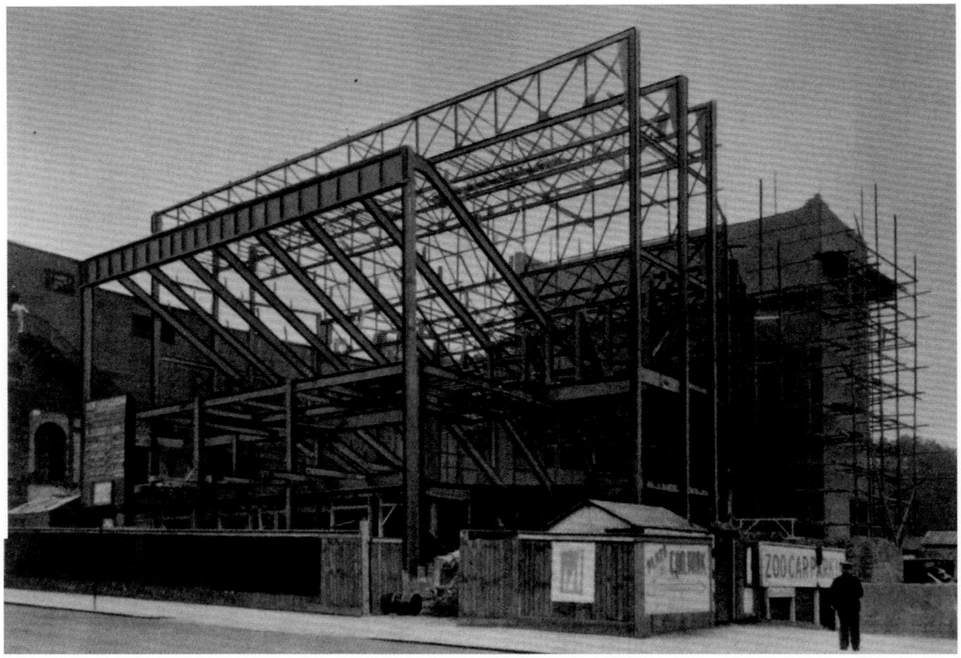

then followed by a Jack Hylton band concert and variety show in the theatre. Unfortunately Ben Kennedy was not well and had to attend the event in a wheel chair, but Bob and Maurice were very much in charge, and Bob welcomed everyone on behalf of his father. Ben also officially welcomed everyone to the new theatre in his preface to the "opening brochure".

The Dudley Herald published a picture of the event in which the small wheelchair-bound Ben Kennedy is dwarfed by the surrounding dignitaries – Dudley Joel, MP, who took the key to formerly open the theatre, Dudley's Mayor, the builder, the architect etc… Was he sitting there feeling that it was the crowning achievement of his long and interesting life, or was he now weary of such things? We have to think about this as 1938 faded into 1939. The theatre was both busy and successful, and innovative, but his declining health may have prevented him from any direct involvement with it. Ben died at his home in Wollaston on 10th April 1939.

News of Ben Kennedy's death was spread by The Express & Star, of Wolverhampton, the Dudley Herald, and the Birmingham papers. The news was usually supplemented with some biographical details – usually sprinkled with the legends rather than precise facts. Newspapers differed on how many times Ben had married and sometimes gave the story a different slant.

Most newspapers reminded readers of the opening of the Dudley Hippodrome; in fact the Express & Star headlined their story: "Death after achieving Life's Ambition."

Ben's funeral and burial took place at Stourbridge Borough Cemetery on Thursday 13th April 1939, not far from his last home which was in Wollaston. He was survived by his widow, Annie, his brother Harry, and by his seven children, and he left a will detailing how the theatrical part of his estate was to be managed by Bob and Maurice for the benefit of the legatees. His estate included the Dudley Hippodrome; the Plaza cinema, Dudley; the Theatre Royal and the Plaza (formerly The Empire), West Bromwich and an interest in The Gaiety in Birmingham.

After Ben's death Harry Kennedy, Ben's brother, became Chairman of the Directors of Kennedy's Theatres Ltd although Ben's sons Bob and Maurice were in charge of the day by day operation of the theatres. Mr. Lyon Clark, a well-known West Bromwich, solicitor was also on the board. Harry had always been somewhat in the shadow of Ben. He continued to live locally, at 380 Bearwood Road, Smethwick and died in June 1947. The Stage reported his death saying, *"He and his brother Benjamin, founded the Kennedy Circuit of theatres and cinemas. He is succeeded by his son Cyril, who is a councillor of the neighbouring borough of West Bromwich."*

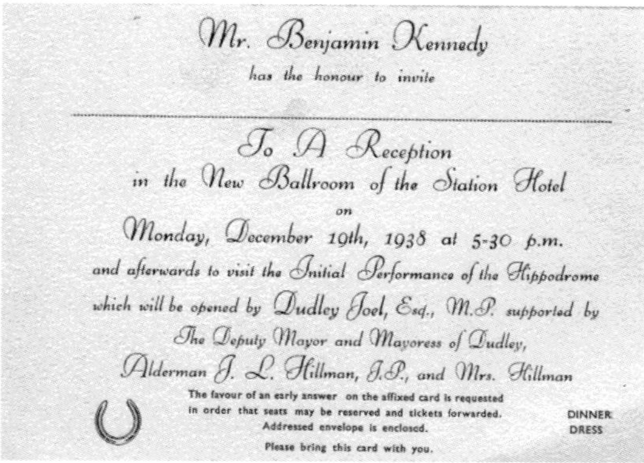

Mr. Benjamin Kennedy
has the honour to invite

To A Reception
in the New Ballroom of the Station Hotel
on
Monday, December 19th, 1938 at 5-30 p.m.
and afterwards to visit the Initial Performance of the Hippodrome
which will be opened by Dudley Joel, Esq., M.P. supported by
The Deputy Mayor and Mayoress of Dudley,
Alderman J. L. Hillman, J.P., and Mrs. Hillman

The favour of an early answer on the affixed card is requested
in order that seats may be reserved and tickets forwarded.
Addressed envelope is enclosed.
Please bring this card with you.

DINNER
DRESS

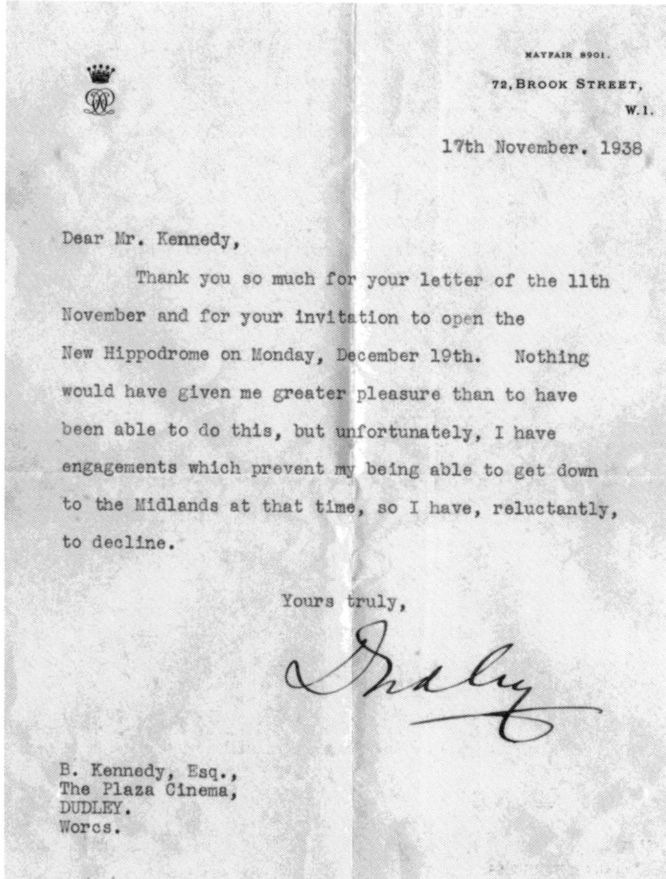

MAYFAIR 8901.

72, BROOK STREET,
W.1.

17th November. 1938

Dear Mr. Kennedy,

Thank you so much for your letter of the 11th November and for your invitation to open the New Hippodrome on Monday, December 19th. Nothing would have given me greater pleasure than to have been able to do this, but unfortunately, I have engagements which prevent my being able to get down to the Midlands at that time, so I have, reluctantly, to decline.

Yours truly,

Dudley

B. Kennedy, Esq.,
The Plaza Cinema,
DUDLEY.
Worcs.

Above, Ben's health may have been failing as preparations were being made to open Dudley Hippodrome but invitations were sent out in his name, and displaying his "horse-shoe" motif. A reception was to be held at the Station Hotel, and then guests would cross the road to see Dudley Joel, Dudley's MP, open the Hippodrome, followed by a Jack Hylton concert.

Right: Ben's reply from Lord Ward, Earl of Dudley, stating that he would be unable to attend.

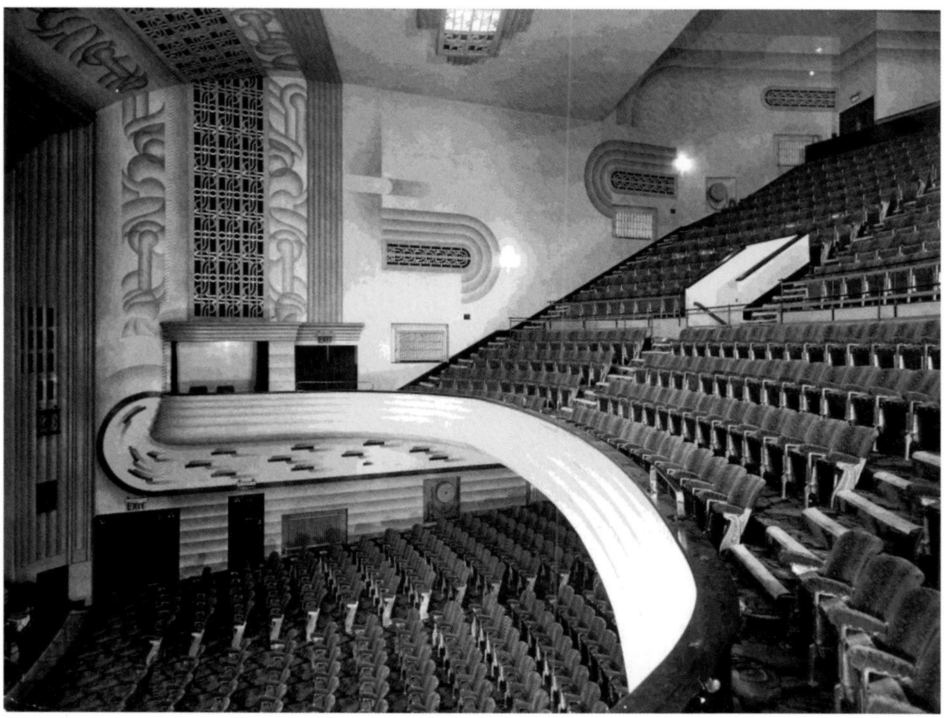

Right: The grand art-deco auditorium of the Hippodrome – which currently, in 2018, probably awaits demolition as a result of the Local Authority's indifference towards it – either in its own right or as a tribute to the work of Ben Kennedy.

Ben Kennedy's Legacy

Ben's sons, Bob and Maurice, had grown up in the business and went on to make a continuing success of their theatre and cinema interests – a story I have told in my book, "Black Country Theatres", published in 2011. They had to deal with the changes and challenges that the business had to face in Post-war Britain – circumstances in which it would be increasingly difficult to run a theatre. They operated as Kennedy Theatres Ltd. while the theatre itself remained the property of the trustees of Ben Kennedy's estate – the management company paying the estate £3250 per annum to rent the building. In the end Kennedy Theatres Ltd. ceased operation in the March of 1958. This left a vacuum in which the trustees had to find someone else to lease and operate the Hippodrome. When no-one was forthcoming they tried selling the theatre by auction, but it failed to reach the reserve. What followed was a complicated period in which the theatre sometimes seemed open and sometimes seemed closed, while lessees tried various ways of making the theatre viable. This included band concerts, and pop concerts, wrestling, amateur operatic & dramatic productions, an annual pantomime, and even occasional "rep".

One lessee, Jerry Jeary, claimed he had bought the building itself and continued the same variety of use, with even more emphasis on weeks of "strip-shows", with jocular titillating names. Really he was still running the theatre on a lease. Having arrived in Dudley in the Autumn of 1962, this is what I discovered at The Hippodrome. I made the mistake of thinking such presentations were best ignored – now I realise I missed an interesting aspect of theatre history, and the experience of going into the Hippodrome while still in theatrical use! It had little to do with the Kennedys, but I would have seen the building in all its surviving glory.

The final curtain fell at Dudley Hippodrome on Saturday 29th February 1964 with the last night of "Glamorous Nights" – a musical show by Ivor Novello, presented by the West Bromwich Operatic Society. While they were leaving the theatre, contractors were arriving to convert the building for use as a club. A Mr. Vic Kendrick was about to reopen it as "The Dudley Hippodrome Casino Club". Ironically, although Bingo had now arrived at the Hippodrome, there followed a period when live entertainment still played a part in the proceedings – bingo running until 9.30pm, followed an half hour later by nightclub activity from 10.00pm until 2.00.am. About 1967 Vic Kendrick sold his lease to

Below: Bob (left) and Maurice (right) Kennedy at the Hippodrome. (A Bob Hosier photograph)

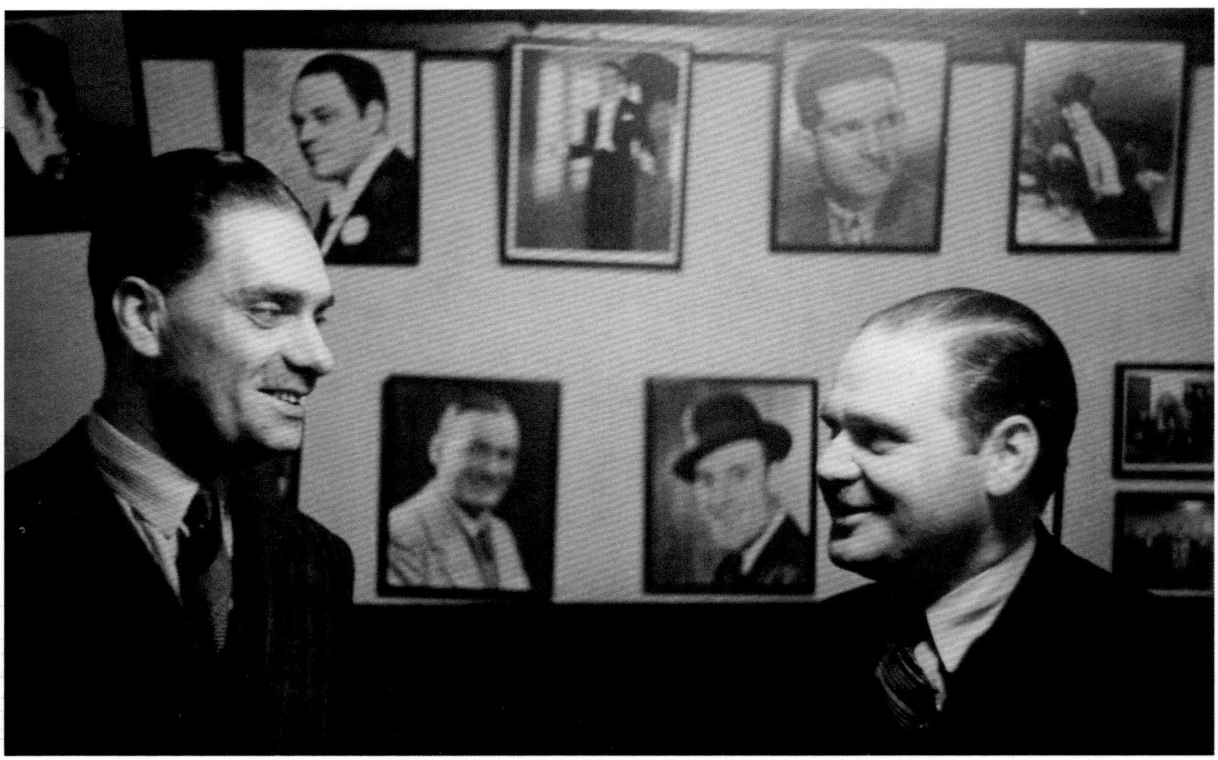

Harry Whitehouse – an interesting character associated with the history of the Avion cinema in Aldridge. Then in June 1968 Harry Whitehouse purchased the Hippodrome building from the trustees of the estate of the late Ben Kennedy for £70,000, and that was the end of the building's remote connection with the Kennedys.

These events were not the end of the story of Ben Kennedy's great building – that continued as a bingo and social club until abandoned by Gala Bingo on 19th September 2009 – forty five years after the last proper stage show in the building, and over half a century after the Kennedy brothers had ceased running the place. I had occasionally visited the building while it was in use as a bingo club and always marvelled at how little some parts of the building had changed since that night in 1938 when Ben had been brought to the opening of his wonderful new Hippodrome.

Since the demise of bingo in the Hippodrome in the Autumn of 2009 the building has stood empty, unused and abandoned. Its compulsory purchase by Dudley Council has not saved the building as successive leaders of the authority have voiced the opinion that it has no future use. A group opposed to its demolition and devoted to rescuing the building and bringing it back to use as a theatre seems, at the time of writing, to have failed to proceed very far with that plan. They were given such a short lease on the building it ruined their chance of obtaining the necessary funding. While all this has been going on I have tried to understand what it is that could be "regenerated", although the preservationists were clear that it would return to full theatrical use – would it have been a monument to Ben Kennedy? Or is Ben now forgotten?

Annie Cora Kennedy died on 3rd October 1983 at the age of eighty five. She was living in Hagley Road West, Quinton but the funeral was organised so that she could be buried alongside Ben at Wollaston, near Stourbridge. Her death was noted by a short piece in the Birmingham Evening Mail but I have not come across an account of the funeral. Bob Kennedy, Ben's first son, died on 3rd December 1989. At the time he was living in Surrey and had been working as Harry Secombe's 'personal assistant and agent' for longer than he had worked at the Hippodrome. He was probably the last person who could have given us a first-hand account and evaluation of his father's life and work.

In the 1890s Ben had become a "variety artiste", in the twentieth century, he had become a very entrepreneurial theatre proprietor and had been a pioneer of "cine-variety". Having been involved in an amazing variety of theatrical ventures and venues, he became the owner of the Dudley Opera House. When that burnt down he built a first class provincial variety theatre on a grand scale. Having died soon after it opened, he left his sons, Bob and Maurice, to try and make it survive into a more "difficult" time. And all this is being written as the Dudley Hippodrome, Ben's monument, faces demolition in the hands of an unsympathetic local authority.

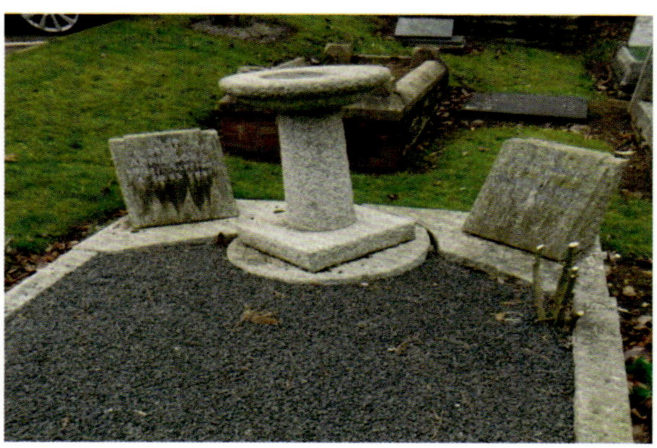

Above: Ben's and Annie's grave at Stourbridge Cemetery, photographed in 2018. (Note the inscription on Ben's headstone, on the right, has been partly erased.) Annie Kennedy had purchased four plots in the cemetery in 1939 but only two have been used.

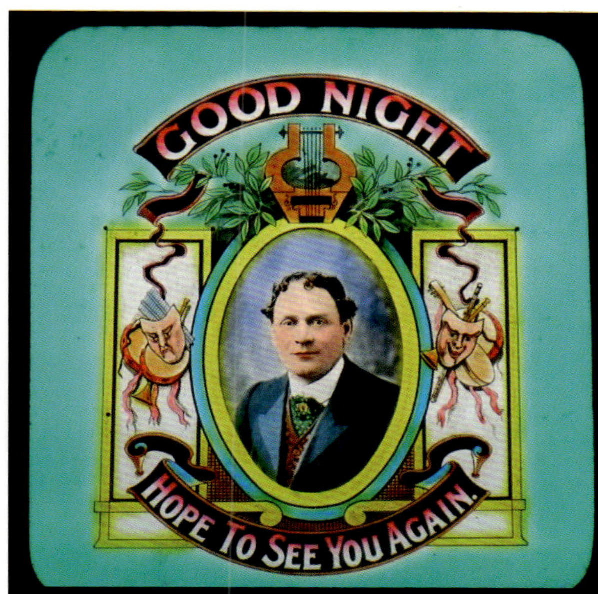

Above: An amazing survivor – a 2 ¼ square glass "magic lantern" slide made for projection at the end of a show in Ben Kennedy's theatres.

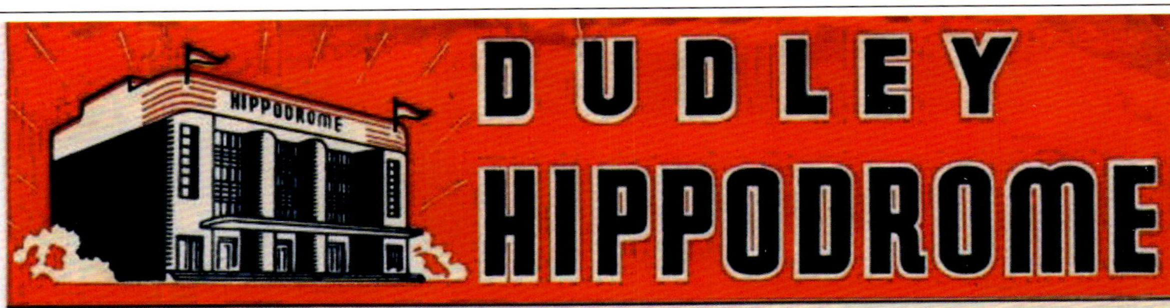

Joint Managing Directors: Robert F. Kennedy, Maurice B. Kennedy *House Manager:* Peter Robinson

FORTHCOMING ATTRACTIONS

The following artistes have appeared at this theatre:

BOB HOPE
FLANAGAN & ALLEN
NELLIE LUTCHER
ARTHUR ASKEY
RED INGLE
GEORGE FORMBY
HERMIONE BADDELEY
TOMMY TRINDER
BARRY K. BARNES
MAX MILLER
ANNE SHELTON
BERNARD BRADEN
DENNIS NOBLE
ROBB WILTON
JEWEL & WARRISS
DIANA CHURCHILL
ALAN JONES
BILLY COTTON
BEBE DANIELS
JOAN CROSS
TURNER LAYTON
VERA LYNN
LAUREL & HARDY
PETER BROUGH
TERRY-THOMAS
REG DIXON
CELIA LIPTON
TED RAY
KITTY BLUETT
FRED EMNEY
DONALD PEERS
JACK HYLTON
RAWICZ & LANDAUER
CARL BRISSON
JACK WARNER
CICELY COURTNEIDGE
JACK BUCHANAN
LESLIE BANKS
ALASTAIR SIM
MAX WALL
BASIL RADFORD
CARROLL GIBBONS
BRUCE TRENT
CAROLE LYNN
FLORENCE DESMOND
LESLIE HENSON
ROBERT MORLEY
NORMAN WISDOM
PEGGY RYAN
CHICO MARX
WEBSTER BOOTH &
ANNE ZIEGLER
HENRY HALL
BARRY SINCLAIR
HARRY SECCOMBE
TESSIE O'SHEA
FRANKIE HOWERD
DONALD WOLFITT
CHARLIE CHESTER
SEMPRINI
CYRIL FLETCHER

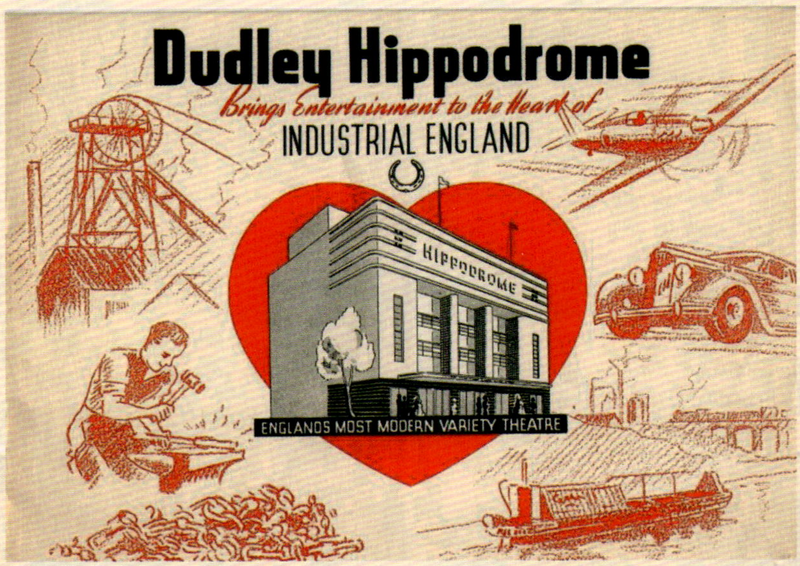

Art work from the Dudley Hippodrome: notepaper, cover of the Eighth Anniversary brochure and programme covers.

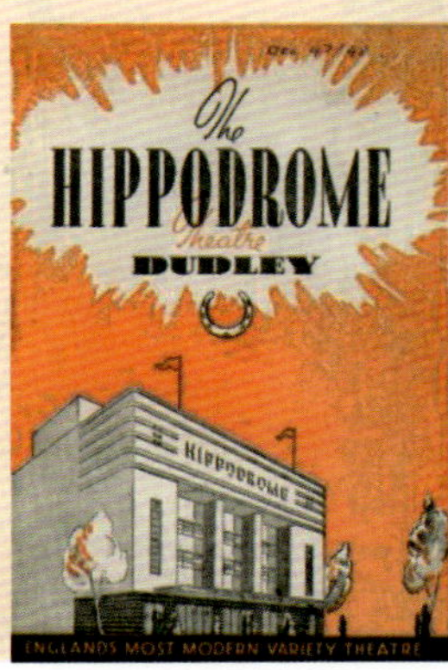

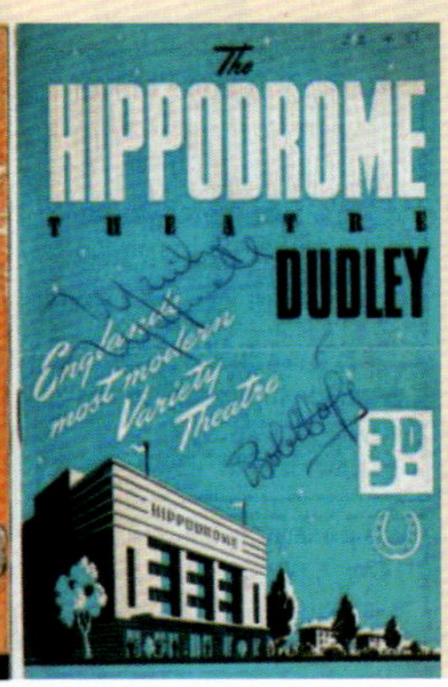

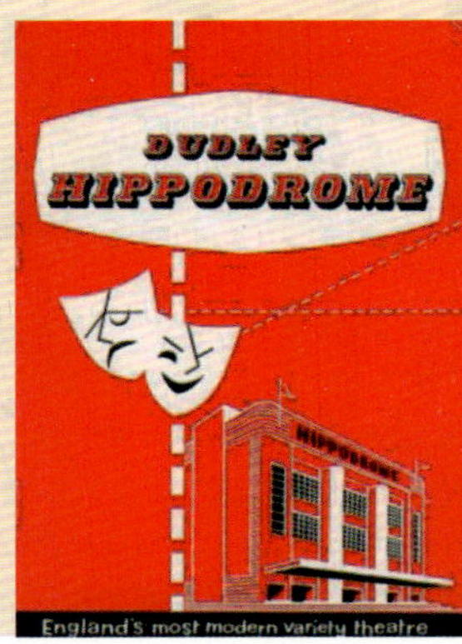

Chapter 7

An Aerialist Without Flaw

Brenda Jones

How it all began…

The people featured in this book generally became known to me by their stage name or pen name and before I could make much progress in knowing more about them I would have to find out who they really were. In Brenda's case it has almost entirely happened in the opposite direction. My enquiries started with her real name and only eventually led to realising that she might be known by other names.

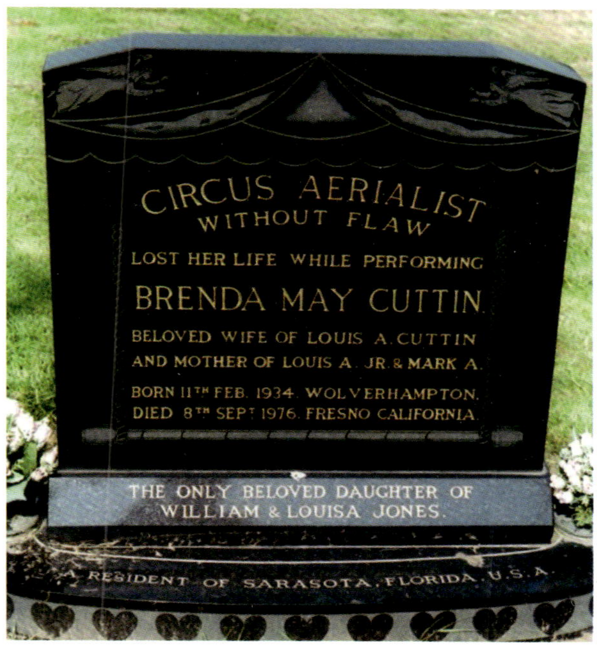

Above: The headstone in Sedgley Cemetery which inspired me to investigate how a "circus aerialist without flaw" could die in the ring, and how a girl born in Wolverhampton in 1934 came to be performing in a circus in California in 1976, and was a resident of Sarasota in Florida. Headstones are rarely so informative at the same time as being so mysterious.

It all began one Monday afternoon in November 2002. I had called on my friends Les and Janet to have a cup of tea and "catch up". They had just returned from a funeral and were bursting to tell me about a headstone they had observed in the cemetery. They had noticed this headstone because it was shaped like a circus 'big top' and they felt the inscription was curious. They suggested I went to investigate immediately. As it happened I arrived at the cemetery on the eastern flank of Sedgley Beacon just as the gates were closing!

My acquaintance with the life of Brenda May Cuttin, nee Jones, began with the sight of her grave in Sedgley Cemetery on the morning of the next day. From its position in the centre of the Black Country, Sedgley Beacon's slope faces the Urals and there is nothing of a similar height above sea level between the two. The slope levels out towards Dovedale Road, and here a modern cemetery has been established. It looks very neat and orderly compared with some local churchyards and the headstones of the graves have a general sense of uniformity. However, one grave did seem to stand out, just as I had been informed. The inscription told me that it was the grave of Brenda May Cuttin, a "Circus Aerialist without Flaw" who "lost her life while performing" at Fresno California on 8th September 1976. Of course anyone reading this would be intrigued to know how an artiste "without flaw" came to die in the circus ring, and would want to know how this death in California led to a grave in the Black Country. The headstone added that Brenda had been a resident of Sarasota in Florida.

The headstone was certainly bubbling with information because it also told me that Brenda was the "beloved daughter of William and Louisa Jones" and provided her date and place of birth. It was also obvious that the grave next to it was the grave of her father, William Jones. I learned immediately that Brenda Cuttin had started life as Brenda Jones in Wolverhampton in 1934: the sort of information usually only discovered long after deciding to find out more about someone!

That Tuesday evening I sent off an email to the American National Circus Museum and Archive in Baraboo, Wisconsin and then twenty fours hour later I had a friendly reply telling me that they did not have a Brenda Cuttin on their files, but they were forwarding my requests for information to friends in Sarasota and Fresno. Such progress was breath-taking! By the end of that week more information had come in from the USA, yet I had hardly made any progress in finding out anything locally. At the time, I was writing short features of local interest for the Wolverhampton-based Express and Star, so I decided to use my column to ask readers what they could tell me about Brenda Jones. Once again the results were dramatic.

As soon as my story about Brenda appeared in the Express & Star I started receiving phone calls from people who knew her and who could tell me something about her life before going to America. There were several striking coincidences. For example one lady, a cousin of Brenda's, exiled to Australia just happened to be visiting her husband's relatives in South Wales when someone from the Midlands showed her the Express & Star and she was also able to ring me! Among other things, she told me that members of Brenda's family were still to be found in Wolverhampton – all I had to do was find them. By the beginning of the following week, only a week after seeing Brenda's grave I was in touch with Brenda's mother, and her brother, Derek, whom it turned out was someone I already knew!

Brenda's mother, Louisa, was not enjoying good health but went out of her way to help me and gave me access to an archive she had collected relating to Brenda's career. This is all the more remarkable considering that my enquiries had painfully reminded members of the family of their loss and I must have seemed like some heartless outsider intruding on their memories and their feelings about Brenda.

As the days went by I also heard more from one or two contacts in America and very quickly I was able to set out some kind of account of Brenda's life while growing up in Wolverhampton, some details of her progress in America, and understand some of the details of her death. All this was such a contrast with the years that had passed in trying to learn more about the other characters brought together in this book.

There were a number of consequences of all this. One was the article I was able to put together for publication in King Pole, the quarterly magazine of the Circus Friends Association in June 2003. Another was that some of the girls who had danced with Brenda in the pantomimes at Wolverhampton's Grand Theatre decided that a re-union should be organised. This subsequently took place at the Grand Theatre with Mrs. Louisa Jones as the guest of honour. From that gathering another reunion was organised relating to a dancing school in Dudley – a group of ex "Latour Girls" held a reunion in 2004 which included a visit to the Dudley Hippodrome, where they had once appeared.

The girls who had once danced with Brenda in the Grand's pantomimes were very keen to share their memories of those times. Fellow dancers Kathleen Thomas and Jean Waterton tried to give me a picture of the hard work involved, the perfection demanded by Madam Leminski, and the camaraderie that they enjoyed. They produced photographs in which one could spot Brenda's impish smile.

As with all the stories told in this book, Brenda's story would never reach a final chapter – there would always be something else to find out, or something could "turn up" unexpectedly. As I began to assemble the stories told in this book I realised that I had never known Brenda's stage name – i.e. the name that has been the starting point for all other stories told here. I had forgotten my contact in Baraboo had not found a Brenda Jones in his files – she was obviously known by another name in the American circus world.

I made contact with Derek Jones again and he was immediately able to clarify this matter – Brenda had often been known as Brenda Peters, and often by other stage-names used when performing a particular act or routine. In the circus world the ringmaster might

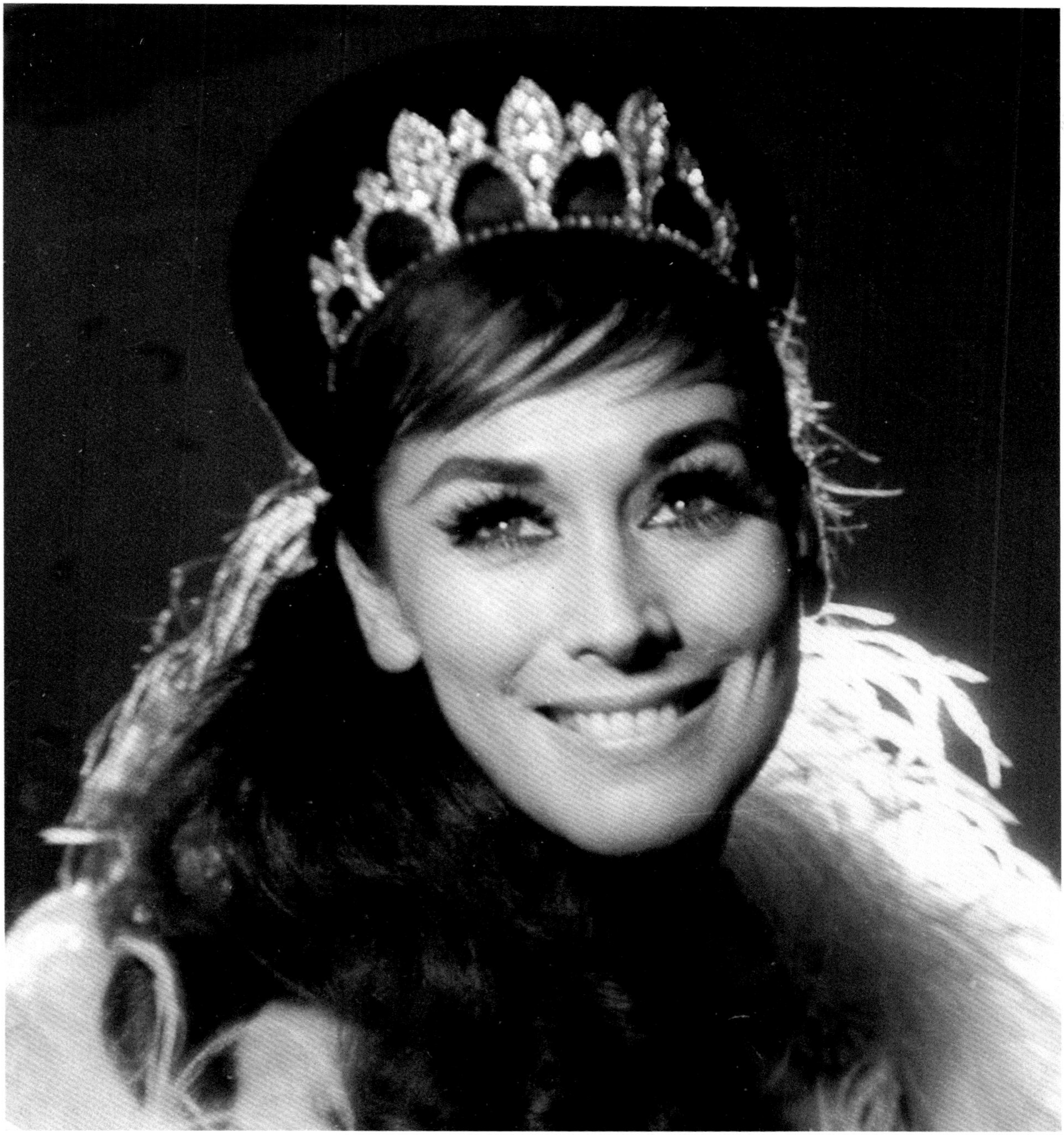

introduce an act as "The Great Rossini Brothers" who, in real life might turn out to be Bill Smith and Fred Green – names in the circus world are often difficult to disentangle. When travelling with Larry Ruhl, for example, they performed as "Michael and Michelle". Because Derek had travelled with his sister in the American circus world in the mid 1960s he was able to provide a fresh first-hand view of events which brought new ingredients of the story to life for me. He has also preserved the archive started by his mother and this might help Brenda's story be perpetuated and passed-on to subsequent generations.

Brenda's story is a reminder that a biography is never really finished and that biographies are fragile if not carefully passed from one generation to another.

The Life of Brenda Jones

Brenda May Jones was born on 11th February 1934, joining the Jones Family of 41 Lawrence Avenue, Heath Town, Wolverhampton. Her father, William Jones, worked for many years at Butlers "Springfield" Brewery, and his wartime service with the RAF is recorded on the Brewery's war memorial which is now preserved at a local Territorial Army Centre. Brenda had two brothers, who, like her, were born before the War, and two younger brothers born after the War. She was christened at Holy Trinity Church in Heath Town on 28th February 1934. Her family had no circus connections, and there was no reason to believe she would lead a remarkable life.

Brenda was at first a rather frail child, but she took up dancing lessons and discovered that she had talent, and this contributed to her self-confidence. She was certainly well known at Prestwood Road Girls School, as proved by the number of phone calls I received from her school-days contemporaries. All testified to Brenda's talent and her attractive personality. She also won prizes for running and athletics while at school.

Brenda was ten when she took her first examination in acrobatic dancing, and was soon tackling ballet and tap at various well-known local dance schools. A certificate survives awarded by the Association of American Tap Dancing, on which the local dance teacher – Ralph Payne – had written "most promising". In 1947 she helped Prestwood Girls School gain a First Class award from the English Folk Dance Society. Other certificates survive recording success in gymnastics, acrobatics, swimming, and many types of dance.

Very quickly she was tackling amateur performances and her mother, Louisa Jones, was battling with Wartime scarcities and rationing to make Brenda's costumes. She joined Margaret Kent in a "sister act" and appeared at local clubs and hostels - earning as much as thirty shillings while still at school, performing as part of the great Wartime hunger for entertainment. At fourteen and a half she appeared in an amateur pantomime presented at Tettenhall Towers.

Brenda left school at Easter 1949 and went to work in a dress shop. (Willson's of Dudley Street, Wolverhampton.) However the girl in the dress shop was not dreaming of becoming a life-long shop assistant. Her ambition was to be selected for the 1949 pantomime at Wolverhampton's Grand Theatre, and in November of that year she was able to tell her colleagues at the dress shop that her dreams had come true. At first she used her Thursday afternoons off to join rehearsals at the

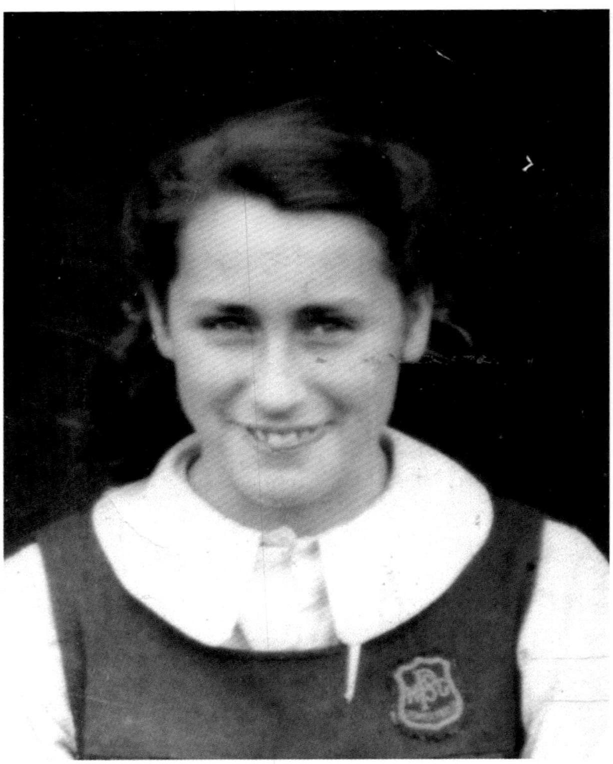

Left: Brenda Jones as a school girl at Prestwood Road Girls School, Wolverhampton, which she attended from 1945 to 1949.

Below: One of the many certificates she received at school. This one was for swimming, others were for athletics, gymnastics and dance.

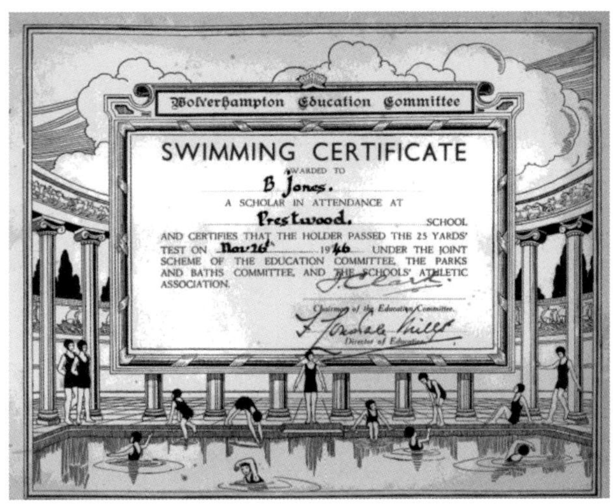

Right: Brenda's school photo taken during her penultimate year at Prestwood Road – 1948. Brenda is third from the right in the back row. Prestwood Girls School survived until the early 1970s when it merged with other schools to create the new Heath Park comprehensive School.

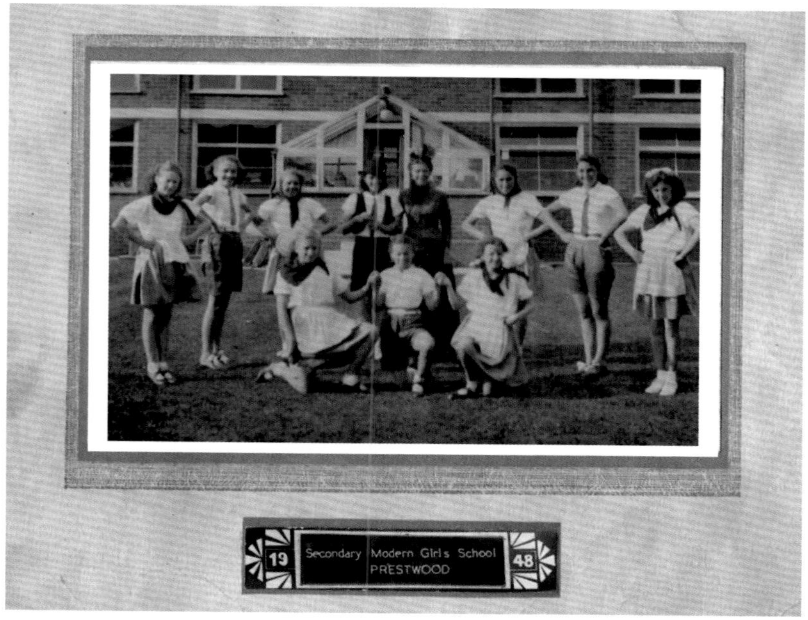

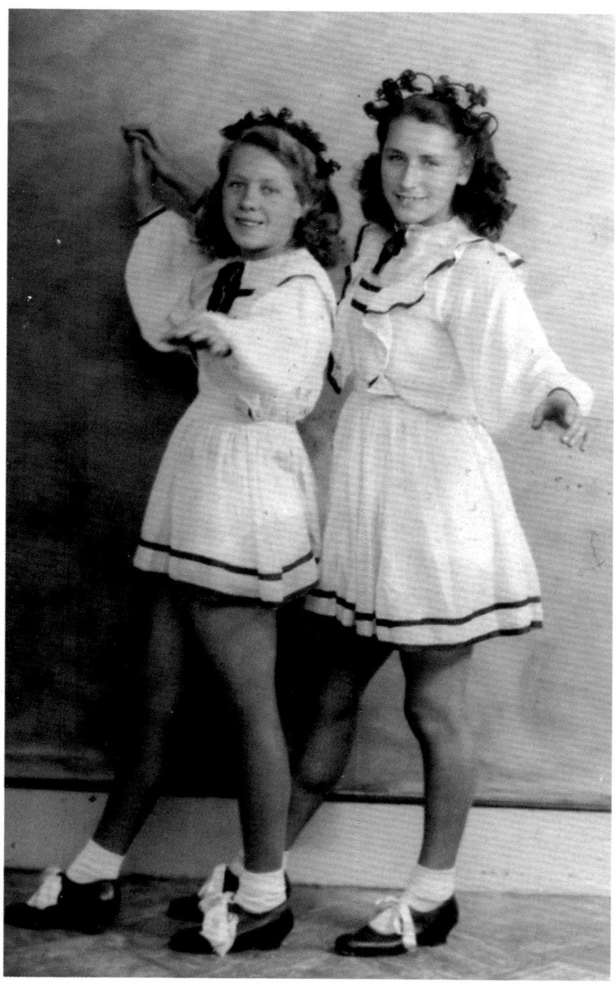

Left: Brenda Jones and Margaret Kent presenting their dance routine as "sisters" while still in their teens. They received payment for appearances in local social clubs and wartime hostels.

Below: Brenda practising in the back garden of hre home in Lawrence Avenue, in the Heath Town area of Wolverhampton.

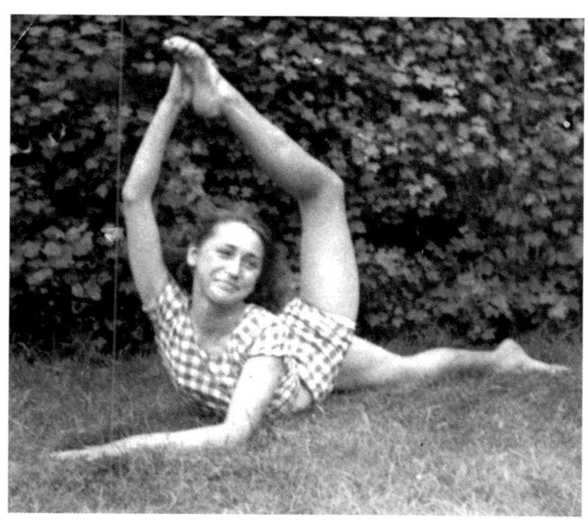

Molineux hotel, but eventually she had to leave the shop and join the full-days of rehearsal that preceded the show. Brenda joined the chorus and dancing troupe with her friend Betty Hadley, and soon made friends with Brenda Owen from Stourbridge. By coincidence Brenda Owen also enjoyed a career that took her into circus and to America.

Wolverhampton's Grand Theatre lived up to its name. It had opened in late 1894 only just over six months since the prestigious laying of its foundation stone. It had been a project by local worthies to provide the town with a top class theatre with great cultural aspirations – unlike the "blood tub" round the corner in Bilston Street! (The Bilston Street theatre was known by a number of names over the years ending up as "The New Theatre Royal", and then as The Clifton cinema.) Four years later the Empire opened in Queen Square to provide "variety". Although The Grand would provide a stage for the likes of Henry Irving and the D'Oyly Carte Opera Company it could not afford to stand aloof from the world of "Pantomime". Its original lessee, Milton Bode, put on "Sinbad the Sailor" after the theatre's first Christmas. By the beginning of the 20th Century there was quite a choice of pantomime entertainment in Wolverhampton.

On the run up to Christmas 1949 there was plenty of entertainment for local people to choose from. Brenda had her sights on appearing in the pantomime at The Grand. Derek Salberg was presenting "Robinson Crusoe" starring Norman Wisdom, with Eddie Leslie as the dame, opening on Boxing Day. The Hippodrome (earlier called The Empire, in Queen Square) was opening on Christmas Eve with Old Mother Riley (Arthur Lucan) in "The Old Woman Who Lived in a Shoe" and over in Bilston the Theatre Royal was putting on a South African Circus. In the Black Country Dudley Hippodrome led the field with Aladdin, followed by an alternative "Robinson Crusoe" at the Plaza West Bromwich. (Both shows presented by the Kennedy Brothers.) The Hippodrome, Wednesbury, was going its own way with a show featuring "Knights". In all these shows there would be at least two dance troupes – one of older girls who were professionals, or semi-professionals, and one consisting of "babes" who were supplied by local dance schools. Many would be hoping that they were taking steps towards show business. (Interestingly, over in Dudley the local Education Authority had forbidden "babes" to appear in "Aladdin" that year and the Hippodrome were trying to recruit young dancers from elsewhere!)

Brenda joined the Lehminski Ladies to be part of the pantomime at The Grand – the ladies mainly being graduates of Madame Lehminski's dancing school in Edgbaston. Madame Lehminski provided dance troupes for the Alexandra in Birmingham and Wolverhampton's Grand – the connecting link being Derek Salberg, producer of both shows, and the then owner of the Birmingham theatre. Brenda Jone's work in the 1949/50 pantomime, "Robinson Crusoe" introduced her to the hard work of the chorus. The work included many costume changes, battling with clothes and shoes that

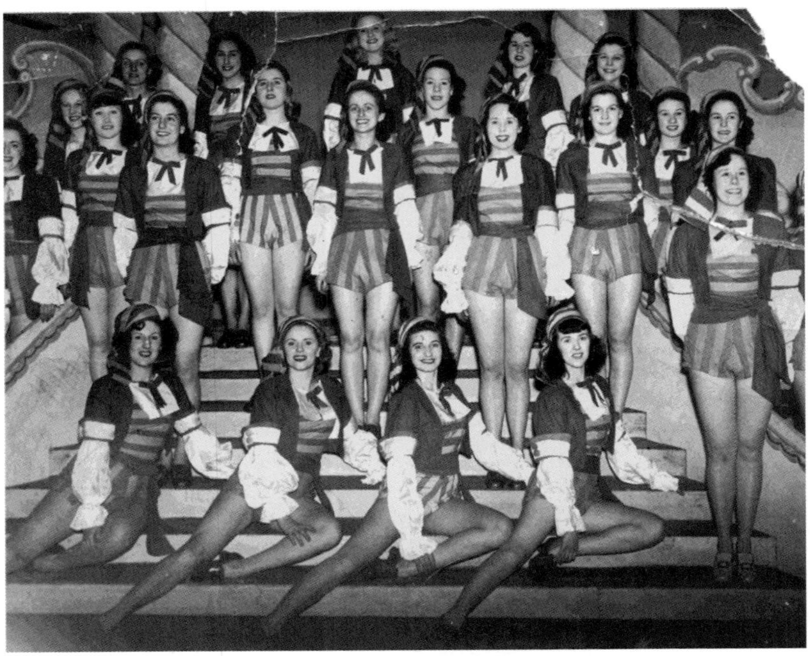

Brenda' pantomime debut on the stage of The Grand, Wolverhampton following Christmas 1949: "Robinson Crusoe". Brenda is second from the left in the back row. Norman Wisdom starred as Billy Crusoe, and the show was presented by Derek Salberg.

Right: The Cooper Twins: Alf and Fred, whom Brenda met while appearing in pantomimes at the Grand Theatre, Wolverhampton. They encouraged Brenda to develop an interest in acrobatics – and – as always, Brenda was keen to learn new skills. Alf Cooper's girlfriend. Maureen Harris persuaded Brenda to become a full-time professional dancer.

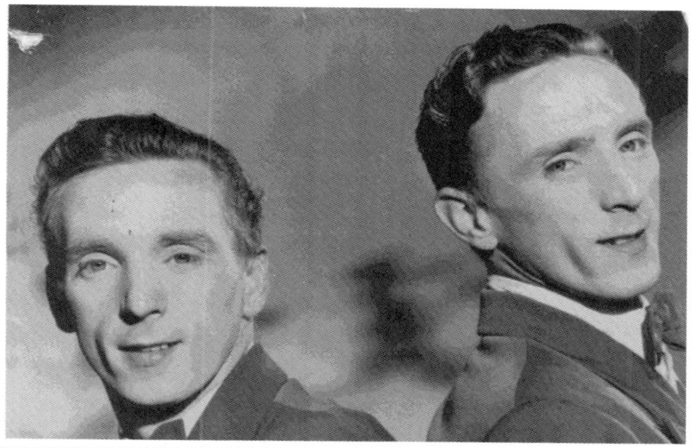

Right: The curtain call at the end of the final scene of "Jack & The Beanstalk" at the Grand Theatre, Wolverhampton, running from Christmas 1950 into 1951.Brenda stands in the back row.

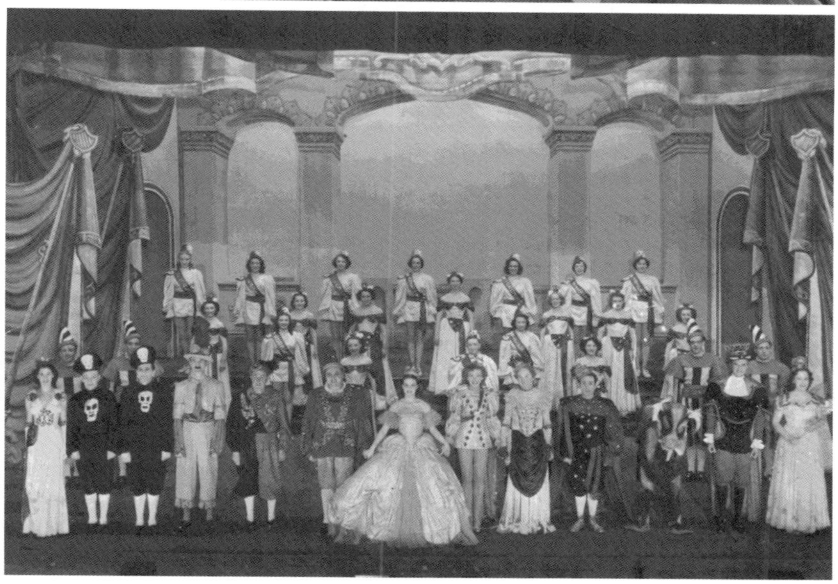

Right: Brenda, on the left, photographed while appearing in the 1951 pantomime at Coventry Hippodrome.("Babes in the Wood")

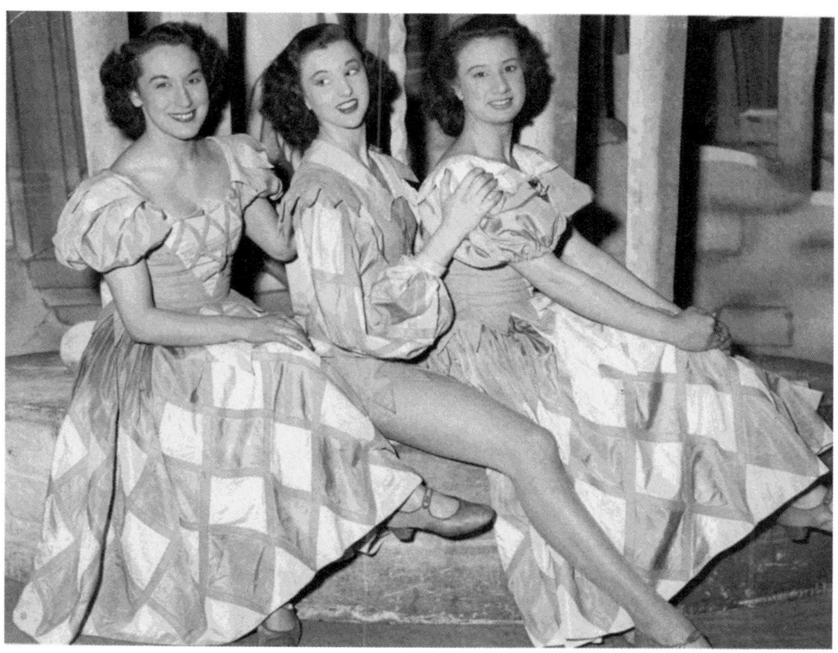

were already well-used, and coping with crowded dressing rooms. Amazingly, everything looked OK on stage under the lights! However, she also used her time at the Grand Theatre to observe the work of an acrobatic troupe appearing in the show, and, with their help, she began to master hand springs, tumbling and head springs. The other girls were gently dismissive. "You ought to join a circus!" was their response.

After the pantomime Brenda returned to the dress shop. The dancing lessons had ceased, but Brenda still practised her acrobatic skills every night before bed. She could hardly wait for the next pantomime and was reassured to find that she was given work in "Jack and the Beanstalk" at the end of 1950. Once again she made friends with the acrobats - The Cooper Twins, Alf and Fred. They taught her skills that she would later use on the trapeze, and tempted her to join them in afternoons at Wolverhampton's Rollerdrome!

With Alf Cooper's girlfriend, Maureen Harris, Brenda set off for London not long after "Jack and The Beanstalk" finished. They joined a dance troupe called the "Marie de Vere Lovelies" and were booked for an eight week season in the Isle of Man. This was Brenda's first sea voyage and lengthy time away from home. To her surprise, when they reached the Isle of Man, she discovered they were appearing in a circus. Although the circus later became the principal focus of her work, her initial reaction to find herself working in the ring was one of horror!

Her circus debut was followed by a twenty week run in a touring review, "Taking Off", and towards the end of 1951 she appeared in "Babes in the Wood" at Coventry Hippodrome with Beryl Stevens. (A few years later Beryl Stevens married Bob Kennedy, the son of Ben Kennedy who is featured in this book.) This was followed by work in Tom Arnold's famous circus which opened in the Harringay Arena in London. She took part in some of the tumbling during the show and started to learn aerial skills. Circus skills were becoming more important than dance skills. While appearing in Tom Arnold's show Brenda began using the stage name "Brenda Peters" for the first time.

Jack Mills of Mills Brothers' Circus of Ohio, USA, came to Jack Arnold's show looking for talented girls with a variety of circus skills. Brenda Jones, and her friend, Brenda Owen, from Stourbridge, were selected and agreed to go to America on a two year contract.

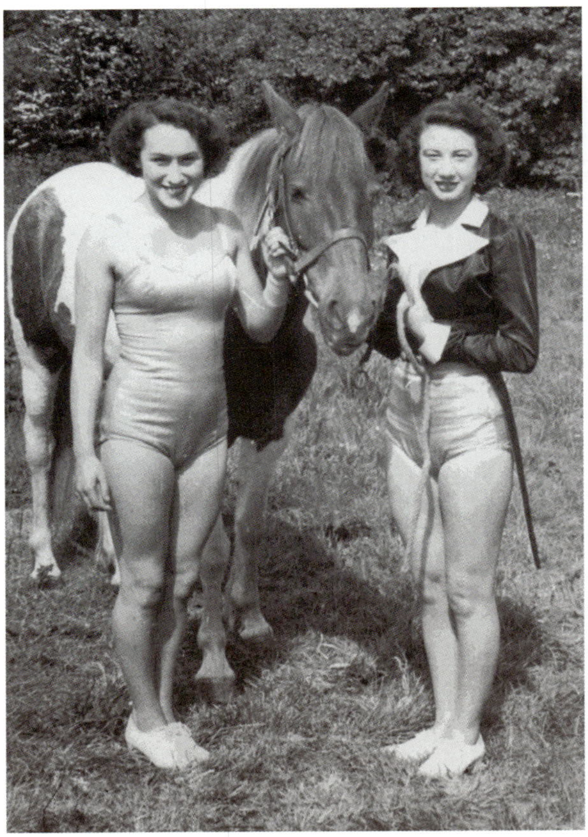

Left: Brenda and Maureen Harris become part of a circus in the Isle of Man.

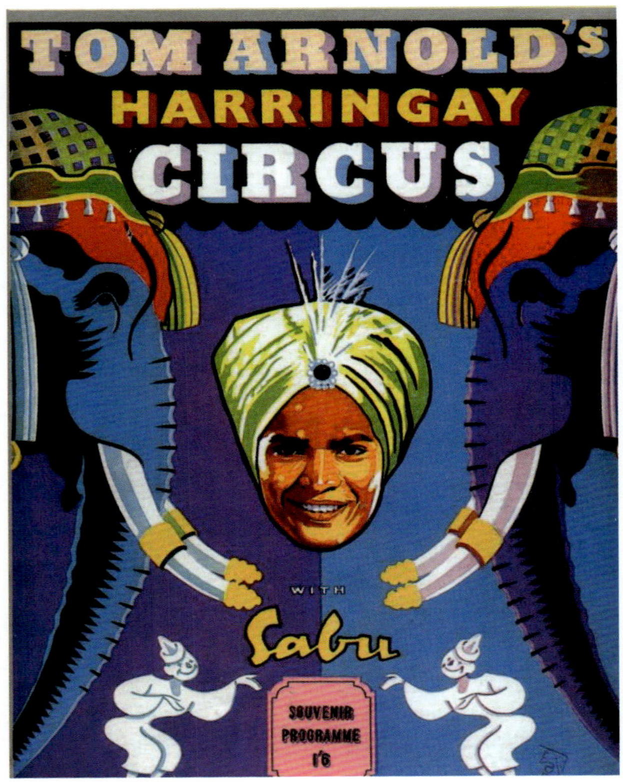

Off to America

The two Brendas from the Black Country joined a party of twenty artistes who set sail from Southampton on the "Ile de France" on 15th March 1952. Their destination was New York, followed by a two-day journey to Greenville, Ohio. Brenda was eighteen years old – reminding us of just how adventurous it was to undertake such a journey. We also have to remind ourselves that this was a time when the usual method of crossing the Atlantic was to go by ship.

The voyage of the "Ile de France", during which the two Brendas from the Black Country entertained the other passengers, was a major turning point in Brenda's life. At each stage of her career the girl from Heath Town had used one performance skill while learning another, looking for new opportunities, always pursuing excellence. She was an attractive brunette, with deep blue eyes and long eyelashes, who could sing, dance, tumble and balance. In the circus world she was what they would call a "useful person". She must have been full of high hopes and aspirations as the ship sailed into New York.

Brenda encountered some disappointments on reaching Mills Brothers Circus in Ohio. In particular she had not been prepared for the frugal living conditions experienced in a "kip truck" shared with seven other girls. But life improved when rehearsals began for a show that was to open on 18th April 1952. Brenda had to learn a difficult tumbling routine, and hand spin, on the "web": a single thick rope. While mastering this and the fairly easy dancing routines, Brenda added to her skills by taking horse-riding lessons.

Horse-riding turned out to be an introduction to yet another area of skills to be mastered as Brenda was quickly identified as someone who ought to learn to work with the elephants. She was not prepared for this, but like many people who meet elephants with an open mind, she was agreeably surprised how helpful and friendly the animals could be. Even so, one less friendly elephant threw her, and poor Brenda sustained injuries to her wrist and face only a few days before the show was to open. She recovered just in time to take part in her first American circus parade and bounced around on a trampoline towed round Greenville.

Below, Brenda, second from the right, joined the "entertainment troupe" on board ship to make her first voyage across the Atlantic.

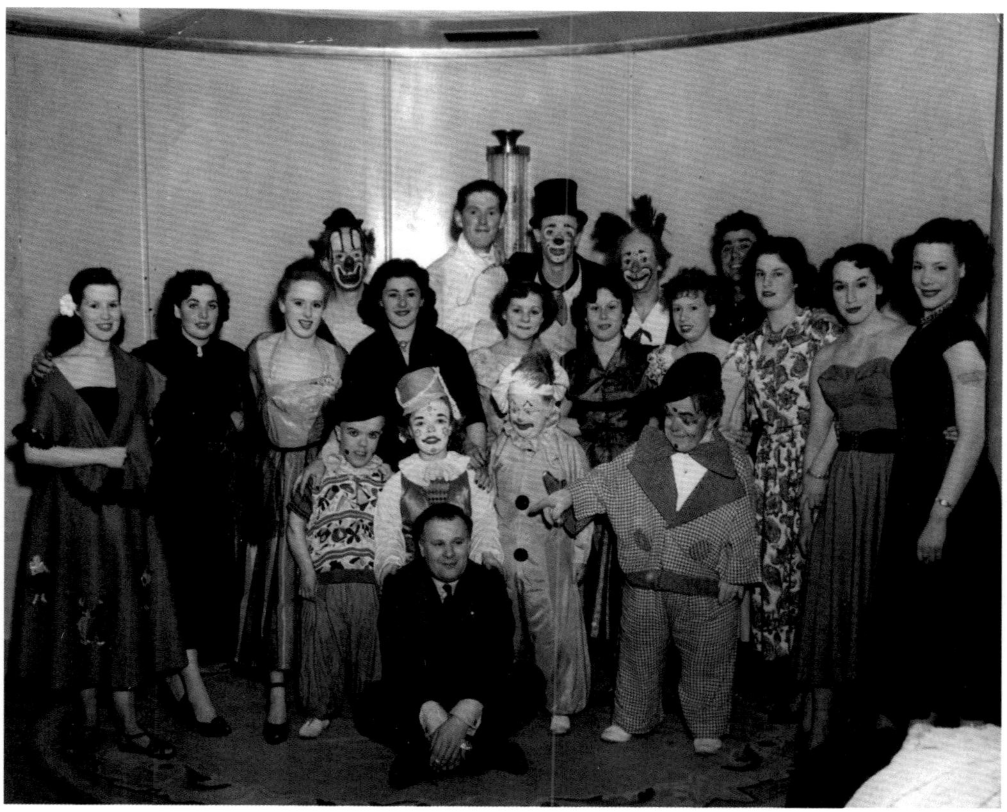

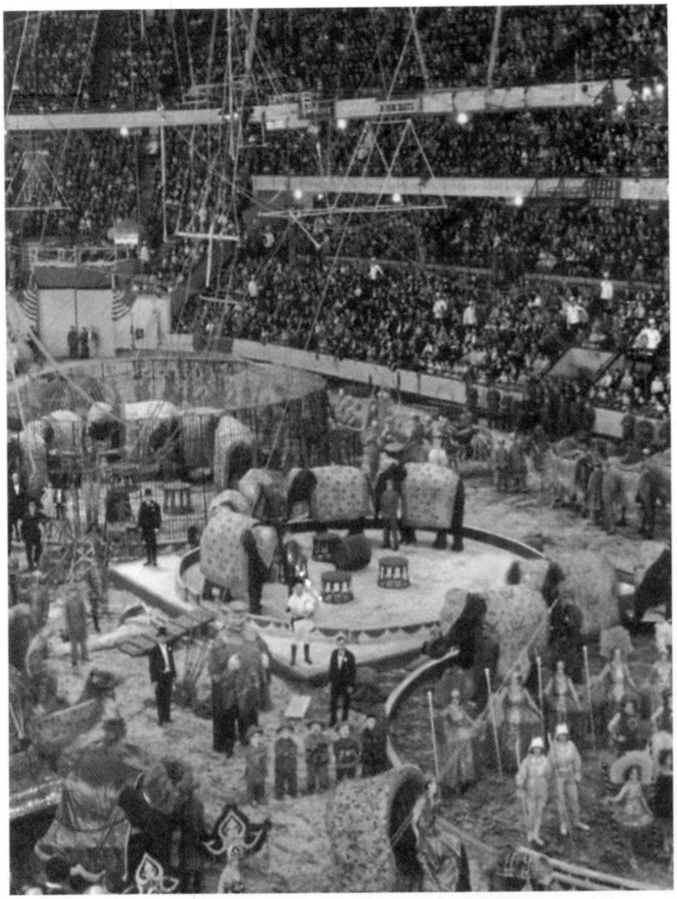

Presentation in a large American circus was going to be a totally new experience for Brenda, and was going to provide her with plenty of scope for learning new skills, from riding elephants to aerial work. As can be seen in this picture, a major American circus would adopt a "three-ring" style of presentation, with activity going on in all three rings simultaneously.
Below: Brenda, in the centre of the picture performs on the slack wire in the centre ring.

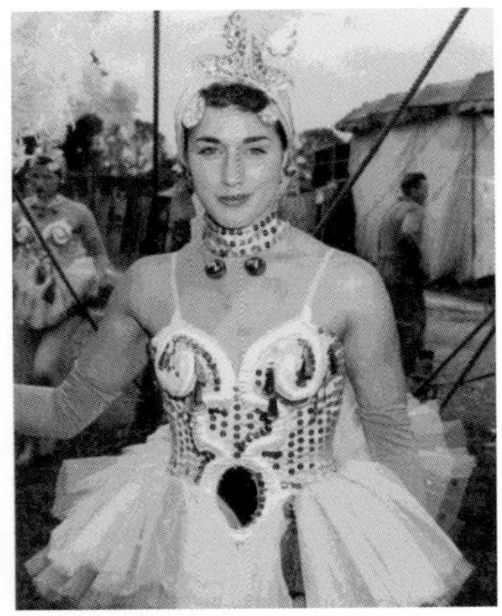

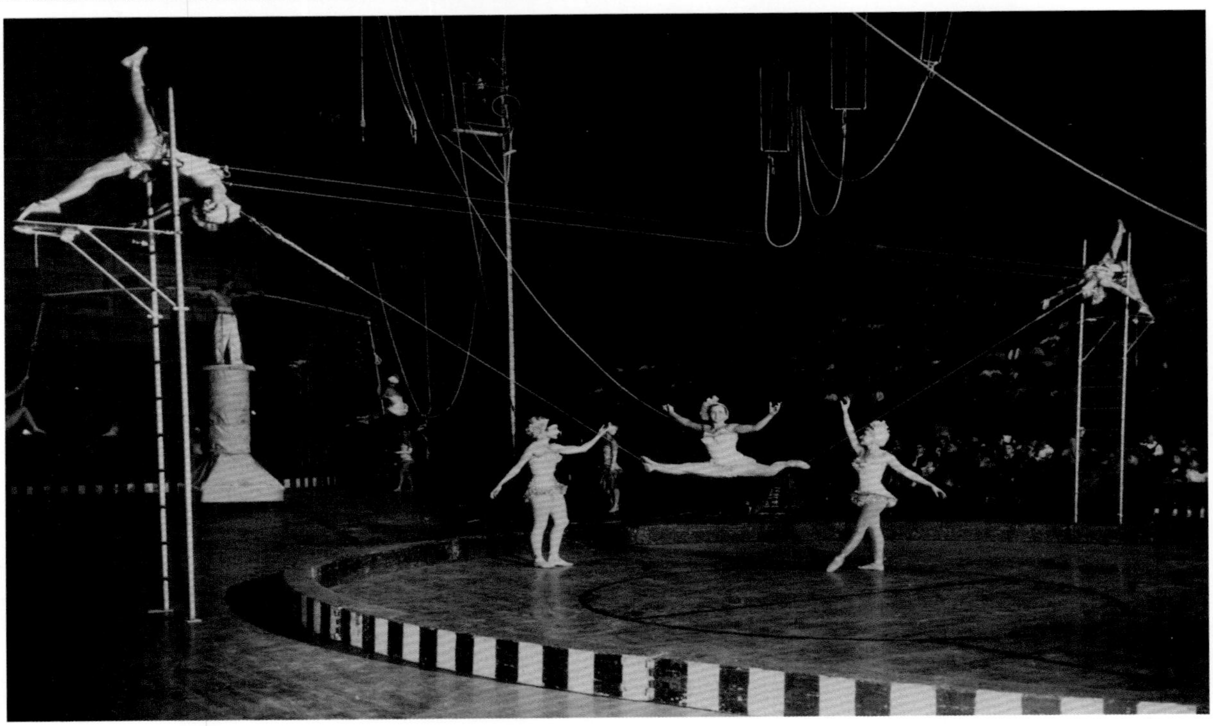

To supplement her eighteen dollars a week, Brenda sold programmes, helped pull down the Big Top and helped load the trucks after the first two nights in Greenville, as well as playing a number of roles in the show. This was followed by an introduction to the horrors of travelling as the show set of for Dayton. This was the beginning of a great adventure - travelling all over America presenting arduous two night stands, living in very primitive conditions, learning new skills and making new friends at a kaleidoscopic rate - and making friends with the elephants once more.

Nearly twelve thousand miles and many adventures later, Brenda found herself touring Florida. One night Mills Brothers were built up on one side of Dade City while Ringling Brothers, America's premiere circus was built up on the other. Pat Valdo, of Ringling Brothers, came to Mills Brothers' Circus to watch their show. He invited Brenda and her friends to join Ringling Brothers on a trip to Cuba. However, Brenda told him that she was looking forward to completing her contract with Mills Brothers and was then going to return home to celebrate Christmas in Wolverhampton! On 27th November 1953 the two Brendas sailed home from New York aboard the "Queen Elizabeth".

Back home in Wolverhampton, Brenda was surprised to find that Ringling Brothers had tracked her down and were sending her a tempting contract at seventy dollars a week. She agreed to return to the USA, and returned on the "Queen Elizabeth" at the end of February 1954. From New York she had to travel to Sarasota, the winter quarters of the Ringling Brothers show on the "Gulf seaboard" of Florida. She was amazed to find luxury accommodation awaiting her, and another shock - she was to be trained as an aerialist.

Rehearsals on the trapeze began straight away and Brenda was expected to master the skills in time to take part in the first show of the company's tour when it opened at New York's Madison Square Gardens. She later said that this was the first time in her life she had experienced real fear. The journey from Sarasota to New York towards the end of March 1954 introduced Brenda to another experience: the Circus Train. Ringling Brothers travelled by rail in three specially built trains, including John Ringling North's own personal railway carriage. Brenda joined over thirty girls consigned to "car 371", but this was luxury compared with the road journeys and accommodation available on Mills Brothers' Circus. The journey in Sarasota began with an impressive "send off" and the legendary ritual of blessing the trains.

Brenda, on the left, as a showgirl on Ringland Brothers, Barnum & Bailey's show.

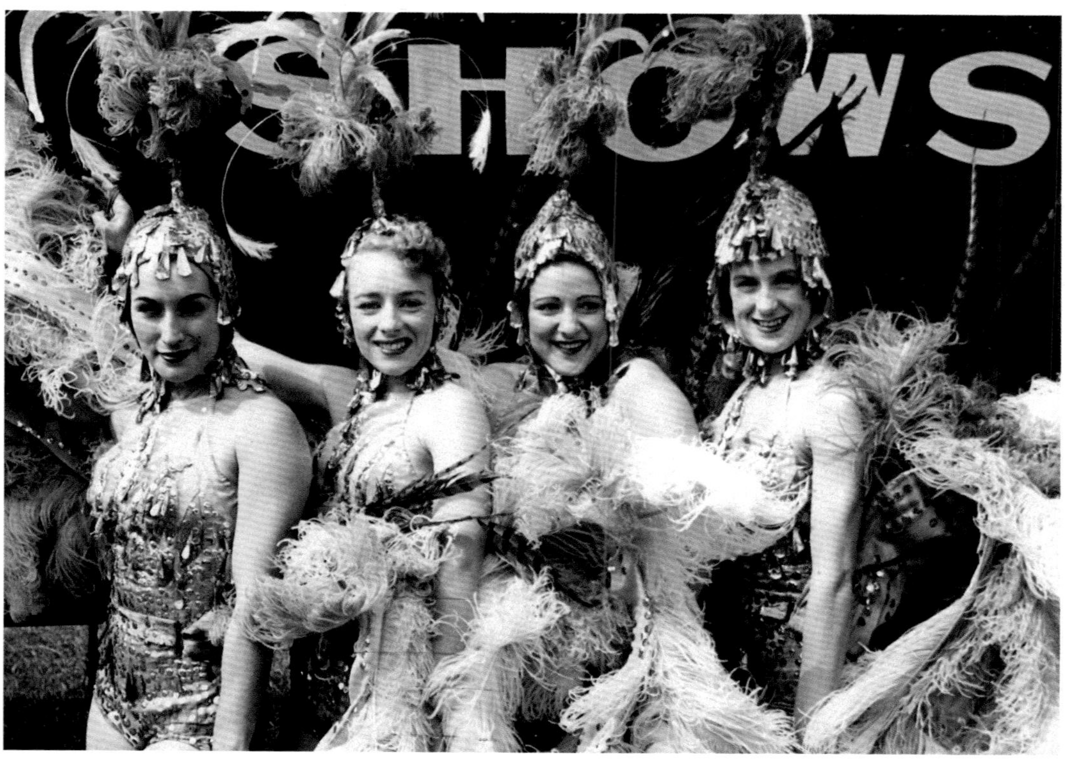

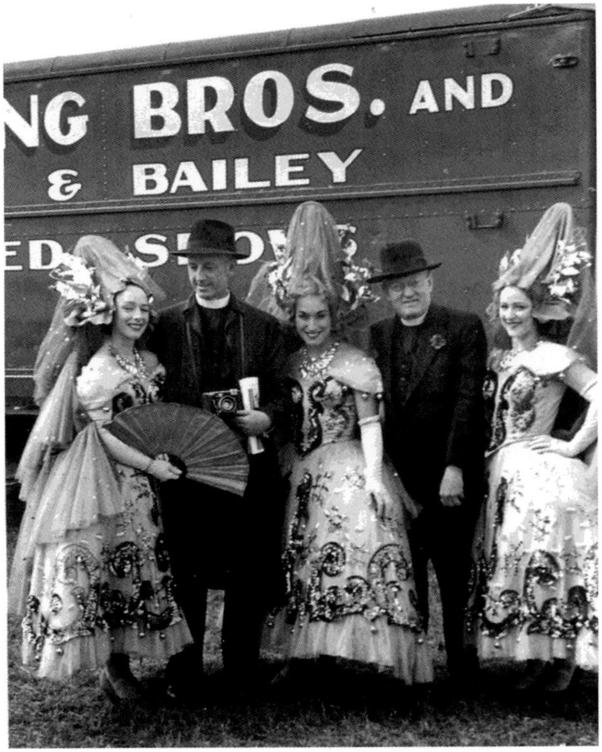

Left: Blessing the circus train at the beginning of a tour. Brenda is in the centre of the picture.

The 1954 season with Ringling Brothers began on 31st March in New York and took Brenda all over the United States. When she returned to Sarasota in December she was offered four weeks work starting on Christmas Eve in Havana, Cuba. This trip provided Brenda with her first experience of flight, as all her previous transatlantic journeys had been by sea.

While she was rehearsing her second year's work with Ringling Brothers, in February 1955, she celebrated her twenty-first birthday. It is amazing to consider the breadth of her experience and achievement before even acquiring the key of the door! (A silver key was sent over from Wolverhampton!) A few weeks later she was back at Madison Square Gardens in New York for the first show of the next tour - watching Marilyn Monroe make a ring entrance on the back of a pink elephant.
On completing the 1955 tour, Brenda returned home to Wolverhampton and gave extensive interviews to Elizabeth Prosser of the Wolverhampton Chronicle. The results of these interviews were presented as a five-part biography of Brenda published in the Chronicle in February 1956. They have provided much of the information included in this account. By the time Miss Prosser's articles were appearing, Brenda was back in America and had joined Polack Brothers' Circus as an accomplished trapeze artiste.

The next ten years formed the core part of Brenda's career as an American circus artiste. She worked continuously and added new dimensions to her repertoire as she had always done. The family's archives include many circus programmes and ephemera from this period, but it is difficult to plot Brenda's progress year by year compared with Elizabeth Prosser's account of progress up to the end of 1955. Working with the Polack Brothers took Brenda away from the world of the "Big Top" and into the world of appearing in halls and open-air arenas.

In Chicago, on 6th March 1961, Brenda married Louis Anthony Cuttin, at the city's First Methodist Church. Louis was a circus "concessioner", who already had two sons, Louis Jnr and Mark, by a previous marriage. He was known to everyone as Buzz because he was always so busy. ("Concessioners" independently sold sweets, drinks, programmes and circus mementoes etc., having paid the circus proprietor for the "concession".) No member of her Wolverhampton family was able to be at the wedding, but three years later her brother Derek was able to go over to America and travelled for a year with his sister and her new American family. He even sold a few circus programmes and balloons! Meanwhile Brenda's aerial work was taking on new challenges.

For at least three years Brenda joined Larry Ruhl as "Michele & Michael". She performed a high perch act at great height, and in stunts such as hanging from helicopters or from high buildings. One newspaper cutting from The Sun, published in Vancouver on 26th August 1969, shows Brenda and Larry swinging from beneath a helicopter. All in a day's work for the girl who had left school in Wolverhampton to work in a dress shop!

Brenda and Larry Ruhl who often appeared as "Michele and Michael". They perfected many aerial stunt feats both in and out of the ring.

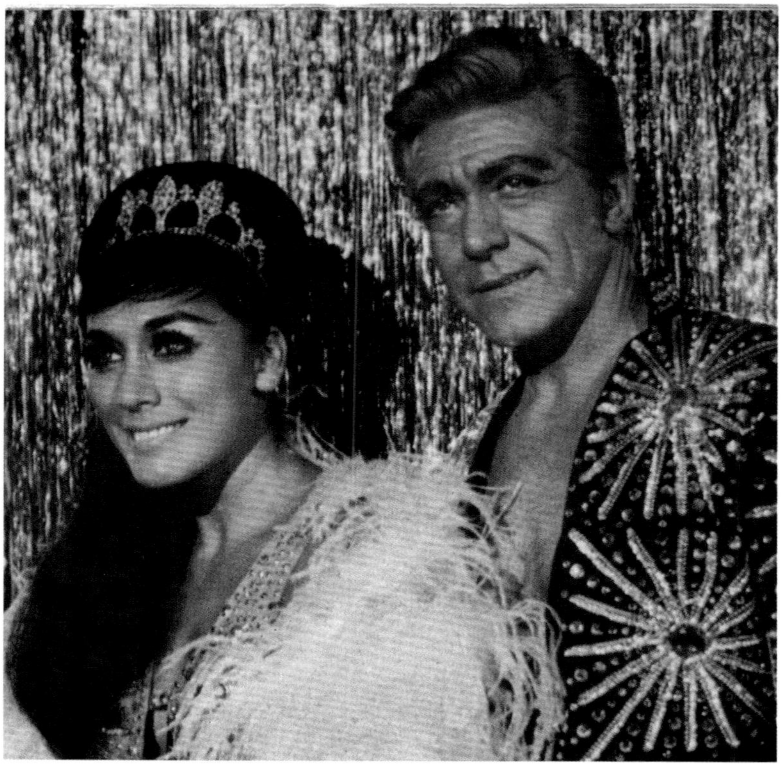

When contacted in January 2003, Larry Ruhl looked back on his partnership with Brenda, and wrote:

"Brenda was my third partner and a fine one at that. She came to Cleveland, Ohio, when she heard that my second partner, Darla, was retiring to get married. I remember having seen Brenda performing a couple of years earlier while she was in a group called Barbette's Girls. Barbette trained girls in web, iron jaw and single trapeze work. Brenda was indeed a natural and well trained, but she had never worked in the centre ring as a starring act. She turned out to be a natural and toured with me throughout the entire United States and all of Canada. During the summer months I had created my own original act performing under a moving helicopter. Brenda took to this act like a duck to water."

Brenda and Larry also travelled with the "Holiday on Ice" shows which toured European cities in the early 1970s. When the USA and USSR concluded an agreement to exchange circuses for the first time as part of a general cultural exchange programme, Brenda travelled to Russia for several months, where her skills were really appreciated. Another "claim to fame" involved a brief appearance in the film "Jumbo".

Throughout her twenties and thirties Brenda filled her life with a varied and successful career. She wrote home regularly and visited her home town every now and again. Brother Derek had visited America again in 1967, and Brenda's mother also made visits. Certainly the people in Wolverhampton who had known her never forgot her and followed news of her life with interest. Avis Bargery, a nurse recalled, *"I nursed Brenda in 1962 at the Queen Victoria Nursing Institution in Bath Road, Wolverhampton, when she came back to England to have a knee operation. She was a lovely girl - I can see her now as if it was yesterday."* This sentiment has been echoed again and again in letters from her school friends from Prestwood Girls School, from lads in Heath Town who watched her grow up, and from fellow dancers with whom she had performed at Wolverhampton's Grand Theatre.

As she grew older, Brenda became an aerialist instructor, but never really wearied of being a performer. She had bought a home in Sarasota and in her early forties was contemplating a retirement in Florida. In August 1976 Elvin Bale asked her if she would stand in for his pregnant wife in an aerial act he was presenting for Ringling Brothers, & Barnum & Bailey's Circus on motorcycle and trapeze. Elvin would be riding the motorcycle high up in the Big Top, Brenda would be hanging by her teeth beneath the motor cycle on a rope.

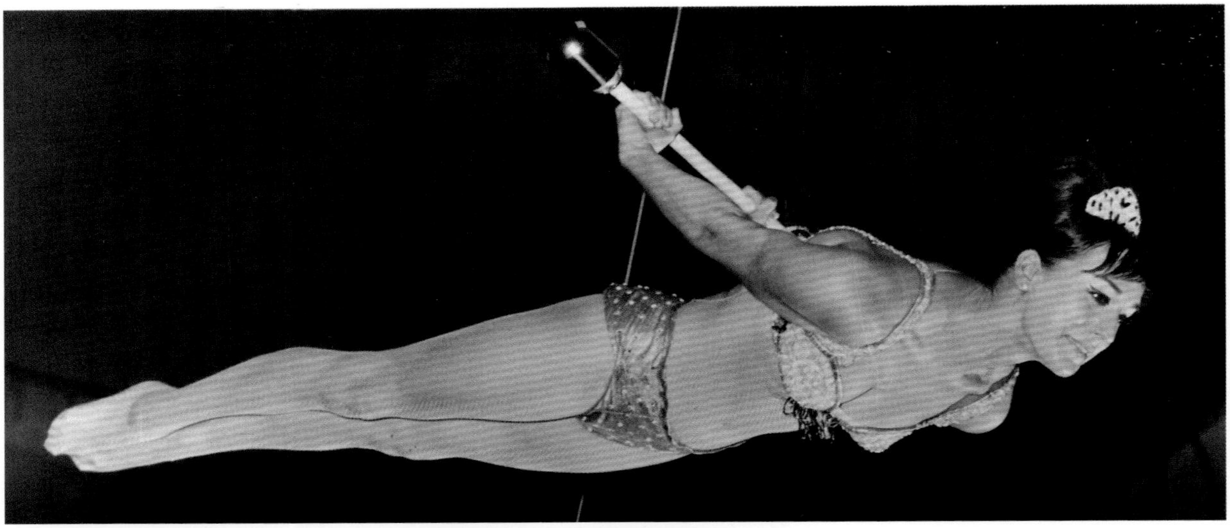

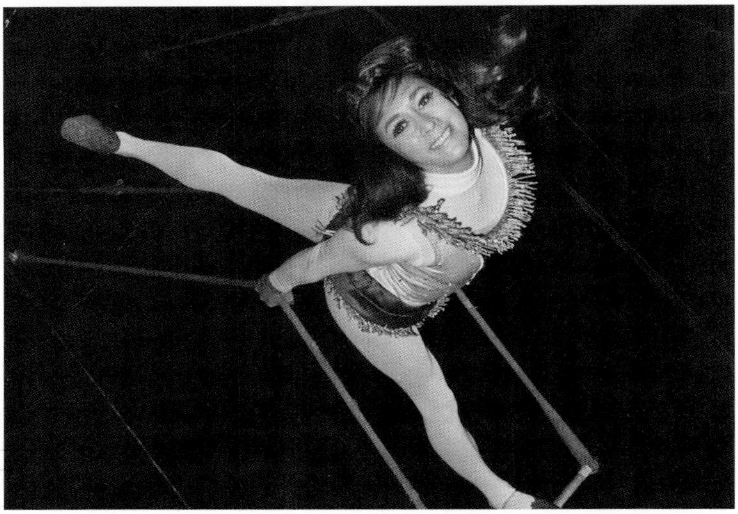

Above and Left: Brenda used all her grace and skill in presenting aerial acts in the American circus world.

Bottom left: A publicity photograph of Brenda and Larry Ruhl.

Bottom right: Brenda, on the right, with Marilyn Monroe preparing to enter the ring in New York's Madison Square Gardens.

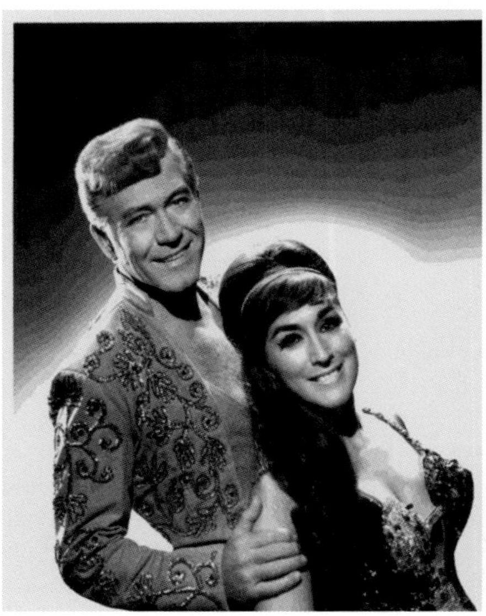

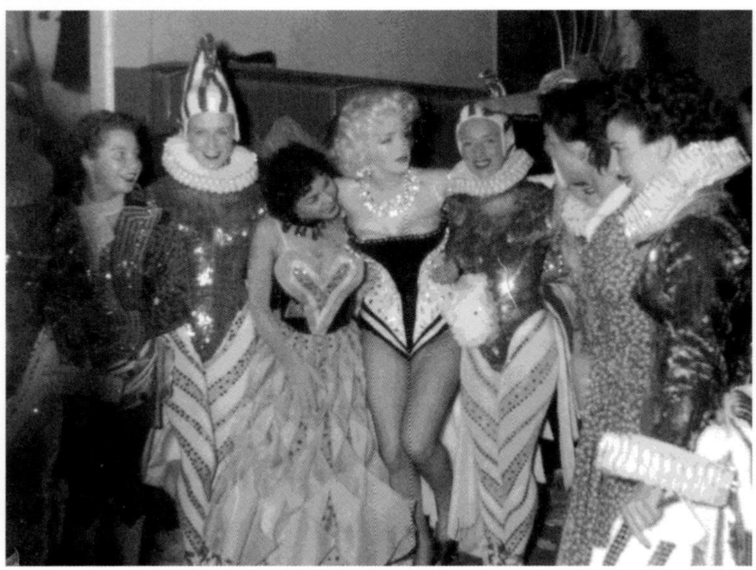

Brenda's circus career enabled her to be 'at home' on the back of an elephant, or hanging by her clenched teeth to a rope suspended from the trapeze high above the ring, or suspended with Larry Ruhl, from a helicopter high in the air.

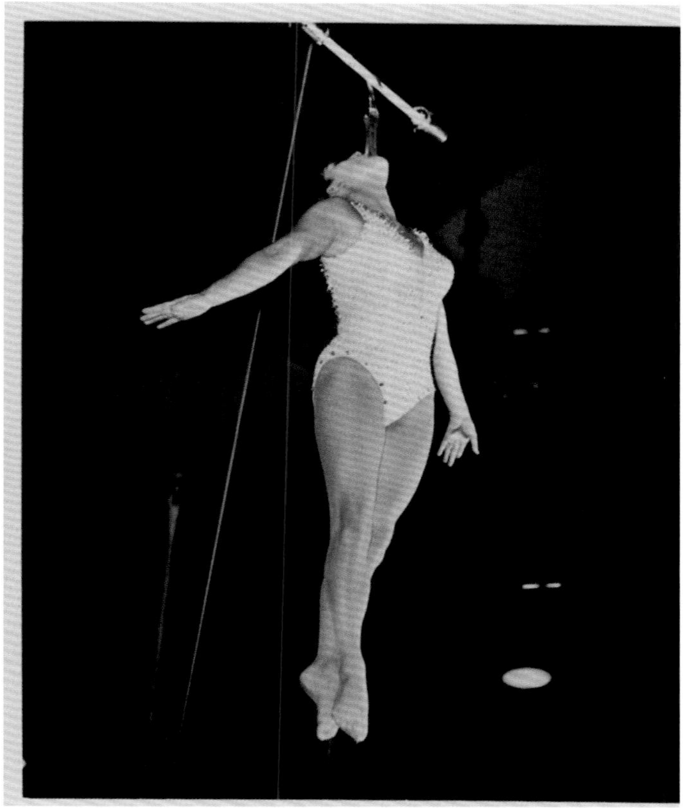

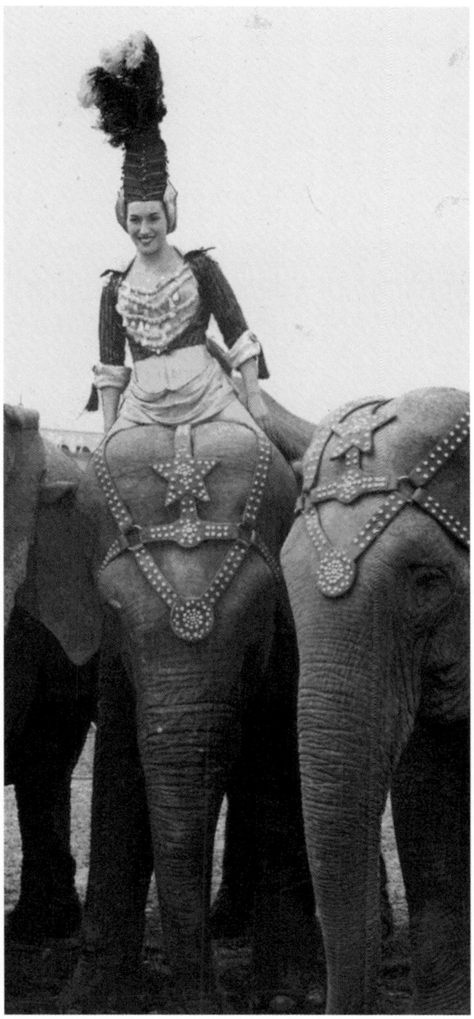

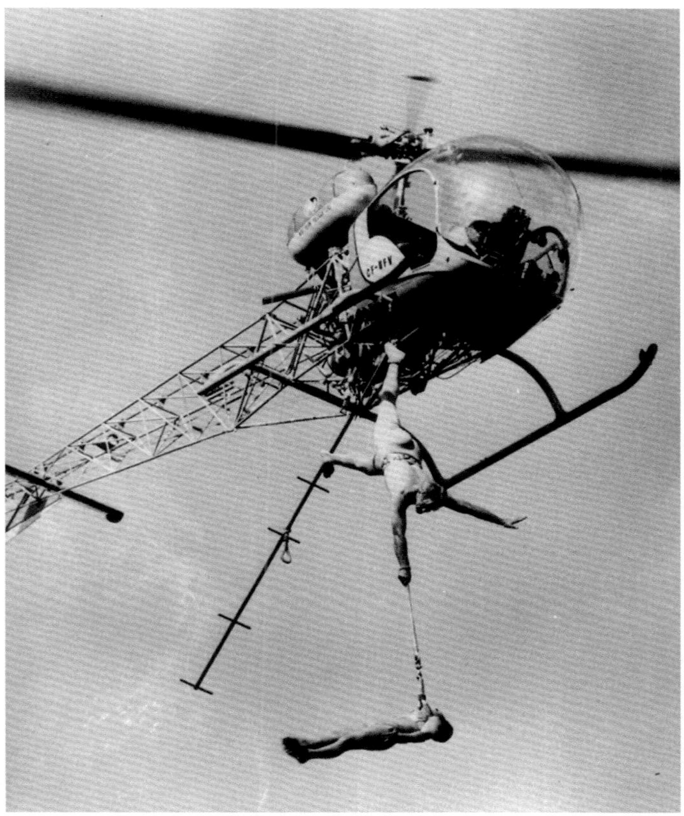

Yet another challenge

Three weeks later, on 8th September 1976, Brenda was appearing with Elvin Bale when his act was being presented at the Convention Centre in Fresno, California. Suddenly she seemed to lose her grip of the loops and fell forty feet to the floor. An hour later, at the local hospital, she was pronounced dead. The rigging was in perfect condition and Brenda herself was a performer "without flaw". Her fellow artistes noticed that she had not called out as she slipped, nor had she attempted to break her fall.

At the inquest it was revealed that she was probably unconscious at the moment when she slipped, and that she had probably suffered a cardiac arrest, rather than made any mistake in the presentation of her act.
Although this happened in Fresno California, there was a quick reaction back in Sarasota where Brenda had made her home. Way back in 1954 she had made friends with Liliane Johnson, fellow circus performer and experienced aerialist. Liliane, meanwhile, had become a reporter on the Sarasota Herald- Tribune. Liliane wrote:

"Brenda is coming home today for the last time. She died on Wednesday night doing something she had always lived for – aerial work. On official records she was Mrs. Louis Cuttin of 700 Seeds Avenue, Sarasota, but for people 'in the business' she was Brenda Jones, the English girl who made friends wherever she went, and who was forever writing letters. If someone was in need, Brenda was near.

She was also the person other aerialists would call when suddenly left without a partner. 'I'm waiting for a call from Elvin', Brenda told me a few weeks ago, 'His partner is leaving the show'. She added that she was feeling great, was practicing again despite dislocating her shoulder earlier. She never lost her strength. She was one of the few aerialists who could take long lay-offs with few penalties.

Now she is dead. She fell to her death during a full-house performance of the Ringling Brothers & Barnum & Baily Circus. She fell while performing one of the easiest aerial acts – at least easy for a woman who performed underneath helicopters. The act Brenda was doing consisted of a motorcycle climbing an inclined cable to a circular platform above the ring. Underneath the cycle is a trapeze or perch. Riding the motor cycle

Below: Brenda Jones married Louis Cuttin, known as Buzz, on 6th March 1961 in Chicago.

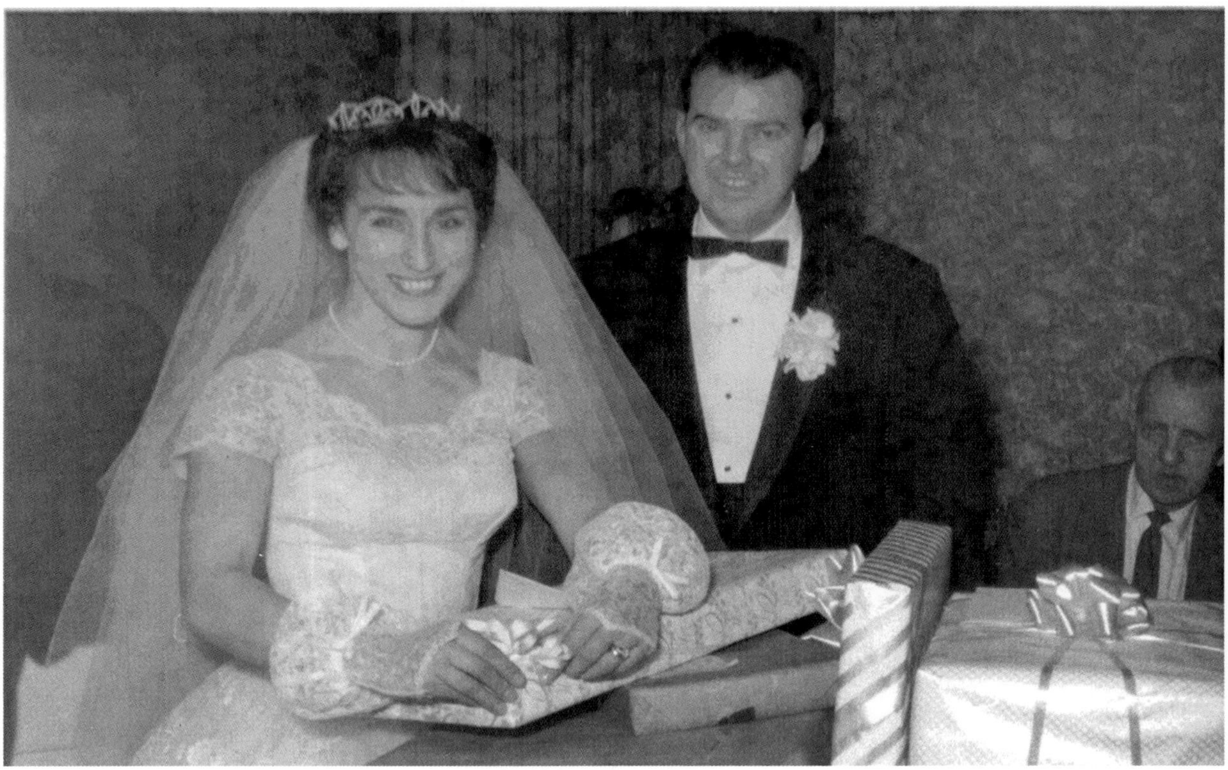

was Elvin Bale – an outstanding trapeze performer. While plummeting to her death, Brenda nearly took Elvin with her. Falling off the bike he hung above the floor of the Convention Centre with only a strong grip on the handlebar of the motorcycle. From the ground his wife and Charly Baumann were able to slide an aerial ladder close enough for him to reach and he was brought down safely. Everyone stayed up all night trying to figure out how she could have gone out of the hand loops as she was such a strong girl.

Aerialists sometimes talk of death. Not in a morbid way, just as a matter of fact. We all have lost friends to falls, and we all have friends in wheelchairs. While in Sarasota, Brenda often took a chair bound girlfriend to shows and other places. 'She has so much courage', Brenda once told me of her friend, 'She never complains – I am just so grateful I'm still performing'.

Brenda did indeed have a home in Sarasota, a town with a huge circus community, but she also still had a home and family in Britain. Brenda was brought back to England and was buried at the cemetery in Sedgley after a funeral service at Holy Trinity Church in Heath Town. It was a large impressive funeral - reflecting the fact that Brenda was both a "local girl from Heath Town", and a star of the American Circus. Local people remember the blue casket in which Brenda was buried and the mourners who seemed to have come from all over the world. She was a well-loved and respected artiste, totally devoted to her work, but also able to endear herself to those around her wherever she went.

Postscript

Elvin Bale was also born in England – way back in 1945. He was born into a circus and variety theatre family and went into the business as a child. His family moved to America in the 1950s when his father took a job as a tiger trainer with Ringling Bros., Barnum & Bailey's Circus. Elvin performed in a variety of acts and finally emerged as an aerialist and trapeze artist. His acts were often performed as stunts in famous locations. After Brenda's death Elvin developed a "human cannonball" act called "The Human Space Shuttle". Later this act was toured internationally. On 8th January 1987 he suffered a serious accident while performing the act in Hong Kong resulting in paralysis in both legs. Nevertheless, he later took on agency and circus management work.

Louisa Jones, Brenda's Mum, died on 15th June 2003, in Wolverhampton. She was buried in the family grave on Sedgley Beacon, next to Brenda's on Tuesday 24th June 2003.

And what of the world that Brenda inhabited in America? Ringling Brothers, Barnum & Bailey's Circus closed on 21st May 2017 after a period of declining attendances coincided with rising costs.

The "combined show" was the result of a merger that took place in 1919, but taking account of its predecessors the show enjoyed a history lasting one hundred and forty six years.

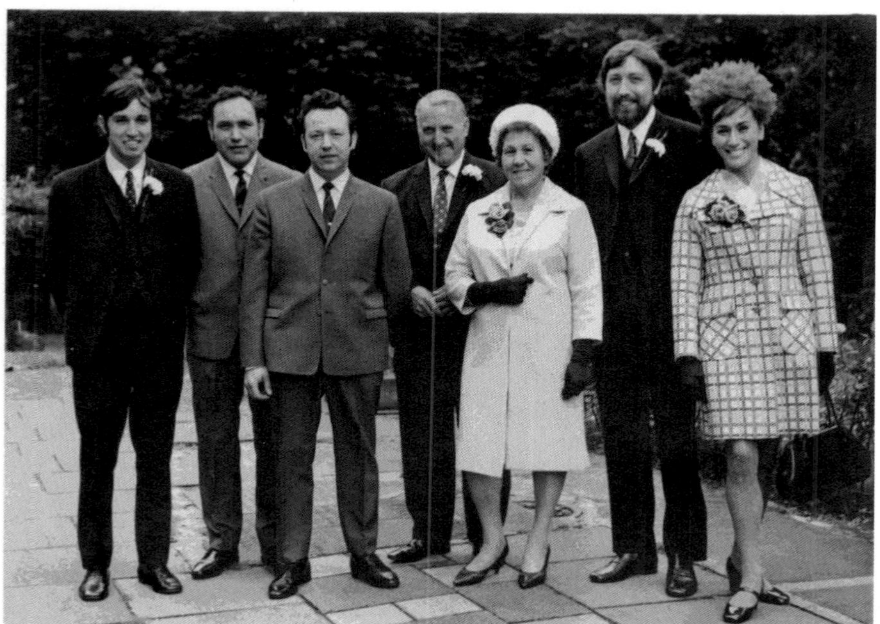

Brenda, on the far right of the picture, made frequent visits back to England to be part of her Wolverhampton-based family. Here she poses with her parents, William and Louisa Jones, and her brothers on a family occasion. Left to right: Peter, Gordon, Ivan, Mr. William Jones, Mrs. Louisa Jones, Derek and Brenda.

More pictures from the Brenda Jones Archive, maintained by her family.

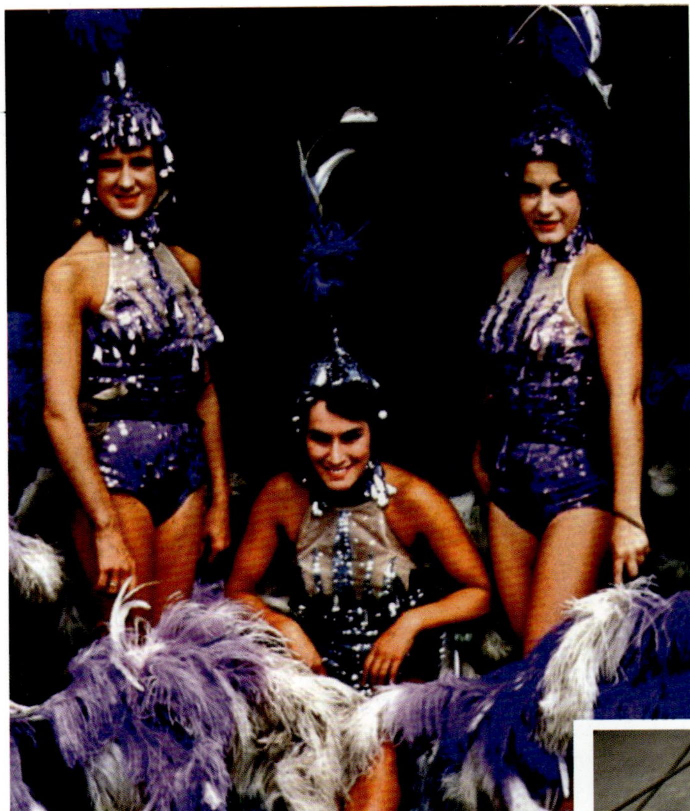

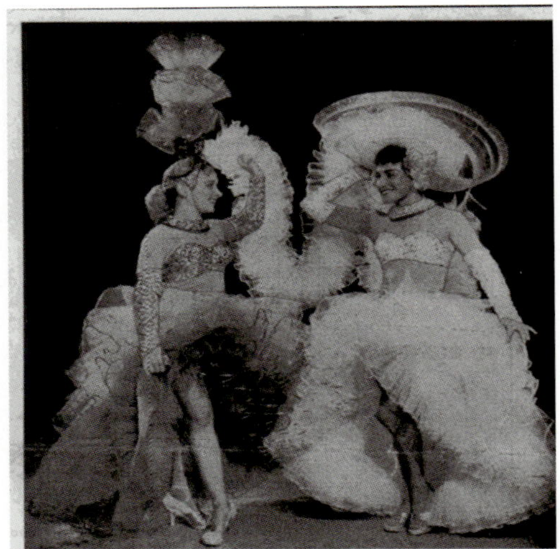

Two of BARBETTE'S AERIALOVELIES (Joyce Breedenbach a Brenda Jones).

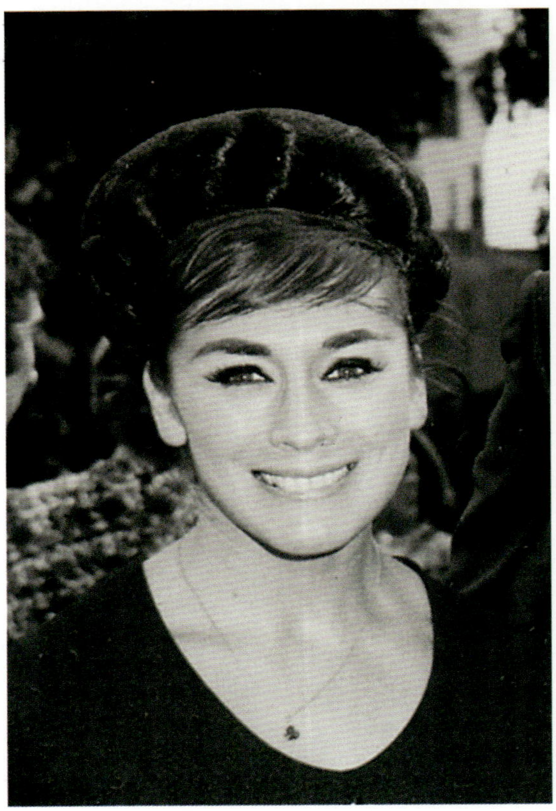

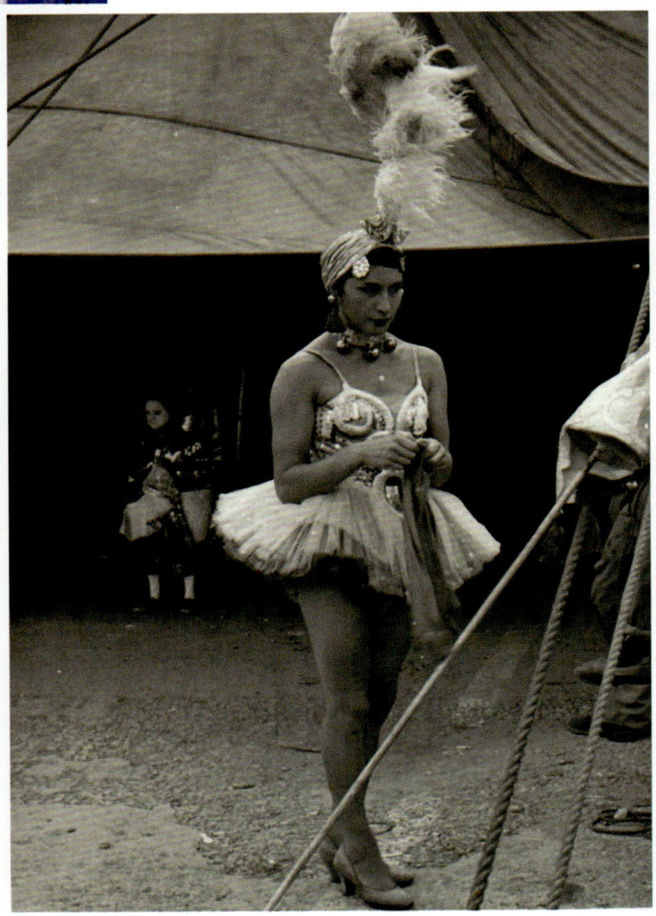

A Scene in Dudley Port

One damp Friday morning towards the spring of 1911, Joe Bate made his way through the dirty mist to a building in Dudley Port, on the corner of Grosvenor Road. As a Tipton lad, born in 1874, Joe had originally encountered the building as a Salvation Army hall, but in 1902 John Morton converted it into a theatre. It was a large corrugated iron building, but that was not a problem to John Morton who had used the very same material to build the Cradley Opera House back in 1893. John Morton gave the iron building the name "Colosseum" spelt in the same way as a rival theatre in Dudley built by the legendary John Maurice Clement. More recently the building had enjoyed life as a skating rink, but it had been taken over by Douglas Phelps who was converting it back to a theatre or cinema. Joe Bate was appointed by Douglas Phelps to be temporary manager of the place, Joe being no stranger to the business of converting existing halls to cinema use. After all, earlier in 1910 he had worked in a hall in Lichfield for Pat Collins, the fairground showman, but the venture had come to a sudden end when the premises caught fire!

Joe Bate was busy opening the building when Douglas Phelps arrived – in one of those new-fangled machines called a motor car, accompanied by his wife, Maude Lynton . They had driven from Stourbridge where Douglas Phelps was the proprietor of the Alhambra Theatre – a building he had purchased from Eliza Patch upon her retirement in 1900. Douglas Phelps obviously liked the name "Alhambra" and was experienced in running a hall which provided both theatrical and cinematographic presentations, and sometimes mixed them together. Douglas had been an actor but had settled into theatre management at Worcester, before deciding to become the proprietor of the "retired portable" in Stourbridge.

His "new" Alhambra in Dudley Port was facing a few problems before it could be opened. The local council had rejected some plans and some modifications that had been made to the building. New plans had been drawn and further alterations had been made. Douglas had called this morning's meeting to share with fellow showmen any experience they had gained in providing entertainment since the passing of the 1909 Kinematograph Act, and its implementation since 1st January 1910. He was looking forward to meeting Irving Bosco who had not only started showing films in Dudley on the first day that the Act came into force, but had experience of converting existing buildings for cinematographic purposes. Ben Kennedy was also coming along and he was in the middle of successfully taking over the leases of several theatres and even in the business of opening new ones.

Neither of these men were the next to arrive. Instead the doors opened and a man in his early twenties entered and introduced himself as Arthur Sellman from Cannock. He had been invited along by Joe Bate as they had many interests in common and both had been close observers of the growth of cinematography in its "bioscope era" – an age that had come to an abrupt end with the passing of the Kinematograph Act. Joe was now 37 and Arthur was only 22 but already they chatted like old men with a love of reminiscing – particularly recalling the travelling shows that had existed before the arrival of the bioscopes. They did not realise at the time but they were both to become regular correspondents for The World's Fair – the showman's weekly newspaper.

Irving Bosco, who had just become a resident of Tipton, was the next to arrive. He was a large, outgoing man, the same age as Joe Bate. In fact both men had worked together about 1896 or 1897 when Bosco was grappling with the potential of cinematography. Both he, and Ben Kennedy, who was the last to arrive, had fingers in many pies, and both believed that "cine-variety" would be the way forward. Their shows would combine real life acts alternated with ten minute sequences of film. As a showman it was a way of hedging one's bets, as everyone was still unsure about the future of film as major entertainment medium; how long could an audience be expected to sit still and consume nothing but the projected image? Even Ben Kennedy with his investment in brand new purpose built theatres, made sure they were also equipped to show films.

Many people were surprised by the number of cinema licences that had been issue during 1910. Everyone present that morning, except Arthur Sellman, had been very busy during that year, and had interests in South Staffordshire, the Black Country, and right into the heart of Birmingham. Douglas Phelps was slightly different in that he devoted all his energy to the running of one location – the Alhambra, Stourbridge - but this new venture in Dudley Port showed that even he was contemplating the possibility of building an empire.
Douglas Phelps had first met Ben Kennedy when the latter had presented a week of film entertainment at the Stourbridge Alhambra in 1903. Everyone present could think of ways that their paths had crossed. In this respect, Irving Bosco was disappointed by the absence of John Swallow who had a base in Wolverhampton. John Swallow had spent part of the previous year touring Ireland and Irving still had interests in a show still travelling in Ireland – it might have been interesting to compare notes.

However the purpose of the gathering was not to enjoy conversation and reminiscence. The task in hand was to help Douglas Phelps solve his problems with the planning authorities. Both Irving Bosco and Ben Kennedy looked forward to the day when they would only operate in new purpose built buildings. As it happened they were able to solve Douglas Phelps' problems fairly quickly and conversation turned to question of the future. Joe was a restless character and would not stay at the Dudley Port theatre for long. Travelling was the thing that satisfied him most and he looked forward to the day when he might own his own show. Arthur also dreamed of owning a show but also longed to be a writer. Irving Bosco looked forward to financial security and even "retirement" in which he would tour the world. They all turned to Ben Kennedy to see what he might say. Ben seemed lost in thought and then he declared that one day he would build the finest theatre in the Midlands.

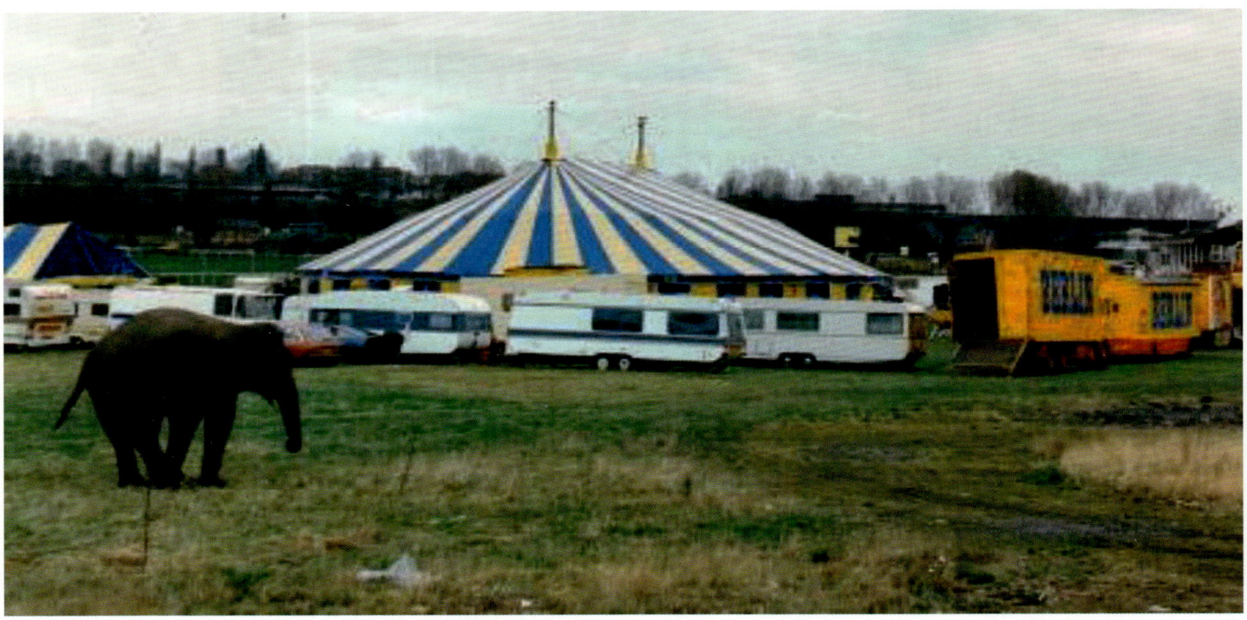

We have not seen many elephants in Wolverhampton in recent years but here we see Rani with Circus Berlin, about 1985, at Dunstall - a stone's throw from Salts' and Sauce's home in Gorsebrook Road, just the other of the viaduct seen in the background.

Epilogue

Looking back at the lives of the people described in this book, it is interesting to return to Rev. Gilbanks' words at the funeral of Eliza Patch when he affirmed that she would be known and remembered *forever*.

It almost seems that the conclusion you might reach on finishing this book is that the lives of our heroes and heroines have indeed become "forgotten". Their achievements can still be researched, but the reality is that as people they have faded into a kind of invisibility that can be a feature of becoming part of the past. Some families have "preserved" them in their family history, others are not able to.

When the Clubbs published their book about John Swallow's elephants I felt much encouraged that Salt and Sauce could be given some immortality via the printed word. I guess I now hope that this book will help maintain a knowledge of the seven people featured in these pages. If elephants can have their place in written history surely a few humans can enjoy the same status.

As well as the lives of the people described in this book being in danger of becoming "forgotten", we also have to acknowledge that the world they inhabited has also gone forever. They lived at a time when entertainment was coping with great change and development and I hope this book will encourage readers to contemplate a world of "shows", of "variety", of exciting fairground rides, of early cinematography and the dynamic world of the circus.

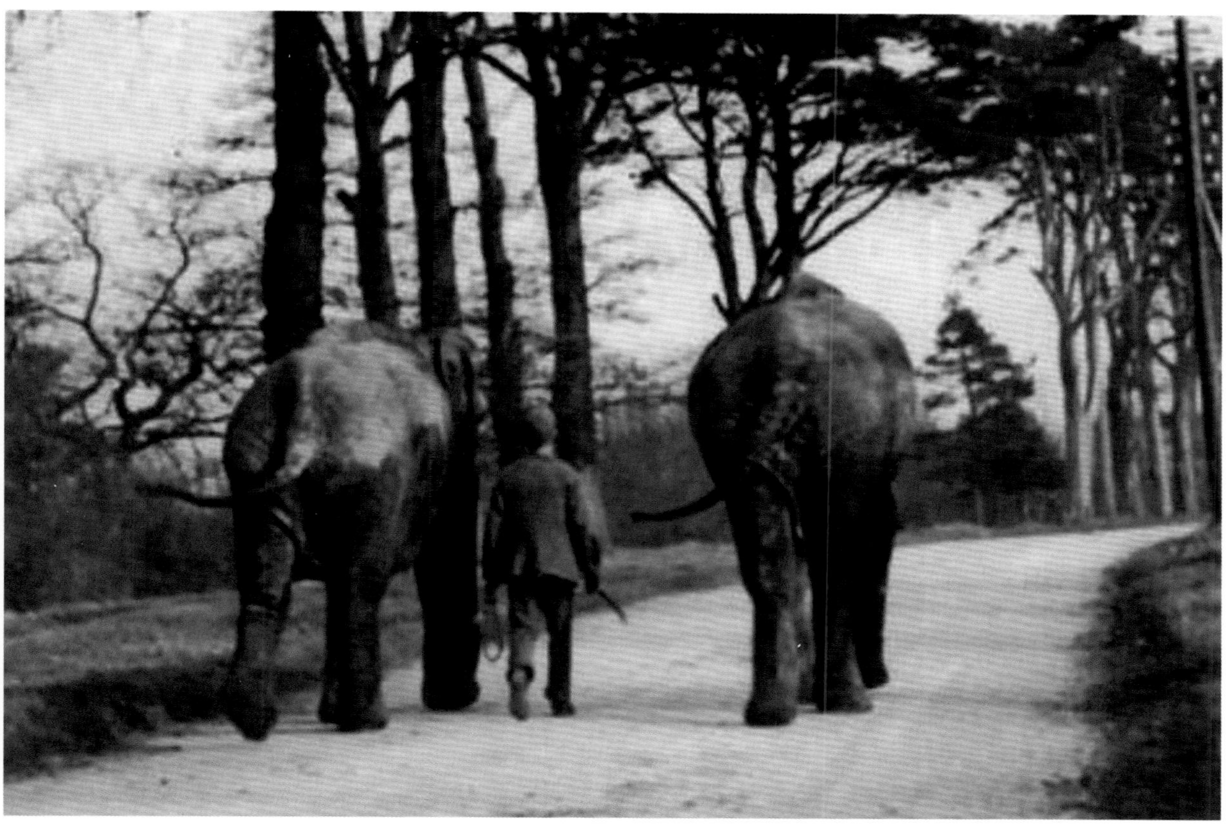

Acknowledgements

Many people have contributed towards the production of this book in supplying information, documents, photographs, and their time and resources.

Firstly I would like to mention the relatives and descendants of the seven people described in this book:

Verity Johnson (nee Swallow): Great grand-daughter of Broncho Bill.
Susan Venus: Grand-daughter of Irving Bosco.
Descendants of Joe Bate.
Jenny Hall: Grand-daughter of Arthur Sellman and her sister, Susan.
(And the other members of the extended family – Laura King, Margaret Gunn and Peter Lane.)
Jane Driver and Penny Shepherd-Barron, both grand-daughters of Ben Kennedy.
(And others who helped in relation to the work on Ben Kennedy, including David Kennedy, and Ivor Burgess.)
The late Ken Shepherd helped me appreciate the history of the Dudley Hippodrome – of which he had been stage manager.
Also the late Bob Hosier assisted me – he had been the theatre's semi-official photographer!
The life of Brenda Jones could not have been told and illustrated without the help of her brother, Derek Jones, and his late mother, Louisa Jones.
In sorting out the family history of the Swallows, I have been assisted by Emma Wraith, Elise Masterman and Howard Mais.

Thanks to my daughter, Kiran Williams, for the drawing at the beginning of the Bennett & Patch chapter. On the home front I wish to acknowledge the help and support of Gill.

Help was also forthcoming from Stephen Smith, editor of "Platform", the quarterly journal of the Fairground Society, and Graham Downie, editor of "The Mercury" – the quarterly journal of the Fairground Society of Great Britain.
Similarly, David Davies of the Circus Friends Association has been helpful, and Ken Rattenbury, a member of the CFA.

All four local archives in the Black Country have been very useful – and helpful – and have made files and photos available over the years.

I acknowledge the support of the editor of The World's Fair who gave me freedom to quote from the pages of that paper. The pages of the World's Fair were examined at the National Newspaper Collection and among the resources of the National Fairground and Circus Archive at Sheffield University. Professor Vanessa Toulmin, who led and developed the archive for many years has always been ready to discuss shows and early cinematography.

Anyone wishing to consider the past and present of the fairground and circus world will find it useful to look at the Archive in Sheffield, and to visit locations such as the National Fairground Heritage Centre at Dingles, in Devon.

Several local fairground enthusiasts are no longer with us, but I always appreciated the help of people like Fred Richardson and Bob Webster. People interested in portable theatres are rare, but I acknowledge the importance of people who have shared their knowledge with me – including Ted Bottle and the late Geoff Holloway.

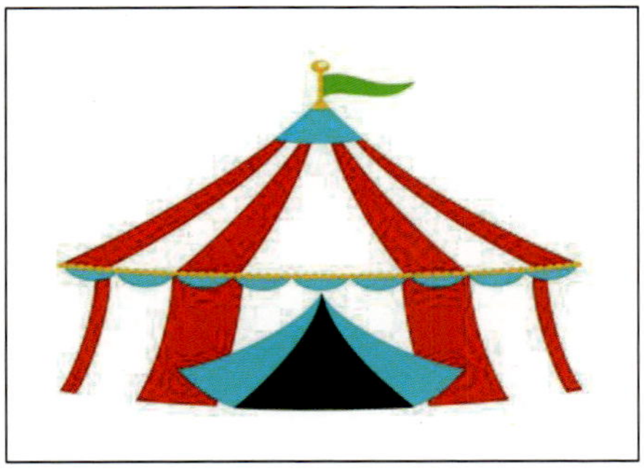

A Reading List

"Black Country Cinemas", Ned Williams, Uralia Press, 2011.

"Black Country Theatres", Ned Williams, Uralia Press, 2011.

"Pat Collins: King of Showmen", Freda Allen and Ned Williams, Uralia Press, 1991.

"Fairs & Circuses in the Black Country", Ned Williams, Uralia Press, 1994,

"The Birmingham Onion Fair", Ned Williams, Uralia Press, 1996.

"A Desert Rat Entertains", Jenny Hall (Arthur Sellman's granddaughter,) Pen Press, 2013.

"The Legend of Salt and Sauce", Jamie & Jim Clubb, Aardvark Publishing, 2008.

"The Travelling Cinematograph Show", by Kevin Scrivens and Stephen Smith, New Era, 1999.

The Lost World of Mitchell & Kenyon", Vanessa Toulmin, BFI, 2004. (Information on A.D. Thomas and other early film pioneers.)

"The Victorian Arena", Vols. 1 & 2. John Turner, Lingdales Press 1995 and 2000.

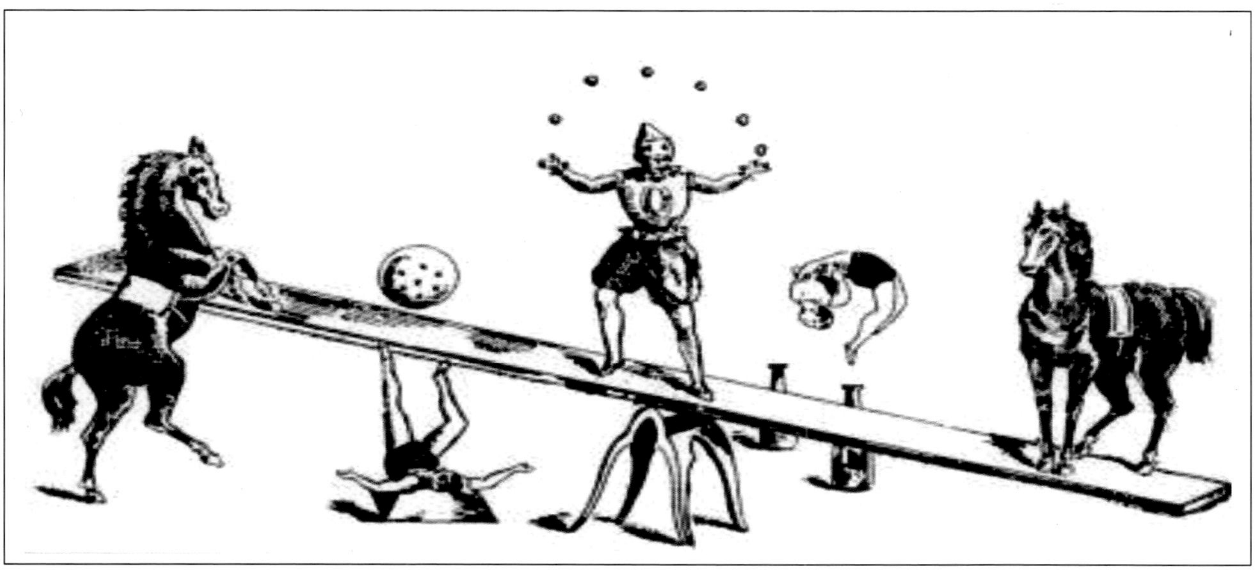

About the Author and Uralia Press:

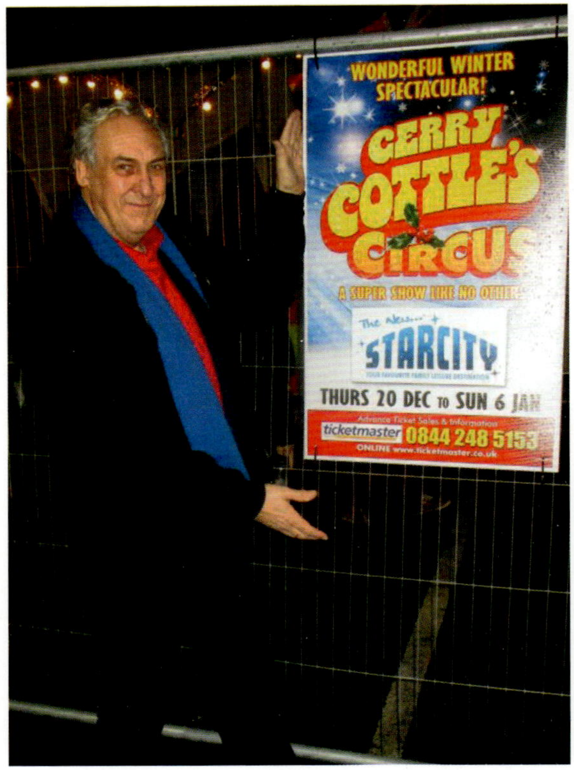

Ned Williams came to the Black Country in September 1962 and since then has produced numerous books about many different aspects of local history while working in various areas of Adult Education. In 1969 he invented Uralia Press to publish local material that otherwise might not ever be published. Since then he has also produced books for The History Press, and all this activity has resulted in this being the fifty second publication. Subjects covered include: Transport (particularly 'railways'), Retailing (particularly the Co-op), Entertainment, and town studies on Dudley, Wolverhampton, Quarry Bank, Netherton, Brierley Hill, and, recently, the Gornals

Most of Ned's books are now out of print but he does buy his own books back from second-hand sources to provide books for folks searching for a particular hard-to-find title!

You can follow Ned's activities via his website: nedwilliams.co.uk

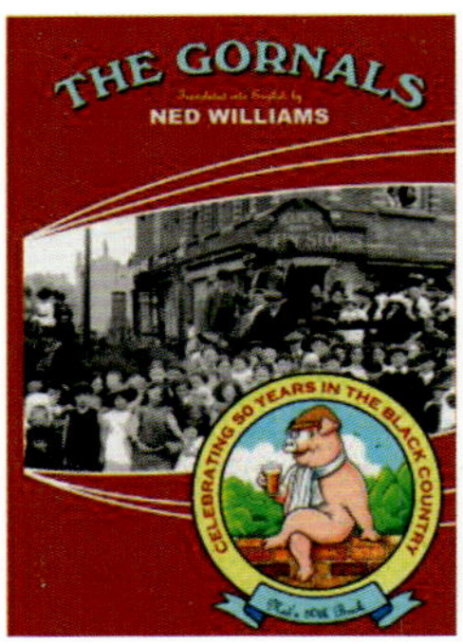

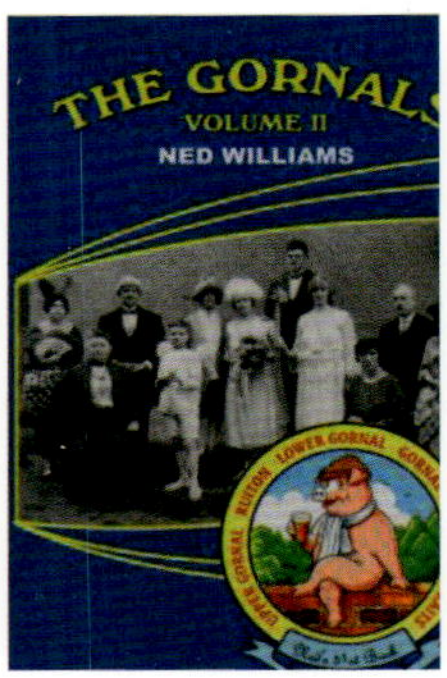

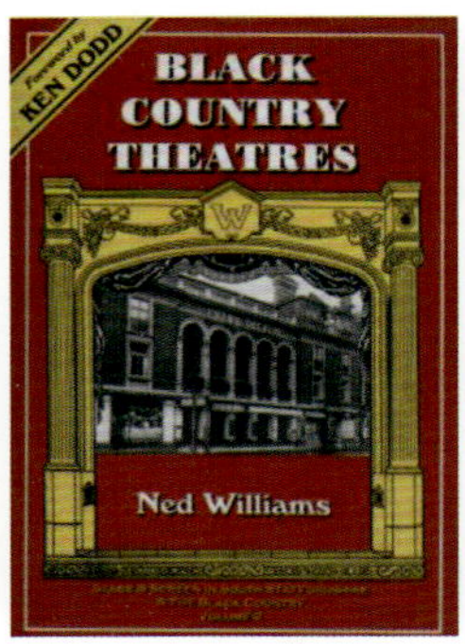

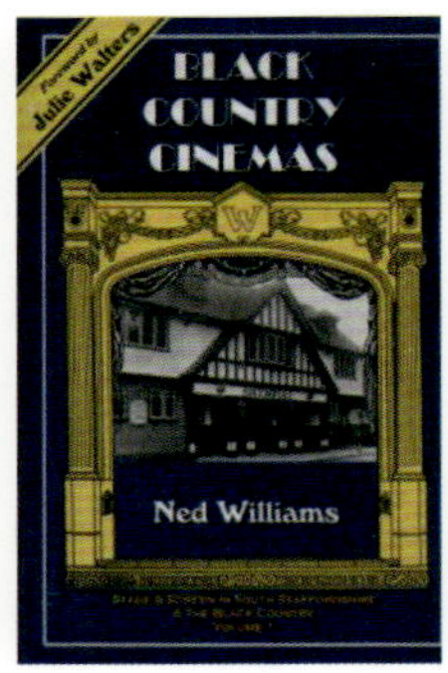

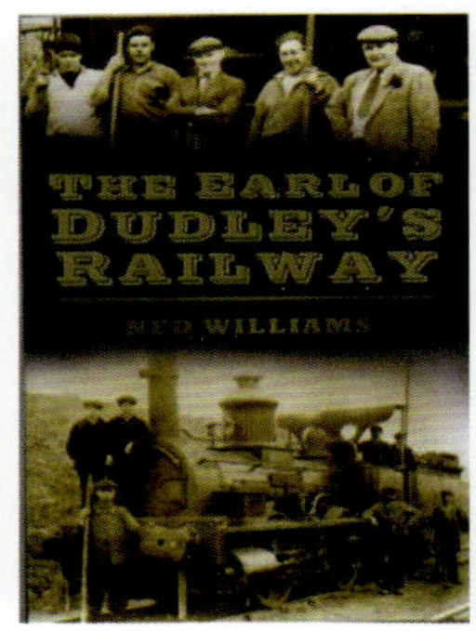

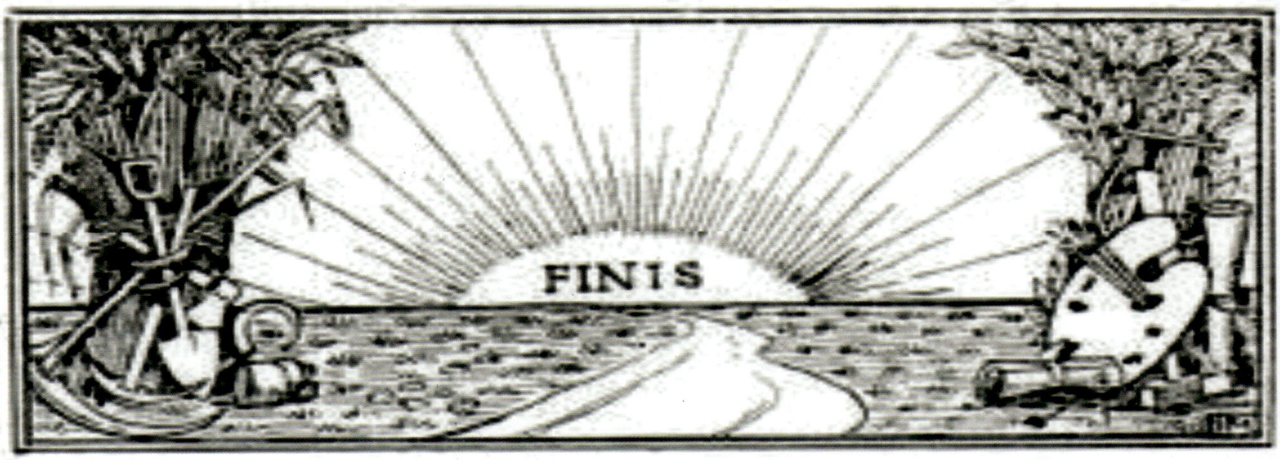